...ers
Speak Out

literacy and schools

CINDY MATA AGUILAR
JANET ALLEN
RICHARD L. ALLINGTON
DONNA E. ALVERMANN
DEBORAH APPLEMAN
NANCIE ATWELL
KYLENE BEERS
RANDY BOMER
DEVON BRENNER
JIM BURKE
LEILA CHRISTENBURY
ERIC COOPER
CHRIS CRUTCHER
HARVEY DANIELS
KATHRYN EGAWA
DANLING FU
YVETTE JACKSON
CAROL JAGO
SARA B. KAJDER
ELLIN OLIVER KEENE
PENNY KITTLE
TERI LESESNE
DONALD M. MURRAY
P. DAVID PEARSON
ROBERT E. PROBST
LINDA RIEF
TOM ROMANO
RUTH SHAGOURY
MICHAEL W. SMITH
ALFRED TATUM
JEFFREY D. WILHELM

Dear J̶

Imagine being invited to a dinner party where you would be able to participate in talk that is excited, passionate, and persuasive about a topic you most enjoy, adolescent literacy. At the conclusion of the party, you leave filled with new ideas that you know in some way will direct what you do next. That's a dinner party you don't want to miss!

We—Kylene Beers, Bob Probst, and Linda Rief—hope you say the same about this invitation—a request that you be a part of an edited collection titled *Adolescent Literacy: Turning Promise into Practice* to be published by Heinemann in the spring of 2007. We are inviting the most influential names in adolescent literacy to be a part of this comprehensive text that we hope not only excites teachers, not only gives them new ideas to consider and new practices to try, but emerges as a leading text at this critical time in the development of adolescent literacy.

A pause to consider what's happening with adolescent literacy right now reveals an inundation of ideas and reports. Reports such as *Reading to Achieve: A Governor's Guide to Adolescent Literacy* (from the National Governors Association), *Reading Next* and *Adolescents and Literacy: Reading for the 21st Century* (both from the Alliance for Excellent Education), *The Neglected 'R': The Need for a Writing Revolution* (by the National Commission on Writing), and *Results That Matter: 21st Century Skills and High School Reform* (from the Partnership for 21st Century Skills) along with reports on adolescent literacy from the National Council of Teachers of English and the International Reading Association show us that the nation—meaning parents, politicians, policy makers, business and community leaders, teachers, and administrators—is looking for answers about how to best address the complex demands of adolescent literacy. Wanting to make sure all students—*all students*—are prepared to be active participants in this changing world, we—meaning those of us who have dedicated our professional lives to improving the literacy of adolescents—have an opportunity now, in one text, to offer a guidebook that helps shape both public conversation and classroom practice.

This is a bold goal. But at a time like this, we need bold goals; we need bold ideas; and we need the most respected leaders to stand together and offer in one volume the re-vision of adolescent literacy. This re-vision is predicated on our understanding that globalization means our middle and high school students will increasingly find themselves living in the "flat" world that is persuasively described in Friedman's best-selling book *The World Is Flat*. It means recognizing that literacy demands are shifting and becoming more complex. It means understanding that automation—a part of our technological world—will change the landscape of the job market (the grocery cashier in the next decade will be the exception and not the rule). As automation expands, different jobs will emerge—jobs that require creating, synthesizing, and evaluating. They will be held by those with ingenuity, imagination, and empathy, those who are willing to take risks and work cooperatively. We should be preparing students for such a world; yet, the politicization of education has resulted in a different agenda where a prescribed assembly-line curriculum asks only that students pass a test. The current focus on high-stakes tests produces students who can answer multiple-choice items but have lost the interest and *agility* to ask probing questions, to conceptualize our new world.

You're an important part of this dinner party, the national conversation this book will encourage. Without you, folks (meaning other contributors as well as readers) will look around the table and ask where you are. So, just say yes!

Our best to you,

Kylene, Bob, and Linda

adolescent
LITERACY

KYLENE BEERS
ROBERT E. PROBST
LINDA RIEF

EDITORS

adolescent
LITERACY

Turning Promise
into Practice

HEINEMANN
Portsmouth, NH

Heinemann
A division of Reed Elsevier Inc.
361 Hanover Street
Portsmouth, NH 03801–3912
www.heinemann.com

Offices and agents throughout the world

The authors and publisher wish to thank those who have generously given permission to reprint borrowed material:

Figure 1–1: "Components of 21st Century Learning" copyright © 2006 by Learning Points Associates. All rights reserved. Reprinted with permission. www.ncrel.org/engauge/skills/agelit.htm.

Credits continue on page 413

Library of Congress Cataloging-in-Publication Data
Adolescent literacy : turning promise into practice / edited by Kylene Beers, Robert E. Probst, and Linda Rief.
     p. cm.
  Includes bibliographical references and index.
  ISBN-13: 978-0-325-01128-8 (pbk. : alk. paper)
  ISBN-10: 0-325-01128-1
  1. Language arts (Secondary)—Social aspects—United States. 2. English language—Study and teaching (Secondary)—United States. 3. Literacy—United States—United States. I. Beers, Kylene. II. Probst, Robert E. III. Rief, Linda.
LB1631.A345 2007
428.0071'2—dc22   2007000688

Editor: Lisa Luedeke
Production: Lynne Costa
Cover design: Lisa Fowler
Cover illustration: © Getty Images 590043
Interior design: Gina Poirier
Typesetter: Gina Poirier
Manufacturing: Louise Richardson

Printed in the United States of America on acid-free paper
11 10 09 08 07   ML   2 3 4 5

Contents

At the same time we must understand the challenges each will face in the context of this twenty-first century

But no matter what the century, writing will always be at the heart of literacy

And at the heart of that literacy instruction is the teacher as writer

That teacher faces the realities of the many demands of writing instruction

And the writing they do is no longer only with paper and pen

Learning is more likely to be meaningful when situated in the questions students ask

And these questions require the deepest thinking from all our students

At some point, we'll want to examine how well our students are doing

We need also to ask how we ourselves are doing

Then, for the times we discover we need some help . . .

*Finally, because adolescent literacy isn't a stopping point, but only a
beginning*

Introduction

First

I STOOD in the hallway of a high school, watching students walk past me, all with great purpose, though I'm sure that purpose varied from calculating the correct pace that would ensure arriving to class mere seconds before the tardy bell to determining the rigor needed to graduate as a National Merit Scholar. I stood there watching and heard a teacher talking in my ear.

"Scares the hell out of me sometimes," he said with more of a chuckle than a tremor in his voice.

"What?" I asked.

"Them. All of them. Who they are now. What they become tomorrow. That they will run the hospitals I'll need when I'm old; that they'll be the ones who are on the city councils, in the police force, in the nursing homes, in the teachers' lounges. They will be the people in charge when I'm old." His words lingered between us as we watched two adolescent girls, each wearing dresses short enough to most assuredly be called T-shirts, walk past. One had too many earrings in one earlobe for me to count easily; the other had tattoos on her arms and painted black fingernails. Both wore enough makeup to encourage me to buy stock in any cosmetics company. And neither carried a notebook, a text-book, or anything that resembled an educational tool, unless you count cell phones and lipstick as required supplies.

They walked past us, saying something about someone being "so not there," and we each decided that surely that conversation was not about us—and of course, it was not, as that would have meant that they were aware of us, thought of us, even *saw* us. We stood there quietly, each wrapped in our own thoughts about adolescents and teaching. Then he said, "Do you think there's any chance of getting it right?"

"What right?" I asked.

"This. All of it," he said, sweeping his hand out over the horizon of teens walking through the halls and toward the classrooms, where teaching and learning were supposed to take place.

"Absolutely," I said immediately, without hesitation.

"Can I get that as a promise?" he asked, grinning as two boys wearing "Vote for Pedro" T-shirts began drumming a complicated rhythm on two locker doors and the assistant principal arrived to urge students on into their classes.

Before I could respond, he had headed down the hall as the tardy bell rang and students slipped into classrooms, leaving me nodding yes to no one.

Later

I stood by the Heinemann booth during the 2004 National Council of Teachers of English (NCTE) convention, watching two teachers talk with Harvey "Smokey" Daniels. He answered their questions, signed their books, and kept them laughing with that quick wit of his. As they walked away, one teacher said to the other that what she liked best about the NCTE convention was that it gave her a chance to see all her favorite authors at the same time in the same place. The other nodded enthusiastically and added that she wished she could have them all in one book so she could re-create that all-in-one-place feeling throughout the year.

Several Months Later

When I finished reading Thomas Friedman's book *The World Is Flat* (2005), I found myself rethinking the "Is there any chance of getting it right?" question from the teacher in the hallway. I wondered if he or I completely understood what the *it* needed to be. I looked at the several reports on the dropout rate and the adolescent literacy crisis sitting on my desk and read them each again, asking myself what in these reports would help teachers and administrators close the reading achievement gap and prepare students for the demands—civic responsibility demands, digital demands, cognitive demands, global demands—of the twenty-first century. While I saw us—as individuals and as a nation—making strides in teaching reading in middle and high schools, I also saw us failing to respond to the more complex demands of educating students for this "flat" world of the twenty-first century.

At the same time, I remembered the teachers at the NCTE convention discussing how important it was to have their favorite authors in the same place. I agreed with their desire and found myself wanting to have a conversation with the brightest educators about what adolescent literacy in the twenty-first century needed to be. So I picked up the phone and called two people who not only have informed my thoughts about adolescents and literacy but have helped many teachers across grades, across the country, and even across oceans: Linda Rief and Bob Probst.[1] We talked about Friedman's book, Daniel Pink's book, *A Whole New Mind* (2005), and the various reports on adolescent literacy; we talked about No Child Left Behind legislation and the demands of adequate yearly progress; we looked through the books on our shelves, through journals, through notes taken at conferences; we asked each other what we knew, what we believed, what we hoped for teachers and students.

The more we thought about the value of synthesis, of collaboration, of working across boundaries, the more sure we became that what was needed was an edited collection where many voices came together to explore the many facets of adolescent literacy: reading, writing, motivation, young adult literature, English language learners, multimodal literacy, civic responsibility, digital literacy, vocabulary, comprehension, and assessment, to name a few. As we chose specific topics to address, we began the difficult task of brainstorming about the people who could best inform our thinking on those topics. After crafting our list, we sent each a letter that said, in part,

> A pause to consider what's happening with adolescent literacy right now shows an amazing influx of ideas and reports. Reports such as *Reading to Achieve: A Governor's Guide to Adolescent Literacy* (from the National Governors Association 2005), *Reading Next* (Biancarosa and Snow 2004) and *Adolescents and Literacy: Reading for the 21st Century* (Kamil 2003) (both from the Alliance

---

1 I want to thank Bob and Linda now for agreeing to join me as coeditors of this project. Though I wrote the introduction, this book was a joint project. I learned much from each of them as we worked together for nearly two years. Linda, a middle school teacher, kept us grounded in the realities of state assessments, odd teaching schedules, too many kids, too few books, late hours spent evaluating student work, and early mornings spent on bus duty. She brought her deep understanding of the reading-writing connection to this project, and Bob and I both benefited from that. Bob did what he does so well: challenged my understanding of what it means to make sense of a text. He was the one who had the perfect question to push our thinking deeper; who immediately saw when something in a chapter needed attention; who kept reminding us that preparing students for this "flat" world is critical. The book became a better book when they agreed to be coeditors with me.

for Excellent Education), and *Results That Matter: 21st Century Skills and High School Reform* (from the Partnership for 21st Century Skills [2006]), along with reports on adolescent literacy from the National Council Teachers of English and the International Reading Association, show us that the nation—meaning parents, politicians, policy makers, business and community leaders, teachers, and administrators—are all looking for answers about how to best address the complex demands of adolescent literacy. Wanting to make sure all students—*all students*—are prepared to be active participants in this new flat world, we—meaning those of us who have dedicated our professional lives to improving the literacy of adolescents—have an opportunity now, in one text, to offer a handbook that helps shape both public conversation and classroom practice.

This is a bold goal. But at a time like this, we need bold goals; we need bold ideas; and we need the most respected leaders to stand together and offer in one volume a re-vision of adolescent literacy practices. This re-vision is predicated on our understanding that globalization means our middle and high school students will increasingly find themselves living in a world persuasively described in Friedman's bestselling book *The World Is Flat*. It means recognizing that literacy demands are shifting and becoming more complex. It means understanding that automation—a part of our technological world—will change the landscape of the job market (the grocery cashier in the next decade will be the exception and not the rule). As automation expands, different jobs will emerge—jobs that require creating, synthesizing, and evaluating. They will be held by those with ingenuity, imagination, and empathy, those who are willing to take risks and work cooperatively. We should be preparing students for such a world, yet the politicization of education has resulted in a different agenda where a prescribed assembly-line curriculum seemingly asks only that students pass a test. The current focus on high-stakes tests produces students who can answer multiple-choice items but have lost the interest and *agility* to ask probing questions, to conceptualize our new world.

For Several Months

Invited contributors responded enthusiastically and began the task of thinking through issues and distilling their thoughts to workable lengths for this book. Each author could have easily written far more on his or her topic, and we thank them all now for their willingness to work through revisions that included prioritizing information so that the most critical was included here. We each learned much as we read their chapters and were always touched with gratitude as they responded quickly and thoroughly to queries. While the impetus for this book rests in a question asked in a crowded hallway and a wish from teachers at a busy convention, the book itself exists because of the expertise and dedication of each contributing author.

Now

You're holding the result of those experts' work: *Adolescent Literacy: Turning Promise into Practice*. We hope it serves as a handbook for middle and high school teachers, school and district administrators, and local, state, and national policy makers. And because we do see this book as a handbook, you are the one who can best decide in what order to read it. Because we anticipate that people will read in the order that best suits their purpose, I'll point out some features that you'll see no matter where you begin.

> *The table of contents.* As you look through the contents, you'll find a note above each chapter title. Reading through all those notes will show you the shape of this book, the story it is attempting to tell.

> *Interludes.* Throughout the book, you'll find shorter essays we've named interludes. These interludes, written by some of the best teachers we know, are each meant to give you insight about some aspect of teaching from a master teacher. We realize that this is a long book with a lot of information, and we wanted you to have a chance to relax from the demands of longer chapters with these shorter interludes. Enjoy!

> *Connections.* Occasionally you'll see a page titled Connections. These pages provide a space for you to jot down your own connections and to connect to other texts we think are valuable.

> *Editors' notes.* In each chapter you'll see editors' notes in the margins. Many of these notes serve to direct you to other places in the book where you'll find comments from another author on a similar topic. Much as a hypertext link takes you to another place in an electronic text, these comments help you make connections among and between chapters. Other editors' notes are our attempt to have a conversation with you as you read. We enjoyed creating these notes and hope you enjoy our over-the-shoulder conversations with you as you read.

> *Pull quotes.* Throughout chapters, you'll find quotes we've pulled out of the text to highlight. While we expect you'll nod in agreement at many of our choices, we also hope you'll find passages that are meaningful for you that you'll "pull" to make your own list of memorable quotes.

> *Appendices.* In Appendix A, you'll find several templates that you can use in your classroom to support student learning. In Appendix B, you'll find several surveys you might want to complete to help you assess your own stage of learning.

> *Study guide.* Many teachers asked us for a study guide to accompany the book. We were reluctant to provide a list of study questions for each chapter, as we know that you'll quickly find what you want to discuss as you read. So, the guide we've created, which is available online at http://books.heinemann.com/adolescentliteracy, offers more general questions that we think are appropriate for any chapter.

We should also point out two things you won't see in this book, no matter where you begin. First, there is no single chapter on reading or writing in content area classes—social studies, history, science, or math. Instead, each chapter addresses how we can improve literacy instruction in *all* classes. Authors address expository and narrative texts and expository and narrative writing side by side. Some artificial boundaries have been drawn around the disciplines, suggesting that some literacy learning is appropriate for social studies but not science, or English but not history, but in today's world such boundaries are blurring. We'd like to push many of them aside and suggest that much literacy development is *not* subject specific. In other words, we don't learn to see cause-and-effect relationships one way in science and another way in history. Instead, we learn the syntactical cues that show us those relationships and use those cues across all content areas.

While we do agree that historians approach a text with different questions (What does the information presented, the artifacts, show me about this culture? How does my understanding of an earlier war affect my understanding of this war?) than a biologist (How does the changing environment affect the life cycle of this species? What characteristics of this group match characteristics of another group?), we see that both types of readers are making connections, noting comparisons, and looking for causal relationships. Though the student in English class might read with an eye toward what a character will do next while the student in chemistry class wonders what will happen when two chemicals are combined, both are predicting. Though students in one classroom might encounter or write narrative fiction while in another, narrative nonfiction or expository texts, they all need to approach the texts they read and write with prior knowledge, all need to have a question in mind, all need to think about audience and point of view and author's purpose, and all need to see value in the assignment for the assignment to be meaningful.

Consequently, we didn't want the history teacher reading just the "Reading and Writing in the History Class" chapter and the science teacher looking only for the "Reading and Writing in the Science Class" chapter. Instead, we want all teachers reading about inquiry and technology and English language learners and comprehension and vocabulary and . . . well, you see the point. In the same way that we want learners reading a variety of texts to synthesize information, we want you to do the same. So, you'll find information about reading and writing a range of genres throughout the book rather than in only one place.

Second, you won't find a chapter that describes a particular intervention program for the most disabled readers. We chose not to include a chapter on reading intervention in this book for several reasons. Primarily, a single chapter would not be enough. I have written extensively about helping struggling readers (see *When Kids Can't Read, What Teachers Can Do* [2002]), as have others. Will the strategies presented in this book help your students who read significantly below grade level? Absolutely—but only if you use the strategies with texts that are at students' instructional and/or independent reading levels. However, this book alone does not provide the in-depth knowledge or expertise that we believe a teacher needs to help students who read significantly below grade level. These students need far more instruction in reading and writing than what can be offered in a regular forty-five-minute class or by the classroom teacher who has not had specific instruction in developing reading abilities.

We do suggest that schools need to re-vision reading and writing instruction as a continuum rather than an either-or situation. We see too many schools that offer remediation or intervention for those students who read far below grade level and nothing for anyone else. This either-you-get-a-lot-or-you-get-nothing method reflects an approach to reading that says once students have some basic skills in place, then they no longer need support. We disagree and believe that all students benefit from different levels of support. We encourage you to think of the literacy instruction in your school as stretching across a continuum.

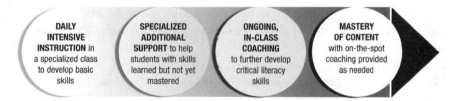

At the left end of the continuum, we see a class for students who read many grades below grade level and lack basic skills in fluency (word recognition, automaticity, and the ability to read with the expression needed for a text to make sense), vocabulary, and comprehension. These students need intervention from a teacher with particular expertise not only in the reading process and in developing word recognition and automaticity in older readers but also in miscue analysis. Buying a packaged program and staffing the class with any teacher who has an open period is not the answer. Nor is it appropriate to presume that the secondary certified English/language arts teacher has more specific knowledge in these areas than the history or science teacher. Schools needing to develop specialized intervention classes must commit to staffing those classes with highly skilled reading instructors. In addition to needing teachers with specific reading-instruction expertise, students also need access to a wide range of reading materials, both narrative and expository, at a variety of reading levels. They need a small class that meets daily for at least forty-five minutes in addition to their regular English/language arts class.

Moving across the continuum, we next see a class students might attend for a semester or even a single grading period to help them gain mastery over particular skills. In this class, students might use their assigned textbooks and literary texts for reading material. While additional material at instructional levels should be used for strategy instruction, this class is geared toward the student who can read required material but needs some special support, perhaps to improve reading rate or hone vocabulary skills. These are students who can read with understanding the information in their history book about the Spartans, but have trouble organizing what they've read in their minds so that they can retell it with coherence or write about it with clarity. Again, a teacher with specific knowledge in the reading process is needed.

Continuing the move across the continuum, we see reading support (as opposed to instruction) now taking place in the regular classroom. Some students in each classroom will always require more help than others on any topic. The same is true for the reading process. The first time students read primary source documents in history class or a lab report in science class or a sonnet in English class, some will need over-the-shoulder coaching on the reading strategies most appropriate for that text. The best person to teach this level of reading is the classroom teacher. Knowledge of reading strategies, fix-up strategies, the writing process, and ways to develop vocabulary helps the classroom teacher coach students through new and increasingly more challenging texts.

At the far-right end of the continuum, we see teachers focusing primarily on mastery of challenging and rigorous content. Students have strong command over a variety of reading strategies and use them almost without thought as they read increasingly more complex texts throughout the year. However, the teacher has the ability to model comprehension, vocabulary, and fluency strategies whenever needed.

While this book largely provides information for the second, third, and fourth types of classes described, teachers in that intensive intervention class will also find much of this book helpful, particularly the chapters by Keene, Allen, Jackson and Cooper, Wilhelm and Smith, Rief, and Daniels.

Next

We began the invitational letter to contributors with the following paragraph:

> Imagine being invited to a dinner party where you would be able to visit with people you most admire, participating in talk that was excited, passionate, and persuasive about a topic you most enjoy. At the conclusion of the party, you'd leave filled with new ideas that you'd know in some way would direct what you'd do next. That's a dinner party you don't want to miss!

We now invite *you* to this dinner party. We trust that you will find the conversation here exciting, passionate, and persuasive. We are confident that you will encounter ideas that will challenge your thinking and change your teaching. After all, that teacher in the hallway lives in each of us, seeking both to understand what our students need and to believe in the promise they represent. Here, we offer answers that will lead to more questions, vision that will lead to action. Read. React. Re-vision. In doing so, you join and enrich our conversation and our community.

> > > KYLENE BEERS

The Measure of
Our Success

In the future, how *we educate our children may prove to be more important than* how much *we educate them.*

—*Thomas Friedman,* The World Is Flat

AUGUST 29, 2005, *a Houston area high school.* "This sucks," Derek said none too softly as he and two of his buddies made their way into the ninth-grade reading class they had just been assigned. The teacher of the remedial reading class tried to make the reassignment from an elective (and popular) teen leadership class to the remedial reading class a positive thing. She talked about students having time to catch up on reading skills, about this classroom being a place where the students would work together to learn together. She reiterated that hard work would pay off with a better score on the TAKS (Texas Assessment of Knowledge and Skills), that the whole school was focused on meeting AYP (adequate yearly progress) this year. "This class will help you make adequate yearly progress," she said a bit too brightly. Then, she asked if anyone had any questions. A voice from the middle of the room asked what the word *adequate* meant.

Kylene Beers began our thinking about this book and therefore her chapter begins this book. Designed to be a handbook on adolescent literacy for teachers, principals, and policy makers, this text can be read in most any order. However, this chapter sets the vision for the entire volume and so beginning your reading of the book with this chapter makes good sense.

—*KB, REP, LR*

"*Adequate* means satisfactory. So adequate yearly progress, AYP, means everyone is making satisfactory progress," she explained.

ANOTHER VOICE: "Making satisfactory progress at what?"

THE TEACHER: "In what you're learning in your classes, like English and math."

ANOTHER VOICE: "So how come I have to be in this class if where I have to make satisfactory progress is in English and math?"

THE TEACHER: "This class will help you with reading, and that will help you in your English and math classes."

ANOTHER VOICE: "So if I make good grades in English, then I'm satisfactory and I can get out of this class?"

THE TEACHER: "Well, you need to make good grades there, but it's on the TAKS that we look to see if you are making adequate or satisfactory yearly progress."

ANOTHER VOICE: "I made C's last year in my language arts class, so how come I passed on to this year if C's weren't adequate but now I have to be in this retard class?"

AND ANOTHER VOICE: "How come just the TAKS means I'm satisfactory?"

ANOTHER VOICE: "So, like, I could be doing good in English but if I fail the TAKS then I'm not adequate?"

ANOTHER VOICE: "Who gets to decide what score you got to make to be adequate?"

DEREK SPOKE UP OVER EVERYONE: "So how come my progress last year wasn't *adequate*?"

The teacher, who had not taken the time to look at the scores from Derek's last two TAKS tests, did not know about the 160-point jump that Derek had made on the reading portion of TAKS. She did not understand that until that moment Derek had not focused on the detail that he was twenty points shy of the score needed to "meet the standard." He had focused on the huge *progress* he had made and, until that moment, had felt good about that progress. But not knowing this, the teacher quieted everyone and gave a lengthy explanation about making sure that all the students in the school showed progress on the TAKS and about how certain goals had to be reached and about No Child Left Behind (NCLB) legislation and testing proficiency and . . .

Derek interrupted her, "Yeah, but you still ain't said why *my* progress wasn't *adequate*." He waited. She said nothing. He asked again, "So how come 160 points wasn't *adequate*?" She started talking again about requirements from the state and NCLB and how everyone in the school has to show he is learning enough each year. Derek put his head down on his desk, pulled the hood of his sweatshirt up over his head, and was done.

> > > > >
An ongoing criticism of NCLB is that AYP not only changes from year to year as states juggle test scores but also varies from state to state, as tests and scoring methods differ. It's likely that Derek would have reached AYP in some states, while in others, like Texas, he would not. The consistency? No state would reward him for his huge *progress*.

—KB, REP, LR

Failing to Note the Progress in Adequate Yearly Progress

Derek's urban high school, facing growing pressure about not reaching AYP for two years in a row, put "low-achieving" ninth graders (i.e., students who did not reach the minimum pass score on the eighth-grade TAKS test) into a "remedial reading class" that proved to be nothing more than a TAKS test-preparation class. It didn't matter that the teacher wanted to teach students reading strategies that she knew would help them in their content area classes (which in my mind include English class); it didn't matter that the teacher knew she needed to teach students with texts at each student's instructional reading level. The principal had purchased a test-prep program that promised to help students reach AYP, and he decided that was the curriculum. When I asked him if he thought that particular prepackaged program was really going to help close the reading achievement gap, especially for the groups of students in his school that were not making AYP (African American students, Hispanic students, and the economically disadvantaged students), he explained, "It's got to. NCLB demands it." *NCLB demands what,* I asked. "That we close the achievement gap," he said. *How do you know when that's happened?* I asked. "Kids pass the damn test," he said, walking off.

> < < < < <
> This point should not be glossed over. Until middle and high school teachers are given the freedom to use texts that are at students' instructional and independent reading levels, then struggling readers will continue to struggle.
> —*KB, REP, LR*

Though school administrators paid a lot of attention to Derek's twenty-point miss-the-mark score, no one attended to the fact that Derek lives in a low-rent apartment project in which five people (he, his mom, and three younger siblings) share a one-bedroom apartment that boasts a lone window air conditioner unit and one bathroom with a perpetually stopped-up toilet. Getting it fixed requires waiting for the project's one plumber or paying a minimum of eighty-five dollars to retain the services of an outside plumber . . . and that's before any work is done. No one addressed the fact that his mother works for minimum wage at a nationally known discount store where she does not receive health benefits. No one noted that she supplements this income with a second job as a janitor in a large office building where she works sixteen hours each weekend cleaning bathroom stalls and waxing the floors. This extra weekend job not only means needed extra income but also means that neither Derek nor his siblings have anyone home on weekends to take them to the library, supervise homework, get them to a classmate's house to work on required group projects, or even sit and enjoy a television movie together. There's little conversation in the home . . . no talking about getting into college, no discussions about what the kids want to be when they grow up, not even much laughter. "We get up, catch the bus, go to school, come home, wait for Mom, eat, go to bed, and do the same thing over and over and over again," Derek explained.

Yes, the school attended to the twenty-point deficit, but no one noticed that Derek, who had been a band student in the fifth through eighth grades, had not continued band because he couldn't afford the high school band fees. No one noted that Derek does not have a computer at home and cannot use the school computers before and after school because his only transportation is the school bus, which runs on a strict schedule.

No one noted that while Derek is eligible for free breakfasts at his school, the same bus that doesn't get him to school early enough to do some work in the library also does not get him there in time for the free breakfast; so, most mornings, he walks into first period having had nothing to eat since dinner—something his mom makes quickly from a box or from cans when she gets home around eight o'clock. He fills up on whatever the school offers for lunch that day. Sometimes one of the cafeteria ladies gives him extra to eat.

The decision to take Derek out of the teen leadership class he had chosen as an elective and put him into a test-prep class was a direct result of NCLB legislation. While NCLB legislation mandates that 100 percent of *all* students in each school pass *all* portions of state-required tests by the 2013–14 academic year (and yes, you should ignore the research that shows the statistical probability of *that* happening), NCLB legislation does not mandate, require, or even suggest that local communities (much less states or the nation) address minimum-wage issues, work to bring the income level of African Americans and Hispanic wage earners to that of white wage earners (at all levels of jobs), make health care coverage available for all, make decent home ownership available for all, eliminate child poverty, make school spending equitable across school districts, or even provide school supplies (not just notebooks and paper that PTAs distribute at the start of the school year but graphing calculators, laptop computers, printers with unlimited ink cartridge refills, and Internet access—DSL preferred) for all school-age children in all schools.

If I sound angry, I am. And I'm not the kid who had to give up my teen leadership class.[1]

---

1. Derek's story has a coda. First, Derek serves as an example of what happens when the system doesn't work. Once it became known that because of bus schedules, Derek was missing breakfast and needed time with school resources, people tried to make adjustments. But rules and regulations trumped and school officials weren't able to make transportation to and from school work any better for him. He continued to arrive after breakfast had been served and had to leave before he could spend time in the library working on school-provided computers. System failure at its worst. On the other hand, Derek's teacher most certainly proved that first-impressions (Derek's impression of the teacher and the class) can be changed. The teacher spoke with me after that first class and admitted that she was embarrassed when Derek asked her about his progress. In this case, the person, not the system, had failed Derek. She had not taken the time to look up information on students, she said with embarrassment and regret. Like students who sometimes chose silence over admitting they do not know the answer, this teacher did the same. However, as the semester continued, she worked hard to prove to Derek that his progress *did* matter and that his huge gains proved that he could do the work. Eventually, the teacher decided to use the test-prep program on Fridays and the rest of the week to teach the strategies for improving comprehension, vocabulary, and fluency that her expertise told her she needed to teach. She used trade books (purchased with her own dollars) that were at students' instructional levels and spent time helping students learn to navigate content area textbooks that, without support, were too hard. Derek eventually raised his head off the desk, and like most kids, proved he was far more willing to forgive than most adults ever are.

The Gap in Closing the Gap

Am I suggesting that students of poverty cannot achieve in school until poverty is eliminated? No. I see students who live in abject poverty make great strides in schools every day. I see programs such as the Comer School Development Program (where I had the great privilege of working for several years) helping stu-dents of poverty achieve; I see programs from the National Urban Alliance (NUA) helping underachieving students of color do the same. And we know that great teachers can and do make great differences in students' academic lives. But I have to wonder what would happen if in addition to demand-ing that schools close the academic achievement gap, No Child Left Behind legislation required that local and state leaders close the poverty gap that exists in their communities, along with the health care gap, the housing gap, the technology gap, the access-to-college gap, and the many gaps that exist between low- and higher-income schools. Did you know, for instance, that low-income schools are more likely to be staffed by less-experienced teachers than higher-income schools, and higher-income schools tend to offer a wider and more rigor-ous array of courses than low-income schools (see Beers 2005)? What *would* happen if NCLB legislation required that business owners completely close the wage-earning gap between races and genders by 2014, that social institutions close the preschool-years preparation gap as well as the nutrition gap between low-income and middle- to high-income pregnant women, and that we all had to examine and eliminate our own gaps of expectation for success among and between races and genders? Close *those* gaps, fix *those* prob-lems, address *those* inequalities and then, *then* teachers will more than willingly talk about what Derek's performance on the TAKS does or does not mean.

> > > > *I have to wonder what would happen if in addition to demanding that schools close the academic achievement gap, No Child Left Behind legislation required that local and state leaders close the poverty gap that exists in their communities, along with the health care gap, the housing gap, the technology gap, the access-to-college gap, and the many gaps that exist between low- and higher-income schools.*

But, of course, NCLB mandates that schools do something that no other institution has been mandated to do. And my fear is not that we *won't* be able to accomplish this, but that we *will*.[2]

< < < < <
Eric Cooper, president of the NUA, and Yvette Jackson, chief executive officer, offer a look at some of the work they are doing through the NUA in Chapter 16.
—*KB, REP, LR*

---

2 I thought carefully about this section. I am writing this chapter during the time when NCLB is up for reauthorization. Daily I receive an email from someone encouraging me to sign a petition that will ask legislators to *repeal* this bill. Daily I delete the petition and refuse to sign it. While I believe NCLB is underfunded and has caused too many to equate learning with testing and define success by the sole criterion of meeting AYP, I also believe that NCLB accomplished something that for too long had been left unaccomplished and, at times, even unconsidered. NCLB requires that all children be taught to the same rigorous standards and explains that gaps in academic achievement between and among groups of students—groups identified by race, by socioeconomic status, and by language—are not acceptable. As a consequence, NCLB legislation compels each of us to examine and eliminate the institutional and individual prejudicial instructional and social practices that did indeed leave some children behind. While addressing the problems with the bill during the reauthorization process is imperative, the move to repeal the legislation that demands such actions is not the best solution.

How and How Much We Educate Our Children

To: Kylene Beers [kbeers@prodigy.net]

From: Paul Sellers [name changed and email removed]
Subject: Helping our high school meet AYP
Date: August 2, 2005

Dear Dr. Beers,

My name is Paul Sellers and I am the principal of ——High School in ——, Florida. I heard you and Bob Probst speak at the NASSP convention last year. I'd like to talk with you both about coming in to work with my faculty about closing the achievement gap. We did not make AYP last year and must this year or we will lose needed funding and risk being taken over by the state. We would like to hire you both as consultants so we can meet AYP. Please contact me as soon as possible.

Bob and I did not go to Florida to help this principal, in large part because the principal's measure of success did not match ours. In a follow-up phone call, I asked what he wanted to accomplish. "Get the scores up," he said. "Do whatever you need to do to get those scores in place." *How does making a certain score help your students with the twenty-first-century literacy demands they face*, I asked. "I don't even know what those are. Just get their scores up," he responded.

A well-respected (and well-funded by the Department of Education) literacy researcher said a similar thing when he attended a think tank on adolescent literacy hosted by the National Adolescent Literacy Coalition in September 2006, a meeting funded in part by the Kellogg Foundation. As chair of this group, I wanted this particular participant there. I respect a lot of the work he is doing in literacy (early childhood and now adolescent literacy), know that reports coming from the center he directs are read by many, and thought his particular take on literacy education would be valuable to the conversation. It was, and I remain pleased that he attended. He did make it clear, though, that his definition of adolescent literacy centered on academic literacy—the literacy needed for students to read (with deep understanding) their school texts and school tests. While I greatly appreciated that he explained that his remarks on adolescent literacy were constricted by the narrower focus of academic literacy, I was dismayed when he said of twenty-first-century literacy skills, "I just can't get my head around what twenty-first-century literacy skills are. But I can identify and help teachers and kids with academic literacy, so that's going to be my focus."

If this well-respected researcher, whose federally funded reports serve as a way to advance the understanding of adolescent literacy, equates the complexities of adolescent literacy with the more limited demands of academic literacy, then I am left to wonder how committed the Department of Education is to preparing *all* students to live and work productively in the twenty-first century. I understand the inclination to default to the more manageable (i.e., testable) demands of academic literacy as the measure of success, but the reality is, literacy demands have shifted and we do our students a disservice if we fail to teach to these demands.

This is indeed my concern—that we'll all default to the demands of academic literacy, that we'll focus on how much we need to teach to make sure kids reach that magical AYP mark, and that in doing so we'll forget (or perhaps never learn) that *how* we teach in this new "flat" world Thomas Friedman so aptly describes in *The World Is Flat* (2005) is probably more important than how *much* we teach. We'll be damned sure that kids reach AYP (after all, doing less means being labeled a failing school, losing needed dollars that might help with instruction, and having the state take over the school). But in doing that, we will have prepared them for the literacy demands of a world that no longer exists.

> < < < < <
> Jim Burke's chapter (10) does a good job of connecting comments Friedman makes about globalization with instructional habits for the classroom.
> —*KB, REP, LR*

The Shift (Once Again) in Literacy Demands

We shouldn't be surprised that literacy demands have shifted once again. Literacy is not a tangible object (like, say, that gallon of milk you may or may not have remembered to buy at the grocery store on your way home); literacy is a set of skills that reflect the needs of the time. As those needs shift, then our definition of literacy shifts (see Myers 1996).

> > > > *This is indeed my concern—that we'll all default to the demands of academic literacy, that we'll focus on how much we need to teach to make sure kids reach that magical AYP mark, and that in doing so we'll forget (or perhaps never learn) that* how *we teach in this new "flat" world Thomas Friedman so aptly describes in* The World Is Flat *(2005) is probably more important than* how much *we teach.*

From colonial America up through the Revolutionary War, literacy was defined as the ability to sign your name— and thus was called signature literacy. Then, through the Civil War, literacy was defined by minimal reading ability and penmanship—thus the focus on keeping slaves from learning to read and write while others attended to letter writing and calligraphy. Literate people wrote long letters and practiced calligraphy. Many of us felt the effects of this level of literacy through elementary school as we practiced making even, tall loops and smooth, round circles while learning the Palmer method of cursive writing. Some of us even remember a section on our report cards labeled "penmanship."

Then, until World War I, literate people were those who had memorized poems, speeches, soliloquies. We now look back and label this time as recitational literacy, in that literacy as penmanship was replaced with literacy as knowing a body of work. We still see the interest in this today through E. D. Hirsch's thoughts on cultural literacy and the (rare) tenth-grade teacher who demands that students memorize something from Shakespeare. But many readers of this text will remember being in school and memorizing "Trees" or "Annabel Lee" or "The Charge of the Light Brigade." When you asked why, you were told, "Because you ought to know these poems." In other words, recitational literacy.

From WWI up through the late 1980s/early 1990s, we saw an increasing focus on analyzing texts, which reached a zenith in the 1990s. This was the golden era of CliffsNotes. The goal was to amass information and have it stored, handy, ready to regurgitate. The text held all the answers and skilled readers could discern that meaning by setting aside their own thoughts and instead focusing on the clues left by the author. As a society, during this time, we were living through the industrial revolution to the technology explosion to the information age. We should not be at all surprised that what was most valued in literacy at this time was that ability to know, to analyze, to explain.

But it's not the twentieth century, and we aren't in the technology or information age. Thomas Friedman (2005) tells us we are living in a flat world. Daniel Pink (2006), author of *A Whole New Mind*, calls this the *conceptual age* and explains that in this age, making meaning and connections will be valued as will focusing on the multiple possibilities of any situation over seeking one solution. In this age, *creative thinking* will be the key to success. Friedman uses different words, but his thoughts mirror Pink's: in the flat world, producing, not consuming, information is the measure of success.

Back to the principal in Florida. I asked him how often students downloaded information from the Internet at his school. He said he had no idea. "Often, I guess," he finally offered. I asked him for examples. "I don't know," he said, more than a bit exasperated. "In their classes, they have to do research and so they download things then. So, it depends on which classes." *And*, I asked, *how often are they uploading their own ideas to the Internet*? "Their own ideas? Why would anyone want to read their ideas? We aren't here to give these students a chance to publish teen diary dribble on the Internet. We're here to teach them the information they need." *They need for what*, I asked. Silence. "That they just need. School. You know. School! You go to school to get information. Information for passing the FCAT [Florida Comprehensive Assessment Test]." The conversation didn't end badly, but it ended. I sat for a long time thinking about his words while remembering Collin.

> > < <

The previous January. I ducked into the high school library to check my email on a school computer. With a mere seven minutes before I had to be in another classroom, I focused on my task and ignored what was happening around me. But when I heard a voice exclaim *No f-in' way*, I decided to take some notice of, if not *what* was happening around me, *who* was around me.

A tall, thin, teenage boy with one earring and long hair pulled back into a ponytail, wearing low-slung jeans and a T-shirt that probably fit him better several years ago, was sitting two chairs away, staring at the next computer screen. With one foot tapping nonstop against the leg of the desk—*tap tap tap tap tap tap tap*—and his pencil eraser drumming against the desktop—*dut dut dut dut dut dut dut*—his eyes never left the screen. Then all sound stopped—no *tap*, no *dut*—silence for a half a beat and then, under the breath again, *There is no f-in' way he can believe that.* Finally he noticed me noticing him. *Yeah?* he asked, in a not-friendly manner.

I decided to ignore the language and focus on the message. "Everything OK?"

"Yeah. Right. Everything is just fine. Except for what this idiot posted on my blog. Who the f— - . . . well, who does he think he is?"

"So, you have a blog?" I asked the tapping, dutting, pony-tailed, earringed, anorexic-looking teenager sitting beside me.

"Name me anyone in this century who doesn't," he said, dismissing me as he began firing off a response to whoever had responded (unfavorably, I'll presume) to his blog posting.

I nodded, hoping that I too had assumed that look of disdain at the mere thought that some people now several years into the twenty-first century had not yet bought or rented or designed or created or posted or set up or whatever it is that one does to or with a blog. As he typed (fast, I should add), I interrupted, asking his name and his English teacher's name. He willingly gave his own name but wondered why I wanted his English teacher's name. I explained that I just wanted to drop by and see what was going on in his English class. He explained that "nothing goes on in there," and then gave me her name and went back to his work.

> > > *"So, you have a blog?" I asked the tapping, dutting, pony-tailed, earringed, anorexic-looking teenager sitting beside me.*
>
> *"Name me anyone in this century who doesn't," he said, dismissing me as he began firing off a response to whoever had responded (unfavorably, I'll presume) to his blog posting.*

Later that day, in his English class, I asked his teacher about his participation and work. I mentioned that he seemed bright and passionate and more than a bit colorful—always a great combination for lively discussion in a classroom. "Collin?" the teacher responded. "Oh, he's failing the semester. He never does anything." I asked how he was with writing. "Pretty bad. He just doesn't try. Lots of errors. Most of the time what he writes is so minimal that it doesn't even make sense." I asked if she knew he kept a blog on environmental issues. She asked if we were talking about the same kid.

When Literacy Goes Underground

Though Collin lived in Texas and therefore had failed the reading portion of the TAKS exam, I was fairly confident that given the chance, he would have scored at the same low level on the Florida state test, the FCAT. Collin didn't value the academic literacy demands his school valued; therefore, while he had not yet dropped out of school, he had dropped out of playing the school game and had taken his literacy underground.

The more Collin and I talked, the more it became apparent that he read a lot (mostly expository texts), wrote a lot (all expository), and viewed reading and writing as important tools for communicating, thinking, persuading, and participating in global issues. The majority of his writing consisted of postings on his blog, which, unlike the majority of blogs by teenagers (as well as adults) that *are* best described as online diaries (the principal wasn't too far off in his criticism), was devoted to environmental issues, in particular global warming. His frustration on the day I met him was a result of a response to comments he had made about President Bush's position on the Kyoto Accord. His teacher's comments were in response to the minimal paper (in terms of quality and quantity) he had turned in on the "style analysis of *After You, My Dear Alphonse*." She saw him as a "struggling reader and writer" and someone who would "struggle with literacy in the real world." He saw her as "just completely out of it" and having "no clue" what he knew or could do.

> > > > >
Both Donna Alvermann (Chapter 3) and Sara Kajder (Chapter 14) offer well-developed ideas about digital literacy.

—*KB, REP, LR*

Collin was in a school that connected literacy achievement to high scores on high-stakes tests. If students met the standard on their state test and if the school met AYP, then students were literate. If not, there was a literacy crisis. In that either-or world, there was no recognition of the literacy abilities he did bring to school—skills that included his ability to synthesize across texts he chose, to create information as a result of that synthesis, and to share that information using digital literacy skills. He, like Derek, was also in a remedial reading (test-prep) class because he, too, had not met AYP. He, like Derek, ignored the class. "Could you pass the test if you wanted to?" I eventually asked Collin.

He shrugged. "Maybe. The test doesn't matter."

"But if you don't eventually pass, you won't get a high school diploma," I reminded him.

"Yeah. Maybe I'll decide to pass it before then. Or maybe I won't. A high school diploma just doesn't mean what it used to mean, you know."

Literacy Learning in the Twenty-first Century

Collin is almost right. I'm concerned that a high school diploma means exactly what it used to mean when we now need it to mean something more. High schools—and middle schools and backing all the way down to elementary schools—need to be places where learning looks different than it did when we were living during the factory age. But I fear it doesn't. We still move large groups of kids from one class to the next with loud, shrill bells, like factory whistles calling large groups of workers back to work after breaks. For the most part, school is still based on show-and-tell (we show and then they tell);

Monday is still the day when spelling words and vocabulary words are distributed, and Friday is still the day when those words are tested. Students are still rated on an A–F system, though most parents couldn't really tell you what an A student in ninth-grade English or seventh-grade social studies knows or does that a B student doesn't know or do. Schooling is still primarily about teachers distributing information and then students giving it back. Some schools understand the importance of inquiry, the value of collaboration, the critical need for creating and questioning and wondering. They understand the learning potential when students self-select writing topics and reading material. They have come to appreciate the absolute necessity for using technology as a tool for learning and not an electronic workbook for remediation, the difference between writing as a way of understanding and writing as reporting, and the inescapable truth that the measure of success must be more than a single state-mandated, minimum-standards test. But most don't.

> > > *I'm concerned that a high school diploma means exactly what it used to mean when we now need it to mean something more.*

But what if schooling looked different? What if we recognized that the world in which we now all work and live is different and what if education were about preparing students to live productively in *that* world? What if learning were interdisciplinary and not arbitrarily divided into forty-five-minute chunks with teachers who rarely have the time to speak to one another, let alone collaborate? What if learning were research based (meaning that learning was tied to what students wanted to research instead of what teachers assigned)?

> > > *What if school were a place for figuring out, where trying mattered at least as much as adequate progress, where learning proceeded at each student's level and pace instead of mandated levels? I think if those things happened, then a high school diploma might mean something, and the something it would mean would be far different than what it meant in 1986 or 1996 or even today in 2006.*

What if students sometimes worked independently and other times worked with others in their school community, local community, state community, or across the globe? What if schooling valued multiple intelligences and the curriculum were dependent on technology and multimedia? What if authentic assessments were more important than multiple-choice state tests? What if asking the probing question were valued more than providing the correct answer? What if students were required to do some sort of service project or community work and what if learning content in the textbook were not substituted for figuring out what to do with that content? What if school were the place where students found their voice, discovered how to think, and saw that what they did and believed and thought mattered? What if school were where students learned a lot (not all, but certainly a lot) about being a part of a democracy, a contributing part? What if school were a place for figuring out, where trying mattered at least as much as adequate progress, where learning proceeded at each student's level and pace instead of

< < < < <
Be sure to read what Randy Bomer has to say about the role of literacy in Chapter 20. Though the final chapter in this book, it's a nice complement to this first chapter.
—*KB, REP, LR*

lock-step pace? I think if those things happened, then a high school diploma *might* mean something, and the something it would mean would be far different than what it meant in 1986 or 1996 or even today in 2006.

Figure 1 is one of the best representations I've seen of what twenty-first-century learning needs to look like. In this figure, academic achievement (which is dependent on academic literacy skills) surrounds digital literacy, inventive thinking, effective communication, and high productivity. For some, this might indicate that academic achievement is the beginning point, something that must be accomplished before moving into the other types of literacy and learning.

I suggest that instead of focusing on academic achievement as something that must precede work on other areas—digital-age literacy, inventive thinking, effective communication, and high productivity—we should view these areas of

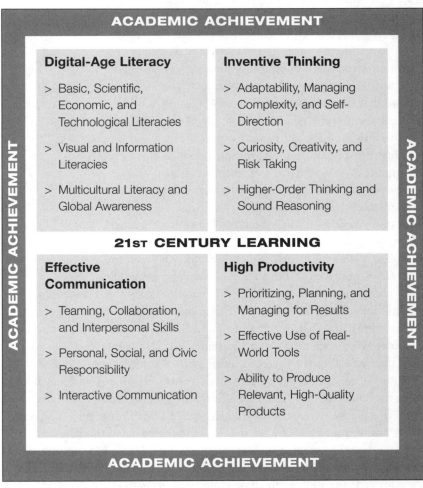

FIGURE 1–1. *Learning in the Twenty-first Century: A Look at Necessary Components*

© 2006 by Learning Point Associates

growth as developing in tandem. In such a school, Collin's curiosity about the environment, his global awareness, his technological literacy, his sense of civic responsibility, and his ability to produce a relevant, high-quality product (his blog) would be more important than his ability to write the style analysis paper his teacher decided he should write. In this school, Collin's passion for the environment would be his entrée into all sorts of learning, and Collin's literacy would be celebrated, not hidden underground. But this school cannot exist without a vision—a practical vision—of what to do.

> > > *This book exists because we believe that in teaching all students, we must first teach each student, and that each student is a promise of a better tomorrow; it exists because we believe that what you do and what you say to the students in your classrooms make an incredible difference.*

Turning Promise into Practice

This book came to be because Bob Probst, Linda Rief, and I believe that in this time of what some have labeled "the adolescent literacy crisis" (Norwood 2006; Moore et al. 1999), we need our most respected adolescent literacy educators to offer a bold vision of what literacy education for adolescents in the twenty-first century should be. It exists because the contributing authors believe that adolescent literacy is bigger than academic literacy and that our current measure of success—a certain score to show adequate yearly progress—is an insufficient measure of real success. This book exists because we believe that in teaching *all* students, we must first teach *each* student, and that each student is a promise of a better tomorrow; it exists because we believe that what *you* do and what *you* say to the students in your classrooms make an incredible difference. This book exists because Derek and Collin and the seven thousand students who drop out of school daily deserve better.[3] And this book exists because we believe students' promise for a better tomorrow begins, in part, with the practices you offer them today.

When you want to know more . . .

Kylene's chapter focuses on helping students grow into literate adults, looking at the political issues that affect literacy education and at the literacies our students are developing, sometimes despite the schools. She's addressed these issues in "Hearing Zach: Matching Reluctant and Struggling Readers with Books," in *English Journal* (2004), and in *When Kids Can't Read, What Teachers Can Do: A Guide for Teachers* (2002).

---

3. This number comes from a study titled "Diplomas Count: An Essential Guide to Graduation Policy and Rates," published by *Education Week* (Vol 25, Issue 41S, June 2006), and in all likelihood will have changed by the time you read this; however, we are unwilling to speculate if that future change represents a lower or higher percentage of students who drop out of school.

Connecting to my thoughts

Connecting to other texts

REPORTS AND RESEARCH ON ADOLESCENT LITERACY*

ACT. 2006. "Reading between the Lines: What the ACT Reveals about College Readiness in Reading."

Alliance for Excellent Education. 2004. "Reading Next: A Vision for Action and Research in Middle and High School Literacy."

Alliance for Excellent Education. 2007. "Double the Work: Challenges and Solutions to Acquiring Language and Academic Literacy for Adolescent English Language Learners."

Center on Instruction. 2007. "Academic Literacy Instruction for Adolescents: A Guidance Document from the Center of Instruction."

National Association of Secondary School Principals. 2005. "Creating a Culture of Literacy: A Guide for Middle and High School Principals."

National Association of State Boards of Education. 2005. "Reading at Risk: The State Response to the Crisis in Adolescent Literacy."

National Governors Association. 2005. "Reading to Achieve: A Governor's Guide to Adolescent Literacy."

National School Boards Association. 2006. "The Next Chapter: A School Board Guide to Improving Adolescent Literacy."

---

* Each of these reports is available online. At your preferred search engine, enter the report's title.

Flying Blind

IN ALL THE YEARS I worked full-time as a therapist, I don't remember a kid over the age of nine or ten who didn't have a teacher somewhere in his life who had saved him. A kid didn't get into my office unless things had turned pretty desperate, or had been desperate from the beginning, and digging through family history for something healthy to serve as an anchor often felt futile. But I could always dig through history and find that healthy anchor somewhere in school. Unfortunately, I could also find its opposite, from teachers who looked at behavior rather than heart to those who refused to understand that rage and bad behavior are more often than not covers for fear—Am I good enough? Will someone discover my secrets and hate me for them? Is there nothing lovable about me? Will I . . . can I hold on?

Brenda, the girl whose voice I used for Sarah Byrnes in *Staying Fat for Sarah Byrnes* (who is now in her mid-thirties), was one of the toughest kids I have known. She wasn't physically scarred like Sarah, but she was emotionally scarred at least as badly. I put her on my client load after she punched out another therapist—one I thought should have been punched out a long time ago for judging his clients. She stood just inside the door to my office during that first session, glaring at me like I just might be next. She dug at the side seam

In a time when "scientifically based research practices" is where some begin their conversations on adolescent literacy, we thought it important to remember what it is we do each day: teach kids—fragile ones, strong ones, funny ones, sad ones, angry ones, happy ones . . . all deserving a life of laughter and hope and learning.

—KB, REP, LR

of her jeans with her car keys for the entire hour, delivering one-word answers to my questions, never moving even an inch toward my desk. I decided to evaluate our progress by how many weeks it took her to come all the way in and sit down (it was four). Only when she felt assured I would not judge or diminish did she begin to open up. Her rage and fear, her anxiety and depression were the stuff of legend. Her home life had been so unpredictable and her treatment with relatives and state caregivers so random that it was nearly impossible for her to make even the most commonsense decisions. Time and again she drifted back to her third-grade teacher, the one person she ever remembered believing her and believing *in* her—her witness. And time and again I anchored my therapy to that teacher's words and perceptions.

After years in and out of foster care and residential treatment institutions, Brenda pulled it together, graduated from high school, applied for student aid and athletic scholarships, and finished college. Shortly after her graduation, I received one of two "special" invitations to her wedding, issued to the two people who, in her words, "saved my life." I was touched but well aware that only one person saved her life, the same person who saved so many of my therapy sessions with her: her third-grade teacher.

> > > *Truth is, every teacher is involved with as many troubled students as not. As if adolescence itself weren't trouble enough.*

The wedding was held outside on a warm summer day. My client was dressed in a gorgeous white wedding dress and running shoes. When Brenda saw that third-grade teacher pull into the parking lot, she shot across the park at full speed, the long train of her dress casting her like a glorious white kite, and jumped into her former teacher's arms. Her teacher held her as if Brenda were her own. It was the first time they'd seen each other since third grade.

Favorite teachers save lives.

What an awesome calling you have come to; what little help and understanding you are being offered from many of those who make the rules. When a middle or high school teacher gazes out over her classroom, she is looking at one in three girls who have been sexually mistreated and one in six or seven boys, depending on which statistic you accept. Approximately one in ten is gay; more are struggling with sexual identity. That's not to mention those engaged in family power struggles resulting in eating disorders, crippling anxiety or depression, and/or self-mutilation. Truth is, every teacher is involved with as many troubled students as not. As if adolescence itself weren't trouble enough.

My email constantly reminds me that so often my books are better than they ever had a right to be because of the history the reader brings to the reading. I used the "gimmick" of a dead narrator in a recent novel, *The Sledding Hill*, largely to give myself the luxury of writing in third person instead of first person. The dead narrator was the best friend of the main character and sought to reassure this friend during hard times by "bumping" him, psychically, I guess you might say. I was playing with the afterlife to give myself a narrator who could see all. Then I got a letter from a twelve-year-old girl whose mother had recently died of cancer. Her father allowed no conversation about the loss in his house; it was to be forgotten. What we don't talk about can't hurt us. The girl said she thought she would go crazy or hurt herself, but then she read *The Sledding Hill* and decided she could feel her mother bumping her. She no longer had to go through her father; she could go to her room and turn out the lights and feel her mother's love surround her. She said that. "I can feel my mother surround me."

A middle school girl wrote to tell me that, though she wasn't a kid with Sarah Byrnes' life ("In fact, I'll probably be a cheerleader"), she thought she might be one of those people who is mean to kids like Sarah. "This story made me want to be a better person." She vowed to take as many friends on that journey as she could get to board her bus.

A high school girl once approached me after a presentation to say she couldn't read my books; she could start them, she said, but they were simply too painful because they were too much like her life. She said she was glad I wrote them and she loved reading the beginnings because she knew where they went and that they reflected her life. If other kids who hadn't had such a hard time read them, they might know her better and understand why she acted the way she sometimes did. Fourteen years old, and more articulate about why she couldn't read my books than I was in writing them. Tears ran down her cheeks like raindrops on a rainy window as she talked, and when I looked at the teacher standing beside her, her hand tucked just inside the girl's elbow, those same tears ran down her cheeks. The girl saw her teacher's reaction and leaned into her as if falling into an elegant hammock. When the girl walked away, the teacher tried to tell me what wondrous material I had written, but I knew the wondrous thing here was her; I had seen the relief on the girl's face when she saw her teacher's complete understanding. That teacher had created a safe enough haven for that girl to approach me, and I knew that long after I was gone, that teacher (and probably others) would be there to help her up each time she crumbled. Healing is possible in a place like that.

Students such as these walk into your classrooms in every size, shape, and color. You can't know their histories because their only control is control of their secrets. You are asked to create a safe enough place for them to learn, and for you to teach, and then are provided with ill-thought-out standards, drawn up by men and women so distant from your theatre of engagement as to be functionally illiterate in its regard. These people demand that you test memory-level

> > > *You are asked to create a safe enough place for them to learn, and for you to teach, and then are provided with ill-thought-out standards, drawn up by men and women so distant from your theatre of engagement as to be functionally illiterate in its regard.*

< < < < <
Chris Crutcher's comments on the difficult lives of adolescents is echoed throughout this book by other authors. Ruth Shagoury (Interlude 1) takes you to the heart of a student from Bosnia; Carol Jago (Chapter 8) shows you the tentative gratefulness of a student from Korea; Yvette Jackson and Eric Cooper (Chapter 16) demand that you see the painful reality of urban youth.
—KB, REP, LR

learning and abandon the staples of *real* education—response, expression, relationship—to chance.

But many of you will refuse to do that, because you did-n't invest years of your life getting an education and gather-ing the tools to follow your passion (knowing you'd never be paid even a fraction of the salary that goes to a CEO—or sometimes the CEO's assistant—or to the pro football player, neither of whom could begin to make the difference you do) to be disallowed the right to make the connection with your students that could change their lives. No child left behind? Only policy makers and politicians need a bill named that to remind them that leaving kids behind isn't a good idea.

> > > *There simply is no tougher job than that of Teacher.*

There simply is no tougher job than that of Teacher. When I was a full-time therapist, I would sit in my office, listening to the stories of some ravaged ado-lescent, and think, "This kid is in a school somewhere in this town. His teacher has no idea what his life is like, and the kid's not going to tell because he can't afford to." His behavior will often look exactly opposite of his true feelings. That teacher has to create a safe place for him *and* must educate him. That teacher is flying blind. But still she cranks up the props each day and takes 'er up. *That's* courage. *That's* how you leave no child behind. *That's* being a teacher.

When you want to know more . . .

Chris is known best for his novels for young adults, of course, but you should also take a look at some of his columns for *Voices from the Middle.* Start with "A Hand Up: Church and State and Spock" (2002) or "A Hand Up: Who You Callin' Diverse?" (2004). And then pick up any one of his novels.

> > > DONNA E. ALVERMANN

Multiliterate Youth in the Time of Scientific Reading Instruction

WHY IS IT THAT precisely at a time when the youth of the so-called Net generation are engaging, often simultaneously, with multiple sign systems (image, print, sound, gesture, digital) and finding their own reasons for becoming literate—reasons that extend beyond reading to acquire school knowledge—there is a narrowing of what counts as reading and how reading is taught? On observing this same phenomenon, Bustle noted, "It's almost ironic that, at a time when young people are becoming credible consumers of mass media and popular culture, curricular standards and pedagogical practices move further from real-life engagements with media to more traditional approaches to teaching and learning" (2004, n.p.).

Indeed, it was this shared sense of irony that partially motivated me to write this chapter. I say partially because somewhat serendipitously, a new book I had read over the summer of 2005 cast several projects in which I was involved in a new light. The book was *Everything Bad Is Good for You* (Johnson

Donna Alvermann expands our thinking about reading by discussing what it means to be multiliterate and by calling to question how multiliteracy competencies fit (or don't) with the more narrow vision of scientifically based research instruction. We chose to set this chapter here, early in the book, to provide a needed backdrop for the issues discussed throughout the book.

—*KB, REP, LR*

2005), and the projects included two grant proposals and a handbook chapter on what constitutes scientifically based reading instruction for adolescents in the United States. Both the proposals and handbook chapter drew from a theoretical perspective that makes use of twentieth-century philosopher-historian Michel Foucault's (1984) notion of genealogy. His is not the type of genealogy typically associated with family trees. Instead, Foucault's approach to writing history looks not only for continuities and origins but also for discontinuities that can disrupt certain claims linking the past with the present. Genealogies attempt to make sense of seemingly contradictory social phenomena, such as in the irony just described in which young people's proclivity for meaning making through multiple sign systems is juxtaposed with narrowed definitions of what counts as reading.

> > > > >
When you finish this chapter, you might want to turn to Chapter 14, where Sara Kajder discusses specific ways to bring digital literacies into the classroom.
—KB, REP, LR

In writing this chapter, I drew from a genealogical perspective in attempting to juxtapose the conditions that support adolescents' digital literacies (practiced primarily outside of school) with conditions that involve them in more traditional, time-honored print literacies (typically associated with formal schooling). My intent is not to reify distinctions between in-school and out-of-school literacies, for to do so, as I have argued elsewhere (Alvermann and Eakle 2006), is to separate these literacies from the very spaces that give them meaning and make them worth pursuing. It also limits what teachers and researchers can learn from students' literacy experiences, at least to the extent that students are willing to share their perceptions of those experiences. Listening to and observing youth as they communicate their familiarity with multiple sign systems across space, place, and time can provide valuable insights into how to approach both instruction and research—insights that might otherwise be lost or taken for granted in our rush to categorize literacy practices as either in school or out of school and thus either worthy of our attention or not.

> > > *What likely set of circumstances coalesced to bring about the present situation in which young people are increasingly engaged in digital literacies (largely through the Internet and other information communication technologies, such as instant messaging, chatting, blogging, emailing, text messaging, and online role playing) at precisely the same time in history when those in authority over school-related reading instruction are moving ever further toward a narrowed definition of what counts as reading?*

Specifically, the question that guides the remainder of this chapter is: What likely set of circumstances coalesced to bring about the present situation in which young people are increasingly engaged in digital literacies (largely through the Internet and other information communication technologies, such as instant messaging, chatting, blogging, emailing, text messaging, and online role playing) at precisely the same time in history when those in authority over school-related reading instruction are moving ever further toward a narrowed definition of what counts as reading?

Times: They Are A-Changin'

Referring to the youth of today as Digital Natives—that is, "native speakers" of the digital language of computers, video games, and the Internet—Prensky (2001) goes on to contrast their several years of practice at parallel processing and multitasking to the experience of the rest of us so-called Digital Immigrants, who like all immigrants retain to some degree our "accent," that is, our foot in the past. In Prensky's words, "the 'digital immigrant accent' can be seen in such things as turning to the Internet for information second rather than first, or in reading the manual for a program rather than assuming that the program itself will teach us to use it" (n.p.).

The importance of distinguishing between Digital Natives and Digital Immigrants for those of us in education, Prensky adds, is this:

> Digital Immigrants don't believe their students can learn successfully while watching TV or listening to music because they (the Immigrants) can't. Of course not—they didn't practice this skill constantly for all of their formative years. Digital Immigrants think learning can't (or shouldn't be) fun. Why should they—they didn't spend their formative years learning with Sesame Street.
>
> Unfortunately for our Digital Immigrant teachers, the people sitting in their classes grew up on the "twitch speed" of video games and MTV. They are used to the instantaneity of hypertext, downloaded music, phones in their pockets, a library on their laptops, beamed messages and instant messaging. They have little patience for lectures, step-by-step logic, and "tell-test" instruction. (n.p.)

Concurrent with this move by youth toward the digital—toward what is popular, highly entertaining, and instant in terms of communicating with one's peers—is another movement, largely driven by policy makers at the state and national levels. Here, the agenda is to make high-stakes testing the impetus driving our students to become better prepared, ready to take their place in an increasingly competitive global workforce. Though no doubt a coincidence, it is interesting nonetheless to note that in the same year in which Prensky (2001) published his article about digital natives and digital immigrants on the Internet, a nonpartisan vote in the U.S. Congress turned the No Child Left Behind Act (NCLB) (2001) into law.

The current drive in this country, fueled largely by NCLB, to make schools accountable, with an emphasis on adequate yearly progress, scientifically based reading instruction, and improved high school graduation rates, has its analog in history. Going back to 1957 and the Soviet's launch of Sputnik, there was a similar push for school reform, one aimed at applying elements of the cognitive revolution to what was perceived as an ailing and decrepit curriculum (Cazden

< < < < <
We found it interesting that Teri Lesesne (Chapter 6) and Donna both use the phrase *times, they are a-changin'*. We didn't want to ask either to rethink what obviously worked for both; we do suggest that you look to Teri's chapter to see additional changes she outlines
—*KB, REP, LR*

2006). Teachers then, as now, were admonished to alter their instruction in keeping with new research and policy mandates into which they had had little if any input.

What was different four decades ago, however, was the view of youth that people generally held. This discontinuity is perhaps most vividly portrayed in Lesko's book *Act Your Age! A Cultural Construction of Adolescence* (2001). Whereas once adolescence was viewed as a period in young people's lives when turmoil, fueled by intrapersonal and interpersonal problems, consumed most of their waking moments, nowadays such a developmentally deterministic and age-biased view has been tempered, largely by the work of scholars (e.g., Amit-Talai and Wulff 1995) who, like Lesko, argue against treating adolescence as a subcategory—one that can be easily labeled and then isolated.

Rather than view adolescents as incomplete, or "not-yet" adults who thus are less competent and less knowledgeable than their elders, scholars of youth culture today are more apt to look on young people as having expertise in areas that have to do with their particular situations and the particular places and spaces they occupy (Hagood 2003; Moje 2000; Morgan 1997; Vadeboncoeur and Stevens 2005). This situated perspective on youth culture argues as well for exploring how people (adolescents and adults alike) act provisionally at particular times given particular circumstances within various discourses.

Language: Necessary but Not Sufficient

Just as the discontinuity in how we view youth today has disrupted earlier claims that adolescents make up a subculture characterized by some (e.g., Appleman 2001) as a purgatory or holding area for not-yet adults, so, too, does the notion of language being necessary but not sufficient to learning disrupt certain claims about print's primacy as a communication tool. Among today's youth, assumptions about the centrality of words and print to meaning making are undergoing considerable questioning and study. Indeed, the young people with whom Jonathan Eakle and I (Alvermann and Eakle 2006) conduct studies in out-of-school settings (e.g., public libraries and museums) rarely, if ever, rely on language as their sole means of communication. Instead, like Short and Kauffman (2000), we have observed that adolescents quite readily integrate art, movement, gesture, and music with language as they talk with their friends, do research on school-assigned topics in the library, peer over each other's shoulders to read a downloaded rap lyric, or chat quietly (and sometimes not so quietly) in front of a museum exhibit.

That youth who engage with multiple sign systems outside of school often blur distinctions between in-school and out-of-school learning is not surprising. Differences in the affordances—those cues that show us how an object functions—that various communication modes offer, whether in formal or

> > > > >
We saw immediate connections between what Donna writes here and what Daniel Pink wrote in *A Whole New Mind* (2005) about synthesis. Stand in the hallway of your school and watch your students. How do they synthesize all the language arts as they communicate with their friends? How do you encourage them to use that same synthesis in their assignments?

—KB, REP, LR

informal settings, are typically of more importance to scholarly inquirers than they are to everyday users of such modes. Moreover, to add to the blurring, there have been throughout history successive and gradual movements from one communication mode to the next: for example, from orality to writing; from reading as sacred and confined to the privileged elite, to a more open and universally accessible practice. With the advent of the New Literacy Studies (Gee 1990; Street 1995) and the convening of the New London Group in the year 2000 came the idea that literacy is singular in neither form nor function. Instead, literacies are multiple and vary according to the social contexts in which they are enacted. As this idea began to take shape, new terms entered the lexicon. One of those terms, *multiliteracies*, is pertinent to this chapter inasmuch as it refers to "modes of representation much broader than language alone" (Cope and Kalantzis 2000, 5–5).

Multiliterate youth are characterized in the popular press as being immersed in the new information communication technologies. For example, "'Go to your room!' sends many kids to a multimedia hub" (Armas 2005). Or, "to read a good book, Japanese pull out their cell phones" (Kageyama 2005). These developments, while perhaps traceable to earlier times, also reflect a discontinuity in the drive toward high-stakes testing, adequate yearly progress, and higher graduation rates at the secondary level. With No Child Left Behind (2001) and the Struggling Readers Initiative (U.S. Department of Education 2006) fresh on many people's minds, how is youth's immersion in the new information communication technologies connected to scientific reading instruction and its many predicted outcomes? In an essay on the pedagogies of globalization, Spring seems to offer a partial, though perhaps unsatisfactory, answer to this question:

> Today, pedagogical methods [such as scientific reading instruction] are primarily determined by the needs of nation states to prepare workers for the global economy. Nations have combined economic and educational planning into an educational security state where pedagogy is controlled through a system of assessments of students and teachers . . . Most national school systems are organized to serve an industrial-consumer state [that] is premised on the idea that a good society involves economic growth resulting from increased production and consumption of goods. In the industrial-consumer state, education is organized to serve the goal of economic growth. (2006, 105)

If this is the case, and if, as Resnick claims, "schools are not the only—or perhaps even the primary—source of literacy competence" (2000, 38), might the popular press' characterization of multiliterate youth be yet another indication that schools are arguably out of touch with the everyday literacies that many young people find relevant? What implication might this state of affairs hold for scientific reading instruction?

< < < < <
Donna is giving us a lot to think about here. Mark this section and return to it after you take a look at Chapter 17, on assessment by Devon Brenner, P. David Pearson, and Linda Rief. When you add comments from the authors of that chapter with hers, you'll want to immediately begin talking with someone about the inadequacies of high-stakes tests.
—*KB, REP, LR*

Thinking About Scientific Reading Instruction Differently

In his best-seller *Everything Bad Is Good for You*, Steven Johnson (2005) reminds us that it was Marshall McLuhan, the well-known Canadian communications theorist in the 1970s, who famously observed that making judgments about new cultural systems on their own terms, such as the video game industry of today, will inevitably be colored by our prejudices of the past. To illustrate how our deeply ingrained preferences for book reading may prejudice our views toward other modes of learning, such as video gaming, Johnson invites us to participate in the following thought experiment:

> Imagine an alternate world identical to ours save one techno-historical change: video games were invented and popularized *before* books. In this parallel universe, kids have been playing games for centuries—and then these page-bound texts come along and suddenly they're all the rage. What would the teachers, and the parents, and the cultural authorities have to say about this frenzy of reading? I suspect it would sound something like this:
>
> Reading books chronically understimulates the senses. Unlike the long-standing tradition of video gameplaying—which engages the child in a vivid, three-dimensional world filled with moving images and musical soundscapes, navigated and controlled with complex muscular movements—books are simply a barren string of words on the page. Only a small portion of the brain devoted to processing written language is activated during reading. . . .
>
> Many children enjoy reading books, of course, and no doubt some of the flights of fancy conveyed by reading have their escapist merits. But for a sizable percentage of the population, books are downright discriminatory. The reading craze of recent years cruelly taunts the 10 million Americans who suffer from dyslexia—a condition that didn't even exist as a condition until printed text came along to stigmatize its sufferers.
>
> But perhaps the most dangerous property of these books is the fact that they follow a fixed linear path. You can't control their narratives in any fashion—you simply sit back and have the story dictated to you. . . . This risks instilling a general passivity in our children, making them feel as though they're powerless to change their circumstances. Reading is not an active, participatory process; it's a submissive one. The book readers of the younger generation are learning to "follow the plot" instead of learning to lead. (19–20)

This glimpse into parallel universes serves as a bit of a discontinuity in itself. We know, of course, that video games were not invented and popularized before books. But had they been, would our prejudices against gaming as a way of learning have been what they are today? In a book titled *What Video Games*

Have to Teach Us About Learning and Literacy, Gee (2003) provides empirical evidence that these games offer something more than mindless entertainment. Gee's argument is not that what young people learn when they engage in video gaming is always good; rather, he specifies that it is in playing good video games that learning often occurs. Understanding just what makes a video game good, of course, would require a full reading of Gee's book in order to learn how he derived thirty-six learning principles from playing video games himself. These principles, which speak to how youth connect different sign systems (words, images, symbols, etc.), how they choose to solve a problem, and how they learn from nonverbal cues, have a lot in common with scientific reading instruction. For example, in both, one finds attention being given to the practice principle, the subset principle, the bottom-up basic skills principle, and the transfer principle, to name but a few of the things they have in common.

< < < < <
To understand more about the connection of video gaming to learning, turn to Jeff Wilhelm and Michael Smith's chapter (15), and look specifically at page 237, where they connect what happens with video gaming to engagement and flow and ultimately powerful learning experiences.
—*KB, REP, LR*

Admitting that online multiple role-playing video games are in their infancy, as far as their educational potential is concerned, Gee also acknowledges that they will never replace books. Instead, he predicts that Internet video games will "sit beside [books], interact with them, and change them and their role in society in various ways" (204). But for now, Gee is content that

> [video games] operate with—that is, they build into their designs and encourage—good principles of learning, principles that are better than those in many of our skill-and-drill, back-to-basics, test-them-until-they-drop schools. It is not surprising that many politicians, policymakers, and their academic fellow travelers who think poor children should be content with schooling for service jobs don't like video games. They say they don't like them because they are violent. But, in reality, video games do violence to these people's notions of what makes learning powerful and schools good and fair. (205)

So what do I make of the coalescing set of circumstances that have brought us to this point—a juncture in which young people are increasingly engaged in digital literacies at precisely the same time in history when those in authority over school-related reading instruction are moving ever further toward a narrowed definition of what counts as reading? Mainly, I see the situation as one in which those of us interested in adolescent literacy would do well to think about scientific reading instruction differently. By this, I do not mean that we should dismiss what good research has shown to be effective for some, though not all, of the young people who sit in our classes or take part in our research. Rather, I would have us take account of the fact that

> the word now shares Web space with the image, and text appears inextricably tied to pictures. The pictures are dynamic, animated, and continually updated.

The unprecedented speed and ease of digital production mounts photographs, movies, and video on the Web. Cyberspace becomes visualized data, and meaning arrives in spatial as well as in verbal expressions. (Heim, cited in Lankshear and Knobel 2003, 170)

I would also have us take note of a challenge that will grow in magnitude as NCLB-driven policies make their weight felt increasingly at the middle and high school levels. That is, it will be important to reconcile narrowed definitions of reading (and hence reading instruction) with the need to develop young people's critical awareness as they engage with multiple sign systems. A review of the literature (Alvermann 2006) on new information communication technologies among middle and high school students in the United States revealed only a handful of studies that analyzed in depth how young people develop a sense of critical awareness about their own implication in the production and consumption of multimodal texts on the Internet. Not surprisingly, multimodal learning is largely ignored by today's advocates of scientific reading instruction and the Institution of Old Learning (IOL)—a tongue-in-cheek term coined by O'Brien and Bauer (2005) to denote the rigidity of certain historically situated practices and organizational structures in U.S. schools. Predating NCLB and its stepchild, scientific reading instruction, by nearly a hundred years, the IOL attempts to fit new information communication technologies into its century-old rigid structures and practices. And when the IOL is successful in such attempts, students are quick to take note of discrepancies between what they are expected to do as readers in school and what they know and do on their own outside of school.

> > > *It will be important to reconcile narrowed definitions of reading (and hence reading instruction) with the need to develop young people's critical awareness as they engage with multiple sign systems.*

Regrettably, while it is easy to critique the IOL in relation to newer literacies and technologies, it is quite another matter to loosen its stranglehold on the mindset of U.S. educators at large. Yet I would argue that if we turn our backs on ideas that seem too far outside the IOL—especially ideas that challenge the status quo—then we will end up supporting a pedagogy that is one-sided. And that would be unfortunate, for as O'Brien's (2003) research on young people's engagement with multimodal texts has shown, learning with multiple sign systems often helps even the least motivated and underachieving readers redefine their literate competence. This would seem to be a point worth keeping in mind when teaching multiliterate youth in the time of scientific reading instruction.

When you want to know more . . .

Donna's chapter challenges our conceptions of literacy and what it means to be literate in this new century. You might want to read more about this in the book she edited with several other scholars, *Reconceptualizing the Literacies in Adolescents' Lives* (2006) and in her *Voices from the Middle* article "Literacy on the Edge: How Close Are We to Closing the Literacy Achievement Gap?" (2005).

> > > ELLIN OLIVER KEENE

The Essence of Understanding

A Wake-Up Call

RAIN WAS pounding Charlotte, North Carolina, as a group of sophomores filed into the classroom. It was early in the morning and energy was low. They tried to look at me without looking at me to assess who I was, what this visitor was doing here, and what kind of a ripple it was likely to cause in the day they hoped would follow the predictable patterns. With the last stragglers, a group of teachers began to file in and seat themselves on folding chairs at the perimeter of the room. The teachers' entrance seemed to add a layer of tension—now what were *they* all doing in here? The kids started to remove earphones and look around at the teachers; whatever was going on, they seemed to have decided that it may be worth muting the iPods—at least temporarily. An impossibly tall young man (was this really a sophomore in high school or an NBA player?) named Greg twisted in the attached desk-chair he'd poured himself into and asked one of the teachers, "What's going on? What'd we do?"

This was a school to which kids came fortified with the accoutrements (iPods and mobile phones) that allowed them to be elsewhere—while appearing

We situated this chapter early in the book because Ellin—while giving us very specific information—helps us think about the bigger picture of comprehension: Just what is comprehension? What does it mean when we say we teach comprehension? What are the dimensions of comprehension and how might each look in the classroom?

—KB, REP, LR

to be present—during class. As I observed in classrooms around the school the day before, I saw kids who could elevate looking disengaged to an art form. Today, that ability to check out appeared threatened. Just what were all of these adults doing in here, anyway?

I was visiting the school to conduct demonstration lessons and to work with teachers who were interested in weaving comprehension strategy instruction into their content area coursework. We had met before school that morning and I had asked the teachers—now assembled in one classroom for a demonstration lesson—to think together about their concerns related to students' understanding of the concepts they taught. I listed the biggest concerns on a transparency:

> Kids don't remember concepts, even a couple days after the tests.

> Kids seem to read the text, finish the assignments, but have no real idea what they've read.

> Kids don't want to engage in discussion about ideas—the only questions I can get them to pose are about the length of the assignment and what's on the test.

> Kids don't apply things they've learned in new situations.

> Kids today don't seem as articulate in their writing or speaking as kids of ten or fifteen years ago.

> When kids are engaged, their focus is on getting the grade, not on true understanding.

> > > > >
Does this sound familiar? Stop and ask yourself and colleagues the same question Ellin asked the teachers in that school: What are your concerns related to students' understanding of concepts?
—KB, REP, LR

Sound familiar? I could have been in virtually any middle or high school in the country. The surroundings may be different and the kids may be less concerned about getting into college, but the symptoms are identical: the kids are disengaged, don't retain and reapply concepts, and don't articulate their thinking.

The teachers expressed concern about the weighty, unmanageable curriculum they were called upon to teach (we coined a term that day—*curriculum obesity*) and understood that the size of the curriculum was at least partially responsible for the kids' lack of retention and reapplication of concepts. Not surprisingly, the teachers were concerned about adding more content—the teaching of reading comprehension strategies—to their already bursting curriculum.

Back in the classroom, in a tenth-grade U.S. history course, I was demonstrating the use of "way-in" texts—picture books and short pieces of text students can use to build background knowledge (schema) and provide a way in to understanding more abstract, concept- and vocabulary-laden texts. I used Toni Morrison's photo-essay *Remember: The Journey to School Integration* (in

WAY-IN BOOKS FOR THE HOLOCAUST AND THE CIVIL RIGHTS STRUGGLE

Holocaust

Abells, Chana Byers. *The Children We Remember*

Bachrach, Susan. *Tell Them We Remember: The Story of the Holocaust*

Bunting, Eve. *Terrible Things: An Allegory of the Holocaust*

Deedy, Carmen Agra. *The Yellow Star: The Legend of King Christian X of Denmark*

Hoestlandt, Jo. *Star of Fear, Star of Hope*

Innocenti, Roberto. *Rose Blanche*

Jacobsen, Ruth. *Rescued Images: Memories of a Childhood in Hiding*

Johnston, Tony. *The Harmonica*

Kaplan, William. *One More Border: The True Story of One Family's Escape from War-Torn Europe*

Mochizuki, Ken. *Passage to Freedom: The Sugihara Story*

Morimoto, Junko. *My Hiroshima*

Oppenheim, Shulamith Levey. *The Lily Cupboard: A Story of the Holocaust*

Polacco, Patricia. *The Butterfly*

Smith, Frank Dabba. *Elsie's War: A Story of Courage in Nazi Germany*

Smith, Frank Dabba (Mendel Grossman, photographer). *My Secret Camera: Life in the Lodz Ghetto*

Tsuchiya, Yukio. *Faithful Elephants: A True Story of Animals, People, and War*

Civil Rights Struggle

Bolden, Tonya. *Tell All the Children Our Story: Memories and Mementos of Being Young and Black in America*

Bridges, Ruby. *Through My Eyes: Interviews and Essays with Ruby Bridges*

Coles, Robert. *The Story of Ruby Bridges*

Haskins, Jim. *Delivering Justice: W. W. Law and the Fight for Civil Rights*

Lasky, Kathryn. *Vision of Beauty: The Story of Sarah Breedlove Walker*

Levine, Ellen. *Freedom's Children: Young Civil Rights Activists Tell Their Own Stories*

Morrison, Toni. *Remember: The Journey to School Integration*

Weatherford, Carole Boston. *Freedom on the Menu: The Greensboro Sit-Ins*

Woodson, Jacqueline. *The Other Side*

Woodson, Jacqueline. *Show Way*

which Morrison writes from the point of view of the subjects in the photos) to help them build schema before they tackled a series of complex essays marking the fiftieth anniversary of the *Brown v. Board of Education* ruling.

I pulled the kids together in a group on the floor (the comments about sitting this way in elementary school lasted less than ten seconds). I wanted them to be able to see the extraordinary photographs around which Morrison has written, and I wanted to create a sense of intimacy, which I find nearly impossible when kids are spread out around the room in desks. I chose to focus instruction on *determining importance*, one of the key cognitive or comprehension strategies that Susan Zimmermann and I wrote about in *Mosaic of Thought: Teaching Comprehension in a Reader's Workshop* (1997).

I began by sharing my sense of the most important concepts in the early pages of the book by reading and thinking aloud, gradually inviting the students to share their sense of the most important ideas. I read the first couple of pages and paused to say, "One of the first things I think is important here isn't the concepts in the text; it's the way it's written—the narration of the book itself. It's fascinating to me the way Toni Morrison has chosen to narrate this book as if she were the subject in each photograph. I have to believe that she chose this very personal form of narration because readers like us who never experienced the effects of school segregation would be able to feel it very personally."

I continued to pause and think aloud three or four times, and before long, the kids had jumped into the conversation, making clear what they thought was important and defending their points of view with examples from the text. The conversation became lively and provocative, and no one had the iPod on. These sophomores engaged in some spirited discourse about the notion of separate but equal and shed light on some aspects of school segregation I honestly had never considered. By the final stages of the conversation, I had become obsolete, removing myself to one side of the room as the students continued their interchange, now oblivious to the observing teachers.

Then I invited the teachers to debrief the experience by asking the students questions. I left it open, and with the first seemingly innocuous question, the students responded with a searing honesty—respectful, but unnerving for the teachers. The teacher merely asked if the students found the lesson significantly different from their normal class discussions. The students proceeded to confess that they almost "*never truly understand*" the concepts they read about and *rarely* understand the concepts teachers lecture about in class. They described a string of experiences across content areas that could only be characterized as "doing time"—attending, doing assignments, working for grades—to get them through high school. Today, they said, was different. In several different ways, they came to the same conclusion—today, they got it.

The students were hesitant at first and qualified many of their statements with "No offense, but . . ." or "I really like my teachers, but . . ." or "I know this is just the way it has to be, but. . . ." The teachers, to their great credit, urged the students on. One teacher remarked, "You guys, we really want to know—what

> > > *The students proceeded to confess that they almost "never truly understand" the concepts they read about and rarely understand the concepts teachers lecture about in class. They described a string of experiences across content areas that could only be characterized as "doing time"—attending, doing assignments, working for grades—to get them through high school.*

> > > > >
Ellin helps us think differently about comprehension. As we consider how we teach students to understand, we might find we need help from people with particular expertise—literacy coaches. Kathy Egawa (Chapter 19) discusses the role of literacy coaches and explains how they help us improve our teaching.

—*KB, REP, LR*

made you get so excited about the ideas in this lesson? I have some of you in English, and kids who spoke today rarely get into the discussion in my class. What made you want to discuss the ideas today when it often feels like pulling teeth to get you to debate an idea in my class?"

A young woman named Samantha said, "After today, I finally get the whole *Brown versus Board of Education* thing. I mean, I didn't really know what *separate but equal* meant the way they define it in the textbooks, but those photographs were unbelievable—it wasn't separate, it was abusive. I wish I'd seen these photographs and read this book earlier."

The tall kid who wondered at the beginning of class what they'd done wrong followed with "Yeah, see for me, it has to do with emotion. If I can feel it, I remember it. If I know how the people felt, I sort of become part of it, you know?" Kids all around him agreed.

Their history teacher, in one of the all-time great questions I've heard directed to a group of kids, ended the discussion by asking this question: "If teachers want you to get more engaged like this more often, what would you tell us to do?"

The kids hesitated a moment before appearing to reach consensus on a spokesperson—Kyla, a girl who had been very active in the conversation about the book, but who had said little in the debriefing. She said, "Well, it seems like if we could just focus more on one thing and have time to talk about it, we'd *really* understand it more."

As the bell rang, one of the teachers stopped her and said, "Exactly what do you mean by *really* understand it?"

Kyla said, "You know, know it for longer than just the test."

As the teachers and I later discussed the lesson in our own debriefing session, I repeated the girl's statement for them and asked them to respond. What does it mean, I asked, to *really* understand a concept?

What Does It Mean to Understand?

I wonder if, in a field where we toss terminology back and forth across a net like a flattened volleyball, we have taken time to think about that simple question— What does it really mean to understand? As we talked, we gradually came to the conclusion that without meaning to, we had settled on, and settled for, a notion of understanding that was little more than *remembering details, answering our questions, and learning a few new vocabulary words* that the text had set in boldface. Could we be surprised, then, that our students had adapted to our expectations? They had learned that in the classroom, understanding meant remembering the facts long enough to answer questions, completing a project, or scoring well on the test. But both the students and the teachers knew that understanding was really something much richer and more complex.

<<<<<
In Interlude 2, Alfred Tatum discusses the importance of seeing the reading our students do as more than simply "remembering details." Rather, we need to think of their reading as a critically important element in their developing concept of who they are and who they might become.

—*KB, REP, LR*

I have found those conclusions confirmed in visits to hundreds of schools, where, in our discussions, in our assignments, in our "learning" materials, we ask students to do little more than (1) answer questions; (2) restate, retell, or summarize text in some way; and (3) learn content-related vocabulary. And when they can do those three things, we conclude that they understand.

There is more to comprehension than merely remembering for the test.

Kyla made it clear that she expected more, even if all she could say about it was that she hoped to remember something longer than the test. She would be grateful, I think, if we—the teachers and the profession—would come up with a richer, more rewarding definition of comprehension and understanding, and then teach from it. That may be difficult to do, but if we succeed, we should be able to lead our students more consistently to deeper and richer readings of texts. The students in the tenth-grade class, after all, had not been promised points, pizza parties, or free periods; instead, they were intoxicated with the intellectual nature of the conversation. They loved making and defending key points in the discussion. They were learning from each other's perspectives. They took the time to bring less-engaged students into the conversation. They even related the cruelty of segregated schools to the dilemma faced by immigrants (legal and otherwise) in this country today. If they can engage and explore ideas like that occasionally, we must conclude they are capable of doing it more frequently, under the right conditions.

> > < <

> > > > >

We each took time to ask ourselves the same questions Ellin lists in this paragraph. We each mentioned how our own understanding of something changed when we had to teach that information to someone. You might stop here now, also, and jot down your own definition of comprehension.

—KB, REP, LR

Listening to the kids in Charlotte that rainy morning inspired me to delve more deeply into the nature and nuances of comprehension. Initially, I had more questions than insights. I wondered . . . What does it look, sound, and feel like when a human comprehends? What is happening in the mind when someone comprehends? Have *I* ever known what it really means to understand as a student, as a teacher? What do we need to do in classrooms to engage kids in the kind of learning that promotes understanding? What are the right conditions for that understanding? And how can we make the pursuit of this understanding an everyday fact of life in our literacy and content classrooms?

One approach to those questions, I decided, would be to examine my own processes of understanding and to observe kids with an eye toward developing and refining a definition of understanding that would help me lead students to higher-level thinking.

Look Inward

Consider a time in your own learning life when you faced a complex problem or difficult concept. Perhaps it was a time when you first tried to read the great Russian novelists, or perhaps it was when you had to write an editorial for a school newspaper that allowed you only a few column inches in which to convince your readers of something. Maybe it was when you felt the concepts your physics teacher was introducing were almost clear, but not quite, just beyond your reach; or perhaps you've faced a cancer diagnosis with a loved one and had to devour voluminous information about a complex medical condition quickly enough to ask the important questions about treatment. As learners, in and out of school settings, we all face complex intellectual tasks that we eventually master. I suggest that we take a few minutes to analyze those circumstances—*what, exactly, do we do, cognitively, in order to understand those difficult concepts or ideas?*

> < < < < <
> We were glad to see Ellin make this point—that reading, even for the most skilled, isn't always easy. Challenging texts require us all to struggle.
> —*KB, REP, LR*

I recall, for example, my first graduate-level literature course, in which we were asked to undertake comparative analysis of several contemporary women authors. I can still picture the desk in my apartment cluttered with Toni Morrison and Margaret Atwood novels and Alice Walker poetry. I found myself *lost in their words* but making no progress until I *reread portions* aloud, *savoring the cadences and rhythms of the language* and *noticing small similarities and differences, patterns* that would have escaped me had I read them in a more traditional way. I was worried that I didn't have the intellectual wherewithal to analyze their work with any kind of insight, but I *struggled* through it, reading and rereading passages I found significant, *listening to my own thinking in the silence* of that apartment, and finally beginning to understand. (Those italicized phrases capture my own process of understanding—what I now call the Dimensions of Understanding. I will elaborate on this shortly.)

I began to think that if we can "give language" to the processes in which we engage (perhaps subconsciously) when exploring a complex concept or trying to understand an overwhelming amount of information, we might apply that language to the classroom—in effect, creating a new definition of comprehension. When you reflect on such a time in your own life, what do you recall? What contributed to your eventual understanding? Jot down some of the things you did to tackle that problem. A new definition of comprehension will begin to emerge—one toward which we can teach with the expectation of a far higher level of student engagement and understanding.

> > > > *I've also found that if we can take the time to analyze students in the moment of real insight and understanding—like the one we saw that morning in Charlotte—we can use their own language and insights to contribute to a new definition of understanding.*

Catch Students in the Act

I've also found that if we can take the time to analyze students in the moment of real insight and understanding—like the one we saw that morning in Charlotte—we can use their own language and insights to contribute to a new definition of understanding. We can, in effect, answer the important question we raised that day—exactly what do you mean by *really understanding*?

If, for example, we scrutinized the Charlotte students' behavior that morning, we would have seen that they *focused intently* for a long period of time on one or two concepts; they *influenced and challenged each other* through their discourse; they *incorporated new information* into existing feelings, beliefs, and knowledge; they *reacted emotionally* as well as intellectually; and the ideas didn't necessarily come easily to them—they *worked hard* to understand. Some of these characteristics or dimensions contribute to understanding, others are by-products of it, but they are all present when people understand at something other than a superficial level.

If we observed ourselves and our students in the act of understanding deeply, we might generate a far more useful definition of comprehension—one toward which students could strive, one that would push them far beyond literal recall, one we might use in considering how we create conditions that lead to higher-level thinking in our classrooms. Consider Figure 4–1, which outlines my conception of comprehension or understanding, which I call the Dimensions of Understanding, culled from observing my own and students' processes of understanding.

Whether you agree in sum or in part with this view of what people do when they understand, it is interesting to consider another question: In our classrooms, do we create the kind of conditions (topics we explore, physical environment, assignments, materials, discussions) that promote these dimensions? If we did take steps to reshape our classrooms to promote these dimensions, what might those steps be? Let's take another look at each dimension, and I'll propose one or two simple steps we might take in the classroom to address it.

Making the Dimensions Come Alive in the Classroom

We *concentrate intensively:*

> Talk with students about times when you have learned with an intensity that propelled you to a higher level of understanding. Tell them about the circumstances—were you studying something about which you were passionately interested? What made you take intellectual risks you hadn't taken before? What was the payoff—what did you understand that you didn't understand before working fervently?

> Talk about developing areas of passionate interest—such passions don't come automatically to all kids. Use individual conferences and small-group meetings to help kids find the ideas that most interest them, talk with them about how to pursue topics of passionate interest. How do you do it in your own life—how might they do it?

THE DIMENSIONS OF UNDERSTANDING

When we understand . . .

We *concentrate* intensively. We are fervent and we lose ourselves in the experience of thought. We work intensively; the world disappears and we work hard to learn more; we choose to challenge ourselves.

We *dwell* in ideas. We need time to be silent and we need time to listen to our own thinking, to reflect purposefully on an idea.

We *struggle* for insight. We savor and learn from the struggle itself; we venture into new learning territory and fight or learn from the influence of our own or others' judgment.

We *manipulate* our own thoughts to understand more completely. We revise our thinking by incorporating new knowledge, beliefs, and opinions; we can describe how our thinking has changed over time, how books and other learning experiences have changed us.

We *explore* as renaissance learners, allowing ourselves to meander through a wide range of topics and interests, texts and genres. We work to understand how ideas are related.

We *discuss*, engaging in rigorous discourse about ideas, and find we have more to say than we thought; we consider the perspectives of others and argue with or challenge them until we understand our own and others' opinions and principles. We surprise ourselves with the clarity of our own thinking.

We *create* models to help us remember. We see patterns; we discover new ways to consider our existing knowledge, to hold our thinking; we generate new knowledge. We work to make a wholly original contribution to our world.

We *feel* because our experience is enriched when we have emotional connections; we seek beauty and understand better when learning includes aesthetic journeys; we seek to create something luminous, something that matters to others.

Ultimately, we *remember* . . . the experience becomes potently memorable to us.

FIGURE 4–1.

We *dwell* in ideas:

> Set aside some chunks of class time for focused, silent work in which students can concentrate on more deeply understanding one idea—give

them time to listen to themselves think and consider subtleties instead of rushing to memorize the next thing.

> Model how proficient readers frequently reread and rethink portions of text. Kids often think that rereading means starting at the beginning and rereading everything—show them how readers pick and choose among the portions of text to explore more deeply.

> Teach kids about metacognition—thinking about one's own thinking— and the seven most common metacognitive strategies (see Figure 4–2).

We *struggle* for insight:

> Create learning opportunities in which you purposefully ask students to tackle a more complex idea or text, and provide more support for their learning than usual—teach them how we break apart or analyze complex problems in order to approach them in a systematic way. Model ways in which you take on a complex text or issue if your goal is to understand it deeply.

> Help kids understand that arriving at insights as a result of struggle is worthwhile.

> > > > >
Ellin defines metacognition as that voice in your mind that speaks while you read. We suggest that these same metacognitive skills are important as you write. Reread this list with writing in mind and see if you agree.
—*KB, REP, LR*

METACOGNITION—LISTENING TO THE VOICE IN YOUR MIND THAT SPEAKS WHILE YOU READ

> *Monitoring for Meaning*—knowing when you know, knowing when you don't know

> *Using and Creating Schemata*—making connections between the new and the known, creating schemata when necessary

> *Asking Questions*—generating questions to lead the reader deeper into the text

> *Determining Importance*—deciding what matters most, what is worth remembering

> *Inferring*—combining background knowledge with information from the text to predict, conclude, make judgments, interpret

> *Using Sensory and Emotional Images*—using images to deepen and stretch meaning

> *Synthesis*—creating an evolution of meaning, combining understanding with knowledge from other texts and sources

FIGURE 4–2.

> Talk about the role (positive and negative) self-criticism plays in learning about complex ideas—think about ways in which learners overcome.

We *manipulate* our own thoughts to understand more completely:

> Think aloud about how you use comprehension strategies as tools to help you understand more effectively—how do you question, for example, to help you focus on a section of text that is complex or meaning laden?

> Ask kids to apply the strategies and keep records of their thinking (records of strategy use) so that you can assess their developing understanding—these can be as simple as sticky notes or as complex as self-assessments of group discussions.

> Talk with students about how books have changed your thinking, emotions, beliefs, and values—how have books and ideas inspired you to take particular actions in your community? In what ways do books and ideas change students' thinking—what actions do they take in their community as a result of their evolving ideas?

> Ask students to create a time line of their evolving thinking and the changes they experience in their knowledge and beliefs throughout a unit of study or on a particular concept.

We *explore*:

> Use a wide variety of materials that include multiple genres to help students understand complex ideas—use way-in texts to work toward more complex readings.

> Encourage student choice and ownership in pursuing questions and texts of particular interest to them.

> Create time for students to pursue particular areas of interest within your topic or content area—move beyond the idea that all students must study the same thing at the same time.

We *discuss*:

> Acknowledge to students that we understand ideas most deeply when we do something with those ideas. For instance, when students talk with others about complex ideas, they are more likely to understand them better.

> Create time for students to discuss ideas in different configurations— whole class, small groups, partners. Ask kids to reflect on how their thinking changed because of the perspectives others shared in discussion.

< < < < <
Jeff Wilhelm and Michael Smith (Chapter 15) tell us more about the relationship between doing and learning. Bob Probst (Chapter 5) emphasizes the importance of conversation in the classroom.
—*KB, REP, LR*

We *create* models:

> Encourage students to create written, oral, artistic, or dramatic representations of their thinking (such as letter writing, think-pair-share, sketch-to-stretch, and readers theater) instead of simply answering questions at the end of the chapter or writing summaries.

> Encourage students to take the lead in teaching an aspect of a text or concept to peers—they can develop a learning plan that accommodates learners with different styles and preferences (e.g., visual, auditory, and kinesthetic) in order to maximize the impact of their "lessons."

We *feel*:

> Use materials, topics, and genres that capitalize on the impact of ideas and policies on people—model ways in which those materials and topics affect you as a learner and what you remember because of their emotional or aesthetic impact.

Ultimately, we *remember* . . . the experience becomes potently memorable to us.

> Focus, focus, focus—make decisions about which concepts matter most for students. Don't be afraid to concentrate your instruction (thinking aloud, modeling, demonstrating) on far fewer concepts over a much longer period of time, giving kids an opportunity to work with the concepts and apply them in a variety of texts and contexts.

When you want to know more . . .

As Ellin argues, there's more to comprehension than learning details, and there's more to it than can be dealt with in one chapter. For more about this issue, you might take a look at her *Mosaic of Thought: Teaching Comprehension in a Reader's Workshop* (1997), coauthored with Susan Zimmermann, and *Assessing Comprehension Thinking Strategies* (2006).

> > > *I can think of nothing so gratifying in teaching as introducing students to a more intellectual life—a life in which text messaging and iPods play a role, but in which time in class is spent in the pursuit of ideas that have intrigued readers and writers, scientists and historians, artists and musicians for generations.*

If we take the time to discuss these dimensions with students and if we look to them as, at the very least, the beginning of a new definition of comprehension, I believe we will set a new standard toward which students can strive—far more consistently. We might even consider having students create their own set of Dimensions of Understanding, asking them to describe not just the experience but the things they did and the ways in which they thought in order to understand. I have found that the level of their thinking, the quality of their discourse, and, not insignificantly, the intensity of their engagement skyrocket. I can think of nothing so gratifying in teaching as introducing students to a more intellectual life—a life in which text messaging and iPods play a role, but in which time in class is spent in the pursuit of ideas that have intrigued readers and writers, scientists and historians, artists and musicians for generations.

Lessons Learned

> > > RUTH SHAGOURY

THE NEED TO WRITE, THE NEED TO LISTEN

A new semester. I enter Virginia Shorey's ninth-grade classroom a little nervous about meeting the students who have joined her ESL (English as a second language) class this term. I will miss some of the students I have come to know in my once-a-week trips to Fort Vancouver High School as coresearcher with Virginia—kids like Birri from Ghana, Tam from Vietnam, Christine from the Ukraine.

As the students file into class, Virginia pulls me aside to tell me, "We have a new student—Zerina—from Bosnia. Try to talk with her today—she's a very interesting writer. She's quiet, though, and won't work in groups. She seems to be pushing everyone away."

I follow Virginia's gaze to a slender girl huddled into herself, sitting alone at a table. On the surface, there is nothing to set her apart from her American-born schoolmates: she's wearing blue jeans and a pale green sweater; her reddish-brown hair is clipped to just about chin length and is tucked behind her ears. But her expression is in marked contrast to the adolescents around her: her face wears a combination of sorrow and defiance that is hard to describe.

> > < <

I did try to talk with Zerina that day, and the next week and the next. She continued to rebuff my efforts as well as her classmates' attempts to include her. When Virginia asked students to get into groups to share their writing, Zerina withdrew further into herself. Often, she snapped at those who tried to reach out to her, harshly stating her preference to work alone.

But she wrote. Her writing gave glimpses of her anguish—a touching poem about her beloved city of Sarajevo, now in ashes and beautiful only in her memory; a freewrite about recollecting the pure evil that sometimes surrounded her during the war. It was this writing that gave us an opening into Zerina's world and into the stories and memories of war that continued to shape her life here in America. Telling the stories of these vivid experiences etched in her mind helped Zerina begin to come to terms with her past and take more control of her present. She needed a genuine audience, willing to listen and to try to understand, and she found that in her reading and writing workshop community.

More classrooms today than ever before are populated with children who may feel that large parts of their lives have been taken away from them. Many suffer from aftereffects similar to those of veterans diagnosed with posttraumatic stress syndrome. Zerina taught me that even when I can't understand the horrors of war that too many children of the world now experience, I can strengthen my resolve to build relationships with all my students—even the prickliest ones—and teach with my heart as well as my mind. And I can reconfirm the importance of writing for our most traumatized children of war.

> > < <

Zerina was in her usual position one morning—her black backpack filling the space on the desk in front of her, hiding her from the view of others. I slid into the desk next to her, and she raised her eyes to mine. "Don't turn on that tape recorder!" she ordered harshly. I put my recorder under the desk and, on an impulse, tossed aside my other constant companions, a pen and notepad.

"Sure, I don't have to record anything if you don't want me to. I really just want to talk to you. Mrs. Shorey showed me a couple of the poems you wrote, and I wanted to talk with you about them. Is that OK?"

Zerina nodded—then asked, "Which ones? Did she show you the one she read to the class?"

We spent the rest of the class in deep discussion about the poems she had written, the process of her writing, and the importance of her student audience in class. After this warm-up, she launched into her wrenching descriptions of life in a war zone. I didn't talk to her teacher to student, trying to work with her writing; rather, I was stunned by what she was telling me and wanted to try to understand what she had been through. In one of her stories, she told me about coming out of the basement bomb shelter even though her parents had instructed her to stay inside. "Then *it* happened! A big explosion! Blood and people dying. I was OK. But not everybody . . ."

"How do you cope with something like that, Zerina? How do you face the next day?" I asked after a long silence.

Zerina quietly explained, "I would wake up and say to myself: 'Today it may be my destiny to die.' I was, you know, accepting, but hoping that I live."

Through the year, Zerina wrote and wrote and wrote, and she slowly began to relate to classmates and make tentative friendships. Though she continued to "sadfully remember," she used her writing to educate and explore with others the terrors of war.

I include here an excerpt from one of her powerful poems, in the hope it will give us a glimpse into the lives of children coping with war's ravages and the lessons we can learn from them.

> > > > *Zerina taught me that even when I can't understand the horrors of war that too many children of the world now experience, I can strengthen my resolve to build relationships with all my students—even the prickliest ones—and teach with my heart as well as my mind.*

Sadfully Remembering

Tears in the eyes of the woman, of the mother . . .
I saw them, and am looking at them right now.
Tears are flowing along her face like two little brooks downhill.

It is summer and it seems like everything froze around her and me.

She lost maybe her husband, son, or maybe her brother.
She is the loser and all of us are.
It is silence around us. Her crying cramps on
her face and her painfully moves telling us everything.

I am looking at her and
through my tears, I see two women, ten of them, hundreds . . .
I see unbroken rows of mothers and all of them are crying the same
     way and raising their hands, and praying.
Their tears are the same, brooks of tears . . .
I am standing faded away in that day of that summer, of still one war year.

When you want to know more . . .

Ruth Shagoury* has written about issues both social and personal, and about the role of writing in coming to grips with them. She's explored those ideas further in "Worlds Beneath the Words: Writing Workshop with Second Language Learners," in NCTE's journal *Language Arts* (see Hubbard and Shorey 2003), and in a book that directly addresses the complex issue of social justice, *Teaching for Justice in the Social Studies Classroom: Millions of Intricate Moves* (Makler and Hubbard 2000).

---

* Ruth Shagoury has previously published under the name Ruth Hubbard.

Connecting to my thoughts

Connecting to other texts

WEBSITES FOR YOU TO VISIT REGULARLY

For great lesson plans developed by teachers for teachers: Read Write Think: www.readwritethink.org/index.asp.

For policy information and educational statistics: National Governors Association (click on Center for Best Practices and then click on Education): www.nga.org.

For information on efforts to transform the high schools: Alliance for Excellent Education: www.all4ed.org/index.html.

For statistical data and the Nation's Report Card: National Center for Education Statistics: http://nces.ed.gov/nationsreportcard/.

For information on literature for young adults: The Assembly on Literature for Adolescents of the NCTE: www.alan-ya.org/.

And, of course, the site for your professional organization.

> > > ROBERT E. PROBST

Tom Sawyer, Teaching and Talking

Teaching Is Hard Work

YOU WOULDN'T THINK teaching would be so hard. After all, it's the student who should be doing most of the work. He's the one who must learn to read and write; she's the one who has to learn to listen and speak. They can't learn those subtle arts by sitting back and watching us work. The weight lifter who sits back and says to his coach, "Show me that one more time," isn't going to grow much stronger until the coach stops showing and hands *him* the dumbbells. The reader won't grow more fluent until she picks up a book and starts turning the pages. Nor will the writer grow more skillful until he picks up a pencil and starts scratching on the paper.

The weight lifter, despite the delaying tactics, probably wants very much to grow stronger and so, perhaps with a sigh of resignation, he will ultimately take a deep breath, grab the weights, and start hoisting. Some of the students in our English and language arts classes, however, seem less eager to learn what we have to teach them. At times, they even seem reluctant to get near the barbells we offer them. We know, and they do, too, that if they're going to learn to read,

We placed this chapter here because Ellin Keene's chapter (4) asked us to reconsider what comprehension means, and in the same way, Bob asks readers to rethink the role of talk in the classroom. We tend to think of reading and writing when literacy is mentioned, but the art of conversation remains critical. Much of the business of the classroom—and of the world—is conducted through discussion. Bob urges us to reconsider its importance and the ways we might teach students to engage in it more productively.

—KB, REP, LR

they'll occasionally have to sit down with a book and read. They know that if they're going to learn to write, they'll occasionally have to sharpen a pencil and grab a sheet of paper or sit down at a computer and start spilling words onto the page or screen. There just is no alternative.

And yet, still, some of them will sit there, compromising with us occasionally by pretending to read, dipping into a book, not necessarily the book we've asked them to study, mind you, but frequently the commercial notes on that book. If writing's the issue, they might dash off a loose paraphrase of an encyclopedia article, botching it up just enough so that it looks like amateur prose and presenting it to us as if they had actually struggled through the task of writing themselves. They have to know that won't work. They would, probably, like to be able to read and write well, but they still lean back, arms folded across their chests, and almost challenge us to teach them—as if that were something we could do *to* them as they sit there silent and inert; as if literacy could be injected into them, like a literacy steroid or linguistic growth hormone requiring a bit of loose cash but no effort. Ah, where are the pharmaceutical companies when you need them most?

Tom Sawyer knew how to deal with that lassitude and immobility. Of course, his motivation was not to teach; rather, it was to get himself out of work that he didn't want to do. But he knew how to get others to do it. With a little modeling and a lot of manipulation, he managed to get his lounging, slouching friends lining up for a turn at the paintbrush and that white picket fence; all he had to do then was sit back, supervise, direct, criticize, praise, and otherwise orchestrate the work of those ragamuffins who had been gulled into thinking that they *wanted* to paint, *could* paint, and, if the others would just get out of the way, *would* paint.

Tom might not be our model of the consummate teacher, but he did know how to get his friends to work. He didn't do it by reducing the task to its basic elements and drilling them for months on it—one week on selecting the right color, another week on stirring the paint properly, another on dipping the brush just so far and then carefully removing the excess paint, a few weeks on brush strokes, and then an extra-credit session on keeping dust off the fence until it had dried. Nor did he do it by threatening them with high-stakes standardized tests, or by promising them advanced placement when they returned to school in the fall. In fact, he didn't seem to promise them anything at all, except the intrinsic reward of doing the task well and a comfortably sociable setting, surrounded by friends, in which to do it.

If I could just learn how to do what Tom did so well, perhaps teaching wouldn't be so hard. I could get things started, hand my students a paintbrush—well, a pencil, a book, or a computer—and sit back and watch. They would labor; I would prop my feet up on my desk and supervise, direct, criticize, praise, and orchestrate. They would be doing most of the work, which is as it should be if they're the ones who are supposed to be doing the learning.

We are, I think, learning as a profession to lure our students into those productive labors, even if it doesn't allow us to prop our feet up on our desks. The workshop model, presented so convincingly by Nancie Atwell and others, has demonstrated its effectiveness in eliciting hard work from students on both their reading and their writing. Allowing students some choice in their reading matter has encouraged them to read more widely and carefully. Giving them some respite from the five-paragraph theme and inviting them to write about matters of interest to them has kept them at the keyboard with a bit more enthusiasm. We've paid a great deal of attention, and with great success, to those dimensions of literacy.

But, curiously enough, the linguistic skill that seems to develop earliest, the one in which we all engage most often and with most enthusiasm, the one we don't resist with all the stubbornness at our command, the one that seems most natural is also, apparently, the skill that we have neglected most seriously in the schools. And that's talk. We seldom address it directly; we seldom teach it explicitly; and we almost never assess it. We do expect it, and we do depend on it, but we don't teach it. I suspect that most of us seldom think about talk, conversation, discussion as something to teach—rather, it is a way to teach something else. We ask our students to discuss the subtleties of onomatopoeia to learn about onomatopoeia, but we don't teach them explicitly about talk as a way of learning, resolving issues, investigating complexities.

> < < < < <
> Getting kids to work *hard*, is, well, hard work. Take a look at what Tom Romano, Chapter 11, and Linda Rief, Chapter 13 have to say about this. Of course, getting this level of work from students is tied to their interest in the work. Teri Lesesne (Chapter 6), Dick Allington (Chapter 18) and Penny Kittle (Interlude 4) each discuss choice and the connection between choice and work.
> —*KB, REP, LR*

Talking—at Least Serious Talking—Can Also Be Hard Work

The unfortunate consequence of not *teaching* talking is that we don't seem to be very good at discourse. We chat comfortably enough, and we can handle simple things like setting up a time for lunch or reminding our kids to do their homework, but the conversations that require us to deal with difficult issues, controversies, complex chains of events, predicting outcomes, marshaling evidence, examining reasoning, and other such subtleties don't seem to go nearly as well. Curiously enough, those who talk professionally, and the most publicly, seem to be the worst, as an hour or two at the television set watching talk shows will demonstrate vividly. There aren't many models of civil discourse for our students to learn from.

And so the schools, in particular the English language arts teachers, need to accept that responsibility and make the teaching of discussion a significant part of the curriculum. We have to find ways, as Tom Sawyer did, of luring the kids, not into painting a fence, but into serious conversations. It shouldn't be a difficult task; talking comes so naturally that we should have an easier job than Tom's in making the transition to more serious discourse. It's important for us to try because at least some of the conversations our students will undertake in the future may shape the society in which we all will live. If they are to participate in those conversations effectively, productively, and for the common good, they have to develop the predispositions, the habits, and the standards that will make such participation possible. Perhaps most important, our students must ultimately take responsibility for their own discourse, because their teacher isn't always going to be there to lead them through it.

Attending to Talk

We are, as a profession, taking increasing interest in the topic of talk. Nystrand's book *Opening Dialogue: Understanding the Dynamics of Language and Learning in the English Classroom* (1997) looked closely at student talk in an effort to find out both what we were doing and what results we were getting. *Inquiry and the Literary Text: Constructing Discussions in the English Classroom* (Holden and Schmidt 2002) and *The Language of Interpretation: Patterns of Discourse in Discussions of Literature* (Marshall, Smagorinsky, and Smith 1995) both focused on discussion in the literature class. A more recent book, *Talking in Class: Using Discussion to Enhance Teaching and Learning* (McCann et al. 2006), offers a great deal of help for teachers who hope to improve conversations in their classrooms. Along with these books, there have also been a fair number of articles and chapters that address this issue.

Early in many of these texts, the authors make the point that much of what passes for talk in the classroom barely qualifies. Nystrand, for example, reported that "most schooling is organized, we found, for the plodding transmission of information through classroom recitation. Teachers talk and students listen. And the lower the track, we found, the more likely this is to be true" (1997, 3). On only the second page of their book, McCann and his colleagues summarize the observations of many researchers in the simple declaration "In other words, *recitation*, rather than *authentic discussion*, is the common mode of discourse in most classrooms" (2006, 2).

The Dimensions of Talk

Our researchers would tell us that recitation is not discussion; interrogation is not conversation; the back-and-forth of question-and-answer is not the same as the give-and-take of egalitarian discourse. Even some of the strategies that we value most highly and that serve us well in the classroom may not qualify as real conversation. Debate, for instance, is one of the approaches we've tried for teaching the art of oral exchange. But the problem with debate is that it is predicated upon the notion that one side must win while the other loses. The debater can't say, in the middle of his argument, "You know, you've persuaded me. I've changed my mind. I think you're right." Even if he *has* been persuaded, the format of the debate requires him to carry on, doing his level best to prevail even if he no longer believes in his argument. That sort of match may be fun, but it doesn't encourage the collaborative building of intellectual concepts that become richer than what either "side" might have come to alone.

Debate, like boxing, is a competitive sport. Its purpose is to produce a winner and a loser. Perhaps some thoughtful member of the audience will wander out into the hallway meditatively, reflect on what she heard, and make some synthesis that clarifies and enriches her thinking, but the debaters will go off to celebrate their victory or nurse their bruises and perhaps refine their arguments. If they've learned anything from their opponents, they'll hide it carefully until long after the debate is over and the scores are in. Conversation should lead to something better for both parties.

Perhaps at the opposite end of the spectrum from debate, a highly structured, rule-bound engagement, is the bull session, a free-flowing, open-ended, ungoverned, often chaotic exchange of whatever passes for thought in the minds of the participants. Often high-spirited, occasionally great fun, these conversations can keep a group entertained for hours, though at the end, the participants may wonder what they've been discussing. Again, conversation has greater potential than that.

In between these two extremes, there are conceivably many forms or contexts or purposes for two or more people in conversation. Consider some of them:

Storytelling—Sometimes, we are just recounting the events of the day or passing along some narrative that we found entertaining.

Agenda Setting—Part of some discussions is the planning of the talk. What, exactly, are we going to address in this conversation with a parent—the child's behavior, or his writing, or his absences, or his health, or all of those? In what order?

Problem Solving—If the agenda setting identifies a problem—say, how do we get your child to do her homework?—then further talk attempts to generate and select ideas that might solve it.

Brainstorming—Solving problems requires ideas; brainstorming is talk devoted to producing them.

Decision Making—Choosing among alternatives requires identifying and applying criteria and then committing to the results.

Surely, there are others, and just as surely these overlap and flow into one another. I may tell you a *story* about what happened in class the other day in order to justify discussing an issue that seems important to me, and at the heart of that issue is a *problem* that I want to solve by inviting you to *brainstorm* ideas with me, so that you might ultimately assist me in making a *decision* about what I might do. Let's consider a small collection of activities that might help us get students involved in good discussions and teach them something about the art.

Setting the Stage

What do we need for a conversation to occur? First of all, the participants need to at least feel comfortable with one another. It isn't easy for most of us to discuss anything more significant than the weather when we are thrown together on an elevator with a few strangers. When sitting in a conference session with fifty or sixty other teachers, many of us feel reluctant to raise our hands to ask a question, much less to make a controversial statement or challenge a presenter. Unless we are unusually bold, we'll probably want to move slowly, gradually test the waters, reassure ourselves that our ideas will at least be given a respectful hearing before we make any revealing or tentative statements.

In the sometimes brutal social world of the adolescent, those insecurities must be even worse. The athletes may not feel comfortable talking with the intellectuals, who may not feel comfortable talking with the goths, who may not feel comfortable talking with the cheerleaders, who may not feel comfortable talking with the thespians, who may not feel comfortable talking with the athletes . . . but they're probably all in the same English class, and sooner or later their English teacher is going to break them into small groups, toss *King Lear* on their desks, and ask them to make something of it. They'll need some help getting started.

Finding the Poem

We need to find those ways of helping—simple activities, or structures, that get conversations started in comfortable, relaxed, nonthreatening ways. For example, one successful strategy for helping students get to know one another at the start of the school year is Finding the Poem, a fairly simple icebreaking activity. For this, the teacher needs a few simple poems. For instance, if you plan to use groups of four, you'll need six or seven poems of four stanzas each. You'd be surprised at how many poems you can find suitable for this activity. A few examples that come readily to mind are "Life for My Child," by Gwendolyn Brooks, "The Child at Winter Sunset," by Mark Van Doren, "My Papa's Waltz," by Theodore Roethke, and "The Road Not Taken," by Robert Frost. A quick glance through whatever anthology you're using for the year plus a few of your supplemental texts should do the trick. If you have the time to look a bit further, glance through collections by some of the contemporary poets like Stephen Dunn, Mary Oliver, Sharon Olds, David Bottoms, Billy Collins, and others. (If you can't find four-stanza poems, break longer poems into four short segments, however crudely.) Print one stanza (or chunk) of each poem in a large, readable font on an index card. Shuffle the cards together and distribute them to students. Then instruct students to move around the classroom, introducing themselves to each other (if done at the beginning to the school year) and comparing stanzas until they find another that seems to fit with theirs. When two students have found a match, they continue to roam as a pair until they find the rest of the poem. When the students are satisfied that they have complete poems, ask them to sit together in their group and put their stanzas in what seems to be the right order. Then you might ask each group to read its poem aloud and tell you something about why they settled on that order of stanzas.

Now, of course, this activity is hardly a rich, full, free-flowing discussion. But it is a start. It gives students a fairly simple task—finding the stanzas that constitute a poem; it requires them to meet other people in the class; it demands that they talk at least briefly about the text they are carrying; and it asks them to solve a fairly simple problem, which is deciding on the order of the stanzas. It's an activity that is neither too threatening nor easily avoided. No one has to say much more than "Hello, here's my stanza. Let's see the one you have." But on the other hand, no one can choose *not* to participate because everyone is needed to complete the activity.

Generating Ideas and Setting the Agenda

We want much more than minimal interaction and thought out of our students, of course. Such an activity as Finding the Poem is intentionally simple, giving the students a short piece of text, posing a simple problem, and requiring only brief conversation. Real conversation requires that participants have ideas, that they articulate those ideas, and that they bring them to the group, decide how to address them, and then engage with one another. The recitation, criticized that McCann and his colleagues, neglected several of those steps. By providing students with the text and then launching right into questions about it, teachers offered little opportunity for students to generate their own questions or articulate their own responses to what they'd read. Students whose experiences in the classroom have been limited to such recitations will need to learn how to identify questions or issues of their own that will sustain conversation.

We need to figure out ways of enticing kids to do just that. Obviously, it's not something that we can do for them, but we might be able to set up circumstances that will encourage them to do it for themselves. If we consider what we, ourselves, do when we begin to read a new book, we may find some clues that will help us figure out how to encourage the same kind of reflection and questioning. What is it that we do? In the first couple of pages of the novel, we will meet a few characters, hear a bit of dialogue, learn something about the setting and perhaps the central character's problem or situation, and begin to wonder . . . Who is this

> < < < < <
> You might take a look at Randy Bomer's chapter (20), where he argues that what we are hoping for in our teaching is to have our students initiate inquiry and discourse. When they accept that responsibility, then we can feel we have succeeded in taking a serious step toward making them independent and responsible citizens.
>
> —*KB, REP, LR*

character? What does he believe and value? Do I like him or dislike him? What has already happened to put him in these circumstances, and what can I anticipate happening in the next chapters?

If we don't begin to at least wonder about some of these matters, even if we don't explicitly articulate and answer those questions, then we probably aren't very engaged with the book. Unfortunately, some of our students are what Kylene Beers calls "read-on-through readers"—readers who pass their eyes over the words, possibly even know all of them, and yet manage to register very little. We need to find ways to get them to pause and reflect, if they are to have anything to talk about.

Annotating the Text

One way to get kids to pause and reflect, simplistic as it sounds, is just to demand it. The demand, however, has to be couched in an activity that makes it manageable for the students. One gimmick that helps, for instance, is the sticky note. Once the class has begun to read—an essay, the next chapter of the novel, a short story, or even a poem—teachers can give students four or five sticky notes each and instruct them to write out three questions that they'd like to discuss about the piece. Three and only three—the extra sticky notes are there in case they come up with a better question as they read.

These have to be *real questions*, although that's a difficult phrase to define. For the time being, it's probably best to define a real question as one for which you would very much like an answer. As time goes on and questions are brought before the class, the group can begin to consider the characteristics of good, discussable questions. They'll learn that the question "What color was the horse?" with its simple one-word answer—gray—is less interesting and discussable than the question "Why was this horse so important to the characters in the story?"

Students then come to class, their texts festooned with their three sticky notes. In groups, they discuss at least one of the questions raised by each of the participants. The first student begins, "I wondered . . . ," and the group talks for as long as the question sustains the discourse. Then the next student presents her question to the group and the talk continues. When all have had a turn, the teacher asks if any of the groups have questions that they'd like to pursue further with the entire class, and with a bit of luck, there will be one or two that the groups have struggled with. Those are likely to be good questions, questions worth pursuing, and the teacher can stick with them as long as they reward the time and energy invested. It's at this point that the teacher might also insinuate his own questions into the conversation, perhaps those he thinks are important but have been neglected. Placing them here, after the students have had time to consider their own questions, allows him to link his issues to theirs, rather than substitute his concerns for those of the students.

> > > > >
We hear echoes of Ellin Keene's comments about the nature of understanding (Chapter 4) in Bob's comments about encouraging kids to pause and reflect so they can have meaningful conversation. Rethink Ellin's Dimensions of Understanding (see page 35) substituting the word "talk" for the word "understand" in the first line. Suddenly we see that Bob's point about the critical nature of talk is on target: talk is intimately tied to understanding.
—*KB, REP, LR*

Afterward, the teacher has an opportunity to point out to the groups what they've done, and it's important to do so if the students are to begin to think about discussion as a behavior that can be worked on and improved. We want them not only to talk but to think about talk. It's something we all do, like breathing, and we usually give it as little thought. Unlike breathing, however, talk is a natural skill that can be improved with attention and effort, just as moving—which every newborn child does naturally—can be elevated, with attention and training, to an art form like ballet.

And what is it, exactly, that they have done? Everyone has

> read the text
> articulated a question
> presented it to the group
> solicited the responses of other readers
> exchanged and examined several perspectives on the question *and* therefore
> come to some agreement about the answer
> decided that they had differing, perhaps irreconcilable, opinions, or
> concluded that they needed to pursue the issue further.

Granted, there is an artificiality to this conversation. We don't go to the bookstore and buy a pack of sticky notes for each novel we pick up. We don't ask three and only three questions about each chapter we read. And we probably don't participate in such a mechanized discussion as this, with each reader presenting a question, taking five or ten minutes to discuss it, declaring her time at an end, and turning the floor over to the next reader. But, artificial as it is, it does require the student to articulate a question, submit it to the group, and talk about it. No student is allowed to read on through the text and wait, empty-headed, for the teacher to ask a question. He has at least taken the first step toward independent, responsible discourse.

Forced Freewriting

There are other ways, of course, of getting students to generate topics and questions that will keep the focus on *their* questions, rather than *ours*. A quick forced freewriting, for example, might work with a short text you're present-ing in class. To generate discussion of a poem (or perhaps a provocative para-graph extracted from an essay or article you're about to have your students read), you might say to the class, "I'm going to read this text aloud two times. After the first reading, I'll pause for about three or four minutes, during which I'd like you to write freely, keeping the pencil moving until I ask you to stop. Say, or ask, anything that came to mind as you were listening. After I've

< < < < <
Be sure to look ahead to Smokey Daniels' chapter (9), where he talks about the conversational side of writ-ing, inviting us to expand our notion of the genres valuable in the classroom to include personal letters and much more.

—*KB, REP, LR*

read it the second time, formulate some question about the text that you think might be worth discussing."

When you've read the text to them, and they've had time to formulate their questions, you have several options. One is simply to put them in groups of whatever size you prefer, probably three to five, and ask them to do just what you asked them to do with the sticky notes—each student presents her question for discussion, taking five to ten minutes to talk about it, until all have had a turn.

A second possibility is to call on a few students at random, ask them for their questions, and quickly write brief versions on the board. If you prefer, you can ask for volunteers. Continue until there are enough good questions to serve as the focal point for as many groups as you want to have, and then break the class up into groups, assigning each group one of the questions to analyze and answer before reporting back to the class.

A third option is to collect the questions and ask the class to give you five or ten minutes of quiet time to review and sort them. They might reread the text during this lull in the activity. You can then hastily and intuitively sort the questions into about five or six different stacks. Those students whose questions are in the same stack will constitute a group. You can move the students into those groups, ask them to quickly review the questions they've raised, identify some central issue or question that emerges from them, and discuss it for a while. This, obviously, is a more challenging task than the sticky note activity. Here, they not only have to formulate a question but also must sift through several questions and either pull them together into something larger or decide which of them they would prefer to consider.

The Quality of Their Questions

As you try activities like these, you're likely to be frustrated at first by the quality of the questions the students raise. Such activities will give you many opportunities, however, to look carefully at questions and discuss what makes a question interesting or trivial, and if you pause frequently to discuss that issue, students will begin to catch on. You can point out that questions that require nothing more than extracting a fact aren't intriguing. On the other hand, questions that call for inference are often powerful and interesting—This poem talks about a conflict between a boy and his father; do girls and their mothers have to deal with the same issues, or is it different for them? Questions that call for comparison can generate interesting talk—What would the writer of a science article be likely to say about that event from the morning news? Questions that invite evaluation and judgment can lead to interesting conversation—Was the decision this character made at this point in the story morally defensible? Questions that bring the text and the students' lives to bear upon one another are likely to lead the class both to impassioned discussion of the issues raised by the text and to the telling of their own stories, stories you might otherwise never hear—Have you ever found yourself in a situation like that in the story, and if so, how was it similar, and how was it different? As you analyze the questions your students raise, you can move them toward more powerful and interesting questions, and thus to more interesting discussions.

Asking Your Own Questions Pushes the Analysis Further

And as they discuss, you can, of course, place your own questions on the table. Once the students know that they can't simply wait for you to raise all the questions, control all the talk, resolve all the differences, and then, just before the bell rings so that they can dutifully write it down in their notebooks, provide the final, conclusive, definitive answer; once they've begun to assume some responsibility for the wondering that must precede thinking; once they have begun to realize that they have to participate actively in making sense of texts and their lives, then there's no reason you can't wonder and question yourself. And as you do so, you both model and push.

> > > The teacher's contribution to the discussion lies in keeping it organized, keeping it flowing, making sure all perspectives are respected . . . but it's also to enrich and deepen the discourse. The teacher's greater breadth of reading will enable her to spot what the students have missed, to raise questions they haven't thought of, to see connections to other events and other texts that the less mature readers won't notice, to recognize the need for more evidence here and a stronger logical connection there . . . so, she will gradually be training students to talk in more sophisticated and intelligent ways.

For example, students reading a difficult story like "She Unnames Them" (LeGuin 1985), a tale about Eve choosing to leave Adam and the Garden of Eden and strike out on her own, may see the allusions to the Bible story, may talk about the differences between generic names (cat, dog, and woman) and personal names (Fluffy, Fido, and Eve), and may talk about the gender issues so obviously raised, but their teacher may spot something else. You might notice those last lines:

> I could not chatter away as I used to do, taking it all for granted. My words now must be slow, as new, as single, as tentative as the steps I took going down the path away from the house, between the dark branched, tall dancers motionless against the winter shining.

You might see in the unnaming and renaming evident in calling the trees silhouetted by the cold, white, winter glow "tall dancers motionless against the winter shining" a metaphor for art, perhaps especially literary art wherein the poet or novelist tries to see things fresh and new, breaking down the categories and classifications we've become accustomed to—*unnaming* them. And then, of course, *renaming* them—searching for ways of seeing them fresh and clear, uncontaminated by preconceptions and stereotypes, renaming them so that we have to concentrate for the moment on aspects and characteristics that we might ignore if she had said simply "trees in the moonlight."

What question could you ask to expand the discussion to encompass that thought? Perhaps "What are the tall dancers?" followed by "I wonder why she doesn't just call them trees, if that's all they are?" And then, if that hasn't led the students into the reflection you're searching for, "In what other parts of the story does she talk about naming—does that help us figure out why she calls the trees 'tall dancers'?"

Pushing the discussion further with your question doesn't ignore or diminish the significance of the students' questions if you're cautious—it simply indicates that you, too, wonder, question, doubt, speculate. In other words, you, too, are a reader who sees the possibility for inquiry in anything you read and seeks others with whom to discuss it. Is this story a metaphor for literary art? Is LeGuin suggesting that writing poetry and fiction is an effort to get more intimately in touch with reality, to break down preconceptions and stereotypes, to see the world more clearly? Is this a story about how language organizes experience, then grows rigid and inadequate, and then must be challenged by new formulations? These are legitimate questions that a sophisticated adult reader might raise about this story, and if your class is sophisticated enough—this is, after all, a difficult text— then there's no reason for you not to bring them up.

> > > *As I said earlier, there won't always be an English teacher around when you need one. Ultimately, the students have to develop some independence. For most of their lives, they'll be discussing politics, ethics, religion, the latest movie, television shows, and, we hope, the books they'll be reading, all without the assistance of a good teacher to organize and manage the discourse.*

There is, in fact, every reason *to* bring them up. If conversation works by bringing various perspectives together, so that they may be compared and contrasted, examined for their strengths and weaknesses, their virtues and defects, with all being refined by the process, then having a more experienced, more insightful, more thoughtful reader in the discussion should serve to move kids along. The teacher's contribution to the discussion lies in keeping it organized, keeping it flowing, making sure that all perspectives are respected, and encouraging as many kids as possible to enter into the flow of talk, but it's also to enrich and deepen the discourse. The teacher's greater breadth of reading will enable her to spot what the students have missed, to raise questions they haven't thought of, to see connections to other events and other texts that the less mature readers won't notice, to recognize the need for more evidence here and a stronger logical connection there, and in doing so, she will gradually be training students to talk in more sophisticated and intelligent ways.

Moving Toward Independence

As I said earlier, there won't always be an English teacher around when you need one. Ultimately, the students have to develop some independence. For most of their lives, they'll be discussing politics, ethics, religion, the latest movie, television shows, and, we hope, the books they'll be reading, all without the assistance of a good teacher to organize and manage the discourse. And so we have to find not only ways of guiding and structuring their conversations so that they may learn the art but also ways of letting go, getting out of the way, leaving them on their own so that they may assume the responsibility.

The Dialogue Booklet

One design that both offers structure and support and begins to move the teacher out of the middle is the dialogue booklet. This is simply a series of questions designed to move a group through a conversation, allowing the students a great deal of control over what they discuss but not abandoning them entirely. You might, for example, write about five to ten questions, like these:

1. Introduce yourself to your partner(s)—where are you from, what are your interests, and so on. Ask any questions you wish.

2. What feeling or emotion did the text give you? Describe it briefly and tell us why you think the text caused that reaction.

3. What memory does the text call to mind—of people, places, events, sights, smells, or even of something more ambiguous, perhaps feelings or attitudes?

4. What did you see happening in the text? Paraphrase it—retell the event briefly. When you discuss, see if there are differences in the paraphrasing.

5. Did the text give you any ideas or cause you to think about anything in particular? Explain briefly what thoughts it led you to.

6. What is the most important word in the text? Explain briefly why you think the word you've picked is the most important.

7. What is the most important phrase in the text? Explain briefly why you think it's so important.

8. What image or picture did you see as you read the text? It might be something you remember and not something in the text. Describe it briefly.

9. What sort of person do you imagine the author of this poem to be?

10. How did your reading of the text differ from that of your discussion partner(s)? In what ways were they similar?

11. How did your understanding of the text or your feelings about it change as you talked?

12. Does this text make you think of another text, song, TV show, or other literary work? What is it and what connection is there between the two pieces?

13. What did you observe or learn about your discussion partner(s) as the talk progressed?

14. If you were to write a few pages, maybe a letter, about your reading of the text, who would you write to, and what would you write about? (Probst 2004)

When you have questions that you like, arranged in an order that feels like the natural flow of conversation, prepare the booklets by duplicating one question in each quadrant of a sheet of paper, so that it can be copied, collated, stapled, and cut, yielding small booklets (see Figure 5–1). Then simply provide students with a copy of the text you want them to discuss, and pass out the booklets, asking the students not to glance through them in advance. Instruct them to turn to the first page, reflect for a few moments on the question or prompt they find, and discuss it with their group for as long as it sustains talk. Tell them that when the talk begins to dry up, they should agree that it's time to move on, turn to the next page, and repeat the process.

As they talk, you can wander around the room, taking notes on what you hear and observing how well the talk is going; this will serve as a basis for subsequent discussion of both the text and their conversations when you call the class back together again.

An activity like this allows the teacher to move to the sideline without abandoning the students. They have a structure for the conversation offered by this sequence of questions, and they have control over the pacing; they're free to let the conversation take new directions unpredicted—and uncontrolled—by the

Dialogue with a text	Dialogue with a text
Dialogue with a text	Dialogue with a text

FIGURE 5–1. *Discussion Questions Formatted for a Dialogue Booklet*

CRITERIA FOR THE EVALUATION OF DISCUSSION	
The student/class . . .	**Notes:**
1. comes prepared to engage in the work of the classroom by having read, written in the journal, conducted interviews, and sought out relevant information or experience.	
2. supports the ongoing discourse of the classroom by contributing to the talk, listening attentively to the offerings of others, and helping, when necessary, to draw others into the discussion.	
3. accepts responsibility for the success of the talk by refraining from sarcasm or insult that silences others and by tolerating digressions from his/its immediate concerns.	
4. is willing to probe and question, to speculate, to take risks.	
5. tolerates the missteps, meanderings, and recursiveness typical of discussion, and explores the possibilities in ideas offered.	
6. attempts to build upon and extend the thoughts of others.	

FIGURE 5–2. *(Continues)*

From *Adolescent Literacy.* Portsmouth, NH: Heinemann. ©2004 by Robert E. Probst, from *Response & Analysis*, Second Edition. Portsmouth, NH: Heinemann.

CRITERIA FOR THE EVALUATION OF DISCUSSION *(continued)*	
7. questions others, exploring the potential of their contributions, and offers clarification and elaboration upon her/its own ideas when necessary.	
8. assumes some of the work necessary to maintain discussion and push it along—i.e., helps by summarizing issues, raising questions, extracting significant points, making connections, setting agenda.	
9. assumes the responsibility for independent and individual summary and closure.	
10. looks for connections—between texts, the ideas offered by other students, and experiences outside the classroom.	
11. acknowledges the structure of the discussion and abides by the patterns implicit in it (brainstorming, storytelling, responding, and problem solving all imply different sorts of talk).	

FIGURE 5–2. continued

From *Adolescent Literacy*. Portsmouth, NH: Heinemann. ©2004 by Robert E. Probst, from *Response & Analysis*, Second Edition. Portsmouth, NH: Heinemann.

teacher. The teacher is still there, of course, observing and taking notes, intervening if necessary to help a group or to teach something about the discussion process.

Evaluating Our Conversations

We do much of the business of the world on paper, of course, but the spoken word is still important enough for us to address directly in our classes. Although there is nothing kids do more naturally and easily than talk, and we don't need Tom Sawyer's cleverness to get them to engage, we do have to search for ways to get them to talk better. And what does *talking better* mean? Obviously, it includes such matters as listening more carefully; calling for, providing, and questioning evidence; accepting and examining other points of view; and dealing tactfully with one another. It might be appropriate for us, at least occasionally, to assess what's going on in conversations somewhat more formally, if only for our own information. A sheet like the one in Figure 5–2 (on page 57), for example, might help us as we observe either an entire class or a few students as they talk. Modify it to suit your students, your course, and your own vision of what good conversation is.

Final Thoughts

Tom used talk skillfully and effectively. So, too, do the cult leaders, the advertisers, and many others who use language to persuade and convince, and occasionally to deceive and conceal. We need to teach our students to use conversation to build better ideas collaboratively than any of us will come to on our own. We need them to be able to watch press conferences and think about the answers they hear and the questions they would've asked themselves, had they been there. We need them to be able to participate in the conversations of a democratic society, explaining their perspective, calling for clarification, requesting and offering evidence for positions taken, examining and perhaps correcting the logic of an argument, changing their minds when appropriate, and digging in to make the case stronger when that's called for. In these past decades, we've paid a great deal of attention to reading and writing, and we've made great progress. I hope that over the next several years, both we and our students will pay as much attention to and make as much progress with the delicate and difficult art of conversation.

> **When you want to know more . . .**
>
> Bob has been arguing that literature is an invitation into a dialogue—with other readers, with the author, with the characters, and even with the teacher—for a long time. He wrote about it in "Literature as Invitation," for *Voices from the Middle* (2000), and in his book *Response and Analysis: Teaching Literature in Secondary School,* Second Edition (2004).

Connecting to my thoughts

Connecting to other texts

BOOKS TO READ ON READING BOOKS

Coles, Robert. 1989. *The Call of Stories: Teaching and the Moral Imagination.* Boston: Houghton Mifflin.

Dirda, Michael. 2003. *An Open Book: Coming of Age in the Heartland.* New York: Norton.

Hamilton, John Maxwell. 2000. *Casanova Was a Book Lover: And Other Naked Truths and Provocative Curiosities About the Writing, Selling, and Reading of Books.* Baton Rouge, LA: Louisiana State University Press.

Manguel, Alberto. 1996. *A History of Reading.* New York: Viking.

Nell, Victor. 1988. *Lost in a Book: The Psychology of Reading for Pleasure.* New Haven, CT: Yale University Press.

> > > TERI S. LESESNE

Of Times, Teens, and Books

I WAS A TEEN when Bob Dylan sang "The Times They Are A-Changin'." His song was a political call to arms letting the "establishment" of adult society know that the world was changing and urging these adults either to step aside or to lend a hand. Dylan's reminder that times are a-changin' seems even more appropriate for the new generation of adolescents who not only witnessed the terrorist attacks of September 11 but now live in a world defined by war and shaped by the effects of global warming, divisive politics (here and abroad), and potential pandemics that shake us all.

But we don't have to look to the world scene to see how times have changed. One glance into the bedroom of any adolescent shows the transformation. Computers, iPods, cell phones, and Bluetooths—this generation of teens more than any other before them is wired to technology of their day. Furthermore, this technology is readily available to more and more adolescents. While previous generations saw new technology emerge slowly through the ranks—the most privileged first—this generation of teens is living through a technology explosion; teens from almost all income levels have access to the same technology at the same time. And they use it!

Learning about what kids will read is always a pleasure and therefore this chapter could have been placed anywhere in this collection. However, we saw special reason to place it here. With some ideas and strategies already presented, you'll want to put those into practice with perhaps some new books. At the same time, it's perfect prereading for what follows as we next move to a discussion of the reading lives of African American males by Alfred Tatum in Interlude 2 and later to a look at twenty-first century demands by Jim Burke (Chapter 10).

—KB, REP, LR

Today's adolescents are connected beyond the walls of their bedrooms and their classrooms through email, instant messaging (IMing), social networking, blogs, and personal web pages. They connect with other adolescents around the world via email. They download music from other countries. They get their news feed via online sources. Adolescence is all about speed and convenience and immediacy. However, there is more to the changing nature of adolescence than that. Terrorism alerts, videos of bodies being pulled from the rubble here and abroad, people stranded on rooftops for days in the flooded areas of the Gulf Coast, and politicians who suggest anyone who disagrees with policy is giving comfort to the enemy—these images, these messages, echo Dylan's words in a most chilling way. Indeed, the times are changing. These changes, I suggest, mean that adolescents themselves have changed.

> > > > >
Be sure to take a look at what Donna Alvermann says about multiliteracy in Chapter 3.
—KB, REP, LR

In addition to negotiating a range of multiliteracy demands with ease, adolescents are also entering puberty at a younger age, pushing them to wonder about issues of sex and identity when some of us wish they were still riding bikes and playing tag. This need to find answers sooner also has an effect on their reading interests. These days, Judy Blume's *Are You There, God? It's Me, Margaret* is more likely to be read by a fourth grader than a middle school student and *The Outsiders* (Hinton) is more likely read in middle school than in high school. This need for more information sooner is also reflected in the growing popularity of nonfiction books, such as *It's Perfectly Normal*, by Robie Harris, and *Hair in Funny Places*, by Babette Cole. The more intense young adult (YA) literature of Chris Crutcher, Chris Lynch, and Robert Cormier is now read by young middle schoolers. Elementary school children ignore the Baby-Sitters Little Sister books to rush through the Baby-Sitters Club series (both by Ann M. Martin), then quickly reach for *The Sisterhood of the Traveling Pants* and its sequels (Brashares). These changes in middle schoolers—their resources, abilities, and interests—have had a major impact on what is being published and for whom.

Publishers have responded to this resituating of YA books in earlier grades. For instance, recommended age levels on most YA literature now read "12 and up." And take a quick glance at the winners of the prestigious Newbery award, a medal given for literary distinction for *children* (emphasis mine). Lois Lowry's dystopian novel *The Giver*, for instance, is better suited for older readers, ones who will encounter Orwell's equally disturbing dystopian world. *A View from Saturday* (Konigsburg), *Hope Was Here* (Bauer), *The House of the Scorpions* (Farmer), and all Newbery Honor books are all novels that require older readers to negotiate the subject matter as well as the characters who populate these books, yet we find middle schoolers reading them all. Yes, times, teens, and books are all changing.

It makes sense, then, that the books we offer this new generation should also reflect this paradigm shift in how adolescents negotiate their interaction with one another, their way through school and life, and their reading. Young adult literature has done just that: it has evolved to include new forms and formats, as well as new voices. This new YA literature tests kids' mettle as it pushes them to think critically and respond personally on issues previously considered off limits in YA books. This cutting-edge YA literature requires thoughtful readers, students who are willing to respond to these texts critically and personally.

The new YA literature differs in both form and substance. Graphic novels, for instance, combine text and illustration in new ways and are, therefore, a logical extension of the picture storybooks enjoyed by students in elementary grades. Stories that combine distinct genres in a seamless blend move beyond the confines of each genre to extend stories in new directions. Casts of characters that represent a greater diversity of the adolescent population can speak to readers who have before been reluctant to read books that did not reflect their life, their culture, and, therefore, their reality. Books that tackle hitherto taboo topics corroborate the evolution of YA literature, and nonfiction's place in the reading lives of adolescents is more prominent than before.

> > > *It makes sense, then, that the books we offer this new generation should also reflect this paradigm shift in how adolescents negotiate their interaction with one another, their way through school and life, and their reading.*

In this chapter, I explore these cutting-edge books and how they can lead our new generation of adolescents to higher levels of literacy. I also examine audiobooks and ebooks, two formats that push the envelope of what we mean by reading. Other media tie-ins to the literature need to be brought into focus as well; books now come with websites, playlists, and much more. Even product placement—inserting a commercial product specifically into a book and reaping the benefits from the company that produces the product (remember the Reese's Pieces scene from *ET*?)—has reared its ugly head in the world of YA literature. And finally, I offer some discussion of how educators can find the books that will motivate students in their classrooms. If we are to be the adults who lend a hand instead of stepping aside, we need to be able to offer our students books that speak to them and reflect their reality.

Get Graphic

Graphic novels have their origins with comic books. Comic books, which began as a simple compilation of individual strips, have certainly evolved over the years. Graphic novels have paralleled their predecessors in their evolution. Unlike comic books, though, graphic novels are bound in the same manner as hardcover and paperback books. Rather than collections of individual strips, each one telling a different story (think the daily entries for *Charlie Brown*), graphic novels possess the same structure as the more traditional narrative, using both text and illustration to create the complete story—much as picture storybooks use both. These graphic novels present readers with complex characters and multilayered plots. For example, Art Spiegelman's groundbreaking

Maus: A Survivor's Tale, which has found its way into most school library collections and more than a handful of secondary English and history classes as well, presents a view of the Holocaust that both the art and the text develop.

On the other hand, like comic books, many graphic novels, especially those in a series such as Bone, by Jeff Smith, feature archetypal characters, nondescript or backdrop settings, and rather predictable plot lines. So, like more traditional novels, graphic novels offer readers both *series* experiences with flat characters and predictable plots as well as *novel* experiences with round characters and textured plots. So, whichever your taste, there is a graphic novel for you. As a result, the audience for graphic novels has grown exponentially. Indeed, the growth has been so remarkable that in 2007, the Young Adult Library Services Association of the American Library Association, or YALSA, will publish its first list of recommended graphic novels for teens.

Understanding the Interest in Graphic Novels

Why a sudden increase in the popularity of this form of YA literature? In part, the rise in popularity of the YA graphic novel reflects the world of today's youth. Certainly, the influence of television, hundreds of channels all running twenty-four/seven, and other visual media account for increased interest in graphic-heavy texts. Another influence on graphic novels in the past decade has been the influx of manga, a Japanese form of graphic novel. The appeal of manga seems to have it roots in the fact that Japanese anime (animated manga) has become increasingly popular with American children. Cartoons using anime techniques from Japan are not new; perhaps you grew up watching the old *Speed Racer* cartoons on Saturday mornings. Today's generation, however, grew up watching *Powerpuff Girls* instead. The figures of these heroines should look vaguely familiar to anyone who has even glanced inside a piece of manga. Today's adolescents, already familiar with the illustrative style of manga from their cartoon days, have taken to this type of graphic novel without batting an eyelash.

Graphic novels may, like novels in other formats, contain mature material. Some publishers are using the same ratings information as music CDs carry. However, it is always best to preview the books you are adding to the shelves of your classroom library to ensure they are the most appropriate for the students in your class. A terrific resource for educators is Michele Gorman and Jeff Smith's *Getting Graphic: Using Graphic Novels to Promote Literacy with Preteens and Teens* (2003).

Just as the language in Japan reads from right to left, so does the text in a manga-style graphic novel. In addition to each page reading right to left, the entire book reads from what we could call back to front (see Figure 6–1). Adult readers find this difficult, to say the least! Reading manga fluently requires almost a restructuring of our neurons. Today's teens, however, do not find it much of a challenge. They accept and celebrate the differences between graphic novels and those that take the traditional manga approach.

TOMARE!

You're going the wrong way!

Manga is a completely different type of reading experience.

To start at the beginning, go to the end!

That's right! Authentic manga is read the traditional Japanese way—from right to left. Exactly the opposite of how American books are read. It's easy to follow: just go to the other end of the book and read each page—and each panel— from right side to left side, starting at the top right. Now you're experiencing manga as it was meant to be

FIGURE 6–1. *Directions for Reading a Manga Book (as found on the opening page of* Q-KO-CHAN: The Earth Invader Girl Book 1 *by Ueda Hajime)*

Graphic novels not only continue to grow in popularity but also continue to evolve as a separate art form in YA literature. Recently, Tokyopop, a publisher of graphic novels and manga, utilized manga-style illustrations in a new nonfiction series that highlights the greatest stars of the NBA. While these are not graphic novels, the influence of the illustrative style of graphic novels and manga is apparent in the pictures in this series. Biographies for the intermediate grades from Capstone Press provide information in text as well as graphic format in a series titled Graphic Biographies. Again, the illustrations demonstrate the influence of the graphic novel artists in their bold brush strokes and even bolder colors. See Figure 6–2 for a list of some of the more popular and recommended graphic novels for adolescents.

GRAPHIC NOVELS FOR ADOLESCENTS

Burleigh, R. 2003. *Amelia Earhart: Free in the Skies*. Illus. by R. Wylie. Harcourt.

Clugston, C. 2005. *Queen Bee.* Scholastic Graphix.

Eisner, W. 2000. *To the Heart of the Storm*. DC Comics.

Evanier, M. 2003. *Shrek*. Illus. by R. Bachs and R. Fernandez. Dark Horse Comics.

Finkel, J. 2005. *Greatest Stars of the NBA: Jason Kidd*. Tokyopop. (There are additional titles in this series.)

Gaiman, N. 1993. *The Books of Magic*. DC Comics/Vertigo.

Gonick, L. 2001. *The Cartoon History of the Universe, Volumes 1–7: From the Big Bang to Alexander the Great*. Broadway Books/Random House. (There are additional volumes in this series.)

Groening, M. 2001. *Simpsons Comics Royale*. HarperCollins.

Hart, C. 2003. *Manga Mania Fantasy Worlds: How to Draw the Enchanted Amazing Worlds of Japanese Comics*. Watson-Guptill.

——. 2004. *Manhwa Mania: How to Draw Korean Comics*. Watson-Guptill.

Japanese Comickers: Draw Anime and Manga Like Japan's Hottest Artists. 2003. HarperCollins/Harper Design International.

Land, D. 2002. *Star Wars Tales, Volume 1*. Dark Horse Comics.

Mizayaki, H. 2002. *Spirited Away, Vol. 1*. Viz Comics.

Satrapi, M. 2003. *Persepolis*. Pantheon.

Slott, D. 2003. *Justice League Adventures*. Illus. by J. Delaney. DC Comics.

Smith, J. 2005. *Bone: Out from Boneville*. Reissue. Scholastic.

Spiegelman, A. 1986. *Maus I*. Pantheon.

Sugiyama, R. 2004. *Comic Artists—Asia: Manga Manhwa Manhua*. Harper Design International.

Takeuchi, N. 1998. *Sailor Moon, Vol. 1*. Tokyopop.

Tezuka, O. 2002. *Astro Boy, Vol. 1*. Dark Horse.

Ueda, M. 2003. *Peach Girl, Volume 1: Change of Heart*. Tokyopop.

Vaughan, B. K. 2003. *Runaways: Pride & Joy*. Marvel Comics.

Whedon, J. 2004. *Astonishing X-Men, Volume One: Gifted*. Marvel Comics.

Winick, J. 2000. *Pedro and Me: Friendship. Loss, and What I Learned*. Henry Holt.

FIGURE 6–2.

How Can I Use Graphic Novels in My Classroom?

It is not enough to simply point out that graphic novels have found a home in YA literature. The question I hear most often has to do with the utility of using these books in the curriculum. How can the use of graphic novels complement the English curriculum? One answer has to do with multiple ways of knowing: multiple literacies. As Schwarz (2002) notes:

> Graphic novels offer value, variety, and a new medium for literacy that acknowledges the impact of visuals. These novels appeal to young people, are useful across the curriculum, and offer diverse alternatives to traditional texts as well as other mass media.

Crawford (2004) notes that the addition of graphic novels to a library collection can play an important role in motivating readers. Reluctant readers—whether reluctant because of lack of interest or limited skills—often find the visual scaffolds are the hook they need to enjoy the reading experience. The scaffold in the form of illustrations helps the reader draw inferences from text by literally providing visual representations of literary elements, such as mood (e.g., darker colors or more subdued tones), character development, flashbacks, and foreshadowing. Current curriculum demands that now include visual and/or media literacy can also be addressed with graphic novels and their variants from other countries. Graphic novels, such as those nonfiction titles mentioned earlier, can contribute much to students' understanding of how to go beyond a simple reporting of information to a more creative way of providing explanation. The possibilities for using graphic novels in school are as limitless as the topics, stories, and subjects of the very novels themselves.

> < < < < <
> Linda Rief discusses telling-boards in Chapter 13 on page 202—a very logical extension of what Teri discusses here.
> —*KB, REP, LR*

Multiple Genres and Other New Directions in YA Literature

While graphic novels represent a completely new format in YA books, other changes in YA literature are less visible but just as critical. In this section, you'll see how the blending of genres and the use of multiple narrators have also changed books for teens.

A Blurring of Lines: Mixing Genres

In the 1980s, books such as *Weetzie Bat* and other novels by Francesca Lia Block brought the genre of magical realism, already making inroads in the world of adult literature, to the pages of YA literature. Block's skillful blend of contemporary realistic fiction with elements of traditional literature and fantasy led to a new generation of books that combine genres to tell stories from unique perspectives. Magical realism makes it possible for a story to be set in the real world and yet take off on occasional flights of fancy. This combination of the real and the unreal grounds a story in reality, important for readers who find a fantasy world difficult to enter or have a hard time suspending their disbelief. Once the reader enters into the "real world" of the novel, the magical elements are less distracting. In the Weetzie Bat books, we see Weetzie for the rather hip LA girl she is. Her belief in the supernatural world seems just another piece of her eccentric character. That grounding in the realistic setting and main character helps readers accept the other more fantastic and ephemeral characters we meet as the series continues.

More than a quarter of a century later, books with multiple genres continue to take YA literature in new and exciting directions. *Whittington*, the Newbery Honor winner by Alan Armstrong, combines the English folktale of Dick Whittington and his cat along with animal fantasy and contemporary realistic fiction, no mean feat. In many ways, this is a logical outgrowth of the magical realism of the Weetzie Bat books. Armstrong combines the realistic tale of the farmer's grandchildren with the magical tale of the farm animals, who speak to one another and to the children, while adding the historical story of Dick Whittington and his cat. This pairing of history and fantasy is evident in many current YA novels.

Jane Yolen's *The Devil's Arithmetic* led the way for books such as *Second Sight*, by Gary Blackwood, which posits the question If you could change history, would you? Two teens race to tell President Lincoln that he is in danger at the theatre. History meets fantasy as one of the teens has ESP that permits her to see the potential tragedy before it unfolds. The blending of history and fantasy is also found in Blackwood's *Year of the Hangman* and Walter Moseley's *47*. Edward Bloor's *London Calling* combines historical fiction and science fiction. This blend of two separate and distinct genres offers new venues for adolescents to explore. The history is real; the time travel pulls in readers and shows them how the world they live in parallels the past. Perhaps this blending of genres that seem to be polar opposites is reflective of today's adolescents, who have become experts at multitasking: talking on the cell phone while IMing another friend and surfing the Web, all at the same time. Other media also blend genres effortlessly. Witness the hilarious scenes in *Mean Girls* where the narrator likens her high school peers to packs of wild animals, after which they suddenly begin to behave in a frenzied animalistic fashion. *Smallville* is another blend, where teen drama meets superheroic action.

Twilight and its sequel, *New Moon*, by Stephenie Meyer, are vampire romance novels that have become incredibly popular. The vampire romance novel is not new; Anne Rice's Lestat novels certainly combined romance and vampires for adult readers. What is new here is that YA literature has entered into this genre blend with positive results. *Twilight* was named as Amazon's top pick for YA novel of 2005. Advance sales for *New Moon* rival that of J. K. Rowling's Harry Potter books. These different types of genre blending are certain to continue in the foreseeable future.

> > > > >
The word that comes to our minds as we read this is *synthesis*. We live in a world where boundaries are, more and more, blurring if not disappearing. It makes sense that the books students read reflect the same change. We need students focusing on synthesizing, putting things together that normally are seen as separate entities. Blended genre books model this in reading. Tom Romano's important text, *Blending Genre, Altering Style* (2000) shows us how students accomplish the same with writing.

—*KB, REP, LR*

Using Blended-Genre Books in the Classroom

What role can these novels that employ multiple genres play in our classrooms? One obvious activity is to have students discuss the elements of each genre represented in the novel. For instance, when reading *47*, by Moseley, have students discuss what elements of the story are based on actual historical events and which elements represent fantasy. When reading *Whittington*, students could discuss how the three separate stories, each in a different genre, parallel each other and intersect at various points in the narrative. Even more important, though, is the value that these more challenging novels have for the skilled readers who sit in our classrooms. It is difficult to locate books that are developmentally appropriate for such readers and yet provide them the challenge they need and enjoy. Teachers sometimes resort to offering these students challenging books that overreach their developmental abilities or interests.

For instance, *Animal Farm*, by George Orwell, has crept into elementary and middle school classrooms as one answer to providing advanced readers a challenge. While students in fifth and sixth grades can certainly decode Orwell's *words*, they simply have not had enough life experiences to grasp Orwell's intent. The level of abstraction needed to fully appreciate the allegory and the prior experiences needed for that allegory to be meaningful are not sufficiently developed in younger readers. *Whittington*, on the other hand, provides the layering of plots an advanced reader will enjoy while situating itself within the life experiences of a teen.

One Book: Many Voices

While books that mix genres certainly appeal to today's teens, another technique also mirrors the world in which they live: multiple narrators. Multiple narrators and unreliable narrators add levels of complexity to a story. A few new books combine novels in verse with multiple narrators. *Street Love*, by Walter Dean Myers, is the story of Damien, a star athlete at his school, and Junice, a teen saddled with the care of both her younger sister and her grandmother, who is suffering from Alzheimer's disease. By including the voices of Damien and Junice along with other characters, Myers provides readers an interesting perspective. David Levithan does this in *The Realm of Possibility* with twenty separate narrators whose stories and lives intersect throughout this novel in verse. Each chapter features multiple points of view and challenges skilled readers to piece together who is speaking and how the different points of view move the story forward.

Multiple narrators are utilized in Lynne Rae Perkins' *Criss Cross*, the 2006 Newbery award winner. The thread that links the multiple narrators and story lines is the main character's missing locket and the journey this locket takes through the neighborhood over the course of a sleepy summer. Amy Koss'

> < < < < <
> And while blended-genre books make us think of synthesis, multiple voice books bring to mind collaboration. Both synthesis and collaboration are critical skills for thinking and working in the twenty-first century.
> —*KB, REP, LR*

Poison Ivy, subtitled *Three Bullies, Two Boyfriends, and One Trial*, is the story of Ivy, a hapless girl who is the target of a trio of bully girls, Ann, Sophie, and Benita. Ms. Gold, their history teacher, decides to instruct her class about the legal system by having a trial accusing the Terrible Trio of bullying. Each student who talks about the various phases of the trial is a microcosm of some typical middle school kid: jock, nerd, clown, and so on. This use of the stereotypes of middle school could lead students to an interesting discussion about the issues and people that make up their own lives.

Finally, the Dark Fusion series, by master storyteller Neal Shusterman, combines traditional literature with contemporary realism. *Red Rider's Hood*, *Duckling Ugly*, and *Dread Locks* have, at their root, a myth or fairy tale, yet each novel is squarely set in the here and now and deals with contemporary issues such as gangs and bullying. Though *Red Rider's Hood* finds its basis in *Little Red Riding Hood* variants, Shusterman manages to involve Grandma as a fighter of werewolves. *Dread Locks* takes on a Medusa variant, while *Duckling Ugly* tells of a hideous teen who is given the chance to make herself over. Here, Shusterman combines the Andersen story with elements of *Sleeping Beauty* and *Beauty and the Beast*.

Using Books with Multiple Narrators in the Classroom

While some activities are immediately apparent—readers theatre with different voices reading different characters or discussions about how the book would change if a particular character's point of view were to disappear—these books provide another focus for discussion. Remember that books with multiple narrators (and, therefore, multiple perspectives) differ from those told in a third-person or omniscient point of view in that there is no guarantee that each or *any* narrator is reliable. Recall Avi's documentary novel *Nothing but the Truth* in which Philip and Ms. Narwin have different takes on similar incidents. Neither tells the whole truth, the very point of this Newbery Honor–winning novel. Because these characters, and indeed all characters who have a part in telling the story, do so from their unique perspectives, these books can provide an opportunity for students to distinguish—or at least attempt to distinguish—between what is true or accurate and what is untrue or distorted. This does, indeed, push readers beyond literal comprehension or even analysis and develops a skill that might prove useful when reading and evaluating campaign literature, propaganda, and political writings. If one goal of education is to prepare students to be active members of a democratic society, then providing them with reading experiences that allow them to discuss distortions and half-truths becomes important. Reading books with multiple perspectives and multiple narrators provides just such an opportunity.

Welcome to the Real World

Not only do today's YA authors provide readers with books that combine genres and offer multiple perspectives via large casts of characters who each tell their own story, but they now give readers characters who reflect the people and conflicts of today. In this section, you'll get an overview of characters and conflicts that mirror the people and problems teens face today.

Guess Who's Coming to Dinner? Or, You'll Never Guess Whom I Met in the Pages of a Book

When I was a teen, the characters that I met within the pages of a book or watched on television were not the same as the people I knew in real life. Adult female characters were, for the most part, homemakers. Girls were studying for careers as nurses or secretaries. There was, of course, the chance that one of them would solve mysteries for a living, but even then I knew the chances of becoming Nancy Drew were slim. But in my real world, my mother, and thus the circle of her friends who were the role models for me, all worked outside of the home. None was a super-sleuth (or even knew a sleuth!), none was June Cleaver (or even dressed like June!), and while some were indeed secretaries, more were teachers or social workers or lab technicians, or even doctors. There was a real disconnect between what I saw on TV and read in books and what I saw in my world. During the last decades of the twentieth century, as women's role in society changed, YA literature reflected that change. Characters began to reflect reality for more and more readers—and not just for our female readers. Multicultural literature offered characters of color, characters of different religions and socioeconomic status, and characters who lived in cities, suburbs, rural communities, and even other countries.

As the literature evolved, stereotypes began to fade. The perky, perfect cheerleader was replaced by angry and injured Izzy in Cynthia Voigt's *Izzy Willy-Nilly*. The parallel image of the dumb jock has been dealt a similar blow by books such as A. M. Jenkins' *Damage* and the novels of Chris Crutcher. Here are athletes whose entire lives are not defined by the playing field. Crutcher's protagonists in *Stotan!* become a cohesive team not only by training to swim as a team but by learning how to function as a team outside of the pool area. Books by Carl Deuker, such as *On the Devil's Court*, a retelling of the Faustian legend, and Mike Lupica's *Travel Team*, about the underdogs of basketball, also do much to dispel this stereotype.

Fairy tale retellings and variants cast aside the damsel in distress in favor of female characters who take fate into their own hands. *Fairest*, by Gail Carson Levine, uses *Snow White and the Seven Dwarves* as the basis for a new variant of the classic fairy tale. Aza, the protagonist, is not the typical fairest-of-them-all,

> < < < < <
> In this section, Teri continues to give us a close-up look at books that allow teens to wonder about their real-world issues within the safe confines of fiction. Alfred Tatum (page 81) also discusses the importance of literature as a way for adolescents to consider their identity and place in the world.
> —*KB, REP, LR*

when-shall-my-prince-come-along heroine. It is Aza, though, with the help of some gnomes, who manages to right the wrongs and gain the love she desires. Other Levine novels are also illustrative of this new direction in traditional tales. *Cinderellis and the Glass Hill*, *Fairy Dust and the Quest for the Egg*, and *Ella Enchanted*, along with *The Beast*, *Spinners*, and *Crazy Jack*, by Donna Jo Napoli, are just a handful of books representative of this new direction.

Characters come in different sizes (*Stand Tall*, by Joan Bauer, and *Freak the Mighty*, by Rodman Philbrick), different shapes (*When Zachary Beaver Came to Town*, by Kimberly Willis Holt, and *Fat Kid Rules the World*, by K. L. Going), and different religions (*Confessions of a Closet Catholic*, by Sarah Littman, *A Brief Chapter in My Impossible Life*, by Dana Reinhardt, and *Godless*, by Pete Hautmann); a variety of races (*The Tequila Worm*, by Viola Canales, *A Step from Heaven*, by An Na, *Kira Kira*, by Cynthia Kadhota, *A Summer of Kings*, by Han Nolan, *Fallen Angels*, by Walter Dean Myers, and *Mr. Chickee's Funny Money*, by Christopher Paul Curtis), countries (*Homeless Bird*, by Gloria Whelan, *Sold*, by Patricia McCormick, *Evil Star*, by Anthony Horowitz, and *Samurai Shortstop*, by Alan Gratz), and socioeconomic groups (*Black & White*, by Paul Volponi, *Ball Don't Lie*, by Matt de la Pena, and *Slumming*, by Kristen Randle); with handicaps (*Tangerine*, by Edward Bloor, *Firegirl*, by Tony Abbott, and *Rules*, by Cynthia Lord), and sexual orientations that reflect the real world in which they live (*Boy Meets Boy*, by David Levithan, *Luna*, by Julie Anne Peters, and *Doing It*, by Melvin Burgess). This explosion of characters by color, by location, by interest, by religion, by sexual preference means that more and more teens have the opportunity to use books both as a mirror (here's a character who looks like me, thinks like me, worries like me) or as a window (here's a character who offers me a different way of seeing the world). Both situations provide readers with chances to learn more about themselves and those around them.

> > > *YA literature discusses difficult topics with a frankness that isn't about didacticism so much as honesty; that isn't about lecturing so much as exploring; that isn't about answers so much as questions.*

The Plot Thickens

Books now do more than present characters that break through the stereotypes; plots can shatter stereotypical ideas and portrayals of prom, peer pressure, drunken driving, anorexia, and other subjects. Laurie Halse Anderson's *Prom* is an antiprom novel in which the main character does not care that the prom at her school has been cancelled. *Shattering Glass*, by Gail Giles, demonstrated that peer pressure is not simply about fitting in with the crowd and being accepted; it can be about murder. *God of Beer*, by Garret Keizer, delivers to adult readers a tough message to swallow about the pervasiveness of alcohol among adolescents. *Speak*, by Laurie Halse Anderson, takes on a deadly serious topic as Melissa deals with being raped at a party. Alice Hoffman's *Green Angel* is set in the aftermath of a horrendous attack (read September 11) that isolates a teen from the rest of her family and community in a landscape that resembles postapocalyptic terrain.

In a time when teens are confronted with difficult issues (no longer do we *not* discuss school violence, war, famine, global warming, terrorism, pandemics, and so forth with kids), YA literature discusses difficult topics with a frankness that isn't about didacticism so much as honesty; that isn't about lecturing so much as exploring; that isn't about answers so much as questions. A look at some specific books reveals the wide range of topics YA books now tackle.

An Up-Close Look at Today's Books

Skin, by Adrienne Vrettos, is the story of Karen, a young woman who deals with all the conflict in her life by becoming anorexic. Karen's story, however, is told in flashback by her brother Donnie, who discovers her slumped in the front hall of their house one afternoon after school. His vain attempts to resuscitate her let readers know early that this novel has at least one tragic character in Karen. But how has Karen's illness affected other members of her family, especially Donnie? How illness and disease affect other members of the same family is a theme also explored in Terry Trueman's *Cruise Control*, a companion novel to his Printz Honor book, *Stuck in Neutral*. Both books, along with *Inside Out*, also by Trueman, deal with characters grappling with illness and disease.

Cynthia Lord's *Rules* features twelve-year-old Catherine, whose younger brother David is autistic. Catherine tries her best to cope with David's condition, but she sometimes thinks she is being ignored by her parents. Then, while waiting for David during one of his occupational therapy visits, she meets Jason, a paraplegic. The life of a young girl dealing with an autistic brother and a paraplegic friend is handled with warm humor and serious concern. Lord strikes just the perfect balance here between Catherine's self-pity (which is never overdone) and her growing awareness that she needs to be more grateful for David and Jason and who they truly are rather than worry about what others think.

Trueman's *Inside Out* tells a story from the point of view of Zach, a main character who is suffering from schizophrenia. And then there is *Diva*, by Alex Flinn. *Diva* tells the story of Caitlin, the young woman who was abused by Nick in *Breathing Underwater*, an amazing novel that told of an abusive relationship from the point of view of the abuser. However, this is not Caitlin rehashing the events of *Breathing Underwater*; this is Caitlin post breakup. She is moving on with her life, auditioning for a performing arts school, where her love of and talent for opera will not be mocked. It is tough for Caitlin to separate her past from the present, but her desire to become an opera singer drives her to move beyond her comfort zone.

Patricia McCormick has certainly tackled some timely topics in novels such as *Cut*. Her latest offering, *Sold*, is set in Nepal and follows the story of Lakshmi, a twelve-year-old girl sold by her stepfather into sexual servitude. Lakshmi nearly loses her own identity as she is degraded by the visitors to the Calcutta brothel she must now call home. However, her dreams of one day returning home keep her hope alive. The emotions presented are so true that readers will find themselves reacting along with Lakshmi as she journeys from Nepal to Calcutta. Today's worldly wise teens will not flinch away from stories set in other countries, and they soon come to realize that the experiences of characters from other countries are just as important to understanding themselves as stories set in more familiar places. *The Red Scarf Girl* (Jiang), *Postcards from No Man's Land* (Chambers), *A Step from Heaven* (Na), *Parvana's Journey* (Ellis), *A Single Shard* (Park), and *Refugees* (Stine) are examples of YA literature that give today's teens an up-close look at people, customs, and cultures from lands near and far.

Taboo Topics

Young adult literature came out of the gate with a focus on topics that had been largely ignored in the past. Teen pregnancy, drugs and alcohol, and rebellion against parents were evident in the first novels of the new genre; good examples are *The Pigman* (Zindel), *Mr. and Mrs. Bo Jo Jones* (Head), and *The Outsiders* (Hinton). Today, authors of YA literature continue to explore new frontiers; as a result, teens are exploring, too, through books that tackle topics as wide ranging as drug abuse, bullying, school shootings, and sexual orientation and identity.

While *Go Ask Alice* (anonymous) introduced YA readers to the harsh world of illegal drugs, new YA books are tackling the abuse of legal drugs, such as alcohol and prescription drugs. *Rx*, by Tracy Lynn, details the growing addiction of a high school student named Thyme who takes Ritalin once to help her focus and study for a test. Eventually, Thyme becomes a statistic: another high school kid who abuses prescription drugs. What makes this story rise above a *Go Ask Alice* sort of cautionary tale is the realistic approach the author takes. Thyme and her friends and family could be living in my neighborhood—or yours. My own teens verify the book's accuracy with stories from school—kids caught with pills or suspended for having aspirin, stories about what kids consider acceptable in terms of drugs. Just as some adults escape pressure with drugs, teens do as well.

Bullying and school shooting stories seem to go hand in hand these days. From Todd Strasser's *Give a Boy a Gun* to Jim Shepard's *Project X*, from *Endgame*, by Nancy Garden, to *Shooter*, by Walter Dean Myers, the stories tell an all-too-familiar tale of young men pushed beyond their limits by bullies. These young men believe the only answer to the intolerable cruelty of their peers is to take up arms against them within the context of school. Certainly these books are a reflection of a new reality for today's adolescents, who have witnessed more violence in schools than any other generation. There are kids in our classes carrying guns for older gang members, kids committing horribly violent crimes. How might these books contribute to thinking intelligently about these matters? How might teachers discuss them in classes? One answer is that in discussing the alienation the bullying characters feel or the embarrassment those bullied often suffer, we give teens with those same emotions a safe context for discussing how "those characters" feel without having to admit they may be describing themselves.

Another topic that often draws the interest of censors has to do with sexuality. Judy Blume's *Forever* still finds readers who are curious about first sexual experiences. Tanya Lee Stone's *A Bad Boy Can Be Good for a Girl* takes Blume's work a step further and actually uses that book in a central scene. Novels about sex and sexuality now deal with gay, lesbian, bisexual, transgendered, and questioning characters. Nancy Garden's *Annie on My Mind* certainly set the stage for the other authors who were to write about this sensitive and volatile issue. *Luna* (Peters), *Boy Meets Boy* (Levithan), and *The Geography Club* (Hartinger) are all honest portrayals of the lives of gay and straight adolescents who are searching for acceptance.

Censorship

Of course, with this new focus on hitherto forbidden topics, there has been a new focus on YA literature on the part of censors. The number of challenges to books in school and public libraries has grown over the past twenty-five years. The new brutal realism in YA literature causes some to be concerned that these books are somehow not appropriate for adolescents. As a member of the National Council of Teachers of English's Standing Committee Against Censorship and an advocate for YA literature for decades, I have made it clear where I stand on this issue. As someone who teaches students who want to go into classrooms and school libraries, I want to make certain these preservice teachers understand the nature of censorship and their role in selecting materials for classroom and school libraries. Censorship is complex; attacks on books come from both ends of the political spectrum and from all the places along the continuum as well. The target of most of the challenges to books tends to be those that deal with sex and drugs. *Forever* has been on the hit list since its publication more than twenty-five years ago. Now it is joined by *It's Perfectly Normal* and *It's So Amazing*, two nonfiction books on the subject of sexuality by Robie Harris. Most challenges to materials come from a true concern for students. However, it is essential to understand the difference between censorship (something we wish to avoid at all costs) and selection, the true nature of how we should be adding books to our libraries.

< < < < <
For more information about challenged and banned books, visit this URL maintained by the Office of Intellectual Freedom of the American Library Association: www.ala.org/ala/oif/bannedbooksweek/bbwlinks/100mostfrequently.htm. NCTE also offers information about book challenges at www.ncte.org/about/issues/censorship?source=gs.
—*KB, REP, LR*

Contrasting Selection with Censorship

Selection occurs when we make decisions about the books we are adding to our library collections. Selection takes into account the needs of the curriculum, the needs and interests of our students, and the need to have a balanced collection that represents all points of view. So, when we approach a new book, we ask questions such as those listed in Figure 6–3 (on page 77). Our answers help us determine which books to select.

While selection is a process of including books, censorship seeks to exclude books from collections. Censors seek to remove books from the hands of all students. Generally, a censor challenges material based on religious, political, or other personal reasons. Unfortunately, the line that separates selection from censorship is microscopically thin. Study the scenarios below titled "Is It Censorship or Selection?" to think about the differences between selection and censorship.

IS IT CENSORSHIP OR SELECTION?

A parent comes to a teacher, asking that her child be excused from reading *Bridge to Terabithia* (Paterson) because there has been a recent death in the family. The parent believes this book is not appropriate for her child at this time because it will be upsetting given recent events. Additionally, this parent is requesting that only her child be excused from the reading. Selection or censorship?

Another parent comes to see you and asks that *Bridge to Terabithia* be removed from your curriculum because of "bad" language and an "inappropriate" relationship between Jess and Leslie out there in the woods. You explain your reasons for including the book as a class reading experience. The parent remains adamant that no one should read this "depressing and immoral" book and goes to the principal, asking for its removal. Selection or censorship?

Audiobooks, Ebooks, and Other Media Tie-ins

Audiobooks are not new or cutting edge, but the technology of audiobooks is continuing to evolve, and books in electronic format are finding their way to library collections. The fact that the American Library Association has created the Odyssey Award to be given to an audiobook for children and/or young adults is testament to the growing use and popularity of this alternative method of reading a book. Cassette recordings of books have been replaced by CD versions, for the most part. Of course, there are a few companies producing audiobooks in MP3 format for downloads to computers and the ubiquitous iPods.

QUESTIONS TO ASK ABOUT SELECTION
AND CENSORSHIP

1. Is this a book that might serve a purpose in the classroom for teaching something in the required curriculum?

   Example: *The Book Thief*, by Markus Zusak, can add much to a social studies classroom studying the Holocaust. *Fairest*, by Gail Carson Levine, is a folktale variant that could serve in a unit on traditional literature. *Punished*, by David Lubar, is a humorous story about a young man challenged to learn more about the use of language, including oxymorons and palindromes, certainly an interesting addition to the English classroom.

2. Is this a book that will appeal to the stated interests of my students? Is it developmentally appropriate for my readers?

   Example: *Endgame*, by Nancy Garden, deals with bullying and a school shooting. Given the continuing problem of bullies in the schools, this novel will likely find an audience. Since the shooting takes place in a high school, it is perhaps more appropriate for eighth-grade readers. *The Amazing Life of Birds*, by Gary Paulsen, is developmentally appropriate for anyone in the throes of puberty or on the verge of puberty.

3. Is this a book that will provide an alternative viewpoint or add to the discussion of a topic that is part of the curriculum or my students' world?

   Example: *The Astonishing Life of Octavian Nothing*, by M. T. Anderson, a gothic novel set during the American Revolution, will provide an alternative view of the role of slaves during the revolution. *Revolve* (Nelson Bibles) is a hip and glossy New Testament that features call-out boxes about topics of interest to adolescent girls.

4. Is this a book that will have some lasting value for readers or one that is simply part of a current fad that might not be popular in a few months?

   Example: Biographies are prime examples of this faddish nature of books. I still have biographies of Paula Abdul and Kirk Cameron in their first incarnations as pop singer and TV series hunk.

FIGURE 6–3.

Playaway furnishes readers with self-contained audiobooks that come complete with headphones and battery. The entire contraption fits easily into the palm of a hand.

Ebooks are already a reality. Books download now to computers, PDAs, and MP3 players. Before long, audiobooks on cell phones will be a reality (they might already be a reality by the time you read this). As technology progresses, the availability of the audio form of books will be more widespread. Do adolescents listen to books? The research is still nascent, but Beers (1998) and I (2006) have noted not only that readers will pick up audio but that audio seems to be one way to address the problems of struggling readers, unmotivated readers, English language learners, and other populations.

Other aspects of technology are also playing a role in YA literature and in the lives of those who read it. Websites in support of books offer readers a chance to delve further into the culture and world of the book. Harry Potter sites abound. For instance, mugglenet.com contains promotional materials, rumors, news, and all sorts of links, including some tantalizing tidbits about book 7 and its possible contents and release date. A recent Web search netted more than eighteen million hits for Harry Potter websites. Of course, there are websites for Lemony Snicket's A Series of Unfortunate Events books as well, including www.lemonysnicket.com/index.cfm. The Watching Alice series has a companion website where readers can search for more clues into the whereabouts of the elusive Alice. At www.alicebrownismissing.com, readers will learn more about evidence in this case.

Add playlists now to other forms of media that can accompany a YA book. What is a playlist? Some authors listen to music as they write. Their choices of music are deliberate. Certain songs and tunes are selected to help develop character, plot, mood, and so on. These choices are called a playlist, and some YA authors share their playlists via websites, blogs, and even in the front matter of their books. Take, for example, Patrick Jones' playlist for *Nailed*, his 2006 YA novel. Originally, Jones had given each chapter a title from an REM song. He burned a CD with these songs to play as he traveled. As of 2006, you could view his playlist at this URL: www.connectingya.com/nailed.html. One activity for readers is to ask them to create playlists for different characters, scenes, or events from the books they are reading.

The blogs maintained by many YA writers mention the music that is a part of their lives as well. Blogs (short for *web logs*) are rather like online journals. These blogs cover a wide array of topics, including YA literature. Authors with blog spots include Laurie Halse Anderson, David Lubar, Tanya Lee Stone, Meg Cabot, Scott Westerfeld, Julie Anne Peters, Alex Flinn, John Green, Cynthia Leitich Smith, Libba Bray, Sarah Dessen, and Ned Vizzini. Librarian Erin Downey has compiled many of these blog spots at her own blog: erindowney.livejournal.com/1742.html. Educators might include snippets from the blogs of authors whose works students are reading and ask readers to comment about their value in gaining insight into the books.

1 Catapult	DOWNLOAD NOW
2 I Don't Sleep, I Dream	DOWNLOAD NOW
3 Crush With Eyeliner	DOWNLOAD NOW
4 Get Up	DOWNLOAD NOW
5 Man On The Moon	DOWNLOAD NOW
6 Everybody Hurts	DOWNLOAD NOW

Adapted from *Nailed*, by Patrick Jones

KEEPING UP WITH WHAT'S NEW IN YA LIT

Any (or better yet all) of the following offer you a fast way to keep current on new YA books.

Review Journals

School Library Journal (www.schoollibraryjournal.com)

Booklist (www.booklistonline.com)

The Horn Book (www.hbook.com)

Voice of Youth Advocates (*VOYA*) (www.voya.com)

Professional Journals That Include Reviews of YA Books

Voices from the Middle (www.ncte.org/pubs/journals/vm)

English Journal (www.ncte.org/pubs/journals/ej)

Journal of Adolescent & Adult Literacy
     (www.reading.org/publications/journals/jaal/index.html)

The ALAN Review (www.alan-ya.org)

Online Lists

American Library Association (www.ala.org/yalsa)

Where Do We Go from Here?

Crystal ball, anyone? Tracking YA literature from its infancy in *The Outsiders*, *The Pigman*, and *The Chocolate War* (Cormier) to its current incarnation with *The Book Thief* (Zusak), *Looking for Alaska* (Green), *ttyl* (Myracle), *The Love Curse of the Rumbaughs* (Gantos), and *King Dork* (Portman) clearly demonstrates that the genre is thriving and changing with the times and with the needs and interests of its audience. As teens continue to push the boundaries of their worlds, the books they want to read will mirror their interests, their needs, and their questions. Perhaps that's what makes this type of book—YA literature— so exciting. While one might argue that books for adults take on new forms more slowly (after all, it is hard to teach an old dog new tricks), books for adolescents must keep up with the excitement and energy of teens. The times, well, they are a-changin', and this new generation of YA literature does indeed reflect the changes of teens and the times.

When you want to know more . . .

If you want some assistance putting all the books you've met in Teri's chapter into the right hands, you might want to pick up her *Making the Match: The Right Book for the Right Reader at the Right Time, Grades 4–12* (2003). And if you're searching for more, you should regularly visit her blog: professornana. livejournal.com.

Connecting to my thoughts

Connecting to other texts

ON THE SCHOOL AND THE CLASSROOM

Booth, Wayne C. 1988. *The Vocation of a Teacher.* Chicago, IL: University of Chicago Press.

Cushman, Kathleen, and What Kids Can Do (organization). 2003. *Fires in the Bathroom: Advice for Teachers from High School Students.* New York: New Press (distributed by W. W. Norton).

Freedman, Samuel G. 1990. *Small Victories: The Real World of a Teacher, Her Students, and Their High School.* New York: Harper & Row.

Hoffman, Marvin. 1996. *Chasing Hellhounds: A Teacher Learns from His Students.* 1st ed. Minneapolis, MN: Milkweed Editions (distributed by Publishers Group West).

Kohn, Alfie. 1993. *Punished by Rewards: The Trouble with Gold Stars, Incentive Plans, A's, Praise, and Other Bribes.* Boston: Houghton Mifflin.

Lessons Learned

> > > ALFRED W. TATUM

BUILDING THE TEXTUAL LINEAGES OF AFRICAN AMERICAN MALE ADOLESCENTS

A pendulum swings both ways for African American males. On one side are hopes and dreams, where the potential leads to promise. On the other side is defeat, where hopes unfulfilled become a record of human tragedy. . . . Teachers must discuss texts with African American male students in responsive ways in order to help them land on the side of the pendulum that swings toward promise and possibility. (Tatum 2005, p. 10)

In this brief essay, I focus on building the textual lineages—those literary and nonliterary texts that are significant in one's development—of African American male adolescents who attend schools in economically disadvantaged communities. They are among our nation's poorest readers. Teachers find it difficult to prepare these young men to comprehend cognitively challenging texts. Some of the difficulty is precipitated by forces beyond teachers' control, such as poverty and the community turmoil it engenders. These factors have a psychological effect on African American male adolescents, who adopt a projected identity—what they can become—that is in concert with their day-to-day lives. The psychologist Carl Jung referred to these factors as "psychic infections." In general, teachers are not ready for these young male adolescents when they appear in our nation's classrooms with underdeveloped literacy skills and an identity partly shaped by community turmoil. This underpreparedness causes many of these young men to be defaulted by their educational experiences. This default occurs when students enter schools with the expectation that something good will happen and the good never materializes. At some point, the expectation of good by the student withers and is replaced by a diminished view of one's potential to become an excellent reader and writer. In addition, teachers experience a diminished sense of efficacy related to improving the reading achievement of these young men.

Students' withered expectations and teachers' lowered sense of efficacy directly affect reading instruction in two significant ways. First, they lead to a deficit model of reading instruction for African American male adolescents attending schools in impoverished communities. In this model, educators do not discuss how reading instruction can align with or counter the historical and immediate variables affecting these students' reading achievement. Instead, educators focus on research-based reading skill and strategy instruction to improve reading scores; they fail to give serious consideration to the role that literacy instruction and curriculum orientation could play in leading these young men to become actively involved in their literacy development and to become agents of change in their own lives. Although skill and strategy instruction is essential, it is insufficiently robust to improve the reading achievement of these male adolescents living in a race-based and class-based society. This deficit model of reading instruction is evident when examining the types of reading materials placed in front of these young men. For example, there is a tendency to place sixth-grade-level reading materials in front of ninth-grade students reading several years below grade level. This decision is predicated on reading level without thoughtful consideration of the student's life level and factors contributing to his emotional, social, and cultural development. Reading instruction must pay attention to adolescents' lives.

There is a deleterious perception that struggling African American male adolescents should accept any form of instruction aimed at helping them become better readers. In some cases, the instruction reinforces their perceptions as being struggling readers or, worse, as students incapable of handling cognitively challenging texts. Like all adolescents, African American male adolescents want to know why they are reading the assigned materials and the benefits of reading the materials. They would like to know how the texts will enable them to be, do, think, or act differently as a result of reading them.

Taking a business perspective, they want to know that there will be returns for their investment. In short, they would like to become smarter about something beyond reading skills. The additional benefits of literacy instruction in students' current place and space and in their future are often not reflected in a deficit model of reading instruction. Teachers may argue that students need to be able to read to enter college. These young men already know this. They have received numerous "pep" talks. African American male adolescents need "prep" talks. That is, they need instruction that helps them become better readers and exposure to a wide range of text that pays attention to their projected identities and ways to counter them. This leads to the next point.

> > > *Teachers may argue that students need to be able to read to enter college. These young men already know this. They have received numerous "pep" talks. African American male adolescents need "prep" talks. That is, they need instruction that helps them become better readers and exposure to a wide range of text that pays attention to their projected identities and ways to counter them.*

Second, the development of textual lineages of African American male adolescents is being severely compromised in an era of accountability. Instead of trying to score with reading with these young men, schools have focused on increasing reading scores. The pressure to meet adequate yearly progress (AYP) has contributed to overlooking young people (OYP). This is problematic with adolescents because teachers can use text to broker positive, meaningful relationships with African American male adolescents during reading instruction. Text, along with knowledge of using research-based reading strategies to address students' reading-related difficulties, can have a significant influence on the lives of African American male adolescents despite some of the psychic infections they encounter in communities of turmoil. Unfortunately, I am finding that African American male adolescents are suffering from an underexposure to text that they find meaningful. This contributes to African American male adolescents accepting a limited view of the role of reading and text in their lives.

Schools must expose African American male adolescents to text that allows them to see the significance of text. They must be able to assess text as having an effect on their lives. I share my own textual lineages to illustrate the point (see Figure 1). These texts became part of my textual lineage during adolescence, mainly in middle school and high school classrooms. The textual lineage began with the autobiography at the top of the chart. I then selected or was assigned the other texts in the order in which they appear. Several of the texts are linked conceptually by the issues described within. For example, Claude McKay's poem captures the residual effects of the America experienced by Frederick Douglass. The texts were significant for four reasons. They contributed to a healthy psyche; they provided modern awareness of the real world; they described the African American collective struggle; and they provided a road map for acting on one's life. Historically, connections among reading, writing, speaking, and action are salient in the literacy development of African American males. Presently, this is not the case. When I ask African American male adolescents to construct their textual lineages, that is, provide a representation of texts that have contributed to who they are and texts that give them direction for the future, they have little or nothing to contribute. These young men have entered middle school and high school classrooms in a public education system in the United States and are unable to identify text they find significant in their lives. This is frightening. They are suffering from an in-school literacy underload. This means that they receive an insufficient amount of text in school to help them critique and understand their experiences outside of school. As a result, many African American male adolescents surrender their life chances before they get to know their life choices.

Essentially, we need to take action and mobilize efforts to build the textual lineages of African American male adolescents in classrooms throughout

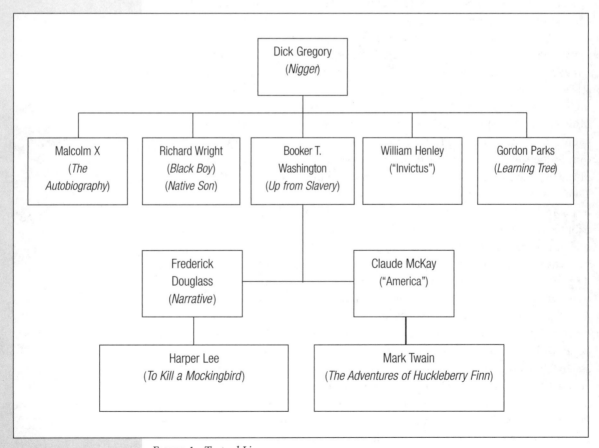

FIGURE 1. *Textual Lineage*

the United States. This requires giving allowance for broader and wider aims of reading instruction in an era of accountability. This also suggests that there is greater need to integrate effective skill and strategy instruction with effective text selection. There is a need to advocate for students at all times when curricular decisions are being made. Educators must continually seek to identify elements of reading instruction that are undertreated or causing disharmony. As a starting point, there is a need to connect text to the multiple backdrops African American male adolescents bring with them into classrooms— community, economic, cultural or gender, national, and personal backdrops. Several texts come to mind. They are *Handbook for Boys* (Myers), *"Yo, Little Brother . . ."* (Davis and Jackson), *Reallionaire* (Gray), and *The Pact* (Davis, Jenkins, and Hunt). I also recommend the poems "If," by Rudyard Kipling, "Invictus," by William Henley and "Test of a Man," author unknown. These young men should read and understand the Declaration of Independence. I also recommend that they read the speech Bill Cosby delivered on the fiftieth anniversary of *Brown v. Board of Education*. The idea is to expose them to more text in a supportive environment. As they come to us each day with undefined expectations, we must be ready with texts that help define those expectations. We cannot wait for African American males to heal themselves; we must contribute to the healing and build textual lineages that move them toward promise and possibility. Too often, for African American male adolescents, the pendulum is swinging in a different direction.

> > > *We cannot wait for African American males to heal themselves; we must contribute to the healing and build textual lineages that move them toward promise and possibility.*

When you want to know more . . .

Alfred deals with a challenging and delicate issue in his chapter, an issue on which we all want as much advice and guidance as we can find. He's talked about it at length in his book *Teaching Reading to Black Adolescent Males: Closing the Achievement Gap* (2005). And he's dealt with it also in an *Educational Leadership* article, "Engaging African American Males in Reading" (2006).

Connecting to my thoughts

Connecting to other texts

ON POLITICS, SOCIETY, AND LITERACY EDUCATION

Brown, Rexford. 1993. *Schools of Thought: How the Politics of Literacy Shape Thinking in the Classroom*, The Jossey-Bass Education Series. San Francisco: Jossey-Bass.

Freedom Writers, The, and Erin Gruwell. 1999. *The Freedom Writers Diary: How a Teacher and 150 Teens Used Writing to Change Themselves and the World Around Them*. New York: Broadway Books.

hooks, bell. 1994. *Teaching to Transgress: Education as the Practice of Freedom*. New York: Routledge.

Kozol, Jonathan. 1991. *Savage Inequalities: Children in America's Schools*. New York: Crown.

Nieto, Sonia. 2005. *Why We Teach*. New York: Teachers College Press.

Tchudi, Stephen. 1985. *Language, Schooling, and Society*. Portsmouth, NH: Heinemann.

> > > JANET ALLEN

Mastering the Art of Effective Vocabulary Instruction

"When I use a word," Humpty Dumpty said, in a rather scornful tone, "it means just what I choose it to mean—neither more nor less."

"The question is," said Alice, "whether you can make words mean so many different things."

"The question is," said Humpty Dumpty, "which is to be master— that's all."

—*Lewis Carroll,* Through the Looking Glass

I SUSPECT MANY readers of this book have faced the dilemma Humpty Dumpty has described here: you spend a great deal of time and research trying to discover a way to master the art and craft of vocabulary instruction, and yet you feel as if the path you have chosen is never the one that will get you to your goal. I know that as a high school reading teacher, I always felt that vocabulary was the area of instruction that mastered me because effective instruction in this area always eluded me. I used a variety

While we'd all stop to read a chapter on vocabulary instruction at any point in this book, we chose to place this chapter here for couple of reasons. First, we've been focusing thus far on the bigger issues of literacy—multiliteracy and comprehension—yet we know that the stumbling block for many readers is down at the word level: just what does that one word mean? And second, Janet's approach to vocabulary instruction is perfect prereading for the next chapter on English language learners.

—*KB, REP, LR*

of programs and always ended up with the same problem: Students memorized the words and definitions for a test but rarely (never?) used them and soon forgot them. In addition, even when studying the words, students had no concept of other meanings and contexts for them. Each year, the promise of the programs never actually became the reality.

In the introduction to Achieve's *Ready or Not: Creating a High School Diploma That Counts*, the authors state: "For too many graduates, the American high school diploma signifies only a broken promise" (2004, 1). As I observe and conduct research in middle and high school classrooms across the United States, it is obvious to me that the "broken promise" to which the authors refer actually stems from a *series* of broken promises. *Ready or Not* connects the broken promise to what a high school diploma represents; I see the broken promises related to educational programs that promise literacy success but fall short. The result of following these literacy practices that don't result in student achievement is a diploma that, in some ways, falls short of representing high levels of knowledge and understanding. While many literacy practices are tied to this issue, vocabulary instruction is at least one of those foundational practices that continues to fall short of meeting its goal: producing students who can read, write, and communicate effectively because they have access to a large reservoir of words. So, how do we turn that promise into reality?

Looking Backward

Fortunately, we have access to a substantial body of research from the past several decades that both tells us what will lead to student achievement *and* serves as a guide to areas needing more research. There are literally hundreds of research studies that provide us with support for instructional practices that would make a critical difference in students' knowledge of words and their ability to continue learning words. For the most part, it isn't a matter of an absence of research. In Baumann and Kame'enui's synthesis of research related to vocabulary instruction, they state: "We know too much to say we know too little, and we know too little to say that we know enough" (2003, 752). What we don't know enough about is how to translate that research into effective, engaging classroom practices.

So, what do we know that would inform our instruction related to recognizing, learning, and using words effectively in speech and writing? To bring context to this discussion, I have compiled a list of what we know and the researchers who provided some of that knowledge (see Figure 7–1). This list is by no means comprehensive, but it serves the purpose of helping me maintain an instructional focus on areas that could really make a difference *if* we used research-based instructional strategies.

WHAT DO WE KNOW FROM RESEARCH?

Knowledge of word meaning is critical to success in reading.	Johnson et al., 1983; Barrett and Graves, 1981; Becker, 1977; Davis, 1972; Hunt, 1957
A rich conceptual base matters.	Johnson and Pearson, 1984
Children learn language through ordinary exposure and instruction.	Beck et al., 2002
Students learn words in a variety of ways.	Blachowicz and Fisher, 2000; Beck and McKeown, 1991; Cunningham and Stanovich, 1991; Nagy, 1988
Students learn words through wide reading.	Nagy and Herman, 1987; Fielding, Wilson, and Anderson, 1986
Students learn new words by learning strategies for understanding unfamiliar words.	Blachowicz and Fisher, 2004; Nagy, 1988; Dale and O'Rourke, 1986
Language/word awareness is critical to learning new words.	Cooper, 2006; Anderson and Nagy, 1992; Beck and McKeown, 1983
Prior knowledge/experience supports increased vocabulary knowledge.	Marzano, 2004; Mezynski, 1983; Anderson and Freebody, 1981
There is a relationship between difficulty of words in text and comprehension.	Graves, 1986; Anderson and Freebody, 1981
Direct vocabulary instruction improves comprehension.	Baumann, Kame'enui and Ash, 2003; Beck and McKeown, 1991; Stahl and Fairbanks, 1986

FIGURE 7–1. *A Quick Reference Guide of Vocabulary Research*   *(Continues)*

WHAT DO WE KNOW FROM RESEARCH? *(continued)*	
ESL students rely more heavily on direct instruction than native speakers.	Gouldman, Nation, and Read, 1990
Context clues vary in degree of "helpfulness" to readers.	Beck, McKeown, and McCaslin, 1983
Knowing a word means more than knowing a definition for the word.	Scott and Nagy, 1997; Dale and O'Rourke, 1986
Repeated exposures to words in meaningful contexts improves comprehension.	Nagy, 1990; Eller, Pappas, and Brown,1988; McKeown, Beck, Omanson, and Pople, 1985; Beck et al., 1982
Discussion leads to vocabulary learning.	Stahl, 1987; Stahl and Vancil, 1986
Semantic mapping improves recall and understanding.	Pittelman, Levin, and Johnson, 1985; Johnson, Toms-Bronowski, and Pittelman, 1982
Teaching word parts improves recall and understanding.	White, Sowell, and Yanagihara, 1989; Dale and O'Rourke, 1986; Fry, Fountoukidis, and Polk, 1985
Instruction toward Tier 2 words can be most productive. (See editor's note below for definition of Tier 2)	Beck and McKeown, 1985

FIGURE 7–1. continued

> > > > >
Tier 1 words are primarily learned through daily spoken language. Tier 2 words are those rarer words that primarily occur in written language that authors expect us to know. Tier 3 words are content-specific and generally aren't encountered until we study that subject. So, "mix" is a tier 1 word while "hybrid" is a tier 2 and "genus" is a tier 3 word.
—KB, REP, LR

Given the breadth and depth of vocabulary-related research, the task of deciding how to actually use it to develop effective vocabulary instruction can be overwhelming. Baumann and Kame'enui (2004) use Graves' (2000) four components of effective vocabulary instruction as a way to organize the chapters in their book, *Vocabulary Instruction: Research to Practice*. These four components are

> teaching individual words;
> teaching strategies for learning words independently;
> fostering word consciousness; and
> providing frequent, extensive, and varied opportunities to engage in independent reading. (2004, 4–5)

These four components extended my thinking into six broad areas that influenced me in terms of translating vocabulary research into practice. The four components Baumann, Kame'enui, and Graves highlighted seemed to be the filling of a vocabulary sandwich: becoming conscious of words, learning new words together and independently, and reading widely. To hold those together, I needed two slices of bread. The one on the bottom is the answer to the question "What does it mean to know a word?" And the slice on top is the answer to the question "How will students use these words meaningfully to demonstrate and communicate ideas and knowledge of content?"

Therefore, as a way of organizing the instructional strategies in this chapter, I have categorized the research in Figure 7–1 into the following six areas:

> What does it mean to know a word?
> How do we learn words?
> What instruction makes words meaningful, memorable, and useful?
> How can we use vocabulary instruction to increase content knowledge?
> How can we provide strategies for students to learn words independently?
> How can we assess vocabulary knowledge as a part of all assessment?

What Does It Mean to Know a Word?

How would you define knowing a word? Do we know a word when we can match a definition to a label, or do we know a word when we can use the word appropriately in a sentence? Is word knowledge dependent on knowing that words have multiple meanings and those meanings emerge from context? Or does one not really know a word until the word's antonyms, synonyms, and key attributes can be articulated? This may seem to wander from the question, but the way we define word knowledge affects how we design instruction. For example, if I define word knowledge as knowing a definition and being able to use that word in a sentence, I will gear my instruction and my assessment of students' knowledge toward that goal. On the other hand, if I believe that knowing a word means knowing that meaning changes by degree and within a context, my instruction and assessment will be directed toward application of the word in multiple contexts. Labov reminds us of the challenge of assessing word knowledge: "Words have often been called slippery customers, and many scholars have been distressed by their tendency to shift their meanings and slide out from under any simple definition" (1973, 341).

Despite knowing that a word may defy an exact definition, researchers tend to agree that there are four stages in word knowledge:

> I've never seen or heard the word.
> I've seen or heard the word but don't know what it means.

> I have some knowledge of the word and could use it in limited contexts.
> I know the word: multiple meanings, multiple uses, contexts, and word forms.

Additionally, Graves and Graves (1994) make a distinction between teaching vocabulary and teaching concepts. Teaching vocabulary is teaching new labels for known or familiar concepts; teaching concepts is teaching students about something for which they currently have little or no understanding or familiarity. Teaching vocabulary takes less time than teaching concepts, as that process simply requires integrating a new label for something already known. On the other hand, teaching concepts requires building the conceptual base *and* adding labels (vocabulary words) to the concept.

For me, these points were critical to my students' understanding of how we were going to learn new words together and independently in our classroom. My favorite way to introduce this process was through a nonsense passage. You have probably read a passage that was written with English words as well as nonsense words. I would write these passages for my students to model the ways we can know a word's meaning from context as well as to remind them that knowing how to *say* a word is not the same as knowing a word's meaning.

Roaf Was Not Bloopy

Roaf was not bloopy.
His bork was flarfing.
Blix saw Roaf.
Why the glork glafe?
"My bork is flarfing," he said.
Blix was bloopy until he gliffed for his bork.
Then he saw Greep morking down the rife with his bork.
Trife that bork back to me, you lafe!
Greep morked even lafer.
"When I tarck you, you will be sholly, Greep!"
Greep morked until he could not mork any longer.
"Tafe your floofy bork," Greep said.
"No bork is worth seeing your glork glafe!"

Interestingly, my students were always able to list the main characters and the conflict; they could even find the action words and the resolution of the conflict. The challenge came when I asked them to discuss the theme or moral of our story. It always provided the basis for our discussion of the difference between a *surface-level knowledge* of a word and *in-depth knowledge* of a word that allows us to extend the meaning in discussion and writing. This then led us to all the ways we could learn new words.

> > > > >
As Janet shows us how to push students to the in-depth knowledge of words, she's really showing us how to make words meaningful to students, relevant to their worlds. You'll see more of this as you continue reading her chapter, but we want you to focus on how often she encourages us to situate new word knowledge against what students already know. Look at what Tom Romano (Chapter 11), Jeff Wilhelm and Michael Smith (Chapter 15), and Yvette Jackson and Eric Cooper (Chapter 16) all have to say about this very same notion of *relevance*. We're struck by how critical this word is when thinking about adolescent literacy.
—*KB, REP, LR*

How Do We Learn Words?

We learn new words and concepts and new names for familiar words and concepts in a variety of ways: experiences, reading, direct instruction, multiple encounters in meaningful contexts, as well as independent research, strategies, and use. In the sections that follow, I emphasize experiences, reading, and independent strategies and use. In this section, however, I want to share some instructional strategies for those words you consider so significant to students' understanding of what you are teaching that you would teach those words explicitly.

A reminder of the necessity for this instruction for what some call "stopper words" was highlighted for us in Lynnette Elliott's ninth-grade classroom. She and her students were exploring a unit on tolerance and intolerance and she mentioned that her students never actually used the words in their writing or discussion. When I suggested that perhaps they didn't know those words, she decided to ask them. Their responses are highlighted here:

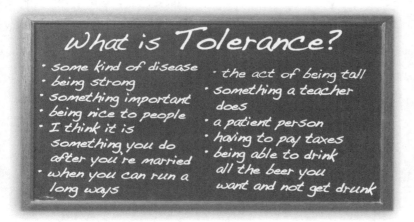

It is obvious to me that Lynnette's students actually did know many of the attributes of tolerance—especially for liquor, husbands and wives, and students! The problem stemmed from the fact that they didn't know this word in relation to what was being studied. For me, in terms of instruction, this can make a word or concept a stopper word. These are the words that should be taught and explored in a word-of-the-day (WOD) activity. I have found that the most effective way for students to explore these critical words in depth is through the use of a graphic organizer that is created to match the ways students will need to know the word in order to be successful in their reading, writing, and discussion.

The graphic organizer in Figure 7–2, Context Plus, was developed for students to explore the target word *malnutrition* before encountering that word in their texts. You, of course, can change the content to address any word or concept. The teacher reads the target word to the students and invites them to

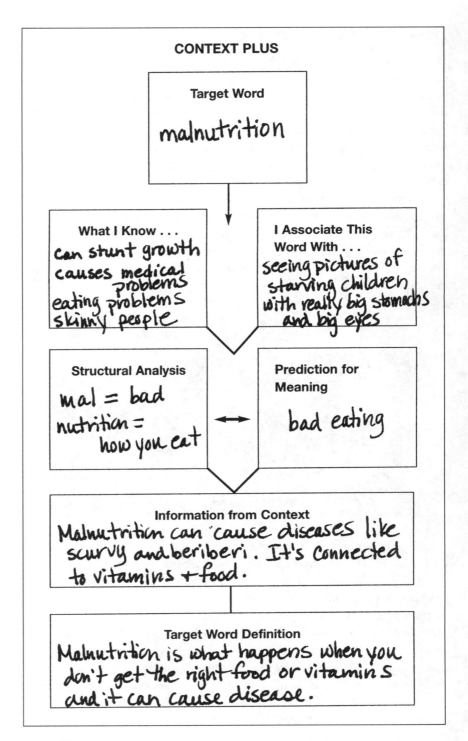

CONTEXT PLUS

Target Word

malnutrition

What I Know . . .
can stunt growth
causes medical
        problems
eating problems
skinny people

I Associate This Word With . . .
seeing pictures of
starving children
with really big stomachs
and big eyes

Structural Analysis
mal = bad
nutrition =
      how you eat

Prediction for Meaning
bad eating

Information from Context
Malnutrition can cause diseases like
scurvy and beriberi. It's connected
to vitamins + food.

Target Word Definition
Malnutrition is what happens when you
don't get the right food or vitamins
and it can cause disease.

FIGURE 7–2.

brainstorm what they know about the word and what they associate with the word (images and/or related words). In a recent use of this graphic, students said they knew that malnutrition could stunt growth, cause medical problems, and come from eating disorders and that it was related to skinny people. They associated the word with pictures of starving children with bloated stomachs and big eyes.

We then asked them to take the word apart—to search for word parts they might recognize to see if those words parts could be added to their background knowledge and result in a predicted definition. Students thought *mal* meant "bad" and that *nutrition* was how you eat or get nourishment; they predicted the definition to be "bad eating."

At that point, we added context for the students by using Haduch's book *Food Rules!* The book highlights aspects of malnutrition: diseases such as scurvy and beriberi, how malnutrition can occur regardless of weight, and its connection to food and vitamins. Students were then able to come up with a target word definition prior to opening their textbooks.

With so many words that are potentially unknown for your students, how do you choose those that will have the greatest impact on their comprehension and writing? McKeown and Beck cite four crucial criteria for this instructional decision:

> > words that will be important for comprehension
> > words that can be defined in terms known to the student
> > words that are useful and interesting
> > words that are of general interest but not crucial to the text (2004, 16–17)

Graphic organizers help students explore the target word(s) collaboratively and add other words and ideas as they have multiple encounters with it in other texts and contexts.

What Instruction Makes Words Meaningful, Memorable, and Useful?

My language is changing. I don't understand it. I read all those books and then I find these words just coming out of my mouth. I don't even know where they come from. Sometimes I feel like I'm in The Exorcist *and have words spewing out!*

—Sarah, ninth grade

Instruction that makes words meaningful, memorable, and useful begins with rich shared experiences. While those experiences can come from discussion and viewing, the most common shared experience in classrooms usually comes from texts that are chosen for common reading. These rich readings provide contexts for words that students might never encounter. This is why I have always been such an advocate of audio-assisted reading. Students are able to read well beyond their independent reading levels with the audio support and, in doing so, encounter words they would never encounter in texts they could read independently. But is it enough just to read the words?

Multiple encounters with a word, particularly if the word is found in meaningful contexts, do affect both the memorability and the usefulness of the word. In Marzano's *Building Background Knowledge for Academic Achievement* (2004), the author highlights three supports for enhancing permanent memory: multiple exposures to information; deep processing (adding details); and elaboration (making associations). These critical aspects can be supported with whole-class and individual (portable) word walls.

> > > > >

Look back at Ellin Keene's comments about deep processing and elaboration (Chapter 4). She uses slightly different language, but she's making a similar point: if we want learning to become memorable, we must move beyond surface discussions.

—*KB, REP, LR*

Most of us have seen word walls widely used in elementary school for years, but word walls have become increasingly popular in middle and high school classrooms as well. When I first started using word walls to support student writing in my classroom, I put the words on the wall in all directions and in random placement. For my most struggling readers, this was word chaos. They couldn't use the support of the word wall because they never could find the words they needed. I found the same to be true in classrooms where there are many English language learners (ELLs). Words need to be organized alphabetically or topically for most students to access them when needed.

> > > *Instruction that makes words meaningful, memorable, and useful begins with rich shared experiences. While those experiences can come from discussion and viewing, the most common shared experience in classrooms usually comes from texts that are chosen for common reading.*

For example, while teaching a Shakespearean play, we might start a class word wall with sight words for Shakespeare (*anon*, *fortnight*, etc). If studying the Revolutionary War in U.S. history, our word wall might have war words, cause and effect words, inflammatory language, and the names of people, places, and events. When I saw the support that the class word wall provided my students, I started asking them to keep their own word walls in their academic notebooks. My students created a simple A–Z chart, but the graphic organizer we are using in content classrooms today is shown in Figure 7–3.

Using such supports, students can highlight and organize specialized vocabulary related to the current topic of study. I provide a place for them to take word notes, as some of the words they highlight in the A–Z area may need examples, drawings, or contextual information in order to be useful. Content area teachers are finding this tool particularly useful for students as they encounter so many specialized and academic words in their units of study.

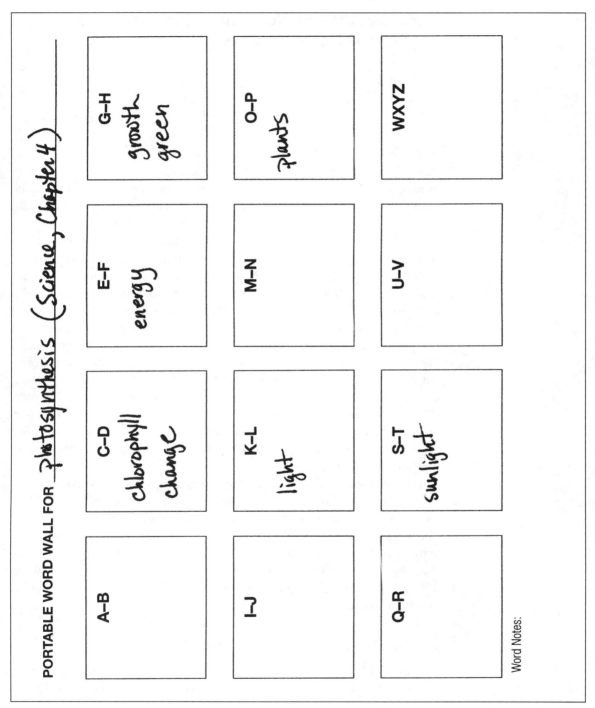

PORTABLE WORD WALL FOR Photosynthesis (Science, Chapter 4)

A–B	C–D chlorophyll change	E–F energy	G–H growth green
I–J	K–L light	M–N	O–P plants
Q–R	S–T sunlight	U–V	WXYZ

Word Notes:

FIGURE 7–3.

How Can We Use Vocabulary Instruction to Increase Content Knowledge?

It's like I always know we are going to get something new when I walk through the door.

—Jose, sixth grade

Most students agree that they always get something new when they walk through the doors into their content classrooms; they also agree that much of it is not understandable to them. Using vocabulary instruction as a way to build background knowledge, support comprehension, and provide a vehicle for students to demonstrate content understanding offers common ground that supports all students in the class. For example, if the textbook we are using contains a great deal of specialized vocabulary, and we know that our students will have little or no knowledge of the meanings for those words, we would want to highlight those words for students prior to their textbook reading. Unfortunately, there are usually so many new and unknown words that word-of-the-day activities can't accomplish familiarity quickly enough. So, where do we begin?

Let's look at the scenario of a science teacher who is about to start the chapter on human digestion in the science book. She could start with some interesting reading related to the content that contains some of the words students will encounter in their texts. Books such as Arnold's *Disgusting Digestion*; Masoff's *Oh, Yuck! The Encyclopedia of Everything Nasty*; and *Ripley's Believe It or Not* provide shared readings that will give students many of the specialized words used in the chapter and generate questions for which the students will want to find answers in the text.

These shared readings can be followed by a simple fill-in-the-blanks activity using a passage from one of the books, such as the one highlighted here from *Oh, Yuck!* As you copy the passage for students, leave out the words you want them to put in the context of their reading. Provide them with a word bank and have them work through the passage in pairs or small groups so they can discuss the words and their appropriateness for the context. When I create these for students, I always leave the first paragraph intact to provide a foundation for the passages that are incomplete.

The Poop on Poop

You have just eaten a wonderful dinner. A thick, juicy cheeseburger, a tall glass of milk, a salad (okay, your parents made you eat that part), and a hunk of watermelon for dessert.

From the moment that _____ touches your tongue, your _____ starts breaking it _____ into smaller and smaller pieces

so that it can get to the parts it needs—the proteins, the _____, and
_____ that _____ your engines. Whatever's left
over after that has got to get _____. (2000, 121)

Once students have completed their reading and discussion, and have filled
in the missing words, they will have encountered many of the vocabulary words
from their science chapter. At this point, they bring enough background knowledge to do a Possible Sentences activity (Moore and Moore 1986), such as the
one in Figure 7–4, page 100. This gives students the immediate opportunity to
use their knowledge of these words to predict possible sentences they will find
when they read this chapter of their text.

In Possible Sentences, students choose two or more of the highlighted
vocabulary words to write a sentence predicting how they think those words
will be used in the context of their reading. Students list their sentences and
then read the text (in a whole group or small group, or independently). As they
read or following their reading, they check their predicted sentences against the
content. If predictions are accurate in terms of content (not word-for-word
accuracy), students highlight with a check or a circle; if they are inaccurate
based on their reading, students revise for accuracy in terms of the text. In this
way, vocabulary instruction has been extended and supported before, during,
and after reading. The multiple encounters with and uses of the words will
ensure that more of the specialized words find their way into students' permanent memories.

How Can We Provide Strategies for Students to Learn Words Independently?

> *Time* catapulted *on—I loved that word from the day it appeared on my*
> *weekly vocabulary list and I put it in a sentence to read aloud. From the*
> *moment I heard it on my tongue, it was somersaults and fireworks to me.*
> —Herschler, *The Darkest Corner*

I was reading a new book, *Tales of the Cryptids,* as I was writing this chapter, and
I was reminded of the power that knowing prefixes, root words, and suffixes
brings to a reader. In their introduction, the authors highlight the definition for
cryptozoology:

Crypto-What?

Cryp·to·zo·o·lo·gy is one big word that is easily decoded. "Crypto" comes from
a Greek word meaning "hidden or covered," and "zoology" is the study of animal life. So, according to the Merriam-Webster dictionary, cryptozoology is

POSSIBLE SENTENCES: THE DIGESTIVE SYSTEM

The following words appear in our chapter on digestion. Work with a partner to write sentences that you think we could possibly find when we read this chapter. Use only two or three words in each of your possible sentences.

Nutrients	Peristalsis	Large intestine	Pancreas
Water	Rectum	Small intestine	Liver
System	Digestive system	Esophagus	Acidity
Proteins	Break down	Foods	Process
Carbohydrates	Mucous	Chemicals	Energy
Fats	Salivary glands	Eliminated	Crucial
		Gall bladder	Digestive tract

Possible Sentences

1. Salivary glands break down fats.
2. Food is turned into energy.
3. Your esophagus is part of the digestive tract.
4. There are no nutrients in water.
5. The large intestine and small intestine process food.
6. The pancrease change food into chemicals.
7.
8.
9.
10.

Using Sentences as a Guide/Modifying Predictions

Each day when you are finished reading, mark each of the possible sentences as true, false, or unknown. When you've finished reading, return to your sentences and see how you could modify them so they are accurate in terms of the content of the passage you have read. In other words, rearrange the words in sentences so they are true in the context of our reading.

1. Salivary glands break down food.
2. True
3. unknown
4. Nutrients come from food.
5. The large + small intestines are part of the digestive tract.
6.
7.
8.
9.
10.

FIGURE 7–4.

the study of and searching for legendary animals—called *cryptids*—to find out if there's any possibilities that these mysterious animals people say they've seen really exist. (4)

In teaching students how to continue learning new words on their own, it is even more critical that the direct instruction and small-group activities we do be related to vocabulary. Stahl and Stahl, in *Vocabulary Instruction: Research to Practice* (2004), highlight Stanovich's (1986) position:

> Stanovich (1986) suggested that children who are more proficient readers tend to read more and read more challenging materials than children who struggle in reading. Because most words that children acquire are learned from reading them in context and because proficient readers read more challenging materials, those which contain rarer or more difficult words, they tend to learn more of those words, enabling them to read yet more challenging materials. Thus, the gap between proficient and struggling readers grows each year. (2004, 61)

With the knowledge of this increasing gap, we know that the importance of teaching students how to learn words independently is critical. Strategy lessons focus on how to learn words from context using internal clues (word parts) as well as external clues (background knowledge, local context, tone, text supports). Strategy lessons on how prefixes, root words, and suffixes can help us learn new words solidify the understanding that, if you know one word, there are probably many other words in that family that you also know. In *Beating the Odds* research (2000), Langer highlights the explicit teaching of strategy lessons, what I call how-to lessons, as one of six instructional moves that can help students beat the odds.

As with all other categories of instruction, the more meaningful the text, the more likely students will be to learn and employ the strategy. Books such as Janeczko's *Top Secret* are great books to help students see that language is always a code, and the more they know about breaking the code, the more capable they are of reading complex texts.

> < < < < <
> Here, Stanovich is describing a situation he's referred to as the Matthews Effect. The Matthews Effect, named from the book of Matthew in the Bible and taken from the quote, "The rich shall get richer and the poor shall get poorer" explains how students who have a slight gap in learning at the beginning of the year end the year with a larger gap. The "rich" students—those who knew a lot—were able to use that knowledge more efficiently and effectively to push their learning. The "poor" students—those who knew less—learned less thereby increasing the gap.
> —*KB, REP, LR*

How Can We Assess Vocabulary Knowledge as a Part of All Assessment?

If you are like me, you aren't looking for one more mandated assessment. On the other hand, we do want to know whether students have a grasp of the meanings of the vocabulary words we have used in our study. Of course, we can test them in various ways, or we can ask them to create projects where they use the words to demonstrate this understanding. Here, however, I'd like to highlight a different activity—Concept Circles. My students successfully used this to demonstrate their understanding of vocabulary. It moved us away from single-word

> > > *The world is a large and wonderful place; words help our students find their way in, through, and beyond the boundaries of their world, to the promise inherent in each.*

definitions and matching quizzes and toward a place where students could truly demonstrate their understanding of the words we had studied. In Figure 7–5, you will see a sample Concept Circles organizer that I designed for students who were reading the textbook chapter on human digestion mentioned earlier.

I was first introduced to Concept Circles in Vacca and Vacca's *Content Area Reading* (1996) and immediately saw potential for assessing vocabulary. Students are given four words or concepts in a circle, and they write about the content using these four words. As part of that writing, students discuss why those four words are in the circle together by looking at relationships between and among the words and concepts. As my students grew more proficient with these, I left one of the quadrants empty, asking them to fill it in and provide an explanation for why they chose that word. As you can see, this type of assessment provides students with individual ways to demonstrate some common understandings of the words you have studied together.

> > > *We could debate programs and practices, and we could highlight strategies and skills for teaching vocabulary. We could even discuss theoretical perspectives that influence the practices we choose. At the end of the day, however, I think we would all agree that language is power, and those who can use language effectively have an advantage over those who can't or don't.*

For the most part, the days of believing that a matching vocabulary quiz can tell us whether students can transfer and apply their knowledge of words have passed. While that might provide some quick check of whether students have surface knowledge of the word, our goal as educators has to include making sure students have access to the words for speaking and writing. This belief that we are teaching content for transfer's sake rather than content for content's sake will influence every instructional decision we make—including those related to vocabulary instruction.

The Value of Effective Vocabulary Instruction

We could debate programs and practices, and we could highlight strategies and skills for teaching vocabulary. We could even discuss theoretical perspectives that influence the practices we choose. At the end of the day, however, I think we would all agree that language is power, and those who can use language effectively have an advantage over those who can't or don't. In *Vocabulary Development: From Reading Research to Practice,* Stahl provides a beautiful summation of the impact of effective vocabulary instruction:

Learning to use a word such as *beret* instead of *hat,* or *pusillanimous* instead of *cowardly,* should make a child think that he has learned a secret code—a better, more mature way to talk and write. After all, teaching word meanings

CONCEPT CIRCLES: THE DIGESTIVE SYSTEM
BREAKS DOWN FOOD

Describe the meaning and relationships between and among the words in the sections of the concept circles.

peristalsis	mucous glands
water	nutrients

Peristalsis pushes food and water through the intestines to pull out nutrients.

salivary glands	small intestine
stomach	large intestine

The salivary glands break down food before it gets to the stomach. Then it moves to the small and large intestines.

FIGURE 7–5.

When you want to know more . . .

For more words on words, look into Janet's book *Words, Words, Words: Teaching Vocabulary in Grades 4–12* (1999). And she has talked about the broader issue of reading and writing in all subject areas in *Tools for Teaching Content Literacy* (2004).

should be a way for students to define their world, to move from *light* or *dark* to a more fine-grained description of the colors that surround us. (1999, 52)

I believe this is what we want for all our students. We know that in these next few years, those students who do not have a facility for interpreting and using language will become those adults who have been left behind. The world is a large and wonderful place; words help our students find their way in, through, and beyond the boundaries of their world, to the promise inherent in each.

> > > CYNTHIA MATA AGUILAR,
DANLING FU, CAROL JAGO

English Language Learners in the Classroom

FROM THE EDITORS: While we could have turned to any one of the three people highlighted here—Cindy Mata Aguilar, Danling Fu, and Carol Jago—to help us understand the complex issues that surround English language learners (ELLs), what we wanted to do instead was put all three of the voices into one chapter. That connection of voices—sometimes in harmony, sometimes not—best represents what you face each day with the collection of voices, of languages, you have in your classrooms.

But we didn't just want a coauthored chapter. We wanted something that suggested the starting and stopping, the rethinking, the interrupting, the contradictions (of self and each other), the hesitations, the silences, the rush of ideas, the spontaneity of the moment that comes when you put three very bright, very passionate, very dedicated teachers into one space. It's the same "noise" that we hope you hear each day when you step inside your classroom. We think it's the noise we must hear when we talk about English language learners, because it's the noise of learning—and we have much, much to learn.

We've set this chapter here because much of the discussion you're about to read is a logical extension of information in preceding chapters. Furthermore, it provides a solid backdrop for what follows in Smokey Daniels' chapter (9) and the chapters on writing.

—*KB, REP, LR*

We chose Cindy, Danling, and Carol for a very specific reason: They represent the diversity we wanted for this topic. There's Carol Jago, a high school teacher from California who works with ELLs on a daily basis. Carol's students—Korean, Hispanic, Vietnamese, Hmong, Chinese, Laotian, Indian, Arabic, African, German, Thai, Japanese, and . . . the list goes on—arrive in her classroom shy, quiet, frustrated, smart, funny, and wanting to fit in. Carol welcomes them all, teaches them all. She gets them through canonical literature, helps them write college entrance essays, prepares them for the California state standards test, helps them learn to read expository as well as narrative texts, and encourages them to speak up, speak out, and speak proudly.

Cindy Mata Aguilar grew up in a Mexican American family in southern Texas. "That's my culture—burritos, tacos, dressing up for Easter, picking cotton for money," Cindy proudly explained. Now she is a senior project director with the Education Development Center, a nonprofit organization with more than three hundred projects that focus on improving education nationally and internationally (see www.edc.org). Fluent in both English and Spanish, Cindy knows up close what the life of a Spanish-speaking student who lives along the Texas border is like. Now Cindy helps us understand the issues of cultural diversity and just what we mean when we say, "It takes a village . . ."

And, finally, we have Danling Fu, a professor in the School of Teaching and Learning at the University of Florida. A native Chinese speaker, Danling taught English in China before coming to the United States to do graduate work. Working extensively with elementary and secondary Chinese students, primarily in New York City (Chinatown) and San Francisco, Danling helps us understand the very specific challenges Chinese students face.

With this broad range of experience—personal, professional, geographical, linguistic, cultural—these three teachers bring great depth to our discussion of teaching ELLs. And the noise they bring to this chapter is exactly what we wanted—rich, fast, and smart. The noise of learning. Each of them had about seventy-two hours to respond online to a series of questions. We offered little time because we wanted immediate responses—just like those you'd give in a conversation at a conference when someone tapped you on the shoulder and said, "I have a quick question." Once they read each other's responses, they inserted other comments as appropriate.

And what did we do during this process? Mostly, we just stayed out of the way.

> < <

EDITORS: We'll start with a question we're often asked. Though we have a single goal for *all* students, regardless of where they begin—that they develop the articulate, reasoned use of language—we know that teaching ELLs must mean something different than teaching native English speakers. What are the differences and similarities in teaching these two types of students?

DANLING: The similar part is that we want to provide all students with a rich language environment that includes plenty of opportunities to use language through reading, discussing reading, writing, and sharing writing. The difference is, ELLs need more specific instruction in language skills and more systematic help in developing their English proficiency (listening, speaking, reading, and writing).

Sometimes, we need to teach them basic language skills—such as vocabulary and pronunciation—which should be separate from concept or content learning. Often, though, they already know the concept, say, for instance, "Tuesday," but they just don't know how to discuss that concept in English. In this case, we simply supply the word without teaching the concept. Other times, they need both. For instance, they don't know *photosynthesis* as a word *or* a concept.

Furthermore, we need to consider that their linguistic and cultural backgrounds may not match our ways of learning and teaching. We need to constantly adjust our approach to meet their potential and needs. For instance, they may not be used to student-centered or interactive ways of teaching, or they may be confused by choice in reading and writing. We should gradually move them toward the approach we believe would help the most, while respecting their need for a "silent period" (according to research, ELLs may remain silent for the first two months; give them time to observe and choose when to join the crowd).

CINDY: I agree that there are similarities as well as differences. It is similar in that teachers should hold both English language learners and native speakers of English to the same high standards. At the same time, it is different in that the standards for ELLs are twofold: language acquisition and understanding of content. Thus, while ELL students are learning the content, they are also learning the language of the content. The first step in setting goals for students is to assess their literacy proficiency in their first language; this information provides the key to the kind of instruction that is required. [Figure 8–1 offers some guidelines for assessing first language proficiency.] If students can read and write in their first language, their ability to transfer from their native language to English becomes easier. However, reading and writing in English are slower for ELLs, since they are simultaneously acquiring English and literacy skills. If a student has not developed literacy skills, a teacher must start with the basics of reading, including phonetic and phonemic awareness, fluency, and so on.

DANLING: Yes, we must remind ourselves to start where the kids are developmentally. For ELLs, that means more than just knowing their English-level proficiency and starting there; it also means knowing that the best starting point is their first language literacy. To respect them as intelligent individuals is to allow them to bring their home language into their classroom learning until they can use English for learning and communication. For instance, we should let them read and write in their first language before expecting them to express themselves in English.

ASSESSING STUDENTS' LANGUAGE PROFICIENCY

Assessing our students' language proficiency is challenging, but it is possible to find sources of assistance. Freeman and Freeman (2002) have developed a teacher-friendly guide that identifies five oral and written proficiency levels:

> *Preproduction*—Students communicate with gestures, actions, yes/no answers, and names. Students draw a picture or dictate a response that the teacher writes.

> *Early Production*—Students respond to either/or questions using words or short phrases. Students copy environmental print, label drawings, or write a simple message.

> *Speech Emergence*—Students respond in longer phrases and sentences. Given a graphic organizer, students write phrases or sentences.

> *Intermediate Fluency*—Students engage in conversation and produce connected narrative. Given a graphic organizer, students produce a narrative with a beginning, middle, and end.

> *Advanced*—Students refine and extend oral ability. Given a graphic organizer, students write several paragraphs with cohesive structure and connected sentences. (65)

FIGURE 8–1.

> > > > >
This notion of leveraging means more when considered against the multiliteracies Donna Alvermann describes in Chapter 3 and the opportunities for using technology (thus improving leveraging ability) that Sara Kajder describes in Chapter 18.

—KB, REP, LR

EDITORS: So teaching ELLs does hold some differences from teaching native English speakers. What about a slight variation on that question: ELLs may come into the classroom with different languages—Spanish, Chinese, Hmong, for instance. Does the home language dramatically affect your teaching approach?

DANLING: I suggest that we do need to adjust our teaching approach to students based on linguistic backgrounds. For Chinese-speaking students, they need to be taught some basic English language features.

EDITORS: Most of us would have to ask . . . what types of features do Chinese speakers need to learn?

DANLING: There are many things, but the basic ones are listed in Figure 8–2.

EDITORS: Thanks. What about Spanish speakers?

SOME DIFFERENCES BETWEEN CHINESE AND ENGLISH

1. Chinese students grew up thinking in terms of characters, not words. So native English speakers think of the word *teacher* as a single word, and later they learn that this single word has two syllables. But Chinese speakers see the word *teacher* as two characters.

2. This leads to another difference that needs to be addressed. English words can have multiple syllables and those syllables can be formed with multiple letters. In fact, rarely are they formed with just one letter. Chinese, by contrast, has one syllable for one character.

3. English words generally end with a consonant sound. In the previous sentence, only *generally* and *a* end with a vowel sound. However, Chinese words usually end with a vowel sound.

4. English sentences all contain verbs. Chinese sentences do not have to have a verb.

5. The basic English sentence structure is subject-verb-object. A Chinese sentence may not have a subject; other sentences might lack the verb. This becomes an issue when teachers try to break Chinese students of the habit of writing in fragments. It's only a fragment in English!

6. English words have features such as tense, gender (his or her), and plural forms. Chinese does not rely on such linguistic markers.

7. English contains some sounds that don't exist in Chinese, such as /l/, /sh/ and /th/. Chinese students will probably also need help with certain pronunciation features, such as word accent, light stress of prepositions in a sentence, and soft pronunciation of word endings.

FIGURE 8–2.

< < < < <
Phonemes—the sounds that graphemes (letters) make—are shown in print by putting slash marks around the letter, as Danling has done here. So, the single letter m is read as the letter m, but /m/ is read as the sound you hear at the beginning of *mat*.
—*KB, REP, LR*

DANLING: They obviously don't need to be taught *those* rules, since Spanish and English share similar phonetic language features. But because the two languages share similarities, Spanish-speaking ELLs tend to mix two languages in spelling and sentence structure. We need to compare and contrast the two languages in our language instruction and help the students become conscious of the similarities and differences between Spanish and English.

I also want to say something about Hmong students. Obviously you mentioned that group in your question just as an example of the range of languages that might exist in a classroom. However, you chose a really interesting one—so it's worth discussing for a moment. For Hmong-speaking students, we should

> > > > >

This notion of writing with pictures and words is something Linda Rief talks about in her chapter (13). She calls this *tellingboards,* a term introduced to her by Roger Essley. While this is a variation of what Danling is explaining, the point that both Danling and Linda see powerful reasons to let kids—all kids—use picture writing as a first step in the composing process is well worth remembering.

—KB, REP, LR

start from oral language (*storytelling* rather than reading aloud) and then move to picture writing (using pictures and graphs to express ideas) and then on to reading and writing with abstract symbols, such as the English language. Book reading and writing can be a new concept to Hmong students, since they come from an oral language tradition. Drama and puppet shows (artistic forms, movements, and music) can be especially helpful as they develop language and literacy skills.

EDITORS: Cindy or Carol—do you agree with these differences, especially for Spanish- and Chinese-speaking students?

CINDY: Yes. There are differences in the alphabet, pronunciation, and semantic structures between Spanish and English, though not as pronounced as between Chinese and English. The Spanish alphabet has additional letters such as the *ll* in *ella* and *ñ* in *mañana.* The English *j* in a word is pronounced /h/ in Spanish and a single *e* is pronounced /ĕh/; thus, the English word *June* would be pronounced /hooneh/ in Spanish. Sentence structures can also be different; *the good man* would be *el hombre bueno* in Spanish, which translates directly to "the man good."

CAROL: I completely agree with the distinctions Danling describes. Native Spanish speakers have the advantage of recognizing cognates in many English words, but sometimes they think they see a cognate where one doesn't exist, which can lead to further confusion.

DANLING: I think that what's important is that all students, regardless of their linguistic backgrounds, need to be immersed in a rich and meaningful language learning environment, but not drills and learning rules out of context. The only

> > > *What's important is that all students, regardless of their linguistic backgrounds, need to be immersed in a rich and meaningful language learning environment, but not drills and learning rules out of context. —Danling Fu*

way to learn a language is to use it authentically, thereby forming a language habit through constant trial and error. Often, when ELLs make linguistic errors, it is not that they don't know the rules, but that they haven't formed a natural habit with the language, or they operate a second language with the habit (linguistic interference) of their first language. The only way to master a language is to use it constantly. ELLs need to have plenty of opportunity to communicate with native English speakers (or people who don't speak their home language). Unfortunately, ELL adolescents often live in neighborhoods that reflect their language background and seek out others who speak their primary language, both at school and in social situations.

EDITORS: That makes a lot of sense to us, Danling, as we've each seen the same thing—students sitting in the cafeteria or walking the halls with others who speak their native language. It's obvious that when they need to discuss issues that are compelling to them (even if that just means who's going out with whom!), they switch to the language they know best. If that's the case, how do we keep them learning at a suitable intellectual level in their classes, including content area classes? How do we address the critical social element in their lives as well?

DANLING: Well, I'm going to say something that will at first glance appear to be a contradiction of what I've just said. I've just said that to become fluent, one must constantly use the language; that's true and I stand by that. But that's only if *all* you want students to do is become *fluent*. If you simply want to get good at understanding the language and speaking it, then you need to practice it all the time. But that's not all we're asking students to do. We're also asking them to learn content—science, math, history, literature—while learning the other language. With that added requirement, we can't ask them to ignore their first language because that means asking them to ignore a critically important scaffold. I do believe the best way to accomplish this is to let them read and write in their first language any time they choose to do so. In fact, I'll go so far as to say they shouldn't stop this, even after they gain the proficiency in English. I'll say that again—louder: The primary language acts as a scaffold to the second language. Removing the primary language means removing the scaffold. Why would we ever do that?

If there are two or three students who speak the same first language in a class, they can have their own study groups during class and even be encouraged to form the same study group after school. We should let them read books, newspapers, or online materials in their native language and then discuss the content and issues among themselves, even presenting their discussion in their home language. Only when they read at their intellectual level can they express their true concerns and discuss the issues that matter to them. Their limited English proficiency can't enable them to do that. As teens, they are just like their English-speaking peers. They have strong feelings and opinions about themselves, others, and the world around them. They have a strong desire to know what is going on at the school, in the community, in the country, and around the world. They don't want to be constrained by their limited English reading, writing, and speaking ability. If they continue to develop their literacy and content knowledge at their literate level, they will learn a new language more effectively.

A lot of doctoral or postdoctoral students from foreign countries (in both liberal arts and science fields) confess that they often don't understand much of the lectures and the textbooks they are required to read when they first come to study in an American university. They manage to do well in the graduate program by reading the textbooks in their native languages (which they have brought from their home countries) and discussing the reading among the students from the

> > > *Only when they read at their intellectual level can they express their true concerns and discuss the issues that matter to them. —Danling Fu*

same backgrounds. Then, when they attend classes, they can follow most of the lectures, pass the tests, and earn their degrees. If ELLs at the graduate level use their primary language as a scaffold to content, why shouldn't we let our ELLs at the secondary level adopt the same method of learning? When I studied Shakespeare in China, I read the Chinese translations of his plays before I read the English originals, which was the only way I could understand the plays and follow the lectures in class.

CINDY: I couldn't agree with you more, Danling. English language learners need more scaffolding in learning the language while learning the content. Since 1997, my colleagues and I have studied schools that provide programs to meet both these needs. For example, Middletown High School (a pseudonym for a high school in Virginia) has an emerging ELL population that includes many Latino, Pakistani, and Chinese students; all are tested for language proficiency at the beginning of each year, and beginners in the English as a second language program have access to three levels of basic instruction. When they have mastered some oral language, they can take concept classes in science, math, and social studies that are taught in English but use language acquisition strategies.

> > > > >
Cindy has written with great specifics about the achievements of students at Middletown High School in an article titled "Middletown High School: Equal Opportunity for Academic Achievement" in the journal *Learning Disabilities Research & Practice* (Aguilar et al. 2006).
—*KB, REP, LR*

For students who are ready to be mainstreamed, "echo" classes in English provide the support needed to make the transition. Students take an English-only course but receive additional support in a class taught in their home language, thus, the *echo*. Summer school provides additional support.

DANLING: I really like that idea of an echo class. That's a smart scaffold that I can see would provide a lot of support. You know, this brings up the other side of the coin. We're focusing on what happens when kids struggle to understand English. What about teachers who speak only English and can't understand what nonnative English speakers are saying when they slip into their primary language? Teachers express frustration when they can tell students are engaged, but they can't follow their discussions or read their responses (if written in the primary language). Teachers need some support as well!

CINDY: Which is, of course, the same frustration students feel!

DANLING: Exactly. I think that as along as we can sense students' passion in learning, we don't have to necessarily understand what they say. It is very much like when we enjoy classic opera—we may not understand a single word, but we can be hooked by the performers' passionate expressions and acting. I love to watch the debates among diplomats at the United Nations, especially when they are angry, though I can't understand a word. I am fascinated by their emotionally charged expressions, with hands waving in the air, body moving back and forth. If ELL teens have chances to demonstrate their intelligence and passion in their school learning, they will want to stay in school and to push themselves hard to learn English as well as content knowledge.

CINDY: That's right. At the same time, though, we can structure activities that build success in English as they use their primary language to think through difficult concepts. For instance, Leonardo Da Vinci Middle School (again a pseudonym to protect students' identities) in New Jersey requires all students to demonstrate their learning through exhibitions such as presentations or discussions. Students with little or no knowledge of English receive their education in the bilingual classroom where the curriculum parallels the general education curriculum. In eighth-grade social studies, both the bilingual students and the general education students study World War II and learn about the Holocaust. Teachers develop thematic units that involve students in researching related topics, and all students read the same texts, such as *The Diary of Anne Frank*—one in English, the other in Spanish. English language learners are learning key content knowledge in Spanish while learning English in their ESL class. Once they develop a working vocabulary, they are mainstreamed into the general education classroom.

CAROL: I've been waiting to jump in, soaking up what you two have been saying. What strikes me is how critical this idea is of letting kids use their primary language as a scaffold, and the notion of starting with their first language, where they can think most deeply, most critically, and with the most focus, and *then* bridging to translating those thoughts into English is at such odds with those who distrust any type of bilingual program.

CINDY: A bilingual program seems better situated not only to provide the scaffold students need for learning the content but also to help them work through the cultural differences students bring to school.

EDITORS: We agree. It seems that ELL students will come to us from cultures that differ in many respects—gender expectations, religious background, sense of personal space, willingness or unwillingness to confront certain issues. Carol, how do you see that these cultural differences complicate our teaching? What must we know to deal with them? How do we keep them from becoming obstacles and instead transform them into opportunities?

CAROL: English learners often feel like outsiders, particularly in a regular English class. They are frustrated by how long it takes them to express themselves and embarrassed by the errors they know they are making at every turn. Like all teenagers, they are self-conscious about how others in the class see them. By thought, word, and deed, teachers need to send English learners the message that they are welcome here. Many teachers fret that they have not been adequately

< < < < <
To read more about Leonardo Da Vinci Middle School, look at the book *Visionary Middle Schools,* by Morocco, Brigham, and Aguilar (2006).

—*KB, REP, LR*

< < < < <
We're glad to see these three discussing the importance of a bilingual program. You'll want to look at the report from the National Literacy Panel on Language-Minority Children and Youth that's titled *Developing Literacy in Second-Language Learners,* edited by Diane August and Tim Shanahan (2006). This meta-analysis highlights the importance of bilingual programs.

—*KB, REP, LR*

prepared to meet the needs of English learners. This unease causes some students to perceive themselves as a problem. Without minimizing the tremendous amount teachers can learn from reading, research, and professional development in English language development, a simple shift in attitude, or even a small gesture, toward the English learners in their classes can help transform an obstacle into an opportunity. One student, Yoo Hyun Kim, was so grateful for a small thing that I did in class—or small in my eyes but huge in hers—that she took the time to write me a poem expressing her thanks. Her words (see Figure 8–3) remind us all that these students are grateful for any help we offer.

A Letter to Mrs. Jago

I was a girl, eager to learn,
eager to catch up with the others.
But the problem was that I was too shy.
One day you asked me,
"What would have Penelope felt after Odysseus returned?"
and I answered, "Very sad."

I was afraid, afraid of letting my voice be heard,
afraid of people hearing my accent,
afraid that the class might think me stupid.

The next day
when I dragged my heavy feet to class,
You softly smiled at me and said "Hi,"
and everything was okay.

It was such a little thing,
and you might not even remember this,
but it will stay forever in my mind.

Now I have more pride in myself,
though not brilliant in my writing.
Mrs. Jago, thank you for understanding
and patiently waiting
until I could find the words.

—*Yoo Hyun (Jean) Kim*

FIGURE 8–3. *Yoo Hyun Kim's poem to Mrs. Jago*

I am always on the lookout for moments when English learners have particular knowledge to share that will enrich the lesson. For example, my tenth-grade class was reading and discussing Michael Pollan's essay "When a Crop Becomes King," an exposé of the big business behind corn production in this country and how it affects the quality of the food we consume. I asked students if the food in other countries seemed to be equally standardized. Oscar Valdez was eager to describe how much better tasting the chicken in El Salvador was and how his grandmother grew all her own vegetables. His story triggered an animated conversation about mass-produced foodstuffs versus naturally grown produce. Oscar went on to write an insightful essay in response to the Pollan article. I could not help but feel that the confidence in his writing was a reflection of the confidence he garnered from being a leader in our class discussion.

DANLING: That's it. So much of this is about confidence. What sometimes gets in the way of students' developing their confidence is not about them, but about us.

EDITORS: *Us?* How?

DANLING: What complicates our teaching when we encounter the students with different cultural backgrounds is we tend to see, hear, and act from our own fixed lenses and perspectives. When our students don't behave, sound, believe, or dress as we expected, we tend to interpret something wrong with them, show our disapproval of them, and try to correct them.

In America, people do enjoy differences; they are bored by cliché in language and fashion. They read books to understand others, pay to try different ethnic foods, visit different countries, and absorb varying styles from different parts of the world in fashion and architecture. We teachers certainly belong to this group of people. But why can't we keep that same openness in our teaching? Students bring their languages, their ways with words, their ways of learning, and their beliefs and lifestyles into our classrooms. If we can see these as resources rather than oddities, our minds, and our students' minds, will open and our curriculum will be enriched. In addition to (or instead of) relying on multicultural books, why not sincerely listen to and learn from the students who come from different cultural backgrounds; they can lead all of us to cultivate appreciation and fascination for differences. Half a century ago, this country worked hard to desegregate, knowing even then that only when people with differences come together will they learn to understand each other, appreciate each other, and live in harmony (see Figure 8–4). Today, we are more than black and white—richer, more interesting, and artful. As teachers, we are obligated to continue this desegregation mission through an inclusive attitude toward diversity, especially in our classrooms.

WAYS TO CULTIVATE CULTURAL HARMONY

> Invite non-English-speaking students to teach their language(s) to the class. (What a great way to learn a language without pressure but for fun!)

> Let ELLs present varying special topics on their cultures and countries: it's better than reading about their countries. For instance, why not let Chinese students talk about Confucius when we study ancient civilization? Let them interview their parents about how Confucianism still affects their life and thinking today.

> Ask them to share with the class the great literature they read in their native language.

> Welcome them to give their different interpretations of texts the class has read and their opinions on certain issues.

> Go beyond holidays, food, and customs when studying different cultures.

> Let *all* students, not just ELLs, listen to each other's thoughts, family stories, and personal concerns and beliefs. Not all the students born and raised in this culture share the same lifestyles and beliefs as those we read about in books.

FIGURE 8–4.

CINDY: It does have to start in the classroom, Danling. I'm thrilled that you bring up that it's our teaching and our inclusive attitude that can make a critical difference. Like you, I too believe that teaching English language learners means understanding and valuing our students' cultural backgrounds and life experiences, as well as knowing their literacy in their home language and schooling experience. I think we can look at this in three steps.

Step 1—Understand yourself. In the mid-nineties, I taught an antiracism course first developed by Dr. Beverly Daniels Tatum (1997), president of Spellman College, that began by asking teachers to unpack their own assumptions, experiences, and feelings about race. It was a very challenging topic to tackle, but we realized that in order to go forward in meeting the needs of our diverse students, we had to step back and examine our own feelings and attitudes about race and ethnicity, and their potential impact on our teaching and expectations. Readings from Peggy McIntosh (1990), Sonja Nieto (1996), Gloria Ladson-Billings (2001), and Lisa Delpit (1995) were only a few of our many sources. We asked ourselves many hard questions: What do I know about my students' culture? What images and/or stereotypes do I have floating in my subconscious? How can I ensure that I respect my students' culture and life experience? Do I really have the same expectations for all students?

Step 2—Learn about your students' cultural background. The next step involves learning about your students. First, we must develop a personal connection. Though language might get in the way, take the time to communicate with your students. Let them tell you their life experiences. Find adults in the school who speak the same language, including the bilingual and/or ESL teachers. Explore the community from your students' point of view. Find the cultural brokers. Identify social and religious resources.

Step 3—Develop successful pedagogy. Finally, teaching literacy skills to students who are learning English is an incredibly complex task that requires multiple elements to be woven together into a cohesive instructional environment. The future academic success of these students hinges on effective pedagogy and a respectful school environment. Interactive teaching that weaves the students' first languages into instructional conversations and curriculum is important. This includes finding materials that are culturally relevant and allowing for the students to use their first languages if they wish. Essential elements are using vocabulary as a curricular anchor and having a print-rich environment that reinforces vocabulary and concept development. Cooperative learning and peer tutoring are also helpful, as is the use of native language in a strategic manner. The goal is to modulate the cognitive demands to allow students to succeed while providing challenging, culturally relevant, and meaningful curriculum.

CAROL: Cooperative learning and peer tutoring are so essential when the students in the classroom talk more fluently with one another than I do with them. Those are powerful strategies for any student, but most certainly for students who are learning English while simultaneously trying to learn content.

EDITORS: We agree, and we certainly support all that you've each said about allowing students to use their primary language as a scaffold to deeper learning—whether in these peer tutoring moments that Cindy and Carol were just discussing or in more informal conversations, as students interpret for one another. But what about when we want students to join the class conversation? How do you encourage ELLs to join in when they are often reluctant to speak out?

DANLING: Well, I think it is very hard for ELLs to speak out like their native English-speaking peers, especially for adolescents as they are at a very self-conscious stage. There are myriad reasons they stay silent: language limitations, fear of sounding stupid, needing more time than the teacher will typically give to form a response, and confusion over the teacher's expectations or directions.

CAROL: I think these reasons from Danling are important and that we get around this by making writing a precursor to any discussion. Too often teachers address a question to the class and call on students with the first hands up.

> > > *Too often teachers address a question to the class and call on students with the first hands up. Speaking on demand can be extraordinarily difficult in a second language. —Carol Jago*

Speaking on demand can be extraordinarily difficult in a second language. Instead, before opening up a question for discussion, I ask students to write for a few minutes. These moments of reflection offer English learners time to think and to compose in English. I then ask students to turn and talk to a partner. This allows English learners to practice saying what they think out loud but outside the spotlight. After this dress rehearsal, I feel comfortable calling on English learners to contribute. Simple wait time alone will never be long enough for English learners. Teachers need to structure lessons so that—without putting English learners on the spot—we treat them as essential contributors to the classroom conversation.

DANLING: That certainly works. If everyone is taking a moment to write, then you are in essence leveling the playing field. I think we also have to remember, though, that even after writing, some kids will still be quiet because silence can be cultural. In some cultures, one is not expected to speak up; interactive learning is unfamiliar, and questions are considered inappropriate. Prior experiences have taught them not to value their own interpretations or thinking, let alone written drafts. They believe the only answer is the right answer, and the only presentation is the perfect presentation. Believing they will fail that, they sit silent.

CINDY: So what does that leave us doing?

> > > > >
Danling's suggestion of making classes highly predictive is important. Don't overlook this powerful way to help ELLs find success.
—*KB, REP, LR*

DANLING: We should make our teaching as predictive as possible so ELLs can be more prepared before class. If they know every time they read a chapter, all students are required to share their interpretation or response, in groups or with the class, they will be better prepared. We should give time for ELLs to practice their oral presentations, which can be read aloud instead of spoken extemporaneously. We should also remember that small-group and partner talk can be good practice for ELLs. The more students talk in small groups, the better they will learn to speak out in class.

Also try to group ELLs with native English-speaking peers. It will help them understand each other and perhaps encourage a friendship. It is hard to speak out among strangers; once they are comfortable with all their peers, it will be easier.

EDITORS: This takes us back to that contradiction you seemed to be making earlier, Danling—that students need as much practice in English as they can get, and yet they need time to process information in their own language. Now you're saying that while peer tutoring in their primary language is helpful, they also need to be in small groups with native English speakers.

DANLING: Yes. It looks like I'm changing my mind, but I'm not. ELLs need both. It's not an either-or question. They sometimes need to work alongside people who speak their language, and they sometimes need to work alongside those who don't.

CAROL: I see this all the time and wonder if the issue isn't about where they are in the process of learning the content. As ELLs are learning new content, perhaps the scaffold ought to be support in their first language; but, then, as they move into the discussion of that content, as they need to discuss ideas about it or plan presentations, they need to be working with native English speakers. Yes?

DANLING: It certainly is that give-and-take. But I have to say that I agree with Carol about writing first. We can prepare ELLs to speak out by first letting them write, then letting them use their written work to practice reading fluency, and last, encouraging them to practice speaking out without looking at their work. Speaking out is a skill, and you can't get better at a skill without practice, but it pays to remember that not everyone enjoys speaking out, especially those from a culture that doesn't value public speech, especially for girls. It may take years before some students get used to speaking out. Don't get too concerned. Some do enjoy silent learning and chitchat among good friends. I know—I am one of those learners.

> < < < < <
> Again, we are struck by the specificity of how we can help. Teach students to speak out by writing first, then speaking from that writing, and finally speaking without the written text.
> —*KB, REP, LR*

EDITORS: Sometimes, though, isn't the problem just not having enough English vocabulary? If that's the case, then how do we help ELLs handle the vast vocabulary issues that confront them each day in every class?

CAROL: I am as concerned about ensuring that the English learners in my care acquire the academic language of classroom discourse as I am with their need to comprehend the particular and often peculiar vocabulary in Poe and Shakespeare. If an ELL courageously attempts to contribute to class discussion, but inadvertently makes a comment that elicits laughter from peers, the student could become convinced he doesn't belong there—when he does! We need to teach students the vocabulary of literary conversations (see Figure 8–5). Together we practice employing phrases like "Another perspective to consider . . ." and "The writer's argument falls apart when . . ." and "This text examines . . ."

Just because a student is in the process of acquiring a second—or third—language doesn't mean she is a second-rate thinker. Many students arrive in this country with high levels of literacy in their home language. My challenge is to help these students acquire the vocabulary of academic discourse so that they can express their ideas coherently in English. Though I make constant use of a word wall and try to use terms repeatedly and in various contexts, English learners are often frustrated by multiple meanings. In those cases, teachers and students need to practice patience, definitions in context, and repetitive talk. Learning vocabulary isn't a simple matching exercise; it is a lifelong enterprise.

PROMPTS TO HELP ELLs ENTER ACADEMIC LITERARY CONVERSATIONS

> This image suggests to me that . . .
> I wonder if the author is implying that . . .
> Where did you see that in the text?
> If I were in this character's place . . .
> Those lines make me feel as though . . .
> When I compare this with what came before . . .
> I can understand how you see it that way, but I . . .
> Does this word have other connotations?
> I was struck by the line where . . .
> I'm unsure. Can you please come back to me?

FIGURE 8–5.

> > > > >

Take a look at Janet Allen's comments on vocabulary in Chapter 7. While the entire chapter certainly will help you focus vocabulary instruction for ELLs, she talks specifically about portable word walls on page 96. Reading Danling's comments about classwide word walls made us rethink how ELLs could use the ABC chart Janet shares.

—*KB, REP, LR*

DANLING: Vocabulary is a *huge* issue at the secondary level for ELLs. While learning the content, ELLs need to spend time working on terminology pertaining to different topics and subjects. A word wall organized by subject and topic is certainly a reachable resource for ELLs. They have to study the vocabulary in context by listening to the teachers use the words frequently. It's like learning music and singing; we have to listen before we can do it on our own. Then we need to require the purposeful use of the terminology in their speaking (group discussion) and writing.

We need to realize that learning vocabulary and learning the spelling of that vocabulary are two distinct things. First, ELLs should recognize new vocabulary through reading and listening to others. Then they should try to use these words in their speaking (content discussion). Only after those two things have happened should students begin to worry about correct spelling.

In order to help ELLs build and expand their vocabulary pool, they need to master key terminology for each topic:

> When they read the text, ask them to pay special attention to the key words and terminology related to the content (reading).

> Consciously use the terminology in your teaching, as ELLs need to hear these unfamiliar words until they become familiar (listening).

> Have students use the words in their group discussions (speaking).

> Then, ask them to take notes and write with those words (writing).

As we systematically move students through these four modes of learning the vocabulary (academic English language), they will gradually build their vocabulary pool. Of course, the best way of enlarging their vocabulary pool is through extensive reading, in which these new words appear often and in many contexts.

EDITORS: Those are some great specific suggestions. What other practical and concrete strategies would you suggest to teachers to support the learning of these students—vocabulary notebooks, preliminary conversations with other speakers of the same language before asking them to join in the discussion in English, avoidance of clichés and idioms in class lectures, clear notes that act as graphic organizers?

CINDY: One practical strategy that is often overlooked is the ability of ELL students in the secondary grades to use technology beyond what is available in school settings. Outside of school, it is very likely that they are using the popular technologies that teenagers love. These popular technologies, which help students communicate with one another and develop social communities, can be incorporated into the improvement of English language vocabulary. Think about making use of text messaging, chat rooms, blogs, and email. These are all tools that connect people with one another. Each has its own vocabulary, language use, and skills. Today's students share pictures, videos, and music with the press of a button. But, we can do a lot without technology (see Figure 8–6).

CAROL: I really like the idea of using blogs and threaded discussions as way to give that silent student a voice. I've also found that it's really important for me to *really* understand the student behind that voice. Teachers of English learners must know their students. It isn't enough to check school records for test scores because tests, even good ones, describe only the level at which a student is performing in English. I need to know more—how long my students have been in this country, the kind of education they experienced in their home country, what language they speak at home with various family members. This information helps me make instructional decisions. Newcomers may be relatively mute in class, but by watching their eyes and smiles, I can often tell they are absorbing an enormous amount of language and content. English learners who have been in our schools for years need and deserve gentle prodding to accelerate their acquisition of academic English. It is critical for me to know when to hold back and when to push. These days, I ask all students in the class to fill out a language survey, being careful to assure them that this is not tied to immigration or intended to determine if they were ready for the class. I assure them that they can ignore any questions they don't want to answer. Their answers help me know what questions to ask and which expectations to set, while reminding me that no two students have the same story, strengths, or needs. (See Figure 8–7.)

< < < < <
Be sure to look at Sara Kajder's rich descriptions about how we can use technology in the classroom (Chapter 14). While she doesn't specifically mention ELLs, Cindy's comments here remind us that technology is a particularly powerful tool for those students.

—*KB, REP, LR*

When you want to know more . . .

The conversation about English language learners and the problems and possibilities of teaching them could go on forever. If you'd like to give Cindy, Danling, and Carol the opportunity to expand the discussion of the last pages, take a look at Cindy's *Schools in the Middle* article "Affinity Groups: A Different Kind of Co-Curricular Activity" (see Gross and Aguilar 1999) and the book she co-authored, *Visionary Middle Schools: Signature Practices and the Power of Local Invention* (Morocco, Brigham, and Aguilar 2006). Danling's *Island of English: Teaching ESL in Chinatown* (2003) will give you some insight into working with speakers of a language dramatically different from English. Take a look, too, at her essay "Teaching Writing to English Language Learners at the Secondary Level" in *The 21st Century's Writing: New Directions for Secondary Classrooms* (in press). Carol's article "Stop Pretending and Think About Plot," in *Voices from the Middle* (2004), and her book *Cohesive Writing: Why Concept Is Not Enough* (2002) will broaden the conversation still further.

STRATEGIES FOR SCAFFOLDING FROM ONE LANGUAGE TO THE NEXT

In their own classrooms, teachers can use a variety of language acquisition strategies that include the following:

> Identify two or three central concepts to the lesson and explicitly focus on vocabulary through the use of word walls, cognates, dictionaries, and word maps. Link key words to images, photos, and drawings.

> Offer students opportunities to listen to and rehearse their new words without fear of embarrassment through the use of computers, tape recorders, and paired reading. Students can listen to the pronunciation of words and practice sounding them out with the aid of technology such as "talking" word processors.

> Provide written and oral summaries of material. In some cases, the publishers have developed brief summaries on CDs that students can use at home.

> Have students engage in real conversations with native speakers (discussion circles, small-group work, pair-shares, and so on).

> Provide reading texts that are developmentally and culturally appropriate for older students. Have students read aloud with one another and/or use computers and tape recorders.

> Provide speaking opportunities such as storytelling, poetry readings, and dialogues with lots of practice and support before student performances.

> Use tools and graphic organizers such as T-charts, Venn diagrams, highlighters, and sticky notes.

> Provide writing opportunities for students to write individually or in groups. They can practice writing notes, lists, and simple sentence structures, gradually advancing to the more complex sentences and the paragraph structure.

FIGURE 8–6.

DANLING: Yes, I support all those strategies. What I want to stress more is that we must let ELLs start reading the books they can understand, with some room for challenge, but not to the point of frustration. Grade-level texts are not appropriate, either, since most secondary ELLs report understanding only 30 percent of those books. Nobody can enjoy learning that way. And no matter the subject, we need to consciously help ELLs develop their listening, speaking, reading, and writing ability in English. At the secondary level, we rush to cover the curriculum, including the textbooks. Remember, to cover less doesn't mean to learn less.

Name: _____

Phone: _____

Email: _____

Dear Student,

I would like you to complete the survey below so that I can be a better teacher to you. Forgive me if I seem to be prying, but the more I know about you, the better I will be able to teach you. Please feel free to skip any question you don't feel comfortable answering.

Sincerely,

Language Survey

What languages do you speak? *Spanish, englich*

_____

_____

What languages can you write and read? *same*

_____

_____

What language do you speak at home? To parents? Grandparents? Brothers or sisters? *Spanish*

Spanish   *both*

_____

What language are you most comfortable in? Explain. *at school you mortly have to speak english but me old my friends we speak spanish*

_____

_____

FIGURE 8–7. *Rudy responds to language survey*   (*Continues*)

Have you gone to school in another country? Where? Through what grade? _Cari zona_
___ _6th grade_ _____

If your first language wasn't English, how did you learn English? _____
___ _at school_ _____

Do you ever watch TV or listen to the radio in another language? Explain. _____
___ _yes, we listen to Spanish music and TV_ _____

When you have children, what language do you plan to speak to them? What language(s) do you want them to be able to speak? Explain. _Both you need to do both_ _____

Comments about your experience being bilingual and/or biliterate? _____
Some teachers are not liking it but it is good and you can read more because it is in ~~two lang~~ Spanish & English.

What else do I need to know about you to be an effective teacher to you? _____
I read slow but it is okay and I am being hard work.

FIGURE 8–7. Continued

Allow students to use their first language or to code-switch in their speaking and writing whenever they feel the need to. We need to learn to read meanings through broken English structure in our ELLs' speaking and writing, and not to correct every error, or they will produce less and learn less. We need to have confidence that by using the language frequently, eventually ELLs will learn the conventions; they will self-correct their "broken language" usage and form the new language habit by using language in meaningful contexts and through real communication.

> > > *We must honor that first language students bring to our classroom; we must understand their culture; we must learn to see—and hear—from a perspective beyond our own. Because, indeed, peace comes in many languages.*
> —*Kylene Beers*

Finally, I'd suggest that we spend less time talking about language, reading, or writing, and let ELLs spend more time actually *using* the language. They don't learn the language rules from listening to lectures or doing language exercises; they learn the rules by using the language in contexts.

> > < <

A last word, an editor's prerogative, from Kylene: Baker, my fifteen-year-old son (as I write this in 2006), has a poster on the wall right *outside* his bedroom door (which you immediately interpret to mean there is no untouched wall space actually left *in* his room). This poster shows a moon's view of the earth with the following words floating all around it: *paz, vrede, ellpήvη, paix, mup, pace, peace.*

I asked him why he liked this poster. He said, "If we're going to ever have peace, real peace, then we probably need to hear all the ways it sounds—Spanish, Chinese, Dutch, Greek, Japanese, French, Korean, Russian, Italian, and English. The words of peace don't come in just English."

Cindy, Danling, and Carol make Baker's point more passionately, more elegantly, and with more conviction: We must honor that first language students bring to our classroom; we must understand their culture; we must learn to see—and hear—from a perspective beyond our own. Because, indeed, peace comes in many languages.

Connecting to my thoughts

Connecting to other texts

ON YOUNG ADULTS AND THEIR LITERATURE

Carlsen, G. Robert. 1980. *Books and the Teenage Reader: A Guide for Teachers, Librarians and Parents.* 2nd rev. ed. New York: Harper & Row.

Monseau, Virginia. 1996. *Responding to Young Adult Literature.* Portsmouth, NH: Boynton/Cook.

Nilsen, Alleen Pace, and Kenneth L. Donelson. 2001. *Literature for Today's Young Adults.* 6th ed. New York: Longman.

Thompson, Jack. 1986. *Understanding Teenagers Reading: Reading Processes and the Teaching of Literature.* Australia: Croom Helm.

One Teacher to One Student with One Powerful Strategy

October 29

Dear Colleague,

Do your students love to write notes to each other, especially during your fascinating presentations? Mine always do. And does your school have a vast underground postal system through which kids distribute those notes around the classroom and throughout the building? (I guess that's why they call it a "passing period" between classes, since kids are both passing between classes *and* passing out notes to each other.) You've probably run across plenty of samples of these missives, discarded on the floor after being delivered and read. Typically, these writings are not very, uh, curriculum centered, are they?

But maybe they could be.

There are lots of elementary teachers who regularly exchange personal notes with their students, writing back and forth about classroom and family events. This simple adult-child correspondence allows the teacher to model good writing, to create a just-right text for each child to read, to see and assess

We've been passing notes like this one back and forth, too, during the writing of this book. And perhaps that's what these chapters are—notes passed back and forth among people interested in literacy. And perhaps books, themselves, might be seen as just long notes passed back and forth over the centuries. In this chapter Harvey Daniels reminds us that all reading and writing are, fundamentally, individuals talking with one another. Literacy is fundamentally personal.

—*KB, REP, LR*

each student's writing skills, and to get to know the student personally—a highly productive use of a few minutes. And when you teach just twenty-five kids, most of whom can write only a few lines, it's both a manageable and a powerful activity. But is there a big-kid equivalent? A way to achieve the same goals when we are departmentalized and teaching five classes a day?

You already sense how potentially important this idea *could* be. At some time, you probably heard yourself say: "You know, kids will say things to me in writing that they'd never say out loud in front of the whole class." Well, if you've expressed that sentiment, then you recognize that there is a whole separate and special channel of communication between you and your students that's just lying there, waiting for you to pick up and use, to teach, to coach, to connect, to guide, mentor, and model. But how? What about the topics, the management, the workload, the logistics, the assessment? Let me try to answer those questions as I also try to convince you that corresponding with your students is worth a careful look . . . or another try.

No matter what subject or grade level you teach, you should be regularly engaged in a lively, individual written correspondence with each of your students. This practice has more power to enhance your instructional effectiveness and to elevate your joy in teaching than any other strategy you could add to your repertoire.

In this chapter, in the upcoming series of letters, I share what I have learned about this old and new, simple yet complex practice after exploring it in my own classroom for—I cannot believe this—thirty-seven years. And I pass along the practical management ideas I have stolen from smarter teachers across the country, as we have compared notes on this backbone activity in our classrooms.

Ready? You've got mail!

Cheers,
Harvey Daniels

Flashback to summer 2006 . . .
June 25
Dear Colleague,

Sometime during my first year of teaching—1969, actually, thanks for asking—we had an inservice workshop. I forget the professor's name, but his university was three states away, so he must have been pretty smart. And that day, what the consultant was preaching was *dialogue journals.*

He said that we should legalize kids' impulse to write notes in class and capitalize on it. We teachers should regularly exchange informal letters with each of our students so that we could get to know the kids better, understand their interests and unique learning needs, and build trust that we could draw upon

> > > > >
Teacher-student correspondence is just one version of a broader family of strategies that might be called written conversation. Be on the lookout for a new book by Elaine Daniels and Smokey Daniels (to be published by Heinemann), in which the authors outline a dozen other versions of letter writing that help students engage, apply, and remember curriculum content.

—*KB, REP, LR*

through the year. Plus, the kids would be getting some good writing practice. It sounded good to me. Still soaking wet behind the ears, I was ready to implement any halfway-plausible classroom strategy the guru recommended.

So the next Monday, I announced to my four English classes and one section of U.S. history that henceforth we would be writing notes back and forth, just to chat about the course, school, life, whatever. I instructed the kids to compose these letters in spiral notebooks and announced that the first batch of dialogue journals would be handed in to me on Friday.

Then, unfortunately, Friday came.

It was gray and drizzling as I schlepped wobbling stacks of spiral notebooks down from my third-floor classroom out to my car, one load after another, and piled them in the backseat. With every curve and stoplight, the dialogue journals lurched, toppled, and slid around. By the time I got home, they were all over the floor. On several of the spiral notebooks, the little wires had already come untucked, and one stabbed me on the wrist. I was already bleeding before I even got the journals into the house.

Do I even need to tell you the rest of the story? It was a long weekend of self-induced torment. Did I read the journals Friday night—or at least get a start on them? Are you kidding? It was the weekend! Saturday? Uh, I had so many other chores and errands to do. The dialogue journals began to feel like a black cloud hanging over my weekend. A beautiful Sunday morning finally came and my wife brightly suggested that we take the kids to the zoo. And I heard myself say, "I can't go to the zoo. I have to read these goddamn dialogue journals!"

Ruefully,
Harvey, aka "Smokey," Daniels

PS: My students were always so diabolically excited when they learned my nickname. They'd holler it at me at football games and around the neighborhood. "Hey, Smokeeeeee!"

June 26
Dear Colleague,

Maybe you have a story like mine.

Most of us have tried some kind of teacher-student correspondence at some time in our classroom lives. Maybe we called it dialogue journals or literature letters or something else. And we probably enjoyed the feeling of closeness—the personalization—that this one-to-one conversation offered. But very often we got overwhelmed with the sheer volume of the mail and the time required to respond to kids thoughtfully and caringly. Sometimes kids would write inappropriate things in their letters that made you want to chuck the whole thing. Maybe a kid sloppily jotted, "This sucks." Or maybe you got a note like the one my colleague Angela received: "Hey, Mrs. A., I have a friend who thinks you are really HOT (except for the pregnancy thing)."

Sometimes we found out things about a student that were hard to handle, that made us uncomfortable or forced us to take action we didn't want to take. In my first month of doing dialogue journals, I learned of one boy's heroin use and had to talk to his counselor and the school psychologist right away. And I felt so stressed and conflicted about this—shouldn't personal letters have a degree of privacy?—that it briefly made me want to abandon the dialogues altogether. It turned out that Max was looking for help anyway—he just used our letters as a way to cry out, and he did not end up resenting me for ratting him out. Still, after experiences like this, or even more likely, feeling the time crunch of responding to so many kids, most of us gave up on dialogue journals.

I think that another mistake we made was defining dialogue journals as containing mostly personal news and general conversation. While this approach certainly let us get to know the kids better (to the extent that they and we were willing to self-disclose), it really had little to do with the curriculum, with the content we were supposed to be teaching. The dialogues were an extra, an option, a grace note in community building, but if they were *teaching* anything, it was mainly indirect, through our modeling and kids getting a little more writing practice. Given this marginal role, it certainly was not surprising that we would drop the letter writing when time pressures and curriculum demands closed in on us.

I almost gave up myself, on that Black Sunday, facing 150 letters to answer. (And no, I didn't answer them all that night. I went in the next day and told my classes it would take me a few more days to get to everyone's notes.) But even in that initial pit of despair, trapped by my own shortsighted logistics, I was captivated by what the kids had to say, what they were willing to share. I heard about what made my class hard or easy, what the kids were reading outside of class, how tough it was to get cut from a team, who had the coolest car, what a pain it is when teachers schedule four tests on the same day, how scary it feels to audition for a part in the school play, how out to lunch parents can be, or appear to be. And, oh yeah, who was dating whom and who done whom wrong.

Above all, I was struck by how complicated and demanding these kids' young lives were. It is a tough job being a person, whoever you are. Even though I was only four or five years older than most of them, I had somehow lost touch with the quotidian realities of teenage and school life. What happened? Did I get amnesia along with my teaching certificate? In order to be the kind of teacher I wanted to be, I needed to stay connected to the kids and their reality. And besides, their notes usually made me feel happy, energized, and somehow, in the flow.

So I kept soliciting letters from my students and writing back. As a true believer in group dynamics, I also looked at this as a part of my community-building efforts. And it seemed to work. My classes were mostly pleasant and hardworking. We seemed to have a sense of esprit and interdependence. When

> > > > >
The notion of staying connected to the kids in their lives flows through this whole book. Chris Crutcher begins with this very point in Chapter 2, and it's emphasized again in Ruth Shagoury's Interlude 1. Alfred Tatum reminds us how important it is to connect our teaching to the lives of our African American male students in Interlude 2. In fact, this idea may be at least implicit in every chapter in the book.

—KB, REP, LR

Don Graves wrote in 1983 that a teacher should know ten things about each student he teaches, I knew I could meet that challenge through my ongoing correspondence with kids.

But it wasn't very academic. I just tried to pen responses that were empathic, respectful, and adultlike. I was mainly being a sounding board, a sympathetic adult, a cheerleader, occasionally an adviser. I kept doing the dialogue journals in my own haphazard way. And then, in 1987, some important guidance came along.

Sincerely,
Smokey

July 8
Dear Nancie Atwell,

I have been working on my chapter in the new Beers, Probst, and Rief book (can't wait to read what you're writing for it!) and have been reminded how much I owe you for being able to develop letter writing in my own teaching and in this article. It wasn't until you published *In the Middle* in 1987 that I understood how to move my teacher-student correspondence from relationship building and general writing practice to something more academically substantial. To use letters not just to connect but to teach.

While the whole book knocked me out (how many times have you heard that?), I learned the most from the abundant samples of *literature letters* between you and individual kids.

> Dear Mrs. Atwell,
>
> I read many chapters in *The Daughters of Eve* over the weekend at my babysitting jobs while they napped or went to bed. The part in the book when the Daughters of Eve are having a meeting you start believing that all men are enemys and you yourself start believing that you hate men. But then when you close the book you have to say to yourself: "This is only a book. Not all men act like that." So the anger that book filled you up with won't be taken out on the next male that's in your sight.
>
> My favorite Duncan book is *Down a Dark Hall* which I read last year. What's yours?
>
> Lilias

> Dear Lily,
>
> I know what you mean. Sometimes a writer creates such a mood that a novel can spin us completely out of our real world and into a world of his or her fiction. It can take a conscious effort to tell the difference and come back to

reality. I'm reading *Good-bye Paper Doll*, a novel about a girl with anorexia nervosa, and feeling very thin and hungry. Then I look down. Lily, I may be hungry, but I'm definitely not anorexic.

My favorite Duncan book is *Chapters: My Growth as a Writer*. I also liked *Down a Dark Hall* and *Summer of Fear*.

Mrs. A (Atwell 1987, 182)

This was the missing structure that I needed. Like me, you were connecting with kids personally, in a playful but grown-up way. But you were also modeling, guiding, and gently directing. You were teaching English in those letters.

So, like so many other teachers back in those days, I put your ideas right to work with my students, literally and methodically. I explicitly reframed our chatty letters as *book talk*. I became far more mindful and intentional with what I was modeling in my own prose. I became more challenging and more directive, not just giving kids handwritten high fives and back pats but asking hard questions and offering more suggestions about their writing and reading lives. And I began to carefully save, and periodically reread, the letters, recognizing that this was perhaps the best evidence I had of my students' growth.

> > > *The inherent privacy and reflectiveness of writing allow us, both student and teacher, to take our time, to think more carefully before we write, and to really talk* entre nous, *just between the two of us, with no one eavesdropping or waiting impatiently in line for his conference. In letters, we teachers model writing powerfully; as they read our notes, students see proficient adult writing unfold before them.*

Today, I see that these dialogue journals or literature letters, with all their complexity and teaching power, are essentially *written conferences*. Of course, we all have out-loud conferences with our students now; they are a nonnegotiable ingredient of a best practice literacy program. When we hold short individual conversations with our young writers and readers, we can take on powerful new roles: we can mentor, guide, and coach young people individually, matching their needs and development precisely. Conferences give us guaranteed teachable moments, one kid at a time, every day. They allow us to truly differentiate instruction, helping every learner to progress toward individual as well as whole-class goals. How did we ever *not* confer?

By conferring in writing, instead of out loud, we add some extra benefits. When we create a special, personalized text for each student, we sure get the kids' attention! After all, it is pretty rare to have a teacher write to you, except perhaps for critical comments at the end of a paper. The inherent privacy and reflectiveness of writing allow us, both student and teacher, to take our time, to think more carefully before we write, and to really talk *entre nous*, just between the two of us, with no one eavesdropping or waiting impatiently in line for his conference. In letters, we teachers model writing powerfully; as they read our notes, students see proficient adult writing unfold before them. What a better use of our time it is to *demonstrate good writing* than to spend the same minutes marking all the errors in a student's paper, so she can toss it in the nearest wastebasket, feeling attacked.

Nancie, I know you never claimed to have invented teacher-student correspondence as a tool of teaching, but you sure paved the way for me, providing models and offering a structure to build upon. And I have since learned more from Donald Murray, Don Graves, Lucy Calkins, Carl Anderson, Katie Wood Ray—and even from institutions like the National Writing Project and the National Council of Teachers of English.

But it was you who kicked my teaching up a notch back in '87, and thanks again for that.

Gratefully,
Smokey Daniels

July 15
Dear Colleague,

Whoops, I didn't quite finish my own crash-and-burn story, did I? We left off with my bleeding wrist and the family going to the zoo without Dad.

The first thing I changed—obviously—was the submission schedule for my kids' dialogue journals. Assigning myself 145 letters to read and answer on a single weekend goes down as one of the dumbest rookie moves ever. Next, I switched to a staggered schedule, where different classes turned in their journals on a different day. But that still left me about 25 letters a day to write—pretty much the same as 150 on a weekend. Duh again.

I felt silently goaded by great elementary teachers like Chris Smith in Elmhurst, Illinois, who somehow managed this load, writing to every kid every day. But Chris' second graders wrote only a few lines; reading time was virtually nil, and she could dash off a student-satisfying response in a single minute. My adolescents were writing much longer entries, which required much more reading time and deserved a thoughtful, proportional response. Every day or even every week was clearly impossible. After a bit more fumbling, I settled into a flow that felt comfortable and doable: five or six students a day, which meant a letter exchange with each kid every four or five weeks. In other words, when my classroom correspondence got smoothed out, I exchanged notes with each student about seven to ten times a year.

Since then, I have talked to teachers all over the country, and we all seem to have come to the same set point. Yesterday, I was working with a group of teachers in Austin, Texas, big letter-writing aficionados. They reported adopting the same rule: for middle and high school, five letters a day, taking maybe two to five minutes for reading and responding to each one. That's a sustainable flow through the year, the Texans had found.

> < < < < <
> Technology may be making such a daunting task somewhat easier. Voice recognition programs such as NaturallySpeaking enable a teacher to read a paper or a letter and speak his responses aloud while reading, letting the computer do the labor of transcribing. Twenty-five letters a day would still be quite a task, even if you're dictating rather than typing, but no matter how many you decide to take on, you might want to experiment with such computer tools.
> —*KB, REP, LR*

But that's if you want to spread the letter writing out, so you are doing a little of it all the time. Another approach is to correspond in bursts, like Angie Andrews does. Four times a semester, she takes ten to fifteen minutes of class time and has kids write letters all at once. Then, she takes the rest of that day and evening to read and write short responses. During part of the next day's class, she hands out her responses and the group shares common elements, concerns, and interests that have popped up in the letters.

Want to hear how this smart first-year teacher worked this—and what the kids wrote?

Stay tuned,
Smokey

August 23
Dear Angie,

Thanks so much for letting me tell your story and for collecting all the written permissions from the kids (and their parents) to use these samples. I think I will mostly just quote you and the kids and tell the story that way. Maybe with a little background first, something like this:

Angie Andrews teaches chemistry to juniors and seniors at Elmwood Park High School, in an inner-ring suburb of Chicago. Yes, chemistry, not language arts or English. Her students are a diverse bunch, as the town's once-monolithic Italian immigrant community is now being infused with Polish and Mexican newcomers. Angie's student load is 130 kids per year, much like that of teachers around the country. But unlike most science teachers, Angie exchanges personal notes with her students about once a month in an attempt to get to know kids better—and to teach them more effectively. Here's how she does it—and why.

"The first time we do this in September, I just give them the first fifteen minutes of class," Angie explained, "and I keep the topic pretty open. I say, 'Tell me what's going on in your life, in school or out, with chemistry or your other subjects.'" The first time she invites these open-ended notes, Angie cautions kids to stick to school-appropriate topics and language ("I don't want to hear about your partying on the weekend. I'm not trying to be your buddy here."). She also warns kids that if they share any information about someone being at risk or in danger, she will contact the appropriate other adults—including the social worker or counselor.

"The first time we do these monologues, they always ask me why we're doing this. And I say, 'Look, there's twenty-eight of you and one of me, and I've only got eighteen weeks in this semester to get to know you—so I can be a better science teacher for you.'" Angie laughed as she recollected: "Kids will actually gasp out loud when I say that; they just go, 'Wow.' Sometimes one kid will say something negative, like 'This is stupid.' But someone always pipes up and says, 'Shut up, she's just trying to help us, you jerk!'"

After the writing time is up, Angie collects the monologues and presses on with the day's lesson. Later, during a free period, she starts to see the range of responses. Some kids, like Rachel, stick with the personal stuff:

Hakuna matata

No worries

I am a pretty laid-back person. *Alwayz* in a good mood. I don't really let things get to me. I'm currently thinking about school and what I want to do with my life. I'm pretty set on wanting to become a doctor.

Amanda offered a full page of lively background:

I love dancing, whether it is at a club or in front of a mirror at home. I like all types of music. I drive a '98 2-door Saturn. It's a stick and a lot of fun to drive. I spend a lot of time at school because I'm involved in a lot of clubs: snowball, band, theater, key club, student council, drama club, thespian society. I'm currently in the musical "Bye Bye Birdie." I'm playing the role of Ursula Merkle, a crazy annoying girl who is in love with Conrad Birdie.

Ian wrote:

So I'm basically going to write you a note. So . . . about Chem II, I'm kinda lost in here. *Damn these smart people!* Kinda getting lost over this subject. I'm not too sure I want to be a pharmacist now. Bio II was really fun and I enjoyed the subject matter. . . . As a senior and 1st time running on a team, I want to make a huge impact (in a positive way) in EPHS. I want to be all-conference for track, impossible but a dream I chase.

Ryan mixed business with pleasure:

This class is pretty simple except that we will have to remember all those elements. Memorizing things doesn't usually come easy for me. Some things it does, but usually it doesn't though. I am also getting a German Shepherd soon. Visited the breeder on Saturday. I am considering training it as a Schutzhund, which is "protection dog." Focuses on obedience, protection and tracking.

And some kids share more global concerns. Chris wrote:

One thing that's been bothering me the last couple of weeks is that I don't know what I want to do after high school. I feel like there's been a lot of pressure on me to keep my grades up and do well on the ACT.

How does Angie respond to and use these letters? First of all, she writes short answers at the bottom or on the back of each student's note and hands them back a day or two later. The kids avidly devour her responses, looking for the personal connections that she invariably offers.

After offering some compliments on Angie's teaching style, Janina took the opportunity to give Angie some course-related feedback:

> I think that we should do more of a review before tests because the wording is usually confusing. I also get nervous before taking a test, which is bad because then I start worrying about grades. I'm always pretty on top of myself for grades because since I was a little kid I've always gotten good grades. I'm aiming for an A but I'm not too sure if that's what I'm going to get.

Angie simply responded:

> Janina,
>
> I will try to slow down. I thought that this stuff would bore you all since you've already done it in Chem I. I'm glad to hear you like this class—it is my first time teaching it.
>
> Ms. Andrews

For other kids, Angie offers a wide range of responses, some more personal and others more academic—and all of them very concise, in keeping with Angie's realistic time constraints.

> My sister and I fought like that, but now she is my best friend (after my husband!).
>
> Stick shift rules!
>
> It's nice to have students with such ambition.
>
> I am sorry to hear about your aunt. Take a deep breath and do what you can do with all the effort you have.
>
> You'll look back at high school and laugh at its simplicity.

Then Angie will bring up a chemistry-related topic that's appeared on several students' notes—like today, when several kids have asked about "sig figs," or significant figures, the policy by which students are required to work out chemical equations to a particular decimal place. "Do we need to go over why this is so important?" Angie asks, and kids nod. She quickly jots some examples on the board, making an analogy to the measurements her carpenter husband makes at work. "He can't just round it off to the nearest inch—or foot," she explains. "The house might fall down."

So Ang, how does that sound? Fair description of your work? Accurate with the kids? The thing I can't really paint in words is the atmosphere in your classroom, the energy and mutual affection that are so palpable, that seem to animate everything. Everyone tells teachers to create something called a positive classroom climate, but you've gone way beyond that baseline standard. The kids come into your room as if they are arriving at a party, happy and eager to be there; they settle right into the work efficiently and cheerfully; they are just as quick to help each other as to laugh. In your room, high school feels not like something to be endured but like something to be savored. How big a part do you think your letter writing plays in this upbeat attitude? I think maybe a lot.

Thanks again for being a pathfinder and a model for all of us. Take care of that bambino and come back to teaching just as soon as you can. The kids need teachers like you so much.

Love,
Smokey

September 14
Dear Colleague,

Does Angie's story make you want to give letters a try—or *another* try? Do you feel ready to enter into a written conversation with your students? If so, let me offer a few suggestions that I've either learned through hard experience myself or borrowed from smarter teachers who've solved the predictable problems we all face. I'll put them in bullets, just to make it easy.

Setting Up

> Lay the ground rules. Make sure kids know what's relevant and appropriate for this kind of conversation. Look back over Angie's directions if you need the right words to say.

> While keeping the door open to personal issues, center the conversation on the topics, the work, the ideas of the class. The personal connections will naturally come along with the content.

> Set a quota and a timetable that's workable for kids and for you. You want to balance between regular, habitual letters and everyone having time to write and respond thoughtfully, patiently, and unhurriedly.

> To create a workshop-style classroom that supports this kind of teacher-student relationship, read *In the Middle* (Atwell 1998).

If you want to make your classroom correspondence more concrete and playful (nothing wrong with that), buy a cheap mailbox at the local home improvement store (under ten dollars if you shop hard) and let students decorate it for you. Kids can have mailboxes too, in the form of folders, cubbies, or shelves in the classroom. Don't have your own classroom? Elaine Daniels tucks her mailbox under her arm and drags it to every room she teaches in.

When Writing to Kids

> Be yourself—meaning, sound like the interesting adult person you are. You can be a mentor and an expert without being distant. This is a chance to bring the real you to school.

> Write informally, just as you might jot a note or an email to a friend or family member. The most powerful letters are *not* superpolished and perfect, but more on the casual side. Slang and abbreviations are fine. It's OK—and actually quite a good demonstration—if the letters show the tracks of the teacher's drafting, even with crossed-out words or phrases inserted with carets. After all, this is personal, one-to-one writing.

> While your notes should be generally correct, they don't have to be perfect. If you think you have misspelled a word, circle it and put "sp?" in the margin.

> Ask lots of specific questions. This is how you help kids to find topics, establish a flow in writing to you, and find a rhythm.

> > > > >
We couldn't help but think about this list of questions as we read Don Murray's chapter (12). He reminds us to write alongside our students. This list of prompts would get anyone started.

—KB, REP, LR

> What makes you think that?
> How did you learn that?
> What would you ask this character?
> Do you see any other sides to this issue?
> What if I said _____: how would you answer?
> But what about _____?
> Can you tell me more about _____?
> What do you mean when you say _____?
> Try to respond to all the questions kids have posed to you.

If it is absolutely impossible timewise for you to answer each kid, you can occasionally get away with a whole-class response instead, along these lines:

Dear 4th Geometry,

Thanks for your inspiring and amusing letters. Based on what Ned, Jane, Jerry, Julie, and Natasha say, we need to go back and look at isosceles triangles again.

On the other hand, it seems everyone has a handle on the equilaterals. And yes, Larry, I do drive a fifteen-year-old pickup truck. I call it Nellybelle and I bought it in college.

Photocopy and distribute the group letter to everyone's mailbox. Try to include as many kids' names and ideas as you can, as a way of honoring and answering them.

When Reading and Responding to Kids' Letters

> First of all, remember that they are kids. Some will say dumb things. Others will be guarded, dutiful, and minimalist. It takes a while to establish a correspondence.

> Do not mark, circle, or correct errors. This is writing to learn, not a formal, public writing assignment. Kids' errors or misspellings will not take root if uncorrected. All of us use a range of text from casual to carefully edited (think of your most recent grocery list). For more on this, see Daniels, Zemelman, and Steineke (2007).

> Do not *ever* use a red pen, even if only to write pleasant responses. Red ink is anchored in negativity for most students.

> Do not evaluate kids' letters qualitatively—the minute you start awarding C-pluses and A-minuses, you'll immediately undermine the authenticity of the conversation *and* commit huge chunks of your time to grading defensibly. There's plenty of other stuff to grade—let this be an oasis for kids.

> It's OK to give *credit* for participation, if you must record something in your grade book. How about ten points for completing a letter, zero for not? No threes, no sevens—it's binary, all-or-nothing grading. All you ever have to remember is the few kids who *didn't* submit or answer a letter—everybody else gets a ten.

> If time simply doesn't permit you to write often to individual students, class letters can fill the gap. In response to kids' individual notes, compose just one letter to the whole class.

Once you get a correspondence established, you may find it valuable for more than just curricular conversations. Letters can be just as useful for privately addressing social or behavioral issues as they are for discussing subject matter. If a student is exhibiting what we now call interfering actions, letters give you a whole new option. Instead of choosing among during-class confrontations, out-in-the-hall corrections, detentions, or phone calls to the parents, you can simply write the kid a note and hand it over at the end of class.

Dear Brenda,

I was concerned today when you were constantly talking while other kids were doing their class presentations. Since you and I have talked about this before, I was especially surprised that you would distract from and interrupt other kids' moments on stage. Did you notice when Sonja and Raoul were trying to hush you up?

Will you make a commitment to work on this? Write back and let me know what steps you're ready to take, OK? By next Monday's presentations, you need to have a handle on this.

—Mrs. Marsh

This kind of feedback (you wouldn't even call it a rebuke) does several things at once:

> It allows the teacher to carefully compose just the right words, instead of improvising in the heat of the moment in front of twenty-five other kids.

> It allows the student the dignity of receiving the feedback in private, later on, when it is less likely the kid will react defensively or feel a need to act defiant in front of peers.

> It puts the burden on the student to reflect upon, write down, and enact a workable plan for improvement—instead of simply feeling attacked or having to serve out a punishment.

Of course, a letter is too slow a tool for a genuine behavior emergency. But most of the discipline problems that plague us as teachers are not sudden, acute crimes and misdemeanors. Instead, they are the nagging, recurrent, water-torture aggravations, like kids who come to class unprepared, who are chronically inattentive, or who are disrespectful of others. For those ongoing ailments—problems that don't require instantaneous intervention—a letter-writing campaign can be a powerful, long-term way to address the issue. At the very least, if things escalate or the problem goes unaddressed, the teacher will have a written record to share with parents, the counselor, or the principal as necessary. But in classrooms where teachers are already using letters as part of their instruction, engagement is often strong enough that fewer interfering actions are happening anyway.

Hope these ideas give you the confidence and the tools you need to get started.

Best,
Smokey

October 29

Dear Friend,

I have been trying to come up with a top-ten list for the advantages of teacher-student correspondence. The problem is I can't boil it down to ten.

Top Nineteen Benefits of Teacher-Student Letter Writing

1. You get to know your students individually.

2. You are reminded of how funny, delightful, and diverse young people are.

3. You get a chance to be playful, be human, have fun, be known, be *you.*

4. You can control your own level of self-disclosure.

5. Students get to know you.

6. People who know each other generally like each other.

7. Mutual acquaintance creates investment in the working relationship.

8. You hear from those shy kids who never speak up in class.

9. You get feedback about the subject matter and your teaching: what's hard, what needs review or reteaching, what's easy, what should be next.

10. You get cues for individualizing instruction.

11. You find out about learning styles and get ideas for reaching different ones.

12. You glean clues for how to match kids in pairs or form them into small groups.

13. You hear kids' often astute self-assessments.

14. You can factor kids' real lives into your assignments, schedules, grading.

15. You use your own writing to model composing skills and conventions.

16. You create just-right, personal texts for each kid to read.

17. You can coach, model, mentor, and help privately, one to one.

18. You may become the "first responder" for a kid who's in trouble and needs an adult to connect him with help. Could any teaching act ever be more important?

19. Other than that, not much.

I'll probably think of more after the book goes to press.

Cheers,
Smokey

October 31
Via FedEx
Dear Kylene, Bob, and Linda,

Happy Halloween! Here at last is my chapter for the new book. I hope it feels like a treat, not a trick.

The four of us have often talked about how hard these last few years have been for teachers. What worries me most about the current accountability-standards-testing frenzy is that it drives a wedge between us and the kids. If *they* don't score well on the big state test, then *we* can get punished, stigmatized, or dropped off the merit pay list. In this insidious scenario, we teachers are at risk of being cut off from the very source of energy and commitment that brought us to this career in the first place—young people.

As more and more external forces disrupt our personal connection with students, the solution is not to step back, to give up on the magic, the enchantment, the I-thou relationship, I would even say the *sacredness* of our work. Instead, we must recommit to the kids, more wholly and more personally than ever. One way to cleave to our calling is to join young people in a lively, honest, and caring correspondence—writing and sharing, one to one.

Thanks for the chance to say this to thousands of colleagues across the country and for inviting me to be part of this unique and timely project.

All the best,
Smokey

From the editors
November 10
Dear Smokey,

You're very welcome, and we thank you for joining the project. Your chapter expresses clearly and powerfully a theme that runs through many of the chapters in the book, we think. Literacy can't be reduced to a collection of discrete and isolated skills; education is more than the list of books read and courses taken; and teaching is more, much more, than covering prescribed content and training kids to take tests. Instead, as you point out, it's a rich and rewarding connection between a teacher and a student. Thank you for showing us a powerful way for creating that connection.

—Kylene, Linda, and Bob

When you want to know more . . .

Smokey writes here about close and effective communication with students. He has dealt with that issue, and others, at greater length in *Best Practice: Today's Standards for Teaching and Learning in America's Schools* (Zemelman, Daniels, and Hyde 2005). His suggestions for talk about nonfiction apply as well to imaginative literature—take a look at *Mini-Lessons for Literature Circles* (2004).

Lessons Learned

> > > DEBORAH APPLEMAN

READING WITH ADOLESCENTS

I've loved to read since I was a child. Reading inspired me to change my name to match the heroines I was reading about—Heidi, Rebecca, Anne, Nancy—you get the picture. Reading propelled me happily through childhood and saved me during a relentlessly bleak adolescence. As I moved from my adolescence to adulthood, my pastime of reading and a few lines from Wordsworth determined my career:

> What we have loved
> Others will love
> And we will teach them how.

How could I not have become an English teacher?

Eventually, I became someone who helps other lovers of reading to become English teachers and to inspire that same love of reading in adolescents. My work over the last fifteen years has focused on reading with young people in two primary ways: teaching them and their teachers to use theoretical lenses—such as feminist theory, Marxist literary theory, deconstruction, and reader response—as they read and encouraging kids to read recreationally in nonacademic settings (Appleman 2006). I've read seemingly countless short stories, poems, and novels—both classic and contemporary—with adolescents and with university students, both with their English teachers and without them. More important, I've listened to students talk about their reading, with me and with each other. What follows are a few of the lessons I've learned from reading with adolescents.

Students are constantly reading the world. They need a place to talk about what they've discovered.

When I first proposed to teachers and teacher educators that students could benefit from the interpretive tools of contemporary literary theory and learn to read the world, many of them were skeptical. I'll confess that I was skeptical myself. Weren't those theories—deconstruction, postcolonialism, new historicism—too sophisticated for adolescents? Wouldn't they resist our expanding notion of what constitutes a text? Wouldn't they be unwilling to submit their own cultural texts to analysis in the classroom? Wouldn't they feel that those cultural texts were compromised if they were treated as school subjects?

What I discovered instead was that adolescents are reading the world all the time and look to us, their English teachers, for the interpretive tools to help them make sense of it. More important, I learned that kids are up to nearly every intellectual challenge we throw at them; they rise to the occasion. As teachers of reading and literature, it is our job to ensure that students have lenses to see the world clearly in order that they might make sense of it.

Students want what they do in school to matter. Students want what they do outside of school to matter.

Relevancy doesn't just capture the heart of this lesson; I mean to suggest much more than that. What students do in school needs to feel important to them, and they need to feel important in doing that work. This feeling of importance is not merely a truism when it comes to adolescence. It is perhaps the central core of our work with them. Constructing significance in their work is not simply a matter of having them read more contemporary texts. It is a matter of creating and re-creating fresh and unrehearsed opportunities to make discoveries about texts, about language, about the world, and about themselves. We need to provide new ground upon which they can make these discoveries, and this ground is not always framed within permabound texts and tried-and-true lessons.

I've learned it is vitally important to help students create their own self-sponsored opportunities for reading and to encourage them to read with depth and complexity. When they have tools to render multiple theoretical perspectives, and when they can apply those tools to things that matter outside of school, the reading we do with them in our classrooms will matter to them more.

> > > *This feeling of importance is not merely a truism when it comes to adolescence. It is perhaps the central core of our work with them.*

Don't underestimate adolescents. They are often much better than we might imagine at finding meaning in a book.

At the beginning of my career as a high school literature teacher, I read and reread the texts I planned to teach. I prepared meticulous study guides and tried to anticipate every question that an adolescent might ask me. Sure, I adhered to a reader-response model that authorized the students' transactions with the text, and I thought about those transactions as the primary source of meaning making in the classroom, but to be completely honest, it was a little bit like Orwell's *Animal Farm* in the interpretive community that was my classroom: all interpretations were equal, but some were more equal than others and, in the end, I considered myself to be the final arbiter in interpretive disputes, or, at the very least, I thought myself to be the person in the room with the most interpretive ability.

I still believe in the responsibility that accompanies being the most experienced reader in the room. I also believe that my classroom, while democratic, is not a true democracy, and that I have a responsibility as a teacher that makes me more than a colearner. Still, I am regularly humbled by the ability of adolescents to perceptively read and interpret literary texts.

I remember, for example, reading Martel's *The Life of Pi* for one of the out-of-class book clubs that I observed. I loved the book, but I was totally confused by it, and I was worried that the students might have also been confused. What was real? What was metaphorical? Was there really a tiger? Who ate whom? What about all of the fantastic figurative language and the allegorical structure and the dense background in religious history? As I slid into a Breakfast Book Club meeting to observe the discussion, I was afraid I would find disillusioned and disappointed readers.

Instead, within the first five minutes of a student-run discussion, all of my questions and confusions about the book were cleared up. I listened—fascinated, impressed, and chastened—as students brilliantly explained what had befuddled me. I should have known better.

Enthusiasm may indeed be contagious, but students won't necessarily like books just because we do.

I suppose this is a contradiction of that Wordsworth quotation that originally inspired me. Sometimes students don't love what we have loved, and that has to be OK with us. *The Catcher in the Rye* (Salinger), *A Separate Peace* (Knowles), *The Scarlet Letter* (Hawthorne), even that nearly sacred text of the high school literature canon, *To Kill a Mockingbird* (Lee), won't always engage, inspire, captivate—or even be tolerated by—today's students. And so in the interest of keeping our classroom a viable space for student engagement, we have to consider whether some of our literary chestnuts may be too anachronistic, or precious, or irrelevant to offer to adolescents in the twenty-first century.

No one is too cool or too old to be touched by the magic of having someone read aloud to him or her.

The language of literature is sometimes musical, sometimes soothing, and sometimes simply exhilarating. There is no better way to hook kids than to read them the first chapter of a book. I've seen it work with all kinds of texts, from the traditional—*Of Mice and Men* (Steinbeck), *The Old Man and the Sea* (Hemingway), *The Great Gatsby* (Fitzgerald), *To Kill a Mockingbird*, *A Separate Peace*, any Shakespeare play—to the unexpected—*Their Eyes Were Watching God* (Hurtson), *The God of Small Things* (Roy), *The Things They Carried* (O'Brien), *The House on Mango Street* (Cisneros). This fascination with hearing the sound of literature is a lesson that all elementary teachers and most middle school teachers have learned well. It is one that high school teachers in particular need to remember.

The classroom isn't always the best place to discuss literature.

Hard brown desks, fluorescent lighting, the close press of peers—why would we think that school is a great place to experience the pleasures of reading? The lesson learned from observing students discussing their ideas in book clubs is that it's not just the actual *reading* of texts that is more enjoyable in comfortable surroundings. *Talking* about reading needs to be more comfortable as well.

Of course, this lesson is not meant to insult the good work of English teachers everywhere who inspire great conversations about great and not-so-great books. But let's face it: students sometimes do a better job of asking each other questions about books than their teachers can, and they can sometimes have more fun talking about books without us. If we truly want students to regard literature not simply as a school subject but as a habit of mind and heart, as a practice essential to leading a literate life, then we need to be more willing to create spaces for students to read—without us.

> > < <

My love of literature as an adolescent was more than a pastime. It was a lesson to be learned: literature can be the site of self-discovery and intellectual growth for adolescents if we, as their literature teachers, help create the spaces, both in the classroom and out, for them to flourish as readers and thinkers.

Adolescents are smarter than we sometimes give them credit for being. They are ready to be more intellectually autonomous from their teachers, they are astute and able readers of both texts and world, and they need the things they do and think and feel and say to matter, both in school and out. And literature will matter to them if we let it.

When you want to know more ...

Deborah's essay mentions both the concept of critical lenses—various ways of looking at a text—and the importance of moving reading out of the classroom, away from the harsh fluorescent lights, and into the students' diverse worlds. She has written more about these ideas in her books *Critical Encounters in High School English: Teaching Literary Theory to Adolescents* (2000) and *Reading for Themselves: How to Transform Adolescents into Lifelong Readers Through Out-of-Class Book Clubs* (2006).

Connecting to my thoughts

Connecting to other texts

ON LITERARY THEORY

Farrell, Edmund J., and James R. Squire, eds. 1990. *Transactions with Literature: A Fifty-Year Perspective.* Urbana, IL: National Council of Teachers of English.

Iser, Wolfgang. 1978. *The Act of Reading: A Theory of Aesthetic Response.* Baltimore, MD: Johns Hopkins University Press.

Rosenblatt, Louise M. 1956. "Acid Test in Teaching Literature." *English Journal* 45, no. 2: 66–74.

Rosenblatt, Louise M. 1978. *The Reader, the Text, the Poem: The Transactional Theory of the Literary Work.* Carbondale, IL: Southern Illinois University Press, 1994 (paperback edition).

Scholes, Robert E. 2001. *The Crafty Reader.* New Haven, CT: Yale University Press.

Teaching English Language Arts in a "Flat" World

ON MOST FRIDAYS, men and women from different professions come to speak in my ACCESS (Academic Success) class, telling us about the world for which my class and our school are preparing them. These people, from all backgrounds and industries, arrive like ambassadors of countries about which my students have heard, but that they cannot imagine themselves joining. These representatives speak a language the students do not always recognize but that I hope they will learn as they listen to and, on rare occasions, visit these people. What is this language? It is the verbs that refer to what kids must be able to do in the future; it is the nouns they will use when they enter that future work; and it is the adjectives that describe how well they had better do if they hope to keep the jobs they will have worked so hard to get. What gives strength and stature to each talk, however, is literacy—not the literacy of school and homework, but the literacy of adult life and work; the literacy that establishes people's value in the marketplace, displaying what they know, what they can do, and how well they can work with others, many of whom are different from themselves; the literacy that enables them to learn other skills and information that will ensure they'll get to keep their job when others lose theirs during hard times.

If you've been reading this book in order, you've completed chapters that discuss comprehension and vocabulary strategies, looked at the needs of specific groups of students, and thought some about engagement and motivation. Now, we decided, is the moment to consider what all this means against the backdrop of twenty-first-century demands.
—*KB, REP, LR*

We do get some distinguished guests to come to the class at times. We have had judges and senators, authors and broadcast personalities; it is the common people, however, and their evolving, increasingly sophisticated literacies that I have in mind when I look at my kids who come to me reading several grades below where they should be. When I think of the literacies of the future, the skills needed not just to survive but to thrive in the twenty-first century, I think of the police officer and firefighter, the mechanic and small business owner, all of whom have come to speak to the kids about the world to come and what they must know and be able to do if they are to find success and happiness there as adults. The police officer, for example, holds up a three-inch-thick book of laws, saying he had to learn them all and demonstrate that learning by passing a test. He goes on to say that he and his colleagues are always learning because of the evolving demands of their work. One workshop teaches the officers to work with people from different cultures; another focuses on terrorist events and the tools they must use to communicate during such a crisis; still a third workshop provides them with new training in how to use technology to solve a range of problems often encountered during an investigation.

> > > *When I think of the literacies of the future, the skills needed not just to survive but to thrive in the twenty-first century, I think of the police officer and firefighter, the mechanic and small business owner . . . they are all workers who must continue to learn as their fields evolve and who must, consequently, be highly literate.*

The other speakers are no different: The firefighter speaks of having begun as one who put out fires, only to discover that he also had to become an expert in medical, structural, and chemical crises. The mechanic began by fixing cars, but he now speaks of mastering the changing technology, keeping up with trends that require ever thicker manuals and longer training sessions, while coping with the increased demands of running his own business and managing all the data that goes with it. These speakers call to mind my father, who entered the printing business at nineteen and learned the basics only to find himself, nearly forty years later, appointed to lead the shift to new digital technology, a shift that made obsolete those people who refused to develop new skills. When my father entered the business, he cut and pasted images with scissors and tape; when he retired, he performed these same skills using a machine that cost more than he made in a year, while the real scissors slept in the dark drawer at his knee. In other words, they are all workers who must continue to learn as their fields evolve and who must, consequently, be highly literate. And the changes are evident, not just in the working world, but for students themselves. When I was a student, for instance, we read, wrote, spoke, and did 'rithmetic; now, according to the poster in the Apple store, kids "Blog. Compose. Podcast. Jam. Share. Photocast. Chat. Switch. Play. Create."

Thinking to the New Literacy Skills

Are these the new literacy skills of the twenty-first century? Or are they new wine in old bottles? In *Learning for the 21st Century: A Report and MILE Guide for 21st Century Skills* (Partnership for 21st Century Skills 2003), the authors focus on "learning skills," identifying three distinct types:

1. Information and Communication Skills

   > *Information and Media Literacy Skills*—Accessing, analyzing, managing, integrating, evaluating, and creating information in a variety of forms and media; understanding the role of media in society.

   > *Communication Skills*—Understanding, managing, and creating effective oral, written, and multimedia communication in a variety of forms and contexts.

2. Thinking and Problem-Solving Skills

   > *Critical Thinking and Systems Thinking*—Exercising sound reasoning in understanding and making complex choices, understanding the interconnectedness among systems.

   > *Problem Identification, Formulation, and Solution*—Knowing how to frame, analyze, and solve problems.

   > *Creativity and Intellectual Curiosity*—Developing, implementing, and communicating new ideas to others; staying open and responsive to new and diverse perspectives.

3. Interpersonal and Self-Directional Skills

   > *Interpersonal and Collaborative Skills*—Demonstrating teamwork and leadership; adapting to varied roles and responsibilities; working productively with others; exercising empathy; respecting diverse perspectives.

   > *Self-Direction*—Monitoring one's own understanding and learning needs, locating appropriate resources, transferring learning from one domain to another.

   > *Accountability and Adaptability*—Exercising personal responsibility and flexibility in personal, workplace, and community contexts; setting and meeting high standards and goals for one's self and others; tolerating ambiguity.

   > *Social Responsibility*—Acting responsibly with the interests of the larger community in mind; demonstrating ethical behavior in personal, workplace, and community contexts. (9)

These skills are evident in the presentation of every speaker who comes to our class, regardless of what field they come from or what level they hold. The woman from In-N-Out Burger and the man from the vocational college emphasize and embody these learning skills as much as speakers from different professions who talk to us.

Focusing on the Skills Needed for the "Flat" World

It is Tom Friedman (2005) and his notion of a "flat" world, however, that I want to focus on here, for his "flatteners," forces that level the playing field in the global economy, represent the most significant challenge to students and their teachers. As Friedman points out, people can participate and compete in ways they never could before, thanks to increased access to advanced technologies (212). In addition to access, people in such countries as India and China have "a very high ethics of education" (213), a quality that drives them to be insatiable learners who are very outcome oriented. What, then, are the core aspects of a twenty-first-century education? Tom Friedman answers this question by identifying the roles and responsibilities that we will need in coming years. Friedman offers eight roles that will create "the New Middle [class]," saying that students need to be great

> collaborators and orchestrators
> synthesizers
> explainers
> leveragers
> adapters
> green people
> personalizers
> localizers

His point, which I examine in the remainder of the chapter, is that a flat world is a competitive world in which, thanks to digitization and the Internet, work will increasingly go to the people with the best skills, who can do it within the necessary time constraints, for the best price, regardless of where they live. Recently, for example, while thinking through a project, I was told that we could save significant money and time if "we had China do the graphics and design." Thus Friedman argues for the eight different roles, all of which will make people more "untouchable" by making their jobs less likely to be outsourced or made obsolete as a result of automation by computers.

The Great Collaborators and Orchestrators

Examples of collaboration in the workplace are omnipresent. The firefighter who comes in to talk to my ACCESS class tells us that while all must have the same set of general skills, each of the firefighters must also develop a specialty to round out the team. It is these different skill sets that require them to collaborate, each bringing their knowledge and skills to the situation to help the others. The FedEx manager spoke not only about delivering packages but also about coordinating and orchestrating a complex operation of people, packages, and equipment distributed across several different locations, all of which have to work together to get the packages to people on time. Still others talk at length about the need to work within systems that can be spread out across geographical boundaries and that are often complicated by cultural and linguistic differences, all of which they and their colleagues must learn to see not as obstacles, but as resources.

What are the implications of all this for me in my classroom? While there are parallels in all subject areas, I focus on language arts and literacy, as these make up the world in which I work as a high school English teacher. To help my students become effective collaborators and orchestrators, I can

> < < < < <
>
> As you think about collaboration in the classroom, and about the complications posed by cultural and linguistic differences, take a look at Chapter 8 by Aguilar, Fu, and Jago, where they discuss these issues at length.
>
> —*KB, REP, LR*

> > use groups or teams in a variety of ways, asking them to come up with multiple solutions to the same problem (e.g., different interpretations of the same text, various ways to present the same information)

> > assign individuals different roles and ask them to collaborate with others to assemble their disparate ideas into a coherent whole that they must then synthesize into a visual explanation, paper, performance, or presentation

> > establish a threaded discussion online through which students must work together to make sense of a topic or text, posing and responding to each other's ideas

> > rotate their seating assignments every three or four weeks, telling them they cannot sit next to anyone they have already sat next to; this ensures that they work with different people and encounter alternative perspectives, including students from different cultures and backgrounds

> > use corporate-style facilitation protocols like Open Space (www.openspaceworld.org) and Save the Last Word for Me (www.nsrfharmony.org/protocol/learning_texts.html) to lead discussions of complex and controversial ideas (participants follow a prescribed sequence of steps that develop the skills needed to contribute to substantial discussions)

The Great Synthesizers

In his book *A Whole New Mind: Why Right-Brainers Will Rule the Future*, Daniel Pink (2006) argues that "symphony" is one of the essential aptitudes in the future global economy. Pink insists that "it is the capacity to synthesize rather than analyze; to see relationships between seemingly unrelated fields; to detect broad patterns rather than to deliver specific answers; and to invent something new by combining elements nobody else thought to pair" (130) that will be valued and rewarded in the workplace of the future. Friedman says it a bit differently, emphasizing that one must be able to not only see or detect seemingly unrelated pieces—of information, systems, concepts—but also combine them in ways no one has considered, thereby making something new. I have come to think of this as a characteristically American concept: *e pluribus unum*. This phrase embodies what we try to do in our classes: take the many (perspectives, texts, ideas) and synthesize them into one new idea and form that draws on all the others that came before it.

Pink (2006) examines this essential skill in the context of what he calls the Conceptual Age, which follows on the heels of the Information Age. Symphony, he argues, requires people to understand the connection between diverse, and seemingly separate, disciplines. He further explains that analogical reasoning, that ability to see the relationship between apparently different things, is a critical skill. Marzano, Pickering, and Pollock (2001) address this skill, insisting that teachers look for opportunities to compare and contrast as a means of arriving at a deeper understanding of the content. In addition, teachers can incorporate and improve synthesis by having students

> > > > > >
It's interesting to think through the roles that Jim explains in this chapter with comments about literacy coaches from Kathy Egawa's chapter (19) in mind. Literacy coaches are orchestrators, synthesizers, explainers, and most certainly leveragers (see below).
> > > > > —*KB, REP, LR*

> consider an idea, event, or problem from multiple perspectives before synthesizing their thoughts through a discussion or presentation

> read a variety of texts and genres in order to explore a topic from different perspectives and then incorporate these different ideas into one paper that integrates the many into one new text

> produce a presentation using a visual representation or a program like PowerPoint that requires they use multiple sources and integrate the different sources into one slide with the three points common to all the sources.

The Great Explainers

As processes and products become more complex in design and function, people will rely increasingly on others to help them understand how the processes and products work. Friedman offers the example of a photography store whose business changed dramatically with the arrival of digital photography. The owners responded by transforming their business into one devoted to training people how to use the new cameras and print their images using the store's high-quality printers. As the business grew, people wanted to learn more complex aspects of digital photography, such as how to manipulate images using software programs, and the store was happy to teach those skills, too—after they found a good explainer to help them understand these processes themselves.

Pink (2006) offers a useful variation on Friedman's role of explainer. He argues that one of the six essential skills for future success will be telling and using stories. Focusing on the role of the right hemisphere of the brain, which considers information in the larger context of the big picture, Pink describes story as "the fundamental instrument of thought" (101), one capable of explaining ideas in ways we will remember if the teller "has the ability to place these facts in *context* and to deliver them with *emotional impact*" (103). Friedman would no doubt say that Pink is an excellent explainer who uses stories to persuade and clarify for others what he means or how things work. Their ideas suggest that students should

> > learn the elements of narrative; after all, the financial analyst should know how to tell a story about the company using numbers, and the scientist must tell the story about how her research can improve the human condition

> > use visual explanations and multimedia applications to tell stories instead of present facts (Atkinson 2005)

> > write personal narratives to refine and reinforce their understanding and use of the narrative elements

The Great Leveragers

Friedman's term *leverager* is a bit abstract, but the idea stresses a crucial skill for future success: managing oneself despite a constantly evolving workplace that demands new skills and abilities from its workers. Leveraging, as Friedman describes it, means making the greatest use of various systems, technology, and processes in order to achieve a desired result. Thus, a great leverager must know more than others about how to use certain tools and processes. Friedman provides a useful generic description: a great leverager will know how to *identify* a problem, *analyze* its causes, *solve* it, then *redesign* that process or system to ensure it does not happen again, in a way others can understand and replicate. Peter Drucker (1999), the great business philosopher who coined the term *knowledge worker*, would sum up this notion by saying that leveragers know their strengths

< < < < <
This notion of leveraging means more when considered against the multiliteracies Donna Alvermann describes in Chapter 3 and the opportunities for using technology (thus improving leveraging ability) that Sara Kajder describes in Chapter 14.

—*KB, REP, LR*

and how to use them to solve a range of problems vital to the business they are in, and thus they are essential to the company for which they work.

The *Learning for the 21st Century* report discussed earlier reinforces Friedman's emphasis on these skills. Teachers can help students manage themselves and discover their strengths by having them

> > identify, through reflection on and various self-assessments of their learning styles and abilities, their strengths and how they can best use those to succeed in school and the workplace

> > listen to speakers from and read about the world of work and the skills needed to succeed there

> > learn the strategies needed to organize and complete their work

> > develop their ability to use a range of tools and means and to choose from among those tools to solve various intellectual problems

> > reflect on the process by which they solved a problem to improve their awareness of their own strengths and weaknesses while focusing on how they could do the same tasks better next time

The Adapters

Perhaps no other skill better captures the essence of the future than adaptability. When the fire chief comes to speak to my ACCESS class, he talks first about what it was like when he joined the department. In short, you had to be a strong man (who worked only with other men) who could aim the hose at the fire until it went out. As other emergency services were established and then began to consolidate, largely because of decreasing budgets, firefighters found themselves having to learn medical skills; as equipment (e.g., computers) with toxic components appeared, the methods of extinguishing fires became more complicated; and, of course, after September 11, firefighters had to learn about biological, chemical, and even nuclear warfare and how they would respond to it in the event of an attack. The fire chief emphasized the constant cycle of learning that now characterizes their work, making firefighters' ability to learn as crucial as their ability to respond, extinguish, and treat.

> > > *What does it mean to be a versatilist? Friedman compares it to training as an Olympic athlete for an event you won't know you are doing until you arrive at the stadium. For education, this skill—being able to adapt—implies not only preparing to do different things or play different roles but also learning to use a variety of tools or techniques to solve emerging problems.*

Friedman says the future demands versatile generalists, those who can adapt their current skills and knowledge to solve the problems and meet the needs of different situations that will arise. In part, this quality is necessary because of a shrinking workforce: companies want one person who can do three things well because they cannot afford to hire three people who each do one thing well. "Versatilists," as Friedman calls them, "can apply depth of skill to a progressively widening scope of situations and experiences, gaining new competencies, building relationships, and assuming new roles" (2005, 289). They not only adapt but continually learn and grow, using these skills and knowledge in ways described in the section about great leveragers. According to Friedman, workers in almost any field must essentially become the human equivalent of Swiss Army knives.

What does it mean to be a versatilist? Friedman compares it to training as an Olympic athlete for an event you won't know you are doing until you arrive at the stadium. For education, this skill—being able to adapt—implies not only preparing to do different things or play different roles but also learning to use a variety of tools or techniques to solve emerging problems. In the past, you could be a hammer and treat the world as a nail; today you must be a toolbox that can ask itself which tool is the best for the job. Moreover, it means being able to adapt your perspective in light of cultural or other factors that may affect the situation. Thus teachers find themselves wondering how to teach adaptability in the class so students will have it when they enter the world. To achieve this result, teachers might

> require students to work within different constraints that challenge them in productive ways

> bring speakers into the class from the work world so students hear what people in different fields must know and how they are expected to work

> ask students to assume a variety of roles within a given assignment

> demand that students do the same assignment in different ways, using different tools or techniques, some of which they may need to learn in order to complete the work

Green People

While not directly related to Friedman's concept of green people, Howard Gardner added to his list of multiple intelligences "naturalist intelligence," which he defines as enabling "human beings to recognize, categorize and draw upon certain features of the environment. It combines a description of the core ability with a characterization of the role that many cultures value" (1999, 48). The "biological renaissance" that Friedman refers to is not a skill set as much as it is an emerging opportunity, "an era in which college students, instead of becoming doctors, might instead focus on bio-derived or bio-inspired solutions to our looming energy and environmental problems" (2005, 293).

What knowledge and skills—what environmental literacies—will be needed, and how might we develop them in our classes? Gardner offers a compelling beginning by focusing on the observational and analytical competencies such an intelligence will demand of people. In addition to integrating opportunities for the refinement of such skills, teachers might incorporate readings and activities that simply develop and sustain an increased awareness of the environment and our impact on it in the past, present, and future. Students in my English class, for example, often take an environmental biology class that requires them to collaborate on and design ecosystems that they must observe, drawing on many of the other skills described previously, but having the primary effect of making them aware of how one element in the environment affects another. Thus they become not ecologists or biologists but systems thinkers, people capable of seeing and working within an existing system that will demand the intelligence of many in the future to keep it healthy.

Passionate Personalizers

In a global world, one in which a college graduate in India might serve as a digital assistant to an American boss, creating presentations, formatting documents, arranging appointments, and scheduling flights—all while his American boss sleeps—the marketplace is more and more about skills and services. Many of these can be handled anywhere, thanks to digital technologies. When my sister ends her shift at an American package delivery service around dinnertime, her work is resumed for the night by a woman of perhaps the same age in India, who uses the same skills my sister does to earn a fraction of what my sister makes doing the same work. It is almost inevitable that soon the work will be done exclusively by such Indian call center workers—until, that is, voice recognition software improves and replaces people altogether. Already we find ourselves talking to machines that can tell us if there is a flight at a certain time or ask us whether our package is ready for pickup. Thus we arrive at Friedman's next skill set: personalizing.

The great personalizers take a basic service and transform it into something only they can do or that meets some local need the community has. It is the extra touch in a service that inspires loyalty in customers or the added value that you cannot get by going outside the community. As Friedman emphasizes, it is a social dimension of service, delivered in a way that customers value enough to pay for. Again, returning to Gardner's multiple intelligences, we might think of personalizing as a manifestation of "interpersonal intelligence [that] is concerned with the capacity to understand the intentions, motivations, and desires of other people. It allows people to work effectively with others. Educators, salespeople, religious and political leaders, and counselors all need a well-developed interpersonal intelligence" (1999, 43).

English teachers might make a note about the need for such personal skills and their implications for communication. Specifically, teachers might have students

> use format, design, and style in documents and other communication products (e.g., presentations, PowerPoint documents) to meet others' needs instead of just their own; students might, for example, design a brochure for someone other than themselves, a client with specific needs and values

> communicate and interact with a range of people through different group protocols designed to best meet the needs of the group

> evaluate, critique, and redesign certain workplace documents to improve their effect on customers

> identify areas of improvement around the community and design signs, services, or products to best meet these needs (One year students in my remedial English class—when such a class still existed—designed and created a community resource directory that they published for local real estate agents and their prospective clients.)

> focus on design (not at the expense of substance) when creating presentations or documents or even the medium they use to convey that information

This set of skills is one we all value. While perhaps it is hard to see how we might teach them, these services help us work well and feel better as we crash through the storm of demands that often haunt our busy days. Passionate personalizers—the real estate agent who remembers me and sends periodic personal notes about houses coming onto the market (houses I will never be able to afford); the woman at the coffee shop who stops to help me figure out which coffee I want and how it should be ground; the mechanic who accommodates my busy schedule; the organization that makes information available online so I don't have to go to their office—are people and agencies who ask how they can meet my needs and thus get and keep my business. There is an ethos to these people and businesses that, while we cannot always directly teach or test in our classes, we can stress as a value in the way we have students work.

The Great Localizers

The last skill represents a paradox of sorts: how to use global resources and technologies to create local solutions. Central to this skill is the ability to find appropriate resources outside of the local context and use them in ways that improve efficiency and reduce costs. Friedman includes the example of the café that offers a range of services—for example, wireless Internet access, a fax machine, space to work and meet—in order to keep customers in their seats longer and thus make more money. He also discusses the local auto repair shop that offers to order supplies for your BMW from Romania for half the cost of ordering the same parts from New York. Thus the localizers are adept researchers, constantly surveying the markets that support their business.

In the future, everyone will have to know how to investigate different subjects for personal and professional reasons. As health care and retirement become more individual responsibilities, as current trends suggest they must, we will all have to find information we can use to make decisions about the products we use, services we choose, or places we invest our money. Such information literacy is at the heart of what Friedman describes when it comes to localization. To that end, teachers of tomorrow's students should today have their students

> generate useful research questions about a wide range of subjects across disciplines

> learn to use a range of search strategies and tools to find different types of information needed to solve an informational problem

> research a topic from multiple angles to find alternative solutions to the problems they are trying to solve

> use various persuasive and rhetorical strategies to create a compelling advertisement or brochure for a real or imaginary business

Implications for the Classroom

In exploring Friedman's ideas here, I have offered representative examples to illustrate what each of these skills might look like when addressed in the classroom. Many of these skills challenge the foundations of the curriculum we have taught for so long, raising questions such as what English language arts should be and how much literature students need to read, given all the emerging skills they will require if our country is to remain the economic power it has been. As an English teacher, however, I won't be arguing for throwing out a discipline I love and that can accomplish so much. Still, we need to develop a new vision— if not a vision of what English language arts offers, then at least a vision of how it achieves its stated ends.

One area that gets more and more attention in research is *discussion*, specifically how to use it to increase engagement and improve understanding (Nystrand 2006). While I have worked to improve discussion in class using such traditional techniques as literature circles (Daniels 2001) and Socratic seminars (Copeland 2005), I have begun to look to two other techniques, both of which offer a glimpse into new ways to have kids work while simultaneously developing some of the essential literacies Friedman outlines in his book *The World Is Flat* (2005). Specifically, I have used technology outside the classroom to complement our work inside the classroom, typically through threaded discussions, email, and a service called School Loop. In addition to such technology-based approaches, I have explored the use of various protocols originally designed to facilitate discussion in meetings and the world of business but which adapt themselves well to the classroom and develop skills kids need to succeed in the world of work. Examples of such protocols are Open Space and Save the Last Word for Me (both of which were mentioned on page 153).

I want to end this chapter by walking readers through two sample threaded discussions, one of which I conducted in my AP English literature class with seniors and the second of which I carried out with my ACCESS class, a group of freshmen who came into high school reading several grades below the ninth grade. Both discussions happened in the opening weeks of school.

Seniors returning from summer had read a number of books with strong women characters and feminist issues. Without going into any detail about feminist criticism, I simply posted the text in Figure 10–1 on School Loop, an integrated communication service for students and teachers (www.schoolloop.com).

I told them they had up to a week to post either a question or a comment. I was completely unprepared for the quality and quantity of the responses from students whose names I was still learning that first week. While we engaged in initial discussions in class about these same texts, the threaded discussion allowed us to extend the conversation beyond the classroom at the same time that it began to enrich it, for students in class discussions began to refer to comments others made outside of class in the online forum.

My most significant concern was what I should be doing to address their needs and ensure that this experience developed some of the skills Friedman says are so essential to their success in the world. As the discussion took off, I found myself observing how they behaved and thought, concluding, as some studies (Grisham and Wolsey 2006) have found, that the teacher's role is to monitor and guide students toward deeper and more elaborate inquiries and responses.

When the week was over, unquestionably the most dynamic first week I've ever had in the classroom, the transcript from the two classes was forty pages long. During that week, I would say I spent about an hour monitoring and skimming their responses; after all, I was busy trying to get lessons planned and do other things, so I needed to know that I didn't have to read every word. Figure 10–2 offers a glimpse into the format and quality of the discussion. In some instances, I responded to an individual student's remarks; on other occasions, I

> < < < < <
> Jim is touching on a critical point here about discussion that is discussed in greater detail in Bob's chapter (5) and Smokey's chapter (9).
> —*KB, REP, LR*

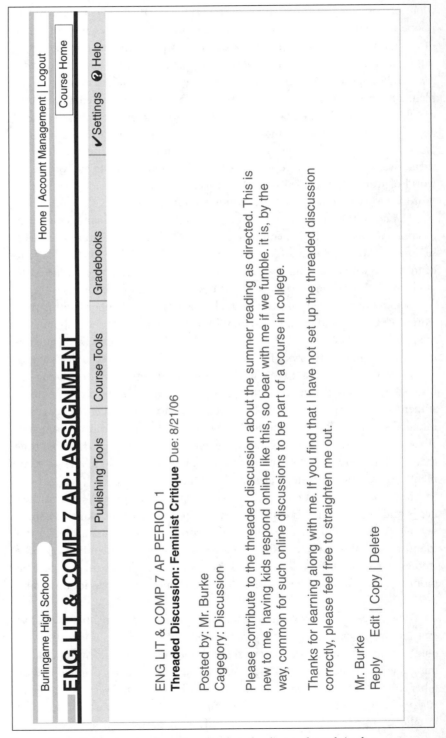

FIGURE 10–1. *Students not only wrote online but also discussed novels in class.*

tried to guide the discussion, making larger observations about the emerging patterns in the hope of guiding them into new and deeper inquiries.

Once the week was up, I asked students to reflect on the experience by responding to four questions. One senior student's response can be found in Figure 10–3.

From: Alexandor Zimmerman
Subject: Re:Re:feminist critique   Date: 8/20/06 11:42 AM

I strongly agree with Rachel and Makenna in this observation of Pride and Prejudice and I'll take it a step further. I believe that Jane Austin puts a real importance in the character of Elizabeth Bennet and she is promoting her kind of attitude towards the imbalance of gender in society. Austen suggests that women like Elizabeth, socially powerful (now married to Darcy) and very opiniative, will become very influential women's rights movements in the future. Women like Elizabeth can be portrayed as the socially powerful figures who supported women's rights movements throughout history, like Abigail Adams and Eleanor Roosevelt. Jane Austen may have intended to spark a realization in her society back in 1813 that more women like Elizabeth and not Ms. Bennet were needed.

Reply to This Post | Reply to Main Post | Edit | Delete

From: Mr. Burke
Subject Boundary between art and propaganda   Date: 8/15/06 10:47 PM

Makenna suggests a new angle on the subject by "making the woman argumentative." Is the writer using literature as a means of advertising what should be, advocating a position for women in the society or reaching for a larger, more universal truth? Does a work qualify as "art" or "literature" if it advances a socio-political agenda for change?

Reply to This Post | Reply to Main Post | Edit | Delete

From: Mr. Burke
Subject: Source of woman's power   Date: 8/15/06 8:41 PM

Several of these posts seem to raise the question of the source of women's power in the stories and their relationships with those around them. An interesting thread that runs through the comments. I wonder if the source(s) of women's power have changed in the last hundred years, particularly in the cultures where these novels are set.

Reply to This Post | Reply to Main Post | Edit | Delete

From: Spencer Currie
Subject: Re:Source of women's power   Date: 8/16/06 9:47 PM

Power has moved from domestic to professional-while money is always a dictator of power. Nora's power stems from her dealings within the home and taking financial matters into her own hands, similar to Mrs. Joe's

FIGURE 10–2. *Excerpt from Threaded Discussion on Summer Reading*

A SENIOR RESPONDS (ONLINE) TO INVITATION TO REFLECT ON THE PROCESS

1. **How does the online/threaded discussion compare to in-class discussion?**

   I think the discussion was more in depth. People in class all have ideas, but are too shy to say anything for fear of getting the "wrong answer." With the Internet as a barrier, you have time to craft a well-developed response and no INSTANT feedback.

2. **Does the online discussion allow for a different way of responding than in-class?**

   See above. You can speak your mind more.

3. **Did the discussion lead you to new insights in the books we discussed? Explain.**

   The online discussion went for around a week (I think). Many new ideas were added throughout the course of that time. It was fun to read all of the responses!! You can't do that type of discussion in a 50-minute period, and even if you continue it to the next day, people won't remember what they say.

4. **Anything else**

   However beneficial an online discussion, I like the human interaction that class discussion has to provide. There is always that "element" missing in an online discussion because you can't really "see" the circumstances in which a person says something for a reason.

   EXAMPLE: Question is asked whether feminism has been lost. One person could have differing opinions from day to day if they experience sexism. It all depends on circumstances.

FIGURE 10–3. *One Student's Reflections on the Threaded Discussion Experience*

It is easy to argue that such an effective exchange is the inevitable result of having an advanced class of seniors. No question. Still, engagement remains a major issue for all students, seniors included. Students from my classes began talking to their other teachers about the experience, telling them they should try it, that the kids found it exciting. Within two weeks, social studies teachers were asking me how to set up a discussion about revolution, and a biology teacher wanted to create a discussion on the ethical implications of certain issues in that field. While the seniors' success matters to me, it is the kids in my ACCESS program, some of whom lack computers at home and the necessary technological skills, whom I most I wanted the discussions to help. They need to learn to communicate in writing, access information, and participate in productive discussions, all of which are essential (Burke 2006) to their success in school and the world for which we are preparing them.

Because I could not assume they had computers, I brought my class to the library to show them how School Loop worked and how to log on to the school system. This proved useful, as their teachers were already posting homework to School Loop and assigning work based on certain websites.

Over the course of the next week, students posted comments and responses, all of which found their way into class as discussion points. Given the concern about the "digital divide" (Trotter 2006), the work we did in the initial weeks in both classes (but especially the ACCESS class) was well worth the time. Students were engaged *and* productive, working at higher levels earlier in the year than I had ever achieved before, and working in ways that made a bigger difference in their other academic classes. As they worked, I thought of the different aptitudes Daniel Pink discusses in his book *A Whole New Mind* (2006): design, story, symphony, empathy, play, and meaning. They seemed present in varying degrees in our work that first week, as if all cylinders of the students' brains were lighting up as they told their stories through an experience I designed in order to create a sense of cohesion within the class. The assignment forced them to work together in playfully intelligent and productive ways that were meaningful to them.

> > > *If Friedman's is a flat world, it is also a brave new world, one in which we are inextricably a part, and where success and well-being go to those who learn how to live in it despite its ever-changing demands.*

We can never do it all, never hit every standard or goal we are reaching for, but if we allow ourselves to be guided by such principles as Pink and Friedman offer, our classes—and our students—will accomplish more. When I sat down to design the weeklong threaded discussions in both classes, I made my decisions based not only on state standards but also on Friedman's eight skills, asking myself how I could get the kids to be great collaborators and adapters; how I could help them be great synthesizers and explainers. I do this in an effort to be, I suppose, a passionate personalizer who uses the global resources available to me as a great localizer, who wants *all* his students to leave school ready to adapt what they have learned in my class to whatever realm they choose to enter. If Friedman's is a flat world, it is also a brave new world, one of which we are inextricably a part, and where success and well-being go to those who learn how to live in it despite its ever-changing demands. This is the world for which I prepare my students; it is this world and this century to which I must adapt if I am to be the teacher who meets the needs of my students and the larger world.

When you want to know more . . .

Jim offers a lot of practical suggestions for helping students into twenty-first-century literacy (or for helping us catch up with our twenty-first-century students). You'll find even more in *50 Essential Lessons: Tools and Techniques for Teaching English Language Arts* (2006) and in *Illuminating Texts: How to Teach Students to Read the World* (2001).

Connecting to my thoughts

Connecting to other texts

WEBSITES FOR YOUR STUDENTS TO VISIT REGULARLY

To help your students interact with the news, visit the Newseum, the Interactive Museum of News: www.newseum.org/todaysfrontpages/.

To bring history alive, go to the Library of Congress American Memory page and click on any of the links, including the Today in History link: http://memory.loc.gov/ammem/index.html.

To help expand vocabulary, send students to the Merriam Webster Word of the Day site: www.m-w.com/cgi-bin/mwwod.pl.

To enjoy a poem each and every day, go to the Library of Congress Poetry 180 site: www.loc.gov/poetry/180/p180-list.html.

To see the world, visit the National Geographic Site: www.national geographic.com.

To hear some of the great speeches of our world, go to the History Channel site: www.history.com/media.do.

Teaching Writing from the Inside

Discovery and Surprise

I BEGAN TO LOVE writing during the back-to-back forty-five-minute study halls we seventh graders ended our school day with in 1961. Since little more than breathing was permitted in study hall, my buddy Jackie and I passed the time by writing stories of war and heroism for each other. The previous summer Jackie had played third base to my shortstop. The more we wrote, the more I grew to like talking on the page, creating a verbal performance that I passed up the aisle to Jackie. He was an appreciative audience. I didn't have to say a word aloud, yet could see Jackie's positive response to my words when he turned his head my way, grinning broadly, eyebrows raised in pleasurable surprise.

These many years later, I recognize the agency I was experiencing as a twelve-year-old, the creator of a fictional world in which my friends and I triumphed. The writing was an expression of my evolving ego, a little of which is requisite for every writer. We must come to believe that our writing is worth reading by others. I also realize that something else was at work in that afternoon study hall: I was taking pleasure in using language to create, in forming

While Don Murray (Chapter 12) shows us how to write alongside our students, Tom Romano shows us all the things we (and our students) need to do to make our writing exciting, make it alive, make it writing that needs to be read. This chapter follows Jim's thoughts on literacy in the "flat" world because no matter the shape of the world, writing will always be critical. And though you might be reading it at any point, you'll want to make sure you read Don's chapter and Linda's chapter (13) soon after reading this one.

—*KB, REP, LR*

meaningful, syntactic units with words and phrases that arose in me, a pleasure just as fulfilling in its own way as stabbing a bounding grounder deep in the hole at shortstop and wheeling to throw to first. W. H. Auden said it this way:

> Language is the mother, not the handmaiden, of thought; words will tell you things you never thought or felt before. (quoted in Murray 1982, 85)

In my state's thick book of academic standards for K–12 English language arts there is no mention of Auden's core truth about the magical power of language. At the seventh-grade level there is a standard for establishing a thesis statement, one for determining purpose and audience, one for varying simple, compound, and complex sentence structures—thirty standards in all about writing. But there is nothing explicit about learning to cultivate and revel in the surprise and discovery that accompanies working with words.

Writers Show Us

One best practice for teaching writing is to heed the behaviors of professional writers (Murray 1990; Ray 1999; Romano 2004). A writer I have looked to recently for guidance is Ken Brewer, poet laureate of Utah at the time of his death in March 2006. I came to know Ken when I taught at Utah State University. We remained friends over the next fourteen years. When he was diagnosed with pancreatic cancer, Ken was at the height of his skills as a poet. He was clear-eyed, tough-minded, and compassionate. Through most of the nine months of his illness, he wrote poetry about what was happening to him. In the introduction to his posthumously published *Whale Song: A Poet's Journey into Cancer*, he wrote, "Writing began to heal my spirit" (Brewer 2006).

Here is a poem Ken sent to me three months after the diagnosis:

Waiting for the Dog

Gus is a black miniature schnauzer
with a red collar. When we let him out
at night in our fenced-in back yard,
still we put a plastic collar on him.
It blinks a pink light so we can see
that he hasn't vanished in the dark.

I understand this need for coming home,
for being safe in the house, as in place
as the couch, the table, the kitchen sink.
Perhaps, I, too, need a collar with lights
to keep me ashore, to let everyone know
that I am here no matter how dark the night.

The poem's unpretentious eloquence moves me. Ken respects simple, tangible things: schnauzer, night, fenced-in yard, blinking light. He describes and explores, imagines and speculates. Since I knew Ken, the poem carries extra emotional impact for me. I didn't want my friend to vanish into that night. My bereavement, though, does not keep me from marveling at Ken's urge—even with darkness clearly ahead—to use the gift of language we all possess to write about his experience.

In an email message to me, Ken described his writing process:

> Tom—I never know where a poem is heading as I begin it. After writing "Waiting for the Dog," I began to think of the title as a subtle hint of "Waiting for Godot" and the metaphor in the second stanza surprised me too. That shift from a light in a dark back yard to a light in a light tower along some coast, bringing in the sea/water image (or symbol). That just came as I was writing, with no plan at all. It's a leap, but I think it works and I don't mind "leaps." I prefer to start a poem with something that gives me image and detail (foundation) right away, then write to expand that to some other level or meaning. Always, the language surprises and teaches me.

Ken does not say that he knows the meaning he is going to express before he writes. He does not say he chooses words to communicate already fully formed ideas. He does not say that the writing process is static. He says just the opposite: "I never know where a poem is heading as I begin it" and "Always, the language surprises and teaches me." Ken describes a dynamic writing process in which writers plunge ahead with faith and fearlessness, keeping on their semantic toes, alert for surprises of meaning and insight, a process in which writers learn what they want to say while they are writing. Ken had a method for how he wrote, though it was hardly a formulaic one: *Start with images and details and follow where they lead.* There is a sense of adventure in that, a willingness, a longing even, to encounter the unexpected. I'd like to see the essence of Ken's credo written into an academic standard for writing: "Students will learn to write expansively, trusting language to lead them to surprises of meaning and insight." That is easily as important as using "organizational strategies to plan writing" and establishing and developing "a clear thesis statement for informational writing or a clear plan or outline for narrative writing" (Ohio Department of Education 2001, 238).

Trusting language to lead to meaning can be hard to embrace. It seems counterintuitive to education, the opposite of what is supposed to happen in school, where the rational, the planned, and the scientific reign. Surely, we decide what we are going to write, plan it, and then carry out the plan. Surely, before we start to

> > > > *Ken describes a dynamic writing process in which writers plunge ahead with faith and fearlessness, keeping on their semantic toes, alert for surprises of meaning and insight, a process in which writers learn what they want to say while they are writing.*

> > > *Language is our canoe up the wilderness river, our bush plane, our space capsule, our magic. Instead of "now you see it, now you don't," using language works in reverse: "now you don't see it, now you do."*

write, we know point A, point B, and point C. The truth, however, is that sometimes writers plan in detail, sometimes they plan a little, and sometimes they don't plan at all. Even when writing is guided by a plan, we have a better chance of producing something interesting, readable, and true if at some point we let go so that language can do what it does best: think. Language is not just for expression and communication. Language is for discovery. Actually putting words on the page leads to meaning, connections, associations, ideas, and refinements of ideas. Language is our canoe up the wilderness river, our bush plane, our space capsule, our magic. Instead of "now you see it, now you don't," using language works in reverse: "now you don't see it, now you do."

What's True for All Writing

I told a friend the story of Ken's email message about the role that surprise and discovery played in his writing process. My friend works for a job-recruiting firm and writes plenty of analytical mini-essays about job candidates. Incisiveness, accuracy, and clarity mark her written voice. "Oh," she said in response to Ken's comments, "but that's creative writing."

She saw a distinction between how language works for creative writing and how it works for, well, uncreative writing. I don't see such a distinction. While I recognize different genres and subgenres of writing, I believe that using language is a generative act of creativity. When I write a letter imploring a committee not to trivialize the use of portfolios in the assessment it devises, I count on the process of using language to lead me to surprises in thinking and persuasive examples to support my stance. When I write a poem, I count on language to help me to see vivid images, to strike upon rhythmical patterns of words, and to make understated assertions. When I create a grocery list, I count on language associations to spark my thinking and stock my pantry: I write *hot dogs* and think asudden of *buns* and *mustard*. Now you don't see it, now you do—that's how language works.

I want writing to become second nature to students. That means they have to write many genres for a variety of purposes. I want writing to be as natural for them as slipping on sandals. I want students to consciously know that language is a mighty ally that stands with them, whether they write from the heart or tackle mandatory writing tasks that have been thrust upon them. Students should be diving into quickwrites without stress or much forethought, this to get into the habit of producing language effortlessly. Students should be writing journal entries, responses to literature, and think pieces about concepts and phenomena in their coursework. Most importantly, just like writers who scratch their own itches, students need time and support in choosing their own topics to write about, time and support to explore with language those physical, emotional, and intellectual experiences that matter to them. Words hold magic. We activate the magic by employing language with faith and fearlessness, by accepting and encouraging the flood of words that volunteers itself when we think. Ken Brewer practiced that magic over a span of forty years. I want students to practice it, too, so that, like Ken, it becomes natural for them to write about their thoughts and feelings.

Teacher as Writer

Those who teach a craft ought to do the craft. When teachers of writing write, particularly in the genres they teach, they develop insider knowledge. They know what makes sense in teaching writing. They know what doesn't. Teachers who write demonstrate to students someone who loves to think, explore, and communicate through writing. Teachers who write know the challenges, failures, and triumphs of composing with words. They know the emotional territory students inhabit when they write.

I can't say that every teacher who writes will be a good writing teacher. Nor can I say that teachers who *do not* write cannot be good writing teachers. Teachers who write, though, have a jump on teachers who don't. They not only have empathy for student writers but also gain credibility in students' eyes.

> > > *I want writing to become second nature to students. That means they have to write many genres for a variety of purposes. I want writing to be as natural for them as slipping on sandals.*

Teachers who write speak with authority. They do not merely exhort students with rules and advice about writing—even sensible rules and advice. They demonstrate how writing is done. I don't ask students to do anything as a writer that I haven't done. Brainstorm ideas? I do that on the board or overhead. Create a compelling lead? I write five leads to a piece and bring them to class to discuss the merits of each. Revise writing to give "second genius" a chance to kick in (Stafford 2003, 36)? I show students my gloriously messy drafts riddled with fruitful expansion, clarifications, and sharpened focus.

I show students how one writer creates. I show them that writing is not done only by distant authors. Writing is also done by someone they know, in this case, someone who respects their voices, someone they have come to trust for solid information, someone who has worked at the labor-intensive, fulfilling process of writing.

I often show students various stages of my writing. Here is an excerpt from my journal that I produced one morning while writing with a group of teachers. I took the prompt to "write about your name." I explored and rambled for a page and a half about the origin of my name and my dislike of *Thomas*, before finally coming to this:

> But I did like to be called Tom. I still like hearing my wife say my name—Tom—and I like hearing my friend from Florida call me long distance to Ohio and the first thing I hear him say over the phone is "Tom!" I can think back 45 years ago, before my father died, and I imagine a long day ending in midsummer, the sun long set, but still just a little light yet to make shadows. I hear my father call out from the top of the steps at the back porch, "Tom! Come on home!" I'd come running, maybe take me a minute from some far off place in the neighborhood and even with just that short time it seemed that by the time I got to the bottom of the steps, the night had grown pitch dark. When I looked upstairs to the screendoor, there was no one behind it, daddy having gone into the house, knowing that his voice—the voice I still remember, though it is long dead—his voice would bring me out of the darkness into the yellow porch light of the yard. His voice would bring me home.

I typed this journal excerpt (see Figure 11–1) so that you could easily read the digging I am doing with language. What I did in the classroom, though, was project the journal page on a large screen. I wanted students to see "raw writing," what Ken Brewer called writing produced in initial drafts with little or no revision.

A teacher who writes can pull back the curtain to reveal ways that writing is made. My journal entry features handwriting that has to be legible only to me. It demonstrates thinking that starts to say something one way, stops, crosses out words, then heads off another way. It demonstrates my mind wandering and wondering, prowling for a memory, idea, or observation that's worth cooking in the process of revision.

The poet William Stafford said that "writers recognize opportunities" (1978, 53). I saw an opportunity in the journal entry. Unexpectedly calling forth my father's voice and a time in my summer boyhood interested me. I typed the entry verbatim and then went through it, fleshing it out with information about my father and sensory details of summer nights. Father's Day was two months away, so I sent the draft to the local public radio station, which uses commentaries by listeners. I got back this email from the news director:

> 4/27/06
>
> This looks pretty good, but it's going to be VERY short. Commentaries are typically 3:00 to 3:30. That's typically 2, double-spaced pages.
>
> Here are some things to consider adding:
>
> Where were you a boy in the 1950s?
>
> I'd like to know more about your father. You describe his voice, but I don't

know much else about him from this piece. After all, this is a story about your father. Describe him. What did he look like? What do you remember most about the man? What do you see in yourself that reminds you of your father?

What village in Italy did he leave in 1914? Why did he leave? How/why did he lose his Italian accent?

Irishman—called me that everytime he saw me with such warmth and affection.

But I did like to be called Tom. I still like hearing my wife call me by my say my name — Tom — and I like hearing my friend from Florida call me long distance from to Ohio and the first thing I hear him say is "Tom!" over the phone I can think back 45 years ago, before my father died, and I can imagine a long day ending in mid summer, the sun long set, but still just a little light yet to make shadows. and I hear my father call out from the top of the steps, at the back porch "Tom, Come on home!" and I'd come running, maybe take me a minute seconds from some far off place in the neighborhood and even with just that short time it seemed that by the time I got to the bottom of the steps, ...

FIGURE 11–1. *Raw Writing Sample*

> > > > >
Tom and Don Murray
(Chapter 12) make the same
point about writing with
students. We'd encourage
content area teachers to
remember this is an
important piece of advice
that isn't just for the English
language arts teacher.
—KB, REP, LR

Why were the whiffle ball games so important? Why was it difficult to go home?

You get the idea.

This is a very *good* start to a very touching story. I'd just like to see more details. Make sure that we get to know a little more about the man you're remembering on Father's Day.

The news director gave me a writing conference via email. His questions helped me clarify my intentions. Some I moved on; some I did not. I was creating a piece that became part memoir, part personal essay, part character sketch, with, I hope, the feel of a poem here and there. When teachers actively pursue writing through the entire process from inception of idea to publication of some sort, they can share with students the insider information they gain through experience. The demonstration will deepen students' understanding, demystify the writing process, and show possibilities for writing beyond the classroom.

Multiple Genres

The world of writing is a mural, not a snapshot. I want students' notions of genre to be expansive, not narrow. In school it is easy to get into a genre rut. We need to examine our courses and school curricula for genre hegemony. Does one genre dominate? Is narrative, for example, the primary genre that our students write? (An easy rut to fall into, since storytelling is so natural to people.) Or do students write only responses to literature? (Another easy rut, since the critical essay of literature was the predominant genre many English teachers wrote in college.)

> > > *I don't want students to become Johnny-One-Genres. I want them to examine and communicate through many genres.*

I don't want students to become Johnny-One-Genres. I want them to examine and communicate through many genres. There is much to learn from seeing and writing like essayists, editorialists, playwrights, fiction writers, poets. Through essays, students learn to explore experiences, mixing description with reflection and analysis. Through editorials, students learn to articulate succinct statements of belief and carry out the logic of them persuasively. Through plays, students learn to question characters and themselves in shaping the dynamic, back-and-forth swing of speech. Through fiction, students learn to dramatize action, imagine possibilities, and explore inner thought. Through poetry, students learn to develop imagery, extend metaphor, seek rhythmic, compact language, and experiment with line length and spacing. Genre is the classroom. Language is the teacher.

I would no more restrict students' writing diet to one or two genres than I would restrict their reading diet to one or two genres. Students should read and write personal essays, memoirs, dialogues, poems of many kinds, flash fiction, position statements, letters of praise or commendation or complaint, letters of sincere emotion to friends and family, reviews of books, movies, and music, family histories, character sketches, parodies, fairy tales, eulogies, and more. Students should experiment with different points of view, different voices, different registers of formality. They should aim their writing at varied audiences. The entire curriculum should be rich in writing diversity. Teachers across grade levels need to coordinate their efforts in planning a rich mix of writing experiences for students.

Shaping Writing, Crafting Voice

My ambitions for writing in school are high. It's not enough for students to believe in the magical powers of language and to write with faith and fearlessness. It's not enough for students to have a teacher who writes and demonstrates writing processes and nurtures them with empathy and an eye toward growth and development. It's not enough for students to write in a multitude of genres. I also want students to become sophisticated about the craft of writing. I want them eager to tinker with their writing to make it sing. I want students to learn to take pleasure in shaping. Taking time to shape writing makes writers thoughtful and deliberate. The page is possibility; students create on it.

What I didn't realize during those afternoons back in seventh grade as I hunched over a desk in study hall writing stories to pass to Jackie was this: I was forging an identity. Those pages I carefully tore from the spiral binder were filled with my cramped handwriting. That handwriting represented my twelve-year-old thinking, values, and evolving way with words. I was developing a written voice. I was embarked on a journey of crafting that voice to match the me I wanted to be. I'm still doing that at fifty-eight years old.

I want my college students and the adolescents they one day teach to have opportunities to create their identities on the page. I want them to write with faith and fearlessness, but I also want them to turn their attention to crafting their voices. First-blurt words are essential for getting writing done, but we can often do better than first blurt. We can shape our language and refine our meanings by becoming savvy about working with words.

What do I mean by savvy? I mean big and I mean little. Big: I teach students to hearken to emotions, images, ideas, and stories that are strong in them. I teach them structures of genres. I teach them how to give and receive response on drafts of writing. I teach them habits of revision. Little: I also teach students about the muscle of active verbs and how to tap the generative power of parallel language structure. I teach them the benefits of simplicity and directness, the power of metaphorical language, the convincing nature of sensory details. I teach students how narrative—even bits of narrative in expository writing—draws readers in. I teach them to emphasize a point by placing it in a short sentence. These craft concerns are just some of the delights of working with writing on a word level. Such word work is what writers do. Students learn to work not merely as pupils who write themes. They learn to work as writers.

Word-level work is small but cumulative. It makes students attentive to language, grammar, and possibility. It makes them weigh intention against accomplishment. Leah, a college student, wrote a multigenre paper about her summer work as a waitress at an exclusive country club. At one point she described a fellow waitress who told her that a loathsome but big-tipping regular customer wanted her as his server:

> "Hey, Leah," Collette follows me hurriedly into the kitchen. "Giovanni requested you."

I'd been prodding students to pump up their verbs and eliminate adverbs. Strong verbs add specificity and vividness. Adverbs often indicate wordiness. Leah paid attention. In tinkering with the passage, she strengthened the verb, eliminated the adverb, and, in the process, added language that sharpened the visual detail and introduced movement to capture the harried work of a waitress:

> "Hey, Leah." Collette scurries behind me as I plow through the swinging kitchen doors. "Giovanni requested you."

Such improvements to writing are little triumphs. We need to slow down our instruction and celebrate them. Word must spread around school:
"Ms. Oliver loves little language moves!"
"Use active verbs—Mr. Collins will be ecstatic!"
"Get rid of adverbs and Ms. Nye will give you a better grade!"

The Teacher Wrote

I've spent my professional life teaching writing. My own writing feeds into that teaching, whether I am writing poems, stories, letters to the editor, book reviews, articles, or memoirs. I want students to see writing as more than completing assignments or learning to use writing effectively in the workplace. Oh, I want students to pass future tests of written proficiency. And I want them to use appropriate grammar, usage, punctuation, and spelling. But if they achieve proficiency and appropriateness and rarely write anything personally meaningful again, then I have failed as a writing teacher.

I'm after the heart as well as the head. I want the intellect to grow in its capacity to perceive complexity, to exercise logic, to solve problems. But I also want students to develop compassionate sides to their intellects, ones that value meaningful experiences and seek to render them in ways that touch others.

I'll end this article with "My Father's Voice," the piece I eventually developed from the journal excerpt. I was aiming to merge head and heart. Through his email questions and advice, the news director moved me to revise so that listeners would "get to know a little more about the man" I was remembering. Maybe if I crafted language a little more, I thought, I could touch listeners across time and space. My goal was not dissimilar to how I sought to reach Jackie when I passed those notebook pages up the study hall aisle.

I offer this writing to you in good faith. Maybe you can use the journal entry, the news director's questions, and this final draft to demonstrate how language leads to meaning, how genre transforms when purpose changes, how writing and voice might be crafted, how one writer—a teacher—practices what he promises.

> < < < < < < < <
We hear echoes of Ruth Shagoury (Interlude 1) and Randy Bomer (Chapter 20) as we read this paragraph. Adolescent literacy surely must be as much about developing compassion as it is about improving comprehension. One without the other would be a literacy without promise.
—*KB, REP, LR*

> > < <

My Father's Voice

I remember my father calling my name on summer evenings in the late 1950s when I was a boy in northeastern Ohio. As night fell, I played whiffle ball with neighbor kids in the yard behind Doc Stires' office. We'd all promised to be home before dark, but no one was willing to break the spell. Our play was summer and friendship and a tad of rebellion to be outside in the descending night, beyond the time our parents said to be home.

Then came my father's voice, short, booming, unmistakable, calling my name.

My father's voice. No trace in it of an Italian accent. He had been in America since 1914 when he left Nola, a village near Naples, he then just a boy of nine.

My father's voice still strong at 54-years-old, though he would be dead at 59, the victim of two drag racers roaring down a public road, smashing head-on into his car.

My father's voice calling from behind the screen door of our apartment over his tavern and bowling alleys. He had owned those businesses since 1940, after years of working in the brickyards that had drawn Italian immigrants to Malvern, Ohio.

My father's voice rising into the night sky, carrying over rooftops, alley, and neighbors' yards to land in my ears where I played with friends in the yard behind Doc Stires' office.

Whe you want to know more . . .

Tom has given us an opportunity to watch writing in process, letting us see where it begins and how it develops. And he suggests ways of inviting our students into the pleasures and pains of writing. You should take a look, too, at his *Blending Genre, Altering Style: Writing Multigenre Papers* (2000), which will help us take our students well beyond the five-paragraph theme, and *Crafting Authentic Voice* (2004), which will help help our students find themselves in the writing.

I ran all the way home, toward the warm yellow light emanating from our apartment. My father had worked hard to be successful in America. And like the Italian accent he naturally left behind when he learned English, he also left behind his ethnicity.

There's a photograph in an oval frame of my father and two of his brothers taken after the family arrived in America: Giuseppe, Antonio, and Felice, my father, all dressed in soft caps with short bills, belted waist coats, white shirts buttoned to their necks, knickers, and sturdy leather shoes laced over their ankles. "Look," says the photo, a print of which was surely sent to relatives in Italy. "Look how well we are doing in America."

I heard my father speak Italian only to immigrants who had come to America when they were adults and never learned English with the ease and facility their children did. Otherwise, my father spoke no Italian. The old country was a distant memory that had little to do with the identity he had forged for himself. He was an American business man. He valued decorum, disliked clannishness, discouraged talk in his tavern about politics and religion. Those led to loud arguments, which were bad for business.

I once asked an uncle of mine—Gigi Chiavari—my father's brother-in-law who lived to be 93, why he had come to America. "Why I come 'cross?" Uncle Gigi said. "Same reason everybody come 'cross. You make a better living, a better home, a better life."

That's what my father had done. Forty-two years now since his death when I was fifteen. Forty-two years since I have heard his voice. But writing this, I hear it now: My father's voice at twilight on a summer evening in small town America. My father's voice calling me home.

> > > DONALD M. MURRAY

Teach Writing Your Way

DO NOT PLAN your next writing course. Do not go to your classroom or home office. Instead, take a pad of paper and settle on a park bench; sit in your car before a favorite view with your cell phone off; take a chair at the lonely table in the back corner of a coffee shop. Make sure to leave all your books on writing and teaching writing—including mine—on the shelf. Leave the files with workshop handouts in the drawer. Keep the notebooks from classes and workshops shut. Do the same with the academic journals that report educational fashion—which composition program is in and which is out.

Now sit quietly and think about your own writing. What topics attract you? What allows your own voice to be heard? What makes your writing easy? Consider the conditions that make it easier to compose: Do you produce better drafts in the morning or at night? Do you write on your laptop or longhand in your notebook? How much do you think about a subject before you write? What genre fits which topic?

Writers do not have to examine their own writing, but teachers who write must pay attention to their craft. In fact, it may be much more important that they understand how writing works than how much they publish. I do think, however, that much more of our professional literature should come from publishing writers, not researchers or scholars who themselves do not write.

Ask these questions when you are writing, before you write, after: What worked well? What didn't work? How did you solve writing problems? How long did it take you to get to the final draft? How many drafts were required? What was the focus of each draft? How did the editor help or hinder you?

> > > *Better yet, banish all assignments.*

To be an effective teacher of writing, you should grow your class plans out of your own experience at your writing desk. When you are in class or making individual responses to students' drafts, you should understand the students' problems because you have met and solved them yourself. And, of course, you should share your drafts with your students, documenting how you are still learning to write. You should share your own moments of satisfaction and despair, your fears, your joys, your delight in writing what you didn't know you knew.

What? You don't write yourself? You teach writing and do not write? For shame.

Would you send your child to a piano teacher who couldn't play the piano? A tennis coach who never charged the net? A driving instructor who didn't have a license? Of course not.

An interesting way to become a writing teacher who writes is to write your own assignments. If you can't do them or finish them in the time you have allowed, you've just taken a big step toward becoming a good writing teacher. I'd suggest you have a class meeting and discuss the problem of assignments. After all, your students have been writing when you haven't. *They* are the authorities; their teacher is the learner. A meeting with your class will help you to devise assignments that can be completed on time. Better yet, banish all assignments.

A great deal of the bad writing we see is the product of bad assignments. Each assignment, after all, stems from the teacher's need to control and a failure to acknowledge that students experience the world, and respond to it, in unique and independent ways. Many teachers of composition, I am afraid, assume that students lead the instructor's life, not their own.

When I am asked to read poorly written papers—be they from students at the university or employees from K–12 government agencies or corporations—I ask to see the assignment. I find that most assignments could not have been completed even by a published writer. These assignments are, I believe, unethical acts that usually only produce more bad writing.

If you can write in response to your own assignments, congratulations. Ideally, when faced with that assignment, you will feel just as your students most likely do. Are you thinking: "I have nothing to say." "I may expose myself." "I may make a mistake in grammar." "I spell so badly that even an online spell checker can't find the word" [my problem]. If your assignment triggers these thoughts for you, and you can still write, sharing your drafts, your problems, and your solutions, you have written a fair assignment and, more important, you have become a colleague, not an A-U-T-H-O-R-I-T-Y. A lack of authority— surprise!—brings respect.

Stop reading. Close the book. Begin writing now. As Gertrude Stein said, "Any time is the time to write a poem" . . . or an essay, a memoir, a short story, a novel, song lyrics, a movie review, a movie, a play, an argument, or, yes, a poem. You might even start writing by drawing a picture. Writing is, after all, a visual art. Until we "unlearn" our young students, they are likely to hand you a drawing as a piece of writing. Of course. The visual nature of writing is clear to them . . . until they go to school.

Case in Point

If you have difficulty getting started, try my most effective writing activity. It is the one I use first with what might become a difficult class. Take a three-by-five- inch card and start writing. Let your pen tell you what to say. In your case, no one is going to see it. Write what you keep thinking about, the same way your tongue finds the place where the tooth used to be. Write what you need to know; write what others need to know. Put words down until they wiggle, snake-like, toward a sentence. Write the sentence. Follow it.

Example: Whimpy . . . in my tent . . . Camp Morgan . . . kept near my cot . . . Whimpy Ellis kept snakes in our tent, and all summer long he did not know I was terrified of snakes. It may have been training for combat a few years later when, as a paratrooper in World War II, I could turn off my feelings, step over the dead or dying, and move forward.

> > > *Writing is not thinking written down after the thinking is completed. Writing is thinking.*

No thesis statement, no assignment, no story starter, no prompt, no out- line—just plunge in and allow the writing to tell you what you have to say. When one side of the card is full, take a new card and start over. Tell the same story again. Then take a new card and start over. When you are finished—it usually takes about four minutes a card—take yet a fourth card and start over again. Take a fifth card if you need to.

Read the last card; then compare it with the first one. You will find you had something important to say, and it is usually not what you expected. You are a writer. Writing is not thinking written down after the thinking is completed. Writing *is* thinking.

I am going to write a column. Why? My Whimpy line has given me a way to deal with the casualty of war few people see—the warriors who have turned off their feelings in order to endure military life and combat . . . and they can never turn them on again.

> > < <

The Boston Globe—Now and Then—September 12, 2006

Donald M. Murray
Globe Correspondent

After the bombs, the firefights, the mines, we have a lifetime of silence. Those who were on the front lines rarely speak of their war.

> And what I was thinking: *This was written over a period of three days, in slices of available time—fifteen minutes, twenty minutes, half an hour. Once I had the first line, I could put it aside and come back to it easily. I did not know where I was going with this. I was writing, trying to understand the silence.*

There are good reasons for the silence. Who could understand what had become ordinary in combat? How could I tell my daughters of what I observed under fire, what I had done under fire?

Only years later did I understand how quickly—a matter of weeks in basic training—I had shut down my emotions. It was shockingly easy.

> And what I was thinking: *Now I have to document the generalization.*

It is the little things that mark this shutting down. Each soldier's story is different; all the soldiers' stories are the same.

At supper the first evening at Camp Edwards, food was served family style. One recruit took too many mashed potatoes. A sergeant who was watching us picked up the heavy crockery bowl and threw it at the selfish recruit's face. He bled but did not say anything. He never let his emotions show—and he never again took more than his share of food.

In the barracks when we were all dressing in the first week of basic training, a soldier touched me in an obscene way. I don't remember any emotion. I just placed my fist against his face with some velocity and the ambulance took him away.

The Drill Sergeant, who disliked me as much as I disliked him, tossed a rifle with a shiny, knife-sharp blade at me. He was unarmed. He told me to kill him and without hesitation. I tried. His bare hands were quicker than my bayonet, but I had no hesitation in trying to kill him. That was in my third week of basic training.

Turning our emotions off was necessary if we were to move forward in battle, stepping over the dead. We became people who showed no emotions, sharing nothing, revealing nothing to each other.

But when we came home, our families wanted the open, vulnerable boy who left home, not this man of silence, withdrawn and private.

And what I was thinking: *Now I am surprised. I didn't expect to focus on the silence after they come home. Give readers who were not in combat a taste of what veterans are trying to forget.*

Years ago, after hearing yet another politician speak of the glory of war, I discovered we were all heroes, all brave, all victorious. I don't know who those brave patriots were. I went into battle with my pants full of fear. And you know what? A part of me hoped that some idiot near me might try to be a hero. I shut my emotions off in basic training, and it carried me through three years in the paratroops. I made a conscious decision to unlock my emotions, but it took decades, and the job may not be finished in this week in which I will become 82.

And what I was thinking: *Now the sermon. Is it too much?*

Understand that after the yellow ribbons are taken down that your son or daughter, husband or wife, father or mother, brother or sister, friend or fellow worker are not the people who went to Iraq or Afghanistan. Their ability to turn their emotions off and do what has to be done is needed in combat, but is it good in the play yard, the living room, the bedroom? Usually not. Ironically, that skill was of enormous help to me when I cared for my wife during 14 years of Parkinson's and eventual dementia.

The boys and girls who went to war and came home men and women will, however, at times be silent, withdrawn, and turn off the news as I do, trying not to remember and usually not able to share a life they hope you will never know.

> > < <

As you write with or just ahead of your students, you make discoveries about writing that will change your lesson plan. All the years I was writing and teaching writing, I found new possibilities in writing, as I still do. I would incorporate them into my teaching as they now affect my writing habit, my voice, my order, my pace.

Discoveries Teachers May Make While Writing
Surprise

Writers welcome surprise. They are happiest when they write what they do not intend. I am never loyal to my early drafts when the text is straining to tell me what it has to say. Notice it is the text speaking, not me—the draft assembles my

< < < < <
Not to disparage planning, but the idea of "discovery" arises in several of these chapters. Don speaks here of the discoveries we make as we write, Teri Lesesne spoke (Chapter 6) of what we and our students might find in the realm of young adult books, and Deborah Appleman (Interlude 3) of the rich insights that might spring from the minds of our students as they discuss their reading. It may be the promise of possible discovery, tomorrow or the next day, that makes teaching so intriguing.

—*KB, REP, LR*

> > > *I am happiest when I write what I do not expect. I seek surprise, contradiction, doubt, challenge.*

thoughts and feelings. I'm not loyal to my draft. Graham Greene said, "Isn't disloyalty as much the writer's virtue as loyalty is the soldier's?" I am happiest when I write what I do not expect. I seek surprise, contradiction, doubt, challenge. Many drafts are failures, but instructive failures. We have to fail in order to write, just as my grandchildren had to learn how to fall in order to learn to walk. Each first draft is a new step into the unknown. It is by drafting (failing) that we uncover our true meaning.

1. We begin in a state of not knowing, of hopelessness that may grow into despair, but as we do the drifty, disorganized thinking that is necessary, the playing with fragments of meaning that bounce off each other, we begin to connect—tentatively at first—as the draft finds its way toward meaning.

2. We develop what we may have to say. This is important. Beginning writers are properly overwhelmed when they think of writing a book, a movie script or play, a historical report that might become eight hundred typewritten pages. So would I. That is why I write a word that interests me and write until that word connects with another word. Then I have a phrase that will give me a sentence, then a sentence that gives me a paragraph. A paragraph that leads the way to a page. I do not write books. I write single pages that pile up until they become a book.

3. We edit to achieve clarity, grace, and spontaneity. Ease and spontaneity come when I read my final draft aloud and edit until the lines appear natural, graceful, fluid. I write until they tell me what I have to say and express it the way I want to say it.

Patience

Patience is not in my genes, but when my wife was diagnosed with Parkinson's, I learned patience. I had always been rush, rush, rush, do tomorrow's task today, but the fourteen years of caring for Minnie Mae had an unexpected influence on my writing. I had less and less time to write and the time I had was interrupted, yet I kept writing and the slowed pace made my writing better.

I wrote before writing. I played with fragments of language, images, unexpected connections, heard a bit of what might become my voice. I didn't write drafts in my mind because this mental play—which takes patience—made me far better prepared to create a draft when I had the opportunity. When I am stuck, I turn off the computer and assign the project to my subconscious or my unconscious, confident one or the other will find a solution.

See, Then Write

The more I write my column, articles, chapters like this one, and poems, ghost-write for corporations, and again—yet again—start *the* novel, the more I realize that writing is a visual art more than a language art. We insist students start with language, but I don't start with language. I start by seeing what is, what isn't, what isn't and should be, what connects, what disconnects, what surprises, what contradicts. This is just as true of nonfiction as fiction. I didn't start this chapter with description, but notice how visual it is.

When we teach language, first words begin like a series of balloons floating free. I never paid attention to grammar and mechanics in school because the rules seemed disconnected from meaning. However, once I found what I wanted to say, I discovered the traditions of language were not only helpful but necessary.

Listen

I never could learn piano, drums, or (embarrassingly) the Hawaiian guitar by lessons or by ear, but I write by ear. I do not *see* what I write—my two fingers are searching the keys—but I *hear* what I say when I type it. Somehow or other, learn to hear your writing. Pause to read aloud often. Hear the words in your head as you type or write. Take a walk and think through the words. Whichever, you may discover that your writing improves when you worry less about how it looks and more about how it sounds.

The quality that attracts readers is voice. They hear an individual human being speaking to another human being. I never begin until I hear my voice speaking in my head with compassion, anger, humor, enthusiasm, nostalgia—any of man's many human emotions. As I write and find just what I have to say and to whom I want to say it, I tune the voice to my meaning. And many times my voice tells me what I must say. More important, the voice often tells me how I really feel about the subject, then points out what should be emphasized and what shouldn't.

> < < < < <
> Don makes an interesting point here about the importance of hearing a text in your mind as you write. Look over to Yvette Jackson and Eric Cooper's chapter (16) to contrast this with what they say about seeing relationships among words when trying to understand what someone else has written. Perhaps what these writers are showing us is, once again, the way reading and writing are flip sides of the same coin. When we're reading, we work to see the text to better understand the writing; but when we're writing, we work to hear the words to create what will become for someone else better reading.
> —KB, REP, LR

Writing Is Rewriting

I never revised in elementary school, secondary school or college. I did not do this as a newspaper journalist when rewriting thirty-five to forty-five stories a shift. In fact, I didn't revise later on when writing the editorials that won the Pulitzer Prize. Of course, I responded to correction by teachers and editors, but the skills of revision were not in my toolbox. Then I attempted to make the step from the daily newspaper to major magazine writing. I submitted a story to *The Saturday Evening Post*, then the best market for a writer.

My editor, Bob Johnson, took seven thousand words to respond to my five-thousand-word article. Then he came from Philadelphia to my home in Wellesley, outside of Boston, spending a whole day going through my draft line by line. At the end of the day, he told me he was assigning the story to another writer. I begged for a second chance. He gave me forty-eight hours. The next two mornings, I rewrote the article by getting up at 3 AM and rewriting until I had to go to work. It was published. In the process, I learned the delights of revision and became a disciple of the rewrite gods. They told me to complete the first draft, then read and revise it ten times. I did. Then my wife typed the tenth version. I read and revised that ten times—thirty drafts in all. I sold many magazine articles. Of course, students cannot be asked to do that, but the central act of writing for me is having live drafts on my monitor that extend and explore my world.

I concluded that I taught best and my students learned the most when I had them write one paper each semester or term. I used many variations, but here is one.

> > > > >
You may be surprised to hear Don suggest having students write only one paper during an entire semester, when so many of the others in this book have recommended that students write regularly and often. His course, however, did keep his students writing constantly, though much of their work was rewriting again and again. Keep in mind that he worked with older students who were perhaps better able to sustain interest in one issue for a long period of time.

—*KB, REP, LR*

Week One: Jot down 150 specific details you discover in observing your world with all your senses.

What surprised you? *Poverty Program director drives new Lexus.*

What connected? *Most people avoid turning left when they drive.* (J. Edgar Hoover, former head of the FBI, would not let his drivers ever turn left.)

Which are in conflict with other specifics? *Football team kneels and prays, runs out on field to injure other team's players.*

Week Two: Pick a topic to study in consultation with other students and the teacher. Do a first quick-write of findings of up to five pages.

Week Three: Same as week two.

Week Four: Create a proposal you would send to a publisher. (Proposal models supplied.)

Week Five: Write 150 potential titles for the paper.

Week Six: Write 50 leads.

Week Seven: Complete a first draft.

Week Eight: Write a second draft.

Week Nine: Write a third draft.

Week Ten: Class publication. Students share their work with others.

Week Eleven: Class publication.

Week Twelve: Write the final draft for a grade.

Difference

In 1992, forty-four years after I started writing full-time on a newspaper, thirty-eight years after I won the Pulitzer Prize, I read a statement by Sandra Cisneros that went right to the center of my life as a writer and teacher.

> Imagine yourself at your kitchen table, in your pajamas. Imagine one person you'd allow to see you that way, and write in the voice you'd use to that friend. Write about what makes you different. (in Arteseros 1992)

If you write, you will find what makes you different, what you have to say that will contribute to the human conversation. If you have discovered your own difference, you will be able to hear the individual difference in each student and offer each student a practical curriculum—based not on theory, but on *your* experience as a writer.

When you want to know more ...

Don was a teacher who wrote, and a writer who taught, and the symbiosis of those roles has led to such books as *A Writer Teaches Writing* (2004) and *Shoptalk: Learning to Write with Writers* (1990). They'll extend the discussion of this chapter still further—and perhaps lure you into more writing, yourself.

Connecting to my thoughts

Connecting to other texts

ON WRITING AND ITS TEACHING

Alliance for Excellent Education. 2007. "Writing Next: Effective Strategies to Improve Writing of Adolescents in Middle and High Schools."

Elbow, Peter. 1998. *Writing without Teachers*. 2nd ed. New York: Oxford University Press.

Kirby, Dan, Dawn Latta Kirby, and Tom Liner. 2004. *Inside Out: Strategies for Teaching Writing*. Portsmouth, NH: Heinemann.

Lamott, Anne. 1995. *Bird by Bird: Some Instructions on Writing and Life*. First Anchor Books ed. New York: Anchor Books.

Macrorie, Ken. 1986. *Writing to Be Read*. Rev. 2nd ed. Portsmouth, NH: Heinemann.

Moffett, James. 1968. *Teaching the Universe of Discourse*. Boston: Houghton Mifflin.

National Commission on Writing, The. 2003. "The Neglected 'R': The Need for a Writing Revolution."

> > > LINDA RIEF

Writing: Commonsense Matters

Words are sacred. They deserve respect. If you get the right ones, in the right order, you can nudge the world a little.

—*Tom Stoppard*

THE IMPORTANCE of writing was underscored for me in 1990, when a group from Estonia invited me to spend two weeks in the small town of Haapsalu teaching seventh graders in one of their schools. The desks and chairs were bolted to the floor. There were few supplies. Even fewer books. On the first day, the students arrived twenty minutes early. They were shocked to find all the chairs in a circle. I had located enough loose chairs around the school to ignore those bolted in place. The students weren't used to facing each other. They weren't accustomed to talking to each other. They were most comfortable with the teacher delivering information and their giving back information exactly as it had been presented. No speculation. No questions. No disagreements. No imagining. Definitely, no critical thinking. At least none that these students dared to voice.

Tom Romano's and Don Murray's chapters on writing (11 and 12, respectively) take you deep into specific topics. With their thoughts in mind, we decided this is the perfect place for Linda's chapter as she addresses a range of topics—from motivation to assessment to the writing-reading relationship.

—*KB, REP, LR*

These students, like all in their community, were still under Soviet rule, as they had been for fifty years. It took a while before the wall—the one of silence in this classroom—began to tumble. It began with a whisper from Irinni, "Are you sure we may say what we think?" Then Tiuu, then Havel. "You want us to write what we think? Will it not be trouble?"

"It will *not* be trouble!" I assured them.

> > > *If we want children to become adults who are articulate, literate, and thoughtful citizens of the world, they must learn to think deeply and widely.*

They talked and wrote. And wrote. I heard their lives. Their disappointments. Their tragedies. Their wishes. Their beliefs. Their dreams. Their questions. They arrived thirty minutes early for class every single day and stayed later and later. No matter how hard I tried, I couldn't get to class before they did. Sitting in a circle, waiting to talk and question, think and write.

I knew then, as I know now, that if we want children to become adults who are articulate, literate, and thoughtful citizens of the world, they must learn to think deeply and widely. They must commit their thinking to paper, learning how to be memoirists, poets, essayists, journalists, playwrights, activists, speechwriters, novelists, critics, scientists, historians. In these roles, they and others can examine those beliefs, feelings, and thoughts; build on the same sentiments; provide the evidence to support the thinking; or argue vehemently against it. The problem is, this is easier said than done!

Getting Started by Considering Some Commonsense Matters

As teachers, what we do has to be based on sound philosophical, theoretical, pedagogical, and humanitarian underpinnings. We must ask ourselves as writing teachers: *What do I believe and why? How do I shape those beliefs into sound practices in the classroom? Who are the students with whom and from whom I learn, to whom I teach, and for whom I care and have a responsibility?*

When we ask ourselves those types of questions, when we think about what is working and what isn't working, when we gather the data of student work over time as evidence to support or challenge our beliefs, suspicions, and wonderings, when we continually ask the students to describe the strengths and weaknesses of all they are doing, and when we use all this evidence to inform our instruction, we are contributing practical, meaningful, valuable, and valid information to the educational conversation.

You will find answers to those questions and issues in your own way—perhaps shaped in part by reading texts like this and discussing problems with fellow teachers. I've done the same thing—read professional texts, gone to conferences, attended classes, participated in writing projects, and talked with colleagues. What I've learned from educators, philosophers, and researchers has been applied to my own practice with my own students—about one hundred eighth graders at a middle school in New Hampshire. I share here my own conclusions about writing as a starting point for conversations with your colleagues.

Writing is thinking.

Writing is not about memorizing a series of facts and reiterating that information on a multiple-choice test or within the response to a contrived essay question, only to forget it all the moment the test is over. Writing lets us think of things we didn't know we knew until we began writing. Writing is one way of representing and communicating our thinking to others, using our experiences, our knowledge, our opinions, and our feelings to inform and negotiate our understandings and misunderstandings of ourselves and the world in which we live.

There is no one process that defines the way all writers write.

Writing is a recursive process in which the writer considers purpose and audience as she shifts back and forth, finding ideas, developing those ideas, and clarifying thinking for the strongest, clearest meaning through intentional revision and editing. Different writers use different processes, depending on task, purpose, audience, and composing styles to develop their pieces of writing.

This is why I developed a process paper—so students could describe the process they went through to develop a piece of writing, all the way from coming up with an idea to revising and editing the piece. Each student has a different way of moving back and forth through a piece of writing. As teachers, we have to recognize and honor those various processes and be prepared to learn from and respond to them as one student works without our guidance and another asks for a lot of instruction.

< < < < <
You can see a copy of this process paper on page 269. Be sure to take a look at Chapter 17, by Devon Brenner, David Pearson, and Linda Rief on assessment, to see how Linda uses this process paper as a part of assessment.

—*KB, REP, LR*

We learn to write by writing.

We do not learn to do anything without practicing. We draft ideas, try to organize our thinking, craft the strongest way to say what we want to say, and write continually for real reasons for a real audience because we won't work hard unless we know our practice is going to be used in a real game.

We have to do a lot of writing to accomplish the best writing.

We should not be judged on every word we put on paper. Pianists don't want to be judged on the wrong keys they strike as they learn to play; quarterbacks don't want to be judged on the bad passes they make in practice while trying to connect with receivers. Our students are learning how to write and should be allowed the opportunity to choose the writing they want to be evaluated after they have done enough writing to make the comparisons themselves. We guide them in those decisions by exposing them constantly to good writing and showing them how it's crafted.

Writers need, and want, to write for real reasons for a real audience.

None of us wants to write for a meaningless exercise. Writing is hard work. We want our efforts to mean something; we want to know that our words made someone think, or feel, or learn. The audience could simply be other students in the classroom, an engaged audience who listens as we read our writing aloud. Or, we might choose to do a dramatic reading or post our work on the walls of the classroom, library, or halls. Or it could mean publishing in a school newspaper or literary magazine, a weekly column for the PTO newsletter, or book reviews or poetry sent to other classes. How about a letter to the local newspaper or to a delighted grandparent or friend? An article for a cyberzine site. A state or national writing contest. We must continually look for ways for students to take their writing public so they begin to realize they do have a voice that affects readers in a variety of ways.

Lessons of craft and conventions are best taught within the context of a meaningful piece of writing.

Try as I might, I could not convince Mark, an eighth-grade student of mine, to use a business format when writing a letter of complaint to the publishers of *Write Source*, a student handbook we use in our classroom. Mark had discovered numerous mistakes in the book's map sections and wanted to let the publishers know via a letter; I'm sad to say, it was not sent in proper business format. However, the publishers still read his letter, agreed with the errors, and sent him an offer to work as a cartographic editor for them. Mark immediately wanted to know how to write that acceptance letter in the correct format. Students are much more willing to revise and edit their work when it is done for a real audience for a real reason. We've known this for a while. Back in 1985, the landmark document *Becoming a Nation of Readers* explained, "experiments over the last fifty years have shown negligible improvements in the quality of student writing as a result of grammar instruction. Research suggests that the finer points of writing, such as punctuation and subject–verb agreement, may be learned best while students are engaged in extended writing that has the purpose of communicating a message to an audience" (see NWP and Nagin 2003, 22).

Writers need choice, time, and models of good writing.

We learn to write by writing. We need to give students ample opportunities to write on a continuous basis, with choices of topics and genres that engage their interest and/or to which they can connect. When writers are engaged in the process of writing something that matters to them, for which they have their own purposes, that writing often surprises, delights, and empowers them, encouraging a stronger commitment to the crafting of the writing.

> > > > >
It is easy to connect the importance of choice to reading, yet we need to remember that choice is every bit as motivating for writing as it is for reading. Penny Kittle says more about choice in writing in her interlude (Interlude 4).

—*KB, REP, LR*

Writers need constructive response while engaged in the process of writing that moves the writing forward and helps the writer grow.

Conferences, whether oral or written, are an integral part of the writing process for our students because they help the writers move the writing forward during the drafting process, not after the fact, when they believe they are done. Using the ideas of Peter Elbow in *Writing Without Teachers* (1998), I designed a specific format in my attempts to help students craft their writing (see Figure 13–1).

> > > *Evaluation should move writers forward, helping them grow by identifying the strengths of the process and the product, as well as those elements or conventions that need to be addressed.*

I always have students read their writing to me in an oral conference. They need to be responsible for what they are writing and how they are reading their work. Often, they will revise and edit as they go, while I am listening for the part they have already identified as needing the most help. This way, I can focus my attention on possibilities for crafting that writing. As a writer, I need to hear first what I did well and then hear the questions that may have come to mind as the reader listened. Helping students revise as a result of oral conferences is not easy. Doug Kaufman spent a year following me as I conferred with every student. His findings are published in the book *Conferences and Conversations* (2000). This book captures the work required to turn talk about a piece of writing into nudges that student authors use to do their own revisions.

Evaluation of writing should highlight the strengths of process, content, and conventions and give the writer the tools and techniques to strengthen the weaknesses.

Understanding the process in which students engage in order to craft a piece of writing is as important as the final product. When students verbalize that thinking through a process paper—How did this writing come to be? Where did you get the idea? What did you do, and why, as you went from one draft to the next? What problems did you encounter? How well did you solve those problems?—it shows teachers the multiple strategies writers use and teaches students to pay attention to that process so they become more independent as they develop skills as writers.

Evaluation should move writers forward, helping them grow by identifying the strengths of the process and the product, as well as those elements or conventions that need to be addressed.

Good writing is not defined by one set of criteria but differs depending on the kind of writing.

At the beginning of every year, I have my students read twenty pieces of writing that eighth graders from previous years have written. Though I of course remove names and other identifying markers, students know the writers were my former

CONFERENCE SHEET

Conference Sheet Name _____ Section _____

Date	How can I help you? Articulated by writer	Like/Hear/Stays with me Written by listener	Questions? Written by listener	What if you . . . ? Written by listener	What will you do next? Articulated by writer

Figure 13–1.

From *Adolescent Literacy*. Portsmouth, NH: Heinemann. © 1991 by Linda Rief from *Seeking Diversity*. Portsmouth, NH: Heinemann students. Then, my current students score these pieces of writing holistically on a scale of 1 to 4, with 4 being the most effective. They list three to five of the characteristics they identified as consistent among the strongest pieces. As a class, we list those characteristics or traits and then use them to help identify the strengths or weaknesses in their own writing (see Figure 13–2). This gives the students insights and understandings into what makes a strong piece of writing. This list also guides my instruction as I teach lessons of craft.

When crafting specific kinds of writing, such as book reviews, informational pamphlets, writing for a test, letters of complaint, short stories, or essays, we look at a variety of pieces in that genre and construct an additional list that serves as a guide for developing a particular kind of writing. This gives students a variety of models as well as ownership in the development and understanding of what goes into writing.

Writers need places to collect their ideas: writer's notebooks, working folders, portfolios.

Having students keep a writing-reading notebook is a good idea. While I like to keep my own journal—as you might, too—it's just a book with blank pages. I've found that this type of blank book lacks the structure some students need and can feel overwhelming. Students tend to prefer a recommended size, a structure to hold onto, and some examples of students' responses from the past. Over the years, I've found that a structure gives the students a sense of security and comfort so they can write more freely and honestly. And, I admit, the consistency in size and structure of the sections of the notebook helps me when reading and responding to more than a hundred notebooks every two weeks.

What's the most important reason for keeping a writing-reading notebook? For me, it's having a place where students can gather their ideas so they don't lose their thinking, or their pages—in a locker, in the hallway. It's a place to look back at what they were thinking about themselves, their reading, and their world that might merit further development. It's a place to collect their thinking as readers and writers.

What are the specifics I use in this notebook? First, I ask my students to use spiral notebooks that are approximately eight by ten inches. Next, we divide this spiral into four sections:

> Response section (the first fifty to sixty pages of the notebook)
> Notes (the next fifteen to twenty pages)
> Vocabulary (the next ten to fifteen pages)
> Spelling (the last six pages)

It is in the Initials/Response section where students (1) write or draw their reactions to books read for nightly homework; (2) do their quickwrites in

CHARACTERISTICS OF EFFECTIVE WRITING

Strong Lead

> grabs your attention, pulls you in, hooks you

> unique/original/unexpected phrasing/topic

> makes you want to read it to find out or know more

> gives a direction (focus) to the writing

Focused, Well-Developed Idea with Interest/Appeal to the Writer

> knowledge of topic thorough

> committed/passionate/honest/authentic voice in creating feeling/emotion/ideas/opinions

> knows appropriate times to linger (to slow down the action), condense, or eliminate information (to speed up or leave some things to the intelligence of the reader)

> original/unique/creative voice/style/perspective/viewpoint

Interest/Appeal to Reader

> reader can relate to/identify with thoughts/feelings/experiences/character

> hook (makes you think, learn, question, or feel something)

> complications (bait on the hook) on way to resolution, make it interesting

> an insight/understanding/feeling stays with you even when finished reading (influenced in some way/affected by writing)

Word Choice

> strong, thorough description/vivid details (sights, sounds, touch, smells, taste)

> creates picture in your mind of setting or characters or situation

> so realistic you feel that you are involved in the writing

> original/creative/unique/sophisticated/simple/clear choice of words

> sounds natural, not stiff or contrived, as if the writer is talking to the reader

> use of strongest nouns, verbs

> sense of natural metaphors and use of repetition

> title thought out/crafted with intent to capture a reader, convey the essence of the writing

FIGURE 13–2.

CHARACTERISTICS OF EFFECTIVE WRITING *(continued)*

Sentence Fluency

> intentional use of clipped, rambling, or fragmented sentences

> steady pace and rhythm that appeals to the ear

> choice of sentence structures conveys the mood and voice all the way through

Organization

> clear beginning, middle, end

> flows well/understandable/sensible pattern or style based on kind of writing (essay, poem, short story, review, song, letter, etc.)

> point/purpose clear and intentional in design, rather than wandering aimlessly (nothing is unnecessary)

> makes you think/feel/learn something

Strong Ending

> sense of closure, but you want to read it again

> unexpected (leaves you thinking, wondering, feeling, knowing, etc.)

Conventions

> spelling, punctuation, usage, structure of sentences constructed/edited with intent

> point of view (I, you, he/she) used with intent

    — first-person makes the writing more personal (I think . . .)

    — second-person speaks directly to the reader (You think . . .)

    — third-person distances the narrator from the reader (She thinks . . .)

> tense (past, present, future tense) used with intent

    — present tense makes it seem as if it's happening now

FIGURE 13–2. continued

response to short pieces of writing I read to them at the beginning of class; and/or (3) record anything that leads them to think as readers and writers. For the majority of students, I expect one to five pages of response per week. For example, Joe wrote:

> I just finished reading *The Greatest War*. It kept me on the edge of my seat for almost the entire time. There was hardly a dull moment. If the author, Gerald Astor, wasn't writing about the extremely intense periods of combat (which he was for most of the time), he was writing about the training of the men high in command giving orders.
>
> Sometimes I think it would be cool to go into the army. I would be able to tell great stories, and if I didn't go into combat, I would make great friends and lifelong connections.
>
> After reading this book, when I look at an ad for the army I get reminded that behind all the glory and heroism, war is a torturous, horrifying, gory, and terribly sad experience.

In the Notes section, students record any lessons I teach directly to the whole class. I added this section to their notebooks several years ago when I realized students were taking notes on random pieces of paper and promptly losing them or were confused about where to keep these notes. By keeping them in this one section, they have a record of lessons taught that they can easily reference, and I can see how well they take and apply the notes they've been given. As they take notes, they add topics to their table of contents in the front.

The last two sections, Vocabulary and Spelling, give students a place to keep up with vocabulary words and spelling rules (yes, we still review spelling rules).

Teachers have to know their students well enough to recognize their distinct strengths, interests, and needs.

Do we know our students well enough each year to help them become the best readers and writers they can be? Knowing their strengths, interests, and needs is essential in putting books *they will read* in their hands and helping them find writing ideas they will care about.

Here's an idea. List all the students in your classes down one side of a page without looking at your roster. Next to each name, write a distinct strength, something each is good at, then one thing that really interests that student, and lastly, a book you might suggest to him. Could I do it? I tried. There are lots of gaps for the one hundred students I have, yet I know you could easily have even more students. What if we could do this for every student? It would help us know them and know what to do for each of them as we work to produce the strongest readers and writers.

> > > > >
Smokey Daniels (Chapter 9) suggests using letter writing as a way to get to know students better. Take a look at his chapter with Linda's comments in mind.
—KB, REP, LR

Writing is reading.

There has been so much focus on literacy *as reading* over the last ten years that I often think we have forgotten, even abandoned, writing. We have forgotten that a person can read without writing, but he cannot write without reading. If we neglect writing, while focusing our attention almost exclusively on reading, it is also *at the expense of reading*. Writers are readers, summarizing, reformulating, synthesizing, reorganizing, and reevaluating all they have done. If we want to teach kids to be the strongest readers, we need to teach them to be the strongest writers. This is common sense.

We need to give students ample opportunities to write on a continuous basis, including short, quick responses to literature on a daily basis: What did this reading bring to mind for me? What did I think or feel or learn as I read? What questions came to mind? What in my own experience is similar or different? How does this make me view the world? They need time to develop longer pieces of wider range and depth, and time to read those pieces aloud to their peers and teachers in conference. They need a choice of topics and genres that engage their interest and to which they can connect.

Given these opportunities to engage, as readers, with their own literature, they will write and read and begin to recognize and craft their strongest pieces of writing. And become stronger readers.

The best writing has voice.

The best writing not only gives us voice but is filled with voice. Tom Romano says,

> Voice is the writer's presence in a piece of writing. My bias as a writing teacher
> is to teach students to write in accessible, engaging, and irresistible voices.
> Such voices . . . have certain qualities in common:
>
> > They deliver interesting information.
> > They often employ techniques of narrative.
> > They exhibit perceptivity.
> > They offer surprising information and observations.
> > Quite often, they demonstrate a sense of humor. (2005, 7–8)

Figures 13–3 and 13–4 show you two examples of student writing that are so filled with voice they shout. In Figure 13–3 (page 200), you'll find Alden's essay. After studying Rick Reilly as a mentor author, Alden surprises us with his observations and perceptions of the adult sports world. In Figure 13–4 (page 201), Ivy and Sarah write a scathing review (with my permission to speak their minds) about a book they have read. In both examples, you see polished writing filled with palpable, convincing voice. Their voices convey astonishment at the world,

A Season to Remember

This year in the NHL was definitely one of the most memorable in a long time. This is the first year in the history of the NHL that every single goalie had a Goals Against Average (GAA) of 0.00 and no players scored any goals. Not even one. Oops, maybe I forgot to mention the fact that the NHL didn't happen this year, and that it was officially cancelled a few weeks ago, when Gary Bettman, the commissioner of the league, announced that the players association couldn't come to an agreement with the NHL about the salary cap limit.

At the point of the cancellation there had been a total of 155 days missed because of the lock-out, and there had been 1,161 games cancelled. During that time, the average person would have taken 3,100,00 breaths, slept for 1,300 hours, watched 600 hours of television, and gone #2 about 150 times. Personally, I think the league should have been cancelled a long time ago, right around the 20th trip to the john. After canceling over 100 games, I gave up all hope and decided that the NHL had absolutely no chance of making it.

But seriously, let's take a minute to stop and figure out what these people are having such a grueling debate about. The NHL proposed a rejected salary cap of $44.7 million. If the money was distributed evenly throughout the team, each player would earn somewhere in the area of 1.9 million dollars a year. 1.9 MILLION dollars! I would die for a salary like that. I'd be blowin' my nose in Benjamin's and wipin' my butt with Grant's if I was rakin' in that kind of dough! (That'd be pretty sweet, huh?) Anyways, after the players rejected that offer, they suggested a $49 million cap. With $49 million per team, each player would get about $2.1 million. Wait! What?! This entire debate has been over 0.2 million dollars! Wow!

Well, at least we Americans can say that the athletes of our era aren't getting greedy. I mean, that would be just so horrible if they were so greedy as to not play for an entire year because they want $0.2 million more on their contracts. The average player makes around $2 million. So it's great that our athletes are mature enough to play hockey instead of arguing over the measly sum of $200,000. I mean $200,000 is only like the salary of five Americans in one year. But that's nothing to the pro hockey players of our day. Adding $200,000 to their salary is only adding 10% to the total. Basically, 10% of a pro hockey player's salary is worth as much as the salary of five Americans. Gee, I sure am glad there's not a massive debate over that kind of money!

I can't wait until I get older, and I have a chance to pursue my hockey career by joining the players' association. Maybe by the time I'm there we can debate over $250,000 when each player is making about $8 million a year. That'd be great! And then everyone in the U.S. would think so highly of me, and I'd be a star!

Pssh! Who am I kidding!? The NHL is a joke! This year has probably been the most pathetic year in the history of our sports. The athletes are getting so amazingly greedy that the entire Great Wall of China would be needed to stop the landslide of greed our athletes created. If I, or any of my children, grow up to be athletes, I'll definitely make sure that our minimum salary is $20 mil and I wouldn't stand for anything less. I mean, that's not greedy or anything, is it?

FIGURE 13–3. *Alden's Essay on the National Hockey League*

Are you feeling extra chilly this winter? Having trouble paying those high heating bills? We have the perfect solution, and all it requires is a quick drive to the bookstore. The book *Molly Bannacky* has a beautiful hard-back cover and thick clean pages, perfect burning material, enough kindling to keep you warm and toasty while you read something more interesting. One cord of firewood would cost you $225, while 100 copies of *Molly Bannacky* books would cost $115.60, $100 less!

Molly Bannacky describes the life of a servant who works for a harsh lord. One day her whole world changes as her obstinate cow (heaven forbid!) spills her pail of milk. When ruled guilty in court for stealing the milk, Molly narrowly escapes being hung by reading from the Bible. Instead, she is sent to America to work as an indentured servant. When her time is up, it is up to Molly to make her way as a single woman in a harsh New World, full of over-accepting neighbors and wilderness adventures. Will her slave mean more to her than she meant to her lord? (Oh, yes, MUCH more!)

Here are the problems with this book. The text does not always match the pictures. For example, on page 2 the writing describes Molly as in the barn, but the picture shows Molly standing in front of the court ready to be tried for spilling milk. Also this book does not represent the normal behavior of people in colonial times and could mislead the unfortunate children for whom this book was written. It portrays a colonial era where everyone has overly kind neighbors and marries their slaves. Even as a biography the writing is kind of dull and the story does not have a high point or climax.

Perhaps the most exciting part in the story is when Molly is going to be hung for her evil deed, because you think the book would end there. But, alas, she survives for another 20 pages. If looking for a good way to introduce history to young children, find a different book. This one was useless, boring, and bland. We suggest, as stated above, that you use this book as firewood instead of reading it.

FIGURE 13–4. *Ivy and Sarah's Book Review*

especially at adult behavior. We can see the power of books changing their lives for the better, and hear the poignancy and honesty about all they notice about themselves and others. This is writing that makes us think *and* feel *and* learn something. This is writing with voice.

What Stands in the Way of Common Sense?

It is one thing to say that writing has voice or that students need choice or that there should be real audiences, and quite another to put those ideas into practice. Sometimes moving from promise to practice means looking at what might keep us from moving. What follows are the impediments I've had to work around.

Not Understanding the Impact of Visual Tools in Writing, or Reason Number 999 That Kids Won't Write.

No matter how hard I worked at trying to get all kids to write, I've never understood why a couple of kids in every class refused to participate. Was it they *couldn't* write? Or *wouldn't* write? Why? What was I doing wrong? I kept asking these questions until I heard Roger Essley, an artist with work in the Metropolitan Museum of Art in New York City, speak at a conference. He was speaking about his dyslexia and difficulty with writing throughout his schooling. Teachers wouldn't let him draw, yet it was through pictures that he represented all he understood or was trying to understand. He talked about *drawing as thinking* (stick figures and key words), not *drawing as performance* (creating a piece of art). I listened hard. I had used pictures and students' drawing *to inspire writing*, but I had never thought about drawing as thinking, where drawing didn't count, and spelling didn't count. I sat up and listened harder. He seemed to be talking about first-draft thinking. His comments led me to ask myself, *What if kids were encouraged to represent what they wanted to say, what they were thinking, through stick figures and key words? Would that act as a scaffold to writing?*

I remembered an article I had read by Judith Fueyo (1991). In it, she explained,

> as language arts teachers we are after words, oral and written, but need they be the exclusive avenue by which we arrive at words? . . . Einstein admitted that he did not think in words, but visual images. His early formulations for the theory of relativity came in images of himself riding a light wave. Only later did he come to words. (13)

With Essley's and Fueyo's comments in my mind, I thought about all the research I had read about reading, and how good readers get visual images in their heads as they construct meaning from their reading. The kids who didn't write also told me they hated reading. They told me they saw nothing when they read. What if students who struggled with writing were invited to use visual tools to tell their stories? Would that help all kids come more easily to words? Would that also help them as readers, if they were invited to draw? Encouraged to draw?

I invited Roger Essley to my classroom. He explained to my students what he meant by a *tellingboard*: a large piece of paper with squares drawn on it. Students draw stick figures and key words on sticky notes and move those sticky notes around the tellingboard (adding, deleting, rearranging) to tell the story in a better way based on what students say, ask, and suggest as the story is told to them (see Figure 13–5, page 203). When the tellingboard is complete, the student uses it to guide her writing.

After students had watched Roger do this, they went home and asked parents to tell them a family story. They then put their story on a tellingboard and shared it with the class. The class pointed out what they liked or heard specific to the story and asked questions about parts that needed clarifying. Students returned to their writing to fill in squares based on questions and missed information. They told their story again. When the tellingboard was as complete as they could make it, they went to writing. I was amazed. Kids who had never written before began writing. They had pictures in front of them to guide the

FIGURE 13–5. *Instructions for using and making a tellingboard.*

writing. And even the most reluctant of writers began to produce. I think we could be taking *drawing as thinking* more seriously in our classrooms as we work with all kids. It may be the best tool they have for showing us all they know and understand as readers and writers.

Shaheen, who had written nothing for six months, until Roger introduced tellingboards, told and wrote the story of his grandfather's escape from the Ayatollah Khomeini in Iran (see Figure 13–6, page 205).

Megan was a good writer but reluctant to revise the writing. It seemed like too much work to have to add information or move information around. But with the tellingboard, she could do that without the inconvenience of having a written draft that needed attention. The pictures made revision easier (see Figure 13–7, page 206).

It quickly became obvious that tellingboards were a powerful tool for helping students move from the difficulty of getting words on paper to compelling pieces of writing we all enjoyed.

Lack of Tools

Few students want to write in longhand, but without the use of word processors on a daily basis, we have to rethink where and when writing happens. Are we providing the tools real writers use? If not, how is that changing the quality, the fluency, and the efficacy of writing?

> > > > >
See Sara Kajder's chapter (14) to see how she helps students use technology to change the way they write.
—KB, REP, LR

A lack of tools presents a huge challenge, but tools used inefficiently are equally pointless. When we don't keep up with the rapid development of technology, we can't really show students, or let them show us, how technology can change their writing.

Scripted Lessons Mandated for All Students, All Teachers at the Same Time.

While we see our students as individuals, and while we recognize the strengths and weaknesses of each one, policy mandates often seem to view students through the same myopic lens, treating all students as if they were the same. Yet *we* know that their differences are their strengths. We know how and when to differentiate our instruction based on the variety of learning styles each student brings to our classroom. We know how to take students from where they are to all they can be. We have to trust ourselves as professionals, hired because we know books, know reading, know writing, know the conventions of language, and know what to do to help each student grow as an individual based on his strengths and needs. We have to continue to work as a professional community to show others what works to keep students learning. Scripted lessons mandating Tuesday's writing be the same for each student in every school are guaranteeing mediocrity. We have to continue to learn and grow as professionals who use our voices to speak out against the standardization of all learning.

First Draft

Second Draft

Third Draft

My Granbpa was in the Iranian military when the Ayatollh khomenii, ~~who was~~ a bictator anb a very unkinb person reigned. Every man who was 16 anb ~~above~~ older was forceb to join the army. If you bibn't follow the rules anb live up to the expectations you were either hangeb or shot on site. My Granbpa was very smart anb brave; he was planning an escape to come to america. The men who trieb to escape were shot or put in military Jail. Even if you bib get far away, people who beleaveb in the Ayatollh's way anb religen, or most people were forceb to beleave, they woulb turn my Granbpa over to the goverment. He coulbn't tell anyone what he was planning. While my Granbpa was running he hab to hibe in people's houses for bays or even weeks at a time. He hib in backs of trucks or got on little faires finally he mabe his way into Europe ~~anb to contact~~ my mom in america who was marrieb,

to my bab. ~~but~~ Neither ~~me or~~ my brother nor I were born yet. She got him ~~some~~ money along with a VISA to come to America. When he finally bib he stayeb with us for a while. He coulbn't bring anything nor anyone; he had to leave behinb his wife, who later came to america after the Ayatollah fell. ~~also~~ he also ~~hab~~ left behinb his 3 houses anb all his money, which he was very wealthy. The money can never be useb or taken to this bay. The houses are rented to other people. ~~which~~ My Granbma goes back to check on the houses, But my Granbpa can never go back to Iran because he was a high ranking Intelligence Officer anb there is a bounty on his heab for $100,000.

Now he lives happily in California with his wife, anb is writing phulosife books.

FIGURE 13–7. *Megan's revisions—addition of squares—before going to the writing.*

More Focus on Reading Than Writing in University Courses and Professional Development Workshops.

The National Writing Project has done more for writing than any other group by expecting teachers to write for themselves and supporting that goal in numerous ways, including offering institutes where teachers learn how to do just that . . . and then teach others to do it. Teachers have worked tirelessly, many at their own expense, to attend summer institutes throughout the United

States—several weeks for learning all they can about themselves and their students as writers. But I know that even now, twenty years after I began learning about teaching and writing, all teachers and all students are not as engaged in writing as they could be, or *should* be. A new report by the National Commission on Writing in America's Schools and Colleges, *The Neglected R* (2006), concludes the same. University courses and staff development must offer more opportunities for teachers to write, if we are to become the best teachers of writing. The insert below offers you a great list of texts that you might turn to for more information on writing.

SOME READINGS ON WRITING

Angelillo, Janet. 2005. *Writing to the Prompt.* Portsmouth, NH: Heinemann.

Atwell, Nancie. 1998. *In the Middle: New Understandings About Writing, Reading, and Learning.* 2d ed. Portsmouth, NH: Heinemann.

———. 2002. *Lessons That Change Writers.* Portsmouth, NH: Heinemann.

———. 2006. *Naming the World: A Year of Poems and Lessons.* Portsmouth, NH: Heinemann.

Barbieri, Maureen. 1995. *Sounds from the Heart.* Portsmouth, NH: Heinemann.

Bomer, Katherine. 2005. *Writing a Life: Teaching Memoir.* Portsmouth, NH: Heinemann.

Buckner, Aimee. 2005. *Notebook Know How.* Portland, ME: Stenhouse.

Fletcher, Ralph. 1993. *What a Writer Needs.* Portsmouth, NH: Heinemann.

———. 1996. *Breathing in, Breathing Out: Keeping a Writer's Notebook.* Portsmouth, NH: Heinemann.

Graves, Donald H., and Penny Kittle. 2005. *Inside Writing.* Portsmouth, NH: Heinemann.

Heard, Georgia. 1995. *Writing Toward Home.* Portsmouth, NH: Heinemann.

———. 2002. *The Revision Toolbox.* Portsmouth, NH: Heinemann.

Lane, Barry. 1993. *After the End: Teaching and Learning Creative Revision.* Portsmouth, NH: Heinemann.

Murray, Donald M. 1996. *Crafting a Life.* Portsmouth, NH: Boynton/Cook.

National Commission on Writing. 2003. *The Neglected R: The Need for a Writing Revolution.* Washington, DC: College Entrance Examination Board.

Ray, Katie Wood. 2002. *What You Know by Heart.* Portsmouth, NH: Heinemann.

Romano, Tom. 1995. *Writing with Passion.* Portsmouth, NH: Heinemann.

———. 2000. *Blending Genre, Altering Style.* Portsmouth, NH: Heinemann.

———. 2004. *Crafting Authentic Voice.* Portsmouth, NH: Heinemann.

Spandel, Vicki. 2005. *The 9 Rights of Every Writer.* Portsmouth, NH: Heinemann.

Zinsser, William. 1980. *On Writing Well.* 2d ed. New York: Harper and Row.

High-Stakes Tests.

Several years ago, I met two young teachers who had to sign a clause in their contracts that if they didn't raise the scores of the students in their classrooms from one year to the next, they understood they would be fired. That is nearly impossible to accomplish—and unfair. New students being tested against former students? Educators need to ask themselves, *Is what I am being asked to do, or telling teachers they must do, good for kids? In what ways? Is this helping them grow as writers? Is what they are learning meaningful, sensible, and valuable?* When the answers are no, then conversations with decision makers in the district are a must. While we all agree that accountability is an important part of education, we must make sure that what we assess does indeed show us what students are learning. High-stakes tests rarely do that—and they most certainly do not show us what students are learning as a result of a thoughtful writing program.

> > < <

New teachers and experienced teachers are worried, bewildered, and angry when what we are told to do does not help the children in our academic care grow as learners. We are concerned when the tests of writing don't begin to show the rigor with which writers tackle a project when they are writing for real reasons for a real audience. That may be the most valid and crucial reason for our need to write—with passion, with conviction, with honesty, with voice—to show what does and does not work with our students.

Writing gives voice to the educators who know kids best, because we work with them every day. Writing ourselves lets us understand what we are asking our students to do. Writing puts energy back into our teaching lives because we have real reasons to write for a real audience. Writing lets us look closely at our students and ourselves—Who are we? Where do we fit in this world? Writing lets us hear the powerful, poignant, compelling voices of our students. It's their writing that keeps us in the classroom and gives us energy, because it offers us such hope for the future.

Having the courage to write, no matter what the issue, may even "nudge the world" enough to actually allow teachers to employ the practices that lead our students to powerful, compelling voices as writers. It's writing—and reading—that matters. It's a matter of common sense.

When you want to know more ...

Linda's vast experience teaching midddle school students to write has led to much writing of her own. You might look into her article "What's Right with Writing," in *Voices from the Middle* (2006), and her book *100 Quickwrites: Fast and Effective Freewriting Exercises That Build Students' Confidence, Develop Their Fluency, and Bring Out the Writer in Every Student* (2003).

>>> PENNY KITTLE

THE IMPORTANCE OF CHOICE

Jared sat staring at his computer.

"Having trouble?" I asked, nodding at the monitor.

"Mrs. Kittle, this is *really* hard," and it was the defeat in his voice that made me drag a chair near.

"What is?"

He narrowed his eyes. "I can't write from my *life*. I've never written anything in the last three years that wasn't about a book." His long fingers gestured at the screen. "I'm sitting here waiting for you to tell me what to write about. But that's stupid."

Jared was a senior, smart, willing, and respectful, able to dash off the five-paragraph, thesis-driven essay with remarkable aplomb; he was a master of literary analysis. He could shuffle literary terms, quote the text, and cite his sources, but there was little life in his prose. His process resembled the dull rub of cloth on an ancient table—the same territories of theme and symbolism, but little life, little voice, little trace of this writer. He'd missed the connection between reading someone's experience and writing his own. To discover this, he had to be freed from formulas and both allowed to and required to choose.

I know students understand reading more completely by writing about it, and there are many creative ways to connect students to ideas in literature. Certainly it makes sense to have students respond to literature some of the time: we want deep readers. But these may be mere writing activities to students, not writing that matters to them. When these papers are nothing but exercises, our students draft and rewrite as little as possible to get the paper done. They are unlikely to value any outcome of this work beyond a grade. They see no audience beyond the teacher, no purpose in their lives outside of school. As another student said to me last spring, "I don't imagine I'll be writing a lot of book reports in my engineering classes next fall." Writers can be completely detached in writing about literature, just stacking sentences into a structure created by the teacher. That is a superficial process that requires little. We need rigor in process, not just products, and that requires an emotional investment from the student.

I try to remember to teach writers, not writing. I want every student in my room on a mission to write well. How do I get there? I connect them to their passions. When students choose their topics, they write more and learn more. Here's why.

Choosing is the hardest part of composition.

I sit down to write a review of the field hockey game my students won this afternoon and I don't know where to start. I have to figure out how to show the players, the action, and the dialogue. The challenge slays me. I want life on the page. What to include? What to leave out? Creative acts are rigorous in the most stimulating and surprising ways. Translating lived experience into smooth and efficient writing is more demanding than repeating Mark Twain's views of human nature. If you don't believe me, try it: choose to write one moment from teaching that represents what you believe about your work.

Choice expands thinking.

When we study argument in my room, we read widely. I am on a constant search for the best model texts to use in class, so that my students hear varied voices and see varied structures in argument. We study what we will write. My students see that structure depends on the choices a writer makes—about topic and audience and evidence. When they are shown the myriad ways writers approach controversy, my students begin to understand the complexities of this genre. They try new modes and explore new territories while expanding who they are as writers and thinkers.

A confident voice is developed through choice.

Words that resonate with readers come from the heart of the writer. Chris wanted to write of standing in his living room—one week after his father died there—watching paramedics try to revive his brother from another attempted suicide. How could he make sense of that moment? He wrestled with choices for days: where to begin?

> > > *Chris wanted to write of standing in his living room—one week after his father died there—watching paramedics try to revive his brother from another attempted suicide. How could he make sense of that moment?*

Chris had failed his prior English courses because his analysis of *Romeo and Juliet* was filled with sentence fragments and incomplete thoughts; his writing didn't improve with journal entries for a character in Golding's *Lord of the Flies* or the multi-genre paper on Fitzgerald's *The Great Gatsby*. He saw no value in the work, so he didn't work very hard. In our workshop he found the place where the energy to write well comes from: his ideas. He labored to write, staying after class, then after school. He started an after-school writers' group for students. Of course he improved; all writing is rewriting. But he learned most of his craft based on the needs of a piece of his own writing. Too often our assignments fill time and grade books but not writers' toolboxes.

Choice feeds writers.

I want to go after my own revelations—not yours, not Fitzgerald's, *mine*. I want to know and understand my world. If writing develops my understanding of all I'm thinking, I'll write harder. I watch teenagers craft their work, narrowing focus and developing voice and spending hours on a piece, rereading and crafting again. Johnny reviews football game tapes because they might help him make his narrative real. Months after he's finished, his coach dies suddenly. The next morning he says, "I need to add a final scene to my football piece, Mrs. Kittle. I walked across the field for the first time since Mr. Millen died and everything felt different." That motivation to write is never going to be about a grade. When we can connect a writer to an inner desire to write, we can teach him anything.

Choice feeds the teacher, too.

I'm sitting on the couch today measuring the stack of papers I need to read this weekend. I know there is energy in those pages. The writing is filled with experience, understanding, and growth. Each one is a window into the thinking of my individual students. I am eager to read their work. As I collected final drafts Friday, Isaak asked, "Can we do this again? I didn't really take this one seriously until I saw what other people were writing." This is the boy who jumped out of a second-story window last year during English. He's a wild pirate child, but he's choosing this week to write about losing his father at age seven. Imagine all the ways he could write that piece. Imagine all he will learn about writing in that process. There is no template that can help, only writing and rewriting and discovery in a constant search for understanding and for his own writing voice.

And one last thing:

Choice prepares students for college.

Yes, our students will analyze information in college, but they'll also write narrative and research and argument and blended genres we haven't even named yet. In each moment they will need an experience—an overstuffed bag full of experiences—in narrowing choices down to the most compelling one for the task before them. They'll need confidence in their ability to make smart choices: they'll need to believe they can write anything.

We must plunge into possibility. We can free adolescents from writing sentences and papers and help them write their lives. What will sit beside them in a quiet, ratty dorm room as they fumble over the first draft of a paper due the next day? The process they used to capture a moment—an experience, a belief—that *process* and the tools they used will be there. We prepare writers by challenging them to think deeply and craft with passion. We prepare writers by offering choices—more, and more, and more.

> > > SARA B. KAJDER

Unleashing Potential with Emerging Technologies

IT CERTAINLY isn't new for English teachers to think closely about how technology can amplify our instruction. Sometimes this means calling out those moments where planning, curriculum, and tools come together to move students in new and powerful directions. Other times, however, it reveals holes in planning, misreading of content, instability in resources, and, most critically, those moments where we have allowed the technology to supersede our instructional goals and students' needs. Teaching is messy, and, despite some of the promises we've heard to the contrary, technology doesn't make our work any tidier.

I firmly believe that valuing and seeing the ways in which kids are engaging with new technologies outside of school can teach us a great deal about possibilities in engaging them as readers and writers in our classrooms. For some of us, this might be a new concept; for me, it's been critical to my own professional growth and to my thinking during my recent work in local schools.

This started for me as I walked down the hall of an urban, high-need high school, led by a proud principal into a teacher's classroom. He introduced the

We've set Sara Kajder's chapter here, after comments from others on writing, because she's extending our thinking about this critical topic as she reminds us that writing takes place at a screen with mouse, not pen, in hand.

—KB, REP, LR

scene (and the teacher) by saying, "She gets how to use technology with kids." What I saw wasn't surprising, but it reflects more of our classrooms than we'd like to admit.

After urging students to keep their individual laptops closed, the teacher moved into a ten-minute, paper-and-pencil grammar warm-up where students were recording "corrections" made to erroneous sentences projected from the overhead. At the close of the activity, students were asked to take out their copies of *Of Mice and Men* and listen closely to her instructions before opening their laptops:

> I'd like you to use the class to think about how Steinbeck works with character. In the class folder on the network, you'll find a Word document titled "charac-ter.doc." For today's work, we're going to open that, save a copy with your ini-tials, and enter the information that links the novel to the ideas in the document.

Students spent anywhere from ten to thirty minutes typing their responses and saving their finished work to the class folder on the network.

So, what's happening here with technology? Students are using a word processor to enter their ideas into a document and are then passing it around, which is largely what we do with technology in school. It's as if our instincts lead us to take what we've done in the past and reproduce the process using different tools to create the same product. It's comfortable. It's familiar. And, it's a way to work around issues of access. So here's the big question—Is that enough? Does doing something old with new technology mean that I'm teaching with technology and that I'm doing so in such a way as to really improve the reading and writing skills of the students in my classroom?

While spending some downtime in the same school's media center, I met Max, a bright student who was taking his second stab at eleventh grade, offering the explanation "This isn't my place." He'd identified my red university badge at the onset of our conversation and pushed to know what had brought me to his school, asking, "What could you possibly think that you could teach a bloke like me about technology?"

As I recovered from the stab of his question, I asked him to tell me how he used technology as a reader and as a writer. He looked at me blankly. Time passed. I broke into the silence by explaining that I was an English teacher. Max's eyes rolled. "Oh, man . . . ," he exhaled.

After more time passed, he suddenly blurted out, "The thing is my reading and writing doesn't happen in here. Anywhere I'd really want to write is blocked, or the stuff teachers ask us to do is so much the same thing again and again that it isn't really writing." Now we had something to talk about.

I turned my laptop to Max and asked him to show me where real writing happened. He pulled up his blog, a site bursting with original images, original video, and text, all written and created by Max to share his ideas and experiences. He explained that he posted to his blog daily, using a variety of modes and media. "Depending on what I have to say, I use different spaces in which to work, as talking about driving doesn't fit a paragraph in the same way that it fits an image that follows me driving down the road." For Max, this is writing that matters, or, as he described it, "2 AM writing." He explained, "It doesn't matter when or where—if I'm thinking and there is something that I'm burning to share or express, I do it." And *this* is writing that has a very engaged audience. "I write as much for getting my ideas out as I do to see the comments and responses of those who are listening and reacting. In school, writing is about handing something in. Here, it's about having something to say."

When I asked Max whether or not this kind of writing lived anywhere in his experience in school, he sat back quietly and shrugged. He eventually shared, "I don't learn about blogs from teachers. They don't know they exist, or they think about what the media tells them—like with MySpace [a reference to www.myspace.com]. School is about fitting things into tight little boxes that you measure with a test. You can't do that and use these tools." Just as telling as Max's words was his surprise at how I wanted to share his ideas with teachers. "My teachers don't have to know where to click. I can teach them that. I just want them to teach me the parts that I'm not thinking about yet."

When I paired Max's ideas with what I'd observed earlier in an English classroom that had been positioned as "high tech," I couldn't help but think that we've missed something really critical. In all of our attempts to move forward, we haven't looked to our kids to see what the possibilities are for merging what they know about technology with what we know about what it means to read and write well. We need to think about what happens when we really invent—and offer students, and ourselves, opportunities to do new things in new ways, taking advantage of the unique capacities of the multimodal tools now at our fingertips.

READING AND WRITING SPACES KIDS ARE ENGAGING IN OUTSIDE OF SCHOOL

> weblogs
> fanfiction
> wikis
> video games
> digital images
> digital video/digital storytelling
> podcasts
> MMORPGs (massive multiplayer online role-playing games)
> social bookmarks

Promise into Practice: New Tools and New Practices

So, what does it look like to do new things with new tools? What does it open up? What pressures does it place on our curricula? What roles does it create both for students and for teachers? In the sections that follow, we'll step into some classrooms that are making big moves toward lots that is new, but that are doing so slowly and mindfully. So much of what we've done in bringing technology into the classroom has been about speed. Emergent technology use is different. It requires time spent deeply considering the instructional value added by new tools and time spent crafting instruction that puts content and instructional goals ahead of teaching the technology.

In order to really consider what you're doing in your own practice, the survey in Figure 14–1 might be useful in bringing forward both what you believe about teaching with technology and the ways in which you put those beliefs into practice. I'm continually surprised by the ways in which I *know* better than I might *do*, but tools like this are helpful in providing me with a space for articulating and thinking about what I value and what I actually do within my teaching.

Each of the narratives that follow will walk us into a different English classroom where teachers and students are working as readers, writers, thinkers, speakers, viewers, directors, producers, editors, collaborators, and listeners. We won't focus on where to point and click; we will talk a lot about how these examples push on the idea of instructional value added and bring students into authentic, engaging learning experiences that wouldn't otherwise be possible.

Class Blog

Mrs. Abel's seventh-period English class maintains a class weblog that gets more daily hits than the school district's website. She began by using the site as a place to quickly post links and ideas, introduce new concepts, and provide students with a forum for discussion about the class. As students began to use the site, Mrs. Abel ratcheted up the task, asking one student per day to serve as the class scribe. The job of the scribe, as explained by Brendan, a student in the class, is "to put together all that happened in class, not as a summary but as a synthesis. . . . My job as scribe is to share where we are but make sure that I do so with one eye on where we've been and one on where we're going." Some posts are written, but many others include images and video, opening up what counts as valued communication in the classroom and broadening the possibilities for how voices can contribute and be present. Alexis shared, "If I'm responding to literature we're all reading, sometimes I can't put into words what I can into a picture—and that is something that I can post for response from the entire class. I'm not one to talk in class, but I can talk here—and through pictures."

WHAT COUNTS IN TEACHING ENGLISH WITH TECHNOLOGY?

Directions: Read each statement twice. First, *circle* the number that represents what you believe. For the second rating, *underline* what you actually do.

1. How important do you believe the following is? Circle the number. ○ 2. How often do you do each? Underline _____	Scale of Importance				
	Not at all	Not very	No opinion	Somewhat	Extremely important
Integrate technologies other than a word processor (e.g., MS Word) or a multimedia presentation tool (MS PowerPoint) into your teaching.	1	2	3	4	5
Provide students with an opportunity to use technologies as readers and writers during class time.	1	2	3	4	5
Critically evaluate the technologies that you are required to use in your teaching—or that are provided in your lab, media center, classroom, and so on.	1	2	3	4	5
Keep up with the technologies that your students are using outside of the classroom.	1	2	3	4	5
Evaluate and articulate what literacy means within your teaching, the tasks you ask students to complete, your classroom culture and environment, and the models that you provide.	1	2	3	4	5
Work alongside students to evaluate how emerging technologies work as reading and writing tools.	1	2	3	4	5
Read blogs.	1	2	3	4	5
Post comments on others' blogs.	1	2	3	4	5
Maintain (regularly) your own blog.	1	2	3	4	5
Provide students with opportunities to create multimodal texts (e.g., digital story, digital video, digital book trailer) in response to what they read or in response to a prompt.	1	2	3	4	5
Require students to use and cite online sources when researching a topic.	1	2	3	4	5
Discuss searching strategies with students prior to integrating online sources into a research project.	1	2	3	4	5
Listen to podcasts.	1	2	3	4	5
Provide students with opportunities to write, record, and upload their own online content (e.g., book reviews, podcasts, wiki postings, weblog posts, digital stories).	1	2	3	4	5
Provide students with opportunities to interact with authentic audiences.	1	2	3	4	5
Use technologies (e.g., epals, podcasts, e-mentoring, fanfiction writing) to connect students with authentic audiences for their work.	1	2	3	4	5
Collaborate with other teachers (or students) to design technology-infused curricula or assignments.	1	2	3	4	5
Learn a new strategy, tool, or structure for integrating technology transparently and effectively into your teaching to do something you could not previously do.	1	2	3	4	5

FIGURE 14–1.

Adapted from Survey of Professional Beliefs and Practices *by Kylene Beers, which is reproduced in Appendix B, page 380.*

Students aren't writing just when they are the day's scribe. Some use the blog to ask questions as they are reading. Some post content from their writing-reading journals that they think might be useful to the discussion. Some post ideas and opinions that emerge from discussion. Enid explained, "We aren't assigned a number. Writing here isn't about that—and, if it is, someone will call you on it. Instead, writing is about having something useful to say. I write to see what I think as well as to see how that plays with where everyone else might be."

Comments to student posts are first sent to Mrs. Abel for review before they are posted. Where this is done in part to protect the community, it's also done out of her own interest. She explained:

> We're getting responses from students in China who are reading my kids' thoughts on *Woman Warrior*. We're getting responses from writers who are pushing my students to think deeply about how they are working with nonfiction. I want to know when those are going up so they become a part of class, and I can ensure that students know how their work is being seen and responded to. I've never had a tool like this.

> > > > >

In his chapter, Jim Burke talks about how he uses threaded discussions to get his students "talking" about their summer reading (see page 161). You might think about what might work best for you—threaded discussions or class weblogs (blogs).

—*KB, REP, LR*

Looking More Deeply

As much as new technologies make possible new instructional practices, the use of a weblog in the English language arts classroom lives in more of a gray area, somewhere between a journal and a multigenre project. In the simplest possible terms, a weblog is an easily created, easily changed and updated website that allows a writer to publish his thoughts online by doing little more than entering text into a window and pressing a button labeled Post and Publish. There are a variety of free tools that allow you to bring blogging safely into a classroom—ranging from www.blogger.com (the uberpopular blogging site now owned by Google) to edublogs.org (an open source site for teachers and students). To be a blog, a site needs a couple of critical features:

> a chronological ordering of posts (so the reader can quickly see what is new content and when it was posted);

> dated and archived posts (so what is posted in September is still readily accessible in December);

> a function that allows for comments to be posted to an entry (allowing for a community that is either wide open or restricted by a unique password and login); and

> a menu or indexing feature that usually looks like a calendar.

What really makes a blog a compelling website is the kind of writing that it ought to contain. These aren't static, disconnected pieces of writing. Rather, these are reflective, responsive posts (often made within the same day) that build from one another. This is metacognitive writing with a clear purpose and point of view. Done well, a blog is about having something really significant to say and sharing those thoughts with a responsive and engaged audience. Blog postings cannot be compulsory—for example, where a teacher would require all students to respond to a specific prompt. Rather, they are artifacts born out of a lively interest.

When I first thought about ways of using blogs in my teaching, I immediately thought about migrating a lot of the projects that I had previously done through email. I often used tools like epals.com or the *electronic emissary* to create collaborations between my students and expert writers, readers, museum curators, filmmakers, screenwriters, and so on. We also would link with other classrooms who were reading the same or similar texts or taking on similar projects. Where in the past I'd filtered all of that communication through my professional email account, moving it to a blog would amplify community and provide students access in a safe, respectful, and productive writing space. I also thought of using blogs as peer editing spaces to support students' writing or as a place for online mentoring of senior research projects that usually had previously involved interactions only between me and my students. Again, the goal was to map the work into the unique capacities of the tool—connective, often multimodal writing (as students can post images, video, etc.) completed for an engaged, responsive community and audience.

> < < < < <
> If you aren't familiar with this term and want more information you might go online to http://emissary.wm.edu/. There you will find rich information about this Web-based telementoring service. Designed to set up electronic exchanges among teachers, students, and mentors, electronic emissary is a powerful way to extend learning and teaching not only beyond our classroom walls but beyond our own expertise.
>
> —*KB, REP, LR*

Stepping into a Classroom

Blogs bring student writers an opportunity to write in an online space for an authentic audience and to take a space where they likely haven't been taught to engage as scholars (not much of that happens in MySpace) and create something richly distinct. From the moment that content is posted to a weblog, it has an audience—whether or not that includes the full class, other classes of students, or a community of experts that the teacher has brought into the fold. Writers who have real audiences listening and responding to their writing learn firsthand how writing is a communicative act; they learn to take responsibility for their words, to defend and modify them based on reactions from the real people sitting around them (Kutz and Roskelly 1991, 263).

And when we do this right, we can push past the kinds of curriculum that Max and his peers meet daily, where the study of language in class is completely removed from the uses of language in and outside of class. Kids are blogging outside of our classroom walls, and they'll continue to blog whether or not we provide a space in our classrooms for them to engage, critically, with blogs as communities, as spaces for discourse, and as spaces for developing voice. To me, there is a great deal of potential in using this space to move the conversation forward and really teach students about writing in online spaces and online communities.

As a classroom teacher, I'm surprised by how our dialogue about writing changes once we start working with a variety of writing tasks that include a responsive audience. I no longer get questions about format. Students don't raise their hands and ask about page requirements or what the repercussions are for using twelve-point font as opposed to ten-point. Class discussion moves instead to having something to say. This is higher-stakes writing, not because of my assessment, but because of the response of the community.

Podcasting

Literature circles (or book clubs) provide classroom spaces in which student readers do the work that proficient, engaged readers do. Students read self-selected, interesting books and seek opportunities for rich, authentic discussion. For Mrs. Jackson, the biggest instructional hurdle was how to be in five circle discussions simultaneously. Through the use of an iPod paired with an iTalk microphone set in the center of each circle, the relevance of students' work has been ratcheted up, as the audience is no longer just the members of the circle or the teacher in the moments she is able to grab while circulating. Students are now required to record, mix, and post their discussions to the class website, allowing students and anyone with access to the class website to be both producers and consumers of content.

What does this mean inside the classroom? Each group discussion is digitally recorded. This has become the students' space to think, to play, and to push. At times, they are asked to upload or podcast the entire discussion. However, more regularly, students are required to mix their file (using free audio tools like Audacity) to extract specific parts of the discussion. On the classroom wall, Mrs. Jackson posts the following list of prompts that students use to focus their work:

1. What questions were left unresolved?

2. Which moments of the discussion were the most compelling?

3. What parts of the discussion might help convince a peer to read the text under discussion?

4. Where did the discussion fall apart or fail?

5. What are the key ideas emerging in your conversation about this text?

Students' podcasts sound like polished radio shows, often beginning with self-recorded or self-mixed audio introductions with echoes of NPR and the

> > > > >

Take a look at the description Kylene Beers (Chapter 1) offers about one student's response to school-based writing and his own blog writing for affirmation on Sarah's points.

—KB, REP, LR

punch of an adolescent's chosen beat. More important, students also add their own frame, either setting up what the audience is about to hear or synthesizing or commenting on the content throughout the file. In doing so, podcasting has invited these students to naturally evaluate their own work and set goals for subsequent discussions. Evaluation has become less about students seeking out their teacher's feedback and more about their own responses to the dialogue, work, and products of the circle.

Looking More Deeply

Amidst the data demonstrating the significant numbers of students who are not finding success in school-based literacy tasks is an emerging trend confirming that students might be reading in school but are not likely to be doing so outside of school (National Endowment for the Arts 2004). In order to be inclined to read authentically, students need opportunities to engage with texts in the same voluntary and generative ways that adults do. To that end, a podcast allows for the creation of readers' artifacts ranging from authentic book talks to literature circle discussions to digital stories. Here, students are creating artifacts of their experiences, thoughts, and interactions as readers and writers around texts.

> > > *In creating audio content, students are scriptwriting, writing questions to stimulate discussion (especially if the recording is capturing a live discussion that might involve participants outside of the classroom), selecting appropriate venues for publishing their work, and responding to comments submitted by listeners. Here, learners evaluate what to say, consider options, and make choices. Learning rests on these risks.*

In creating audio content, students are scriptwriting, writing questions to stimulate discussion (especially if the recording is capturing a live discussion that might involve participants outside of the classroom), selecting appropriate venues for publishing their work, and responding to comments submitted by listeners. Here, learners evaluate what to say, consider options, and make choices. Learning rests on these risks. Such podcasts can be used to invite students to naturally evaluate their own work and the work of their peers; allow for rich oral history archiving; archive student discussions, think-alouds, and fluency drills for analysis over time; publish original work; and provide a space for reflection, synthesis, and continued dialogue. Here, curriculum builds on providing students with agency, choice, and an authentic audience, all of which build motivation and learning engagement. As Dyson argues, "Children's contributions contribute substantially to intellectual development in general and literacy growth in particular, given tasks worth talking about and permission to talk" (1983, 5).

Podcasted audio content also provides students with the metacognitive challenge of editing recorded texts, selecting what will be included in a finished product, splicing content so that it cleanly conveys intended meaning, and polishing presentation by framing the podcast with introductory and closing content.

Creating a podcast requires that students have access to a tool that allows them to digitally record content. That can range from using a computer with a microphone plugged into it, to a digital voice recorder, to an iPod with a microphone plugged into the base, to an audio conversation using skype.com and a third-party tool to do the recording. Students then take that audio file, possibly edit it, and post it online for sharing. As with many of the tools that are discussed in this chapter, students bring a great deal of knowledge to the task, making instruction a lot less about where to point and click and much more about content.

Stepping into a Classroom

In regard to the instructional uses of podcasting in the literacy classroom, there are three big ideas to consider that significantly affect both the student reader and the learning environment. In making audio or enhanced podcasts, students are creating a literacy artifact—of a specific reading or experience or story—at a specific time in their own understanding or growth. Where English teachers have done this using a variety of tools (e.g., tape recording, portfolio construction), the podcast invites examination for patterns across artifacts by both the classroom teacher and the student. The electronic nature of the file allows for ease in manipulation and bookmarking.

Second, this kind of work brings teachers into the reading of their students. This is no small feat since reading, unless made public through round-robin reading or a performed read-aloud, is typically a private, internal process that is personal (and often mystifying) to the individual student. Through the use of a podcast of a read-aloud or a student's participation in a literature circle, the teacher is allowed to listen in. This isn't about grading as much as it is an opportunity to hear students' connections, struggles, questions, and ideas. Here, quieter students can have more voice in classroom work, and all students are able to see their own work, and role, as readers in the classroom.

Last, examining their podcasts as artifacts allows students to explore and evaluate their progress across tasks in a course. Where we've looked to portfolios and other assessment tools to do this kind of work, the multimodal nature of the podcast permits students different entrance points into their own work as well as different possibilities to stretch, should they see that their work is predominantly situated within one mode or a pairing of modes or within one type of text or textual response.

> > > > >

If you've read Cynthia Aguilar, Danling Fu, and Carol Jago's chapter on English language learners (8), you know that they too discuss this issue of the quiet student. Take a look at what they have to say about how writing can give that student a louder voice and then look at how their idea becomes even more powerful when connected to Sara's point here.

—*KB, REP, LR*

Writing a Wikibook

The students in my fifth-period eleventh-grade honors English class simply struggled when it came to reading Camus' *Stranger*. Each year, as quickly as I distributed the text, I saw students pulling tattered and highlighted copies of

CliffsNotes from their backpacks. After talking with kids, it became clear that this was as much a factor of the mythology surrounding the reading of that novel as a part of the rite of passage of an eleventh grader as it was a factor of the actual reading skills and confidence of these students. They'd been told that they couldn't possibly think their way through the text without some sort of support, and they trusted the sage voices of those who had come before them more than they did their own voices as readers.

In an attempt to combat this thinking, I offered up a challenge. Before doling out the texts (and watching the yellow edges begin to creep from behind novels and the corners of notebooks), I asked students to join me in an experiment. Instead of reading this text and relying on what had already been written to guide us, I wanted us to create the reader's guide for the novel, incorporating what we brought to the text along with what we uncovered and were able to learn over the course of our study together.

Using the wikibooks.org website, we were able to set up an annotated text to work alongside our study of the novel. The wikibooks site required that our work include various kinds of study aids for reading, understanding, and teaching the text, including but not limited to explanatory notes, introductions, summaries, questions and answers, charts, lists, indices, references, wikilinks, pictures, and audio. Students were initially hesitant, but once we started moving forward, the site took on a life of its own. Initially, they made obligatory posts (yes, I started by counting points for contributions). However, something happened about a week into the project. I received an email from a teacher in Seattle (we were in Charlottesville, Virginia) requesting that her students be allowed to email my class questions and ideas that they had in using our site as they read the novel.

When I shared the request with my class, Gerald was the first student to reply. "You mean that someone is reading this? Not just us?" Within three days, content was exploding on the site. Students had added videos that offered enactments of scenes. Some were podcasting their literature group discussions. Others were linking to every bit of relevant content that they could find. And, in class, I'd never had more participation. By the end of our study of the novel, we'd created a reader's guide to *The Stranger* that was multimodal, completely owned by each of the students in the class, and receiving a large, and validating, number of hits each day. Sam explained, "This is the first time that what I thought meant more than fishing around to figure out what someone else was thinking about what I read. . . . I think that makes this the first book I've *really* read."

Looking More Deeply

The Web is no longer a read-only environment. Instead, tools like wikis make creating content almost as easy as consuming it. In other words, it's just as possible that students in Missouri are turning to the Web to learn about Mark

> < < < < <
> Take a look again at Chapter 8, "English Language Learners." On page 121, Cindy Aguilar makes a point to mention how writing in blogs, chat rooms, and technologically sophisticated realms is helpful to English language learners. We appreciate Sara's discussion of what this might involve for all students; likewise, we appreciate that Cindy thought to highlight the use of this tool with ELLs.
> —*KB, REP, LR*

Twain as it is that they are contributing what they know about his presence in their hometowns, their histories, and their curricula. In the read-write Web, students have the capacity to create content that teaches us—and a much larger community of readers—what they know.

A wiki is a website that allows readers, users, and writers to easily contribute content or edit existing content that is viewable online. Sometimes this requires a login and registration, and sometimes it does not—that just depends on how the site is set up. *Wiki* is a Hawaiian word meaning "fast," though some refer to it as a backronym for "what I know is."

Both of those definitions really come into play when we consider how this tool lives in an English classroom. Wikis are collaborative writing spaces where a community of users are creating content by reading, writing, and editing a shared document (see Figure 14–2).

Publishing happens fast here; once a user submits changes to the content of a page, the page immediately updates. Adding content or making changes to the page is as simple as it is quick. Every page in a wiki has a link that reads "edit page." By clicking on that link, users are brought to a page that presents the text within an editable area where one can delete, revise, and add new content. It is no more complicated than the text box used for entering the content of an email. Finally, each wiki page also has a page history where changes can be tracked along with the identity of the writer who made each change. So, if need

> > > > >

A backronym is a type of acronym that begins as a normal, ordinary word and is later interpreted as an acronym. How do we know that? We went to www.answers.com, which functions as an "encyclodic-tionalmanacapedia" and is a great reference tool.

—*KB, REP, LR*

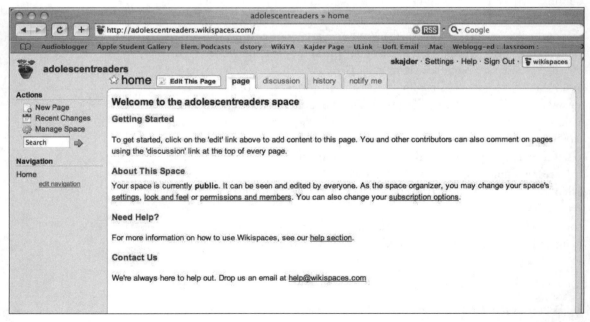

FIGURE 14–2. *A Sample Wiki*

be (and we know that can happen when working with kids), you can use the history page to revert to a previous version.

More often than not, as soon as I begin talking about wikis with teachers, we rapidly move to talking about ways of making sure that little Sara in period three doesn't go on a rampage and vandalize a class-run wiki. Some wiki tools (take a look at pbwiki.com or www.wikispaces.com) will allow for the use of a password. Although the content of the wiki is viewable to anyone who knows the URL, a user must have both a login and a password in order to contribute, edit, change, or comment on content. That said, I've found that in order to foster genuine collaboration, it's important that I give students in the class responsibility for and ownership of the site. If it's something that I police, the work will go only so far. If it's something that the community polices, students learn how to publish content as well as how to negotiate meaning and genuinely collaborate.

Stepping into a Classroom

There are a few things that make this work really unique. Here, the teacher as informed reader directs, guides, and promotes inquiry by engaging in it herself. I wasn't a grader. I wasn't the uber-reader in the class who had all the answers. My writing was merged with my students' writing. Our thoughts were collective. No matter how hard I'd tried to get that kind of balance in class dialogue, this was the first time I was able to make it happen, and the tool had a great deal to do with that. Also, writing in our wiki wasn't publicly identifiable by anyone but me. That's part of what led to the 100 percent participation rate that I had across the class—students were able to write and contribute more safely than in other writing spaces, and the dialogue around their ideas kept them moving forward.

Students saw this as a different kind of writing than what we usually engaged in during class. In part, I believe that had to do with the idea that we were compiling a guide that included lots of different resources, not just a five-paragraph essay. They identified a more dramatic motivation, though, when they shared that this was writing that captured their emerging thinking throughout their reading—writing that changed and brought revision to life in new ways. Rebecca shared, "Here, writing allows us to put it all down . . . so we can return and rethink it." Further, the work here was generated from the class as a whole group, as a series of groups, and as individual readers, each doing real work, moving toward new understandings about significant parts of what was studied. And, students had an almost unprecedented amount of authority over their own learning as we were creating a knowledge artifact valued by others outside of our class community.

< < < < <
Don Murray helps us understand what happens when we write with our students, complete the same assignments we give our students (Chapter 12). We were struck by how Sara pushed our thinking on this in this section as she shows us how generative writing can be for all of us—teachers and students—when technology is a part of the process.
—*KB, REP, LR*

Book Trailer

It is my expectation as a teacher that all students have rich, robust, and complete literacy lives. Reading, writing, speaking, listening, and viewing need to matter deeply outside of our classroom. To that end, I regularly assign projects and tasks that span time outside of class. Ting named one of these projects the Shaking Books Awake assignment. Essentially a remix of an independent reading project, this activity has students independently select and read a work of adult or adolescent literature and then create a two- to three-minute movie trailer that presents images, commentary, and ultimately, a review meant to lead peers to either select the text or allow it to remain in slumber on our shared shelves.

For her first trailer, Ting, a quiet student new to us from the ESL program, focused on sharing her reading of Pete Hautman's *Godless*, a book that either hooks student readers immediately or leaves them a bit cold. She explained, "That's the challenge . . . if I'm really going to move others to this book, why choose something that doesn't push me to do so?"

Her trailer opened silently, with print questions unfolding on the screen, reading, "What happens when your faith is shaken? What do you do with the questions that awaken? Where do you go for answers?" The usually rowdy class was curiously still as the screen filled with words and the lilting sound of Ting's soundtrack, a series of chords and harmonies she recorded herself, playing on the home piano.

The still was broken as a rapid succession of images appeared, each following the other at a dizzying pace that was almost too quick for the viewer to piece together. Then, Ting's voice began to walk us through the characters, the central tensions, and the reasons that she kept reading. And, as she spoke, the images returned; this time, paced slowly as she unpacked what she wanted us to see both by the motion on the screen and her words. The images she used for characters were pictures of close friends whom she'd envisioned as she read, despite the book's use of male characters. Henry, the nemesis of the book's protagonist, appeared as Ting's older sister as she spoke about rivalry and feeling flattened. As a review, she offered, "This book isn't about religion or God . . . it's about being a real teenager, having real questions, finding out some of the suckier answers, and discovering crushes, play, and shared things to laugh at."

After class, six students signed up to borrow our single class copy. More important, Ting left beaming as three students she didn't previously know asked if she'd help "consult" on their trailers. She shared later, "I had something to say that I couldn't do on paper, and the kids who do paper didn't know how to do that. To them, I was a writer. To me, I was a writer who was heard."

Looking More Deeply

A digital book trailer is a concise two- to three-minute digital video in which students are challenged to meld still images, motion, print text, and soundtrack (both narration and music) in communicating ideas, insights, and discoveries about a self-selected text. Students in this class used iMovie to build their digital videos as we were working on Apple computers. In a classroom with PCs, we could have just as easily done the project using Microsoft MovieMaker, another piece of software that allows the user to create and edit digital videos. What matters is that students are working with a digital video editor that allows them to work with a time line. (See Figure 14–3.)

I've used book talks to invite and incite student reading throughout my years of teaching. Some caught. Some fell flat, becoming performances for a grade or points rather than an excited reader's opportunity to share a discovered text with the class. This time, when I asked students to visually represent both their thinking and those elements of the text that made it a compelling or essential read, it was as if new life were breathed into the assignment. Here, we could use technology to engage students who might not otherwise be interested, and do so in a way that took us somewhere better.

The in-class portion of this work has everything to do with selecting texts and then compiling the reader's reactions, thoughts, and representations within the book trailer. The actual reading happens outside of the class. Scripting and initial writing also happen outside of the class, after the class has screened a range of examples—including those who really used the medium so effectively, I wanted to head directly to the media center for the book, and those that were still working to get readers to that place. Most scripts are less than a page in length, challenging students to allow the visuals and sound to carry some bit of the narrative and also demanding a significant degree of precision in the writing.

> > > *I do not teach the technology. I don't teach them where to click. What I do teach is how to ensure that your product conveys the meaning that you intend. I teach multimodal composition— ways of working with multiple modes to create a rich, compelling product.*

I require students to have completed a storyboard and draft script before they can secure time in front of one of the classroom or lab computers. Simply put, I don't have the luxury of instructional time that would allow for them to compose from scratch in front of the computer. Instead, I need them to get in, get it done, and get out. I plan as if all of my students need to have access inside of school in order to get the project complete. As much as technology has permeated our lives, many of my students still don't have access outside of school or library walls.

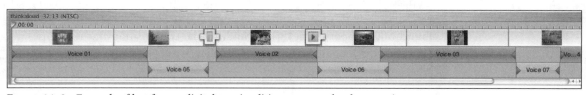

FIGURE 14–3. *Example of bar from a digital-movie editing program that lets you time segments.*

It's essential that in doing this work, you value the knowledge that students are bringing to the task. Students don't come into my class as empty vessels waiting to be filled with knowledge about multimedia technologies or digital video tools. The bonus? *I do not teach the technology.* I don't teach them where to click. What I *do* teach is how to ensure that your product conveys the meaning that you intend. I teach multimodal composition—ways of working with multiple modes to create a rich, compelling product. I teach students that the literacy knowledge that they bring into the classroom is varied and valued, and that we all have a next step that we're working toward.

Stepping into a Classroom

So many class projects end at the submission date and aren't seen again until portfolio time. Instead, this project resulted in an artifact that students considered a resource, one that fed our class library or our reading outside of class. As Allison described, "This is our 'what's next' reading . . . I think we should be creating these throughout the year. Otherwise, aren't we saying that we only read when it's assigned?"

I asked students to reflect on what they learned about themselves as readers that they didn't know or see as clearly when this work started. Some talked about the fact that they didn't want the trailers they created to define or limit what others would think of the text. Others talked about seeing their interests and dislikes in an amplified way. Gus explained, "I never saw it, but I come at books in a certain way. If I'm not there in the first ten pages, I don't go anywhere. But that was really clear here, as after page 10, I didn't have anything more to say." Shelia shared, "I'm only ever reading books that I know I can get through before I actually read them. It is comfortable reading. And that comes out loud and clear in my trailer. I need a stretch." For the most part, students were selecting books that were new reads, explaining that "rereading is almost like cheating" (which gave me an immediate place to go to unteach a perception that I felt was limiting their work).

In doing this work, kids learn how to be learners and readers. We weren't looking to the technology to do anything more than provide a different kind of composing space and, more important, a different kind of a product. The filmic nature of the trailers positioned independent reading in a really engaging light, where, for most students, it had previously been a task that they'd trudged through and for which they were rarely held accountable. Although we couldn't do this work with everything that students were reading, students found other opportunities where multimodal composition fit. In a sense, we expanded the tool kit for writing as much as we expanded our thinking about what counted as valued reading.

Big Ideas with Even Bigger Possibilities

Posted next to my computer is a quote from Hephzibah Roskelly that fuels and inspires so much of my work. It reads: "Emerging occasions emerge only if teachers look" (Kutz and Roskelly 1991, 308). Teaching with technology in the English classroom is about always looking, whether it's seeing kids and the range of talents and literacies that they bring into our classrooms or it's seeing the possibilities in a new tool that allows me to amplify curricula for the better. As the literacies that kids bring into our classrooms change (alongside the literacies that they need in order to be productive and competitive in the world outside of school), there is a very real pressure to make sure that what we teach is relevant and helps to push them to develop the skills needed to be self-directed, ubiquitous learners. I cannot do that without providing opportunities for them to read deeply, think critically, and write closely for responsive audiences that span the globe. New technologies challenge me to create openings.

> > > *Teaching with technology in the English classroom is about always looking, whether it's seeing kids and the range of talents and literacies that they bring into our classrooms or it's seeing the possibilities in a new tool that allows me to amplify curricula for the better.*

Perhaps more significant, they challenge me to resee what I teach in the context of a new classroom/community culture with each new group of students. That means looking closely at what I value as a teacher—and what skills I bring to each tool and task. I wrestle with each new technology that I encounter, in part because the pointing and clicking doesn't come naturally to me and in part because I demand that a new tool take me and my students somewhere better and richer in our work as readers and writers. As a foundation, teachers need to know enough about the tools both to affirm students' uses and to design the kinds of instruction that will move them to use the tools authentically, purposefully, and effectively. From there, the possibilities expand as we think critically about what possibilities new tools afford us. There's no denying it. We're past the point where we can keep doing old things with old tools, or old things with new tools. Students simply won't allow it. No matter how savvy they might be or not be, they are all looking to us to push them, to stretch their thinking, and to teach them to use the tools of the truly literate in a rapidly changing world.

When you want to know more . . .

We've probably all been intimidated, at one time or another, with rapidly developing technologies. If Sara has offered some assistance here, you'll find further help in *Bringing the Outside In: Visual Ways to Engage Reluctant Readers* (2006a). She offers suggestions for helping readers create their own stories in "Meeting Readers: Using Visual Literacy Narratives in the Classroom," from *Voices from the Middle* (2006b).

Connecting to my thoughts

Connecting to other texts

On teaching English

Foster, Harold M. 2002. *Crossing Over: Teaching Meaning-Centered Secondary English Language Arts*. 2nd ed. Mahwah, NJ: Lawrence Erlbaum.

Moffett, James. 1981. *Coming on Center: English Education in Evolution*. Montclair, NJ: Boynton/Cook.

Purves, Alan C., Theresa Rogers, and Anna O. Soter. 1995. *How Porcupines Make Love III: Readers, Texts, Cultures in the Response-Based Literature Classroom*. White Plains: Longman.

Elbow, Peter. 1990. *What Is English?* New York; Urbana, IL: Modern Language Association of America; National Council of Teachers of English.

> > > JEFFREY D. WILHELM
> MICHAEL W. SMITH

Making It Matter Through the Power of Inquiry

Introduction: Understanding the Flow

Given all the findings about how infrequently boys read and how they under-achieve in all areas of literacy (see Smith and Wilhelm 2002 for a review), we were surprised to find in our *"Reading Don't Fix No Chevys"* study that all of our young male informants engaged intensely and with great enjoyment in all kinds of literate activity. What motivated that activity were the conditions of flow experiences articulated by Csikszentmihalyi (1990). When the conditions of flow were present, the boys embraced literate activities. When those conditions were absent (as was the case in most of their school-based literacy activities), the boys rejected literate activity.

Csikszentmihalyi argues that we are most fully engaged and happy when we are in the flow, in other words, when we are experiencing something so intensely that nothing else seems to matter. He identifies eight characteristics of flow experiences that we think can be usefully collapsed into four main princi-ples. According to Csikszentmihalyi, flow experiences occur when they provide a sense of control and competence, a challenge that requires an appropriate

If you're reading this book in order, then you've just read Sara Kajder's chapter (14) and seen powerful ways to use technology to engage stu-dents, not just motivate, but truly engage. We've placed this chapter after Sara's because engagement is tied to inquiry, the topic Jeff and Michael discuss. Sara's chap-ter expands our understanding of engagement through tech-nology while these two focus our understanding of inquiry. This chapter also serves as powerful pre-reading for the following chapter on working with underachieving students.
—*KB, REP, LR*

< < < < <

You've now read the name Csikszentmihalyi three times and either "flow" over it easily because you can pronounce it or are skipping it because you can't pronounce it or are spending too much time on it trying to figure out how to pronounce it! We'll step in here and offer a phonetic pronunciation so that when you discuss with others his principle of flow, you'll not only be able to discuss the ideas but can use his name:

chick-sent-mih-high

—*KB, REP, LR*

level of skill, clear goals and feedback, and a focus on the immediate experience. These four principles plus one that we added—the importance of the social—resounded in our data. Here's a quick summary of each:

1. *Competence and Control*—When competence (the ability to do something well) and control (the sense of having meaningful choices and exerting one's individuality) are part of an activity, then engagement is higher and more sustained. The boys in our study wanted to make choices, state opinions, and create and do things that displayed their individual identity through competence. Situations were motivating when the boys were clearly becoming more competent and exercising ever-increasing control and independence over what they were doing.

2. *Appropriate Challenge and Assistance to Meet the Challenge*—When people feel challenged, in such a way that makes achievement difficult but attainable, and when the necessary help is provided in the context to meet the challenge, then motivation and learning are fostered. This condition was met when the boys were assisted (by teachers, collaborators, the situation, rituals, practice, etc.) to meet a meaningful challenge that was neither too easy nor too hard. Interestingly, the boys complained more often that school was too easy rather than too hard.

3. *Clear Goals and Immediate Feedback*—When the purpose of an activity is clear, and feedback is continuous and immediately usable, flow and learning are promoted. The boys wanted to have a clear and important purpose that, in their eyes, mattered and had a functional value; at the same time, they needed (and enjoyed) clear, visible signs of their progress on a continual basis.

4. *Immersion in the Immediate*—Total engagement and immersion are the *sine qua non* of flow. Situations that were motivating allowed our boys to lose a sense of time and place by requiring their full engagement and participation. They preferred tasks that provided fun in the moment and that addressed immediate needs and concerns over those that prepared them for some distant goal, like college or life after school.

5. *The Importance of the Social*—Our data support the idea that when learning is relational it is always more engaging and richer than learning when alone. The boys in our study were consistently motivated by the social dimension of the activities in which they engaged. The social dimension, in this context, involved far more to our informants than simply talking or collaborating with friends and classmates; it also involved using activities to pursue relationships, over time, with families, authors, characters, teachers, and important ideas and social projects.

Many groups and commentators have indicated that student motivation is the primary challenge facing teachers (see, for example, www.literacytrust.org.uk). As we have explored elsewhere (Wilhelm and Smith 2006), the research on motivation tends to focus on either the origins and effects of individual students' interests—what and why someone does something—or on situational interest, that is, "the environmental . . . and contextual factors that elicit . . . interest across individuals" (Hidi and Harackiewicz 2000, 152). We argue that addressing individual interests in an attempt to engage students, though doubtless valuable, can be extremely time-consuming and is probably too difficult to achieve given the various students in each classroom and the many constraints placed on teachers. Situational interest, however, works for all students no matter their individual tendencies.

We believe that the findings about flow in our *"Chevys"* study demonstrate how to create situational interest that will work to promote the engagement of all students, regardless of their multifarious individual interests. (As a quick for instance, though you may not be able to focus on Ben's passion for rocketry or Jamie's for anime, through your instruction you could create an inquiry unit around the question "What are civil rights and how are they best protected?" that would meet all the conditions of flow and therefore satisfy the conditions for situational interest.) In particular, those findings have led us to three conclusions that have strong implications for classroom practice. As teachers, we must

1. structure instruction to directly and explicitly address questions of genuine importance

2. expand notions of text and curriculum, and what counts as meaningful reading and learning

3. expand notions of competence, especially *student* competence, and find more ways to highlight, celebrate, name, and extend it

In this chapter, we explore each of these points in turn.

Structure instruction to address questions of genuine importance.

Teachers can meet these situational conditions of engagement or flow by constructing inquiry units that both address students' needs for personal relevance and promote disciplinary understandings that clearly count and have functional value in the world (see Wilhelm 2007). Inquiry is not simply thematic study, but the exploration of a question or issue that drives debate in the disciplines and the world. Our work shows us that kids need to find both personal connection and social significance in the units and texts we offer them.

< < < < <
You might want to pause here and skip ahead to Chapter 18, where Dick Allington also talks about situational interest. Adding his perspective to Jeff and Michael's will help you understand the importance of situational interest.
—*KB, REP, LR*

Here is an example of such a unit. Jeff's daughter, Fiona, is a high school student. Her literature anthology includes an excerpt from Defoe's *Journal of a Plague Year* and her high school reading list includes Camus' *Plague*. Neither reading appeals to her for a variety of reasons. Instead of teaching these as discrete texts without personal context, why not ask, "How should we prepare for disaster?" That one inquiry question motivates by setting the stage for discussion, additional reading, research, and projects that students can approach with more specific inquiry questions of their own.

Such a unit should begin with front-loading as a way to develop students' competence. For example, asking students to rank the potential for certain kinds of natural, manmade, or health disasters helps them tap their prior knowledge. Students can then propose possible precautions and preparations for such disasters. This would naturally lead to additional reading—a newspaper article about local parents who do not wish to inoculate their children or a magazine feature on preparations for the avian flu pandemic. These activities help customize the topic for individual students while meeting the criteria of providing an appropriate challenge, appropriate texts, and appropriate assistance in reevaluating their original response to the topic (as they return to their rankings and proposals and update them).

> > > *Having students read different texts around a common question actually benefits everyone. Learning becomes more social, expertise is shared, and motivation stays higher.*

Some students may go on to read the central text; others will read alternative, and potentially even more challenging, texts, such as Jim Murphy's nonfiction book *An American Plague* or Laurie Halse Anderson's historical fiction *Fever, 1793*, about the yellow fever epidemic in Philadelphia. Having students read different texts around a common question actually benefits everyone. Learning becomes more social, expertise is shared, and motivation stays higher.

Even in cases where common readings (such as Defoe or Camus) are used, they can still be usefully paired with various shorter texts on a similar topic, as long as appropriate challenge and assistance are supplied. These shorter articles— they could be about Ebola, quarantining, AIDS in Africa, or social policy, for example—could all be read as part of the unit, thereby giving students quick and visible signs of accomplishment. Students could create semantic feature analyses regarding health disasters, past and present, and compare them according to causes, effects, and ways that were successful and unsuccessful in preparing for or addressing them. A semantic feature analysis, or SFA, is simply a chart that lists the things to be compared on the left column and the features on which you wish to compare these examples along the top of the chart. (See Figure 15–1.) A final project could involve a policy argument about how individuals and communities should prepare for health disasters. Arguments and proposals could be shared in a school forum, through multimedia displays, Internet postings, and the like. Students could plan and enact social action by preparing their home and school for such emergencies. In this way, students' needs for immediate relevance, control, social work, clear accomplishment, and feedback are met. Though some teachers might think such a unit too time-consuming, we've found that combining skills to be taught—essay writing, grammar lessons, and finding theme—allows teachers to accomplish a lot all under the heading of a single inquiry unit.

Inquiry could be undertaken with any unit. As another example, instead of studying civil rights or just having students read a text like *Roll of Thunder, Hear My Cry* (Taylor), *Mississippi Trial, 1955* (Crowe), or *Coming of Age in Mississippi* (Moody), teachers could contextualize such texts in a unit framed by the question How are we implicated in injustice and what can we do about it?

> *What Our Boys Taught Us*: Situating learning in inquiry units that build over time instead of just moving from one activity to the next fosters motivation and understanding.

< < < < <
Don't forget Ellin Keene's concept of way-in books (page 29) as you think about using trade books as a part of an inquiry unit.
—*KB, REP, LR*

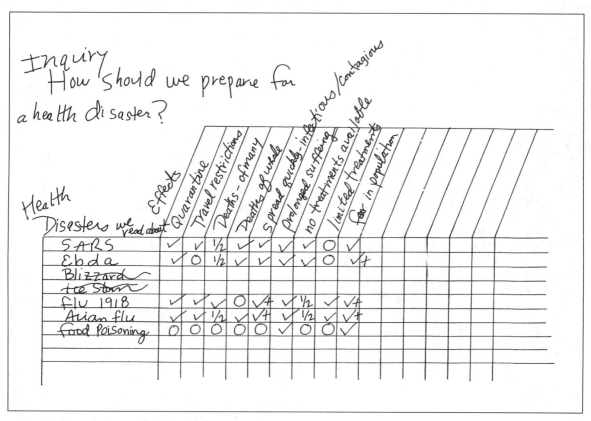

FIGURE 15–1. *SFA Chart*

Expand notions of text and curriculum, and what counts as meaningful reading and learning.

The use of an essential question to frame inquiry immediately encourages teachers and learners to promote the five principles of flow that we have outlined. However, it is important to recognize that some texts provide immediate pleasures and are immediately rewarding, apart from an extended study or inquiry.

As we were discussing how to frame this issue in this chapter, Michael was reminded of reading about a food critic who left his job. In his farewell column he said something like the following: "Being a food critic has been the best position in the world, but I had to quit because I was dying for a pizza." He decided that his life was poorer because he didn't have the time (and spare calories!) for enjoying all kinds of meals in different kinds of settings. His job required him to eat out constantly, to focus on fine food, and to critique instead of enjoy. It strikes us that his situation is similar to that of students who are made to read and appreciate only one particular kind of text: canonical "lit-er-a-chur" that was written for adults and that rewards highly nuanced interpretations.

> > > *In English language arts, what tend to be read are literary texts—often extended, complex, and textured—that reward subtle and nuanced interpretation. These are the reasons such texts are canonized and valued by teachers. Unfortunately, these texts are often outside the independent reading level of students.*

Now we don't mean to say that electronic texts are junk food. In fact, we think they have great value to engage and help students to work with substantive processes and ideas. We do mean to say that we, as teachers, should provide and promote all the pleasures and possibilities of textual engagement.

One of the most important insights our young men taught us is that different texts do different things and have various unique powers. One frustration of the boys was that school is too monolithic and emphasizes too few kinds of texts at the expense of many others that also have value, use, and especially the ability to engage. Often, these marginalized texts are the very ones the boys are most familiar with or drawn to.

> > > > >
You'll want to read what Teri Lesesne (Chapter 6) said of books that these boys would probably most enjoy. At the same time, look at Alfred Tatum's comments (Interlude 2) about the types of books his research has found to be most important for African American males.

—KB, REP, LR

In English language arts, what tend to be read are literary texts—often extended, complex, and textured—that reward subtle and nuanced interpretation. These are the reasons such texts are canonized, included in textbooks and reading lists, and valued by teachers. Unfortunately, these texts are often outside the independent reading level of students. Therefore, the very reasons the texts were selected provide a reason for boys to reject them.

We, like many English teachers, tend to love literary texts because they provide us with what Kenneth Burke calls "equipment for living" through our engagement with a unique and powerful way of knowing. As Wayne Booth (1988) suggests, the amount of time we spend reading an extended literary text allows us to engage in relationships with characters, authors, and ideas in a way that approximates the relationships we have with our oldest friends. We are convinced of the value of literary texts and have devoted much of our professional lives to exploring new ways of teaching them.

But as valuable as literature may be, literary texts often work against a desire for an immediate functional value, and they certainly don't provide other kinds of value that students often seek. Frequently, the texts students find immediately rewarding lean toward the humorous—be they cartoons, jokes or gags (e.g., *Captain Underpants*), or satire and irony (when one is a knowing insider, e.g., *The Simpsons*). Musical texts like rap lyrics explore interesting issues that are close to home and encourage students to stake their identity in their rejection of or support for certain artists or styles. Visual texts such as movies, magazines, and graphic novels offer various kinds of visual assistance to help the reader comprehend complicated issues or plots, thereby placing these texts more readily within existing regimes of competence (Gee 2003). Newspaper articles and websites offer immediate satisfaction by providing answers, if one knows what to look for and how to find it. How-to guides offer immediately functional information, too, all nicely fit into clearly articulated inquiry units.

In short, we found that various kinds of texts provided pleasures and/or immediate gratification that canonical literature does not always provide. For example, many students found a kind of psychological satisfaction in fantasy, where real situations could be addressed through a backdoor or through a unique perspective. Mysteries, too, were popular, offering an immediate challenge and the satisfaction of learning whodunit.

Electronic texts deserve special consideration. One type of electronic text often dismissed by educators is that of the video game. Video games typically involve lots of reading, involve characters, and are embedded in an overarching narrative. They offer interesting and immediately engaging vicarious experiences that are always problem oriented, are often analogous to real-life issues, and always develop and demonstrate growing competence. Control is promoted as gamers are coproducers of their game: the roles they select, the characteristics they choose for their role, and all subsequent decisions and moves they make affect what will happen later and how they must deal with the challenges that arise. Video games are also expertly designed for assisting the player to become better at the game (see Gee 2003). In cognitive science, content is seen as largely procedural. In other words, what is learned involves learning how to do things. Video games offer a perfect example, in that participants encounter considerable content as they progress through the levels of the game. They learn ins and outs of reading directions, situations, and characters; strategies for solving problems and collaborating with other characters; tips for organizing, analyzing, and using data from the game to make decisions; and techniques for making inferences and evaluations in the context of the game. Hypermedia texts (such as Internet URLs) likewise provide the reader with

> < < < < <
> Donna Alvermann also discusses video gaming in her chapter (3). Compare what she said with what these authors offer here.
>
> *—KB, REP, LR*

navigational control, assistance for competence, and coauthorship that conventional print or linear texts do not.

The boys we came to know through our study made it clear that fun and humor were irresistible attractions—in texts and in our discussions about the texts. Since many of the texts that exhibit those characteristics are often disregarded or dismissed by schools, we learned a strategy: use them anyway. In fact, one of the great benefits of organizing units around inquiry is that inquiry units (as we illustrated earlier) create an obvious space for a wide variety of texts to be paired with more canonical and conventional school texts. We also learned to encourage students to pursue free reading of texts that we might have dismissed before conducting our study. In short, we learned from our boys that to maximize textual power and diversify literate skills, we need to put different kinds of texts with different readerly demands and rewards together in conversation with each other.

The boys also helped us appreciate the pleasure provided by a wide variety of texts, including many that are seldom taught in school. We believe that we must help boys understand and experience the pleasure and power of the texts that matter most to us. Traditional literacies provide a way of navigating and negotiating the world that counts in school and in the world. Alternative texts already count in the world and in students' lives; let's connect these to the meaningful projects we should be pursuing in school that also count in the world.

Our boys were often cynical about the fact that what was read in school was not what they saw being read in life. Why not make English class a smorgasbord in which many texts are offered and where these various texts can be brought into conversation with each other? Don't be afraid to let your students teach *you* to appreciate the pleasure.

> *What Our Boys Taught Us*: We need to widen our notion of texts; doing so will widen our repertoires of teaching and what curricula can uncover, and will promote students' strategic reading and widen their textual expertise.

Expand notions of competence, especially *student* competence, and find more ways to highlight, celebrate, name, and extend it.

Buda, one of the participants in our study, had this to say: "School teaches you for how you are dumb, not for how you are smart . . . and school teaches you how you are dumb, not how you are smart."

Buda's comment highlights a problem with school and how it is at odds with the reality of life as an adult, a reality in which we gravitate toward doing things that we are already good at and that will extend our expertise in some rewarding way. For instance, Michael would prefer to help a friend paint his house rather than roof it. Why? Because he has some preexisting interest and expertise in painting, and he doesn't want to stand around being useless and displaying his incompetence at roofing.

Even in areas where we have some expertise, we seek an appropriate challenge that shows us how we are expert and offers ways to display and extend this. For instance, Jeff often plays basketball with the college students at Boise State. But when he has the chance, he prefers to play with other professors. Why? Quite simply, because playing with the young men continually communicates to Jeff that he is getting slow, can't jump, and is easily stuffed. When he plays with people his age, he has the chance to experience the pleasure of competence; he drives to the hoop, steals the ball by anticipating a passing lane, and so on—any of which could lead to disaster when playing with his more athletic students.

Naturally, in school we are trying to teach our students new concepts, new strategies, new stances and attitudes. But this impulse can lead to the problem Buda alludes to: students are being forever confronted with what they do not know and cannot do. Given the headlong push for coverage, exacerbated by information-driven standardized tests, students are often unable to develop competence and control, or display it in any visible way, before being asked to once again confront their ignorance head-on as the next disconnected topic is introduced. In short, who enjoys feeling dumb all the time?

Jeff's daughter Fiona once again provides an example. As a high schooler, Fiona had been a straight-A student and had always enjoyed history, until, that is, she took a class on Western civilization, in which she earned a low B. She then announced that she would not take AP U.S. history, although she had been looking forward to it. Why not? "I don't think I'm very good at history," she explained. Why did she think this? "I don't know anything. I used to think I knew some things but now I see I don't. Plus, I'm an A student in everything else, but I'm a B student in history." Unfortunately, what Fiona took away from a challenging course in an unfamiliar subject was not just information about the evolution of Western civilization but the unmotivating conclusion that she is dumb in history.

What might happen instead if Fiona's teacher recast his job as helping Fiona develop the skills a historian needs rather than as providing her with historical information? The teacher could then embody the five M's of promoting competence: model, mentor, monitor, and provide multiple modalities and measures (Wilhelm 2007). That is, he could model how he would read the textbook as a historian as well as how he would question it, supplement it with the reading of

> < < < < <
> When we first read this chapter we were struck by this simple thought: who does enjoy feeling dumb all the time? Then we turned to the chapter by Yvette Jackson and Eric Cooper, which we've set after this one. In that chapter, Yvette and Eric repeatedly discuss what happens when we teach in a way that helps underachieving adolescents discover they are "smart again."
>
> —*KB, REP, LR*

primary documents, build and apply historical expertise, and so on. He could then mentor and monitor his students' use of similar strategies, highlighting, naming, and celebrating how students came to use strategies of historical thinking and understanding in their own reading, classroom debates, historical dramas, proposals for current policy based on past historical events and thinking, and so forth. And finally, he could use these various techniques and culminating activities, such as arguments, proposals, debates, drama work, and museum exhibits, to develop and measure growing historical understanding.

His efforts to recast his job would be supported by creating an inquiry context in his classes. If the class were examining the question Is the history of Western civilization a history of progress? then studying, say, the rise of the textile industry in the Middle Ages would make some sense—because it led to wealth, the Hanseatic League, political alliances, and so on. Fiona could be asked to brainstorm what current industries will be written about in future textbooks and why, and to find articles in the newspaper about the rise of certain industries and the potential costs and benefits to the wider culture.

Framing the course as inquiry would invite the reading of alternative texts and welcome Fiona's preexisting interests and competencies as a questioner, connection maker, and person interested in social problems and how to solve them. The class would also build and display her (and others') competence in visible ways as she became more expert at reading, thinking, talking, and acting like a historian. As many theorists have argued, all learning is social. Fiona can learn to *do* school and be successful at it, but if she is not learning to *do* history in the way historians do it, she is certainly not learning history. In any discipline, the learner is expected to continually proceed toward doing and thinking about the discipline more like experts do. In a like manner, at the end of the disaster unit, students should be thinking, reading, and writing more like public health experts. This is called the *correspondence concept*, meaning that at the end of any activity, reading, or instruction, the learner should have something in her head that more nearly and identifiably approaches what an expert has in hers, or learning and competence have not been achieved (Bereiter 2004; Nickerson 1985).

Reframing the course as a series of inquiries would also necessitate revising the teacher's approach to assessment. The assessments in Fiona's class are multiple-choice tests and an occasional written quiz. Fiona comes home and often explains to Jeff why she chose the wrong answer and why she thinks her answer is better than the one the teacher chose. Imagine what would happen if the teacher allowed her to write appeal letters explaining her reasoning and displaying the competence not shown on the test. Imagine if the teacher began to scrutinize those quizzes and tests once he saw how his past assessment of his students' historical understanding didn't jibe with his students' demonstration of their historical understanding in debates, projects, proposals, policy arguments, and the like.

> > > > >

Teachers, like their students, are learners; therefore, we, too, are expected to continually think more about our discipline. Literacy coaches are helping us all think more about literacy for all disciplines. Read more about literacy coaches in Kathy Egawa's chapter (19).

—KB, REP, LR

> > > > >

You'll want to look at what Devon Brenner, David Pearson, and Linda Rief have to say about assessment (Chapter 17). In particular, we think that Jeff and Michael would nod in agreement at the process questions Linda asks students when they finish a writing assignment (page 269).

—KB, REP, LR

In our study, we found that all literacy work and learning was a form of identity work (Smith and Wilhelm 2006). Learners required a sense of self-efficacy—a belief that they could be competent as a certain kind of reader, writer, thinker, problem solver, historian, mathematician, and so on, before they would be motivated to learn the strategies and attempt the tasks associated with that identity. Developing the strategies and stances of a reader or writer depended upon first seeing connections between one's current identities, values, and strengths (as a gamer who likes to make decisions and is good at evaluating choices, for example) and the new identity to be developed (as a reader who can see implied patterns and therefore discern subtexts that will help one understand irony, for example). Trying to do something new means trying to *be* something new. It requires taking on the mantle of a "novice expert" (see Wilhelm and Edmiston 1998) or a "virtual identity" (student as a historian, public health expert, expert reader of argument or interpreter of irony; see Gee 2003).

> > > *Competence may be the reason for engagement. But maybe it's the other way around. Maybe engagement is the cause of competence.*

Many of the boys in our study had a "damaged learner identity" (Gee 2003) because they were allowed to conclude that they were dumb. The same thing, we're afraid, can be said for many girls. Fiona, for instance, may very well be seeing her potential identity as a historian or historical thinker as one that is less attainable to her than she might have perceived it before her Western civilization class. As Gee asserts, "If children cannot or will not make bridges between one or more of their real-world identities and the virtual identity at stake in the classroom (e.g., being a particular type of scientist)—or if teachers or others destroy or don't help build such bridges, then learning is imperiled" (61).

To develop a new identity, you must not only believe that you can be successful at exercising the competence required but also experience initial success, build more competence, and then experience more success at increasingly difficult and challenging iterations. The boys in our study were willing to expend considerable effort on tasks that they valued, that promoted their identities in some way, and that helped them become more competent and exercise more control. Although we were disheartened at how rarely school worked to identify and develop competence, we remain hopeful. So much could be done if we expanded our conception and measurement of competence.

What Our Boys Taught Us: Teachers must provide a wide variety of differentiated opportunities to develop competence and become competent, to practice, participate, and be successful as a certain kind of reader or writer, and to name and celebrate our students as readers, writers, thinkers, and disciplinary problem solvers.

When you want to know more . . .

Jeff and Michael have brought together two interesting issues—the significance of gender in literacy learning and Csikszentmihalyi's ideas about flow. They explore both of these topics further in *"Reading Don't Fix No Chevys": Literacy in the Lives of Young Men* (2002), and in *Going with the Flow: How to Engage Boys (and Girls) in Their Literacy Learning* (2006).

> > < <

The language of crisis is often used to characterize the state of literacy in America, but that stance doesn't serve us as teachers because it keeps us from seeing what students *can* do, what texts they *do* enjoy, and how to build bridges from the literacies they have to the literacies they need. When Michael heard John Guthrie speak on motivation at Rutgers University a few years ago, Guthrie cited the high correlations between competence and engagement in reading. He argued that the relationship between these two was so close that it was unclear in what direction the causal error goes. Competence may be the reason for engagement. But maybe it's the other way around. Maybe engagement is the cause of competence. If we think hard about motivating our students, if we devise units that address questions of genuine importance, expand our notions of text, value meaningful textual engagement and textual pleasure, and broaden our notions of competence, our students are sure to profit.

> > > YVETTE JACKSON, ERIC J. COOPER

Building Academic Success with Underachieving Adolescents

WHEN Kylene, Bob, and Linda approached us about writing this chapter, we immediately thought of all the things we'd have to set aside to accomplish this work: namely, *other* work. Perhaps we could pass on this one project, we thought. But then we thought of two things—the title of this book, *Adolescent Literacy: Turning Promise into Practice*, and a number we think of often: seven thousand. From the beginning, we were drawn to the title. This goal of turning promise into practice is what we do at the National Urban Alliance (NUA) daily. We help students turn their promise into practice; we help teachers do the same—for themselves and for their students. How could we not pause from critical responsibilities to talk about something we believe in so very much? And then there is that number seven thousand. This is the number of students who drop out of school daily in the United States. That's right: seven thousand teens.[1]

This chapter appears here because we saw it as a natural extension of what Jeff Wilhelm and Michael Smith tell us about engagement. Yvette Jackson and Eric Cooper hone our thinking and our understanding about how we make that engagement meaningful with underachieving students.

—KB, REP, LR

---

1. It's likely that when you read this chapter, this number will have changed. This number comes from a study titled "Diplomas Count: An Essential Guide to Graduation Policy and Rates," published by *Education Week* (June, 2006). We hope that as you read this chapter, this number is experiencing a downward spiral, and a fast one at that. But until that number hits zero, we'll remain committed to our cause—helping underachieving youth turn their promise into practice.

These seven thousand students are more likely than not to be students of color, are more likely to live in poverty than in financial ease, and are more likely to call a large urban government-funded housing project home than a place in the suburbs—that picket-fenced, chocolate-chip-cookie-scented, ranch-style, single-dwelling home we'd like to at least *believe* our students go home to daily. They are more likely to be male than female, more likely to have failed at least one grade, and are more likely to read significantly below grade level than their peers who stay in school. These seven thousand students consistently score in the bottom quartile of any standardized test, have in all likelihood failed their state assessment so that their high school day is filled with reading (and math) remediation classes instead of the rich diversity of subjects we'd like all teens to experience, and often find themselves expressing their frustration in ways that result in anything from in-building suspension to alternative schools to complete disengagement with learning. They drop out long before they stop arriving at the schoolhouse doors. Most tragically, these seven thousand students not only never realize their promise but believe a myth that suggests they have no promise.

At the National Urban Alliance, we work daily to overcome this myth. This work has resulted in success stories that do not surprise us (we've *always* believed in the promise of underachieving adolescents) but that do inspire us. Because we're a nation of numbers, Figure 16–1 shows the test scores from some of the districts that put strategies we support into practice.

These test scores are not a result of a new kit each teacher bought; they are the result of collaborative work between teacher and student. They are a result of the hard work teachers do—*you* do. In this chapter, we offer you a snapshot of the most essential strategies we find that do turn promise into practice. We applaud you for always believing in the promise of your students, *all* your students.

> > > > >

For more information on how the National Urban Alliance is helping in schools across the country, be sure to visit its website at www.nuatc.org.

—*KB, REP, LR*

Listening to Adolescents

A tenth grader from an inner-city high school brought us up short when she answered the question What do teachers need to know to motivate students? with an original poem that began like this:

> To you I might just be another child lost in society's universal negativity.
> I suppose now is the time for heads to turn away and shoulders to shrug.
> Know this . . .
> Stereotypes can only go so far,
> Last so long, and mean so much.

This student went on to write about how one teacher, *one* teacher, motivated her because the teacher refused to believe the stereotypes, refused to believe that the solution is that exasperated shrug of shoulders, the dismissive

EXAMPLES OF SCHOOLS THAT ARE CLOSING THE ACHIEVEMENT GAP

The table below is based on four-year data from the primarily African American and Hispanic American 15th Avenue School in Newark, New Jersey. It shows the percentage of students reaching state standards in the fourth grade over the course of four years.

School Year	Language Arts	Math
2000–2001	11.8%	5.9%
2001–2002	52.9%	20.5%
2002–2003	59.9%	59.2%
2003–2004	73.7%	76.3%

There are other examples. Dr. Duncan (Pat) Pritchett, immediate past superintendent of Indianapolis Public Schools, wrote to me [Eric Cooper] recently, "The progress is happening for our kids. Our African American students now in grades 3, 4, and 5 are above the average of African American studens statewide, and approximately twenty of our schools are now performing above state average."

In Seattle, research conducted by the school system has found that African American students who have been part of the literacy training conducted by the National Urban Alliance for Effective Education for a two-year period or more, double the achievement of African American students not trained. In Minneapolis, Nell Collier, principal of Cityview Performing Magnet Middle School, has written: "Our students have definitely increased in achievement on a state assessment in reading and math. Our school went from the 33rd percentile to the 54th percentile in reading on the Minnesota Basic Skills Test (MBST) and from the 22nd to the 34th percentile in mathematics. We are an urban school with much diversity in our student body. We have a free and reduced lunch count that is at 91 percent." And again in Minneapolis, the Northeast Middle School experienced an increase in the percentage of students passing the Minnesota Basic Skills Test from 56 percent in 2004 to 68 percent in 2005.

< < < < <
As we moved from manuscript to page proofs for this book, Seattle's Superintendent Raj Manhas, in conversation with NUA leadership, indicated that Seattle students have gone from 67 percent meeting the WASL state standard to 81 percent in the 2006 school year. The superintendent attributed gains to the Seattle NUA literacy professional development initiative.

—KB, REP, LR

FIGURE 16–1.

turn of the head. Her words have stayed with us as we've worked with urban adolescents across this country. The stereotype of what these children can (or cannot) accomplish can only, indeed, "last so long, and mean so much."

While some would suggest that this stereotype will be set aside when *students* work harder, we would suggest that teachers must first work smarter. We start that smart work by first learning to listen to our students and second learning the strategies that help underachieving students learn best.

Educators comb through research to make judgments about how to improve adolescent learning, but they rarely use the most valid, informative source to determine student needs: the students themselves. Standards on teaching adolescent literacy include the ability of students to form critical responses based on evaluation, and yet the most critical question—What's most needed for you to learn?—is seldom asked of the students. In other words, we aren't providing the authentic opportunity for them to apply what we're expecting them to be able to do (think critically to evaluate) to the very thing we judge them on—their learning. If these abilities (thinking critically to evaluate) are important enough for us to use as a basis for judgments about students, then eliciting these abilities to evaluate their own learning needs is equally critical. In our work at the NUA, we find it is critical to ask students such questions not only because they are the true clients of school but because the most important factor involved in motivating adolescent students to learn is engagement.

> > > . . . *the most important factor involved in motivating adolescent students to learn is engagement.*

The type of engagement so vital to them for school learning is the engagement that comes through relationships with their teachers—

> relationships that they believe appreciate their identity and honor them as individuals;

> relationships that are built on genuine dialogue in which students and teachers communicate what's meaningful and relevant to them both; and

> relationships in which teachers demonstrate the ardent belief in the potential of their students by bridging required content to students' personal frame of reference.

> > > > >
Yvette and Eric make a compelling case for how this type of engagement motivates urban youth. In her chapter on comprehension (4), Ellin Keene explains that when students listen to teachers talk with passion, with *fervor*—to use Ellin's word—then they begin to understand what comprehension really means.
—*KB, REP, LR*

Pedagogy predicated on such bonding relationships is the ultimate catalyst for inviting and motivating urban adolescents to engage in literate behaviors because it instills such behavior with genuine purpose: to construct and communicate their own meaning with someone who cares.

Teachers in urban districts want very much to connect to their students and enrich their learning with challenging experiences and feedback students crave (Jensen 1998), but the current culture of education promotes fear of standardized assessments, in both teachers and students. This fear causes a narrow definition of literacy instruction focusing on reading, writing, and learning facts through textbooks. These textbooks do not contain references to the daily experiences of the students, nor to the world affairs they see on the news, nor to the digital modes of communication they use every day. This climate of fear has caused us to forget or ignore what we all know are pivotal factors in turning adolescents on, or what Kylene, Bob, and Linda have labeled as *turning promise into practice*: personal connections (relationships) and what Piaget (in Furth 1981) referred to as personal centering (i.e., Who am I in reference to the world?). So adolescents feel disconnected, unknowledgeable, or, as many have shared with us, dumb. This is a stereotype that, as the student-author of the poem said, can only go so far.

What exacerbates this situation is that textbooks are loaded with technical content language that increases the reading level of the textbook (sometimes several levels within the same book), minimizing students' comprehension while raising their frustration level; it leaves students feeling disconnected from learning and just plain dumb. Teachers see the problem and tell us that sometimes as many as 85 percent of their students can't read their textbooks at an independent level. Yet, with fear of failing to cover what might be needed for the tests, teachers still give assignments that require students to read independently from these textbooks, with the result that nothing gets read and students end up less prepared, not more. The sad reality is that all too often, this situation is interpreted as students not caring, when in truth, they care very much (Jackson 2001).

Simultaneously, some teachers, recognizing the mismatch between students' independent reading levels and textbooks' reading demands, put the textbook on the shelf. They've decided that the book is too hard and students shouldn't be required to struggle through it. They tell students information, put notes on the board, and distribute handouts that cover the material in easier syntax, with more accessible vocabulary. The problem with this is that teaching down to students provides content without rigor. Dumbing down the curriculum is not now, has not been, and will never be the answer for helping underachieving students catch up, keep up, and move ahead. What, then, is the answer? The answer begins with expectations—yours.

Begin with High Expectations: Pedagogy of Confidence

Confident teachers use strategies that empower adolescents. They adhere to the pedagogy that is the platform of the NUA's professional development for reversing underachievement: a Pedagogy of Confidence. Pedagogy of Confidence is based on the fearless expectation that all students will learn. The goal of this pedagogy is high intellectual performance from our urban adolescents. When teachers practice this pedagogy, they do not doubt the potential of urban adolescents,

< < < < <
Eric and Yvette make an excellent point here that is confirmed in a recent report titled *Reading Between the Lines* (ACT 2006). This report explains that while textbooks are difficult reading, we do students a disservice when we choose to set them aside instead of teaching students the necessary skills so they can read them. Go to www.act.org/path/policy/pdf /reading_report.pdf for an online copy of this important report.
—*KB, REP, LR*

< < < < <
You'll find additional information about vocabulary instruction in Janet Allen's chapter (7).
—*KB, REP, LR*

and they switch their instructional focus from *what must be taught* to *what kinds of teaching will maximize learning*. Maximizing learning to reverse underachievement in literacy for our adolescents requires a change in the very definition of literacy itself; we must embrace a definition of literacy that

> > fosters engagement of behaviors vital to adolescents (making connections, inquiring, giving personal perspective, critically evaluating situations);

> > incorporates authentic literacy—literacy relevant to students; and

> > recognizes the critical role of a student's frame of reference in literacy development, enabling them to feel smart again.

Elliot Eisner's definition of literacy does just this. Eisner (1994) defines literacy as an individual's ability to construct, create, and communicate meaning in many forms (e.g., written text, mathematical symbols, all forms of the arts). We are hard-pressed to find an adolescent who doesn't do these things: however, we're saddened that so many of today's teens—especially those who struggle in school—fail to see themselves as people living a literate life, engaging in "smart" literate behaviors. Sadly, they have lost their sense of smartness because their self-motivated literate behaviors and experiences are not recognized or valued in the narrow scope of "discipline literacies" valued in school, the "sanctioned literacies" (Weinstein 2002). To reverse underachievement, we not only have to demonstrate to adolescents that we value their *literate* behaviors and perspectives but also must validate their behaviors and perspectives, so that they see the connection between what they know and what is being taught, thus making them feel smart again. Additionally, we must become more aware of the effects of widely held negative stereotypes regarding the intellectual capacity of schoolchildren and youth of color (Herrnstein and Murray 1994; Seligman 2005). The work of Claude Steele and his associates at Stanford speaks clearly to the deleterious effects of "that corrosive feeling among students that they are not good enough to [intellectually] succeed solely because of their gender, race, ethnicity, or background" (quoted in Froning 2006, 72).

Cooper (2005) writes about the pernicious effects of tracking on students' self-concept, resulting in what we previously have called feeling dumb. Adolescents understand the intellectual stratification that occurs in schools; they know which group of students is considered smart and which ones are considered dumb, solely based on the academic track they follow. We have experienced countless examples in our work throughout the nation where teachers have cited the upper-track students as the "hope of the nation," and the lower tracks as those who will need societal support. Building on this perceived need for custodial care for low-performing Americans, Herrnstein and Murray have gone so far as to propose the establishment of a "custodial state . . . [where] we have in mind a high-tech and more lavish version of the Indian reservation for some substantial minority of the nation's population, while the rest of America tries to go about its business" (1994, 526). We refuse to acquiesce to such cynicism (as tongue-in-cheek as it may be); instead, we staunchly believe in the capacity of people to succeed when nurtured, guided, and strengthened through education reform. We embrace the foundations of an American value that a nation doesn't give up on people. And though it is popular today to declare that education policy should be data driven, we hold that policy should be driven by values and vision that are informed by data.

We nurture literacy a la Eisner by zeroing in on the interdependency of literacy and the learning process of adolescents. Learning happens when the brain makes connections among engaging experiences. Adolescents are engaged when they are actively involved and understand what they are studying. Dewey (1933) described this understanding as the ability to construct meaning, to see something in relationship to something else familiar, and to make connections to the real-world context. The brain naturally constructs meaning when it perceives relationships (Caine and Caine 1994). Constructing meaning is the major requisite to learning and the key to engaging adolescents—connecting to their personal experiences and personal centeredness (seeing the world from their perspective).

At the NUA, we've found it helpful to use a symbolic representation to characterize all we must do as we translate learning and literacy issues into daily practice: $L: (U + M) (C1 + C2)$. This formula is our shorthand for what we must do to guarantee our students' success. Here's what it means. For learning and literacy to develop, students have to understand what they are expected to learn (L). There is voluminous brain research that supports an inseparable connection between understanding and motivation (U + M). Additionally, competence (C1) and confidence (C2) significantly affect motivation. Using this symbolic representation as the basis for planning literacy instruction keeps the focus on adolescent learners, engaging them in their own development. This representation forces us to think of the following factors:

> strategies that will be applied to ensure understanding;

> catalysts that engage the students, bridging to their experiences;

> skills or background information needed to guarantee comprehension; and

> opportunities that will be provided to enable students to communicate with competence and confidence the meaning they have constructed.

So what strategies will ensure understanding and application, and what catalysts will create that bridge between engagement and motivation on one side and curricular content on the other? How do we help students cross that bridge between what they know and what they don't know?

Step One: Zeroing In on the Mission

For students to excel in the disciplines, they must be able to construct meaning from textbooks—a critical part of teaching and learning. Constructing meaning happens when students can make a link to what is relevant and meaningful to them. We may not be reading teachers, but given this reality, we must be teachers of text comprehension if we expect students to learn from the text.

> > > *We may not be reading teachers, but . . . we must be teachers of text comprehension if we expect students to learn from the text.*

And yet comprehension is a cognitive process that involves a repertoire of skills and strategies—tools that don't constitute a final destination but rather serve us in reaching one. The scope of the skills can range from highly specific, narrowly focused teaching-learning approaches to broad ones; from strategies that emphasize group interaction to those primarily content and learner specific. The goal for adolescents is to be literate in the disciplines to such a degree that they not only are equipped and motivated to perform at the high levels of thinking required by the discipline itself but also can internalize new knowledge and process it sufficiently for application to a real-world context. Building literacy in a discipline requires the ability to construct and communicate meaning using the conceptual understanding of the discipline. In order to do that, the students' frame of reference must be engaged, enabling connections between what students know and what they perceive as relevant and meaningful. This requires students to

> perceive an experience to be personally relevant;

> have sufficient prior knowledge to bridge the gap between what is known and what is not known;

> recognize patterns or relationships that are related to previous learning; and

> perceive a personal connection or experience an emotion that makes the new information meaningful and memorable (Bruner 1960; Bransford, Brown, and Cocking 1999; Jackson 2004).

Step Two: Making It Real

Urban adolescents do not usually consider the content of schooling to be relevant to them, to have meaningful patterns or relationships, to connect with things they already know, or to be especially memorable. Cultural experience is what makes something relevant and meaningful. Teachers of urban adolescents are successful when they situate learning in the lives of their students, utilizing the culture of the students as a bridge between the content to be taught and what is real for them. This is, in fact, the basis of student engagement and the definition of *culturally relevant teaching*.

Frames of reference based on concepts from the disciplines provide the entry points for bridging student culture to curricular content. Moving from these entry points to activate a pedagogy of confidence that engages adolescents' learning and expands their literacy requires *mediation*. Mediation is an interactive process that bonds the teacher and the student in a nurturing relationship, which is so culturally important to urban students. The goal of mediation is to elicit from the students a personal motivation for learning. The teacher engages the student around purposefully selected activities that build confidence by guiding discussion toward the critical analysis of concepts and the identification of relevant connections and applications to personal experiences. Through this discussion, the teacher builds background in the understandings of the discipline or text to be studied. This dynamic interaction between the teacher and the student is the most important aspect of the mediation process, for it allows assessment of understanding and learning to be part of the instructional process. The cognitive functions developed by mediated learning form the foundations of literacy and are necessary for achievement throughout life. These include

> focusing on problems or issues
> inferring connections
> organizing information
> labeling
> sorting relevant and irrelevant information (Jackson et al. 1998)

Mediated Learning through Thinking Maps®

Thinking Maps® are eight visual-verbal tools that work together as a language for thinking and learning. The model was initially developed by David Hyerle and is now used as a foundation for professional development (Hyerle and Yeager 2007) to support the brain's natural learning process by helping students identify patterns and relationships in their thinking as well as in textual material. They are based on the eight fundamental cognitive processes that form the core of cognition and learning:

> defining a concept
> describing qualities or attributes
> comparing and contrasting
> sequencing
> classifying
> part–whole relationships
> cause and effect and
> seeing analogies

< < < < <
Take a look at what Jeff Wilhelm and Michael Smith have to say about flow and engagement and the importance of inquiry in their chapter (15). You'll see that though these authors are using slightly different language, their points are in harmony and challenge us to rethink what we are doing (or not!) to connect students to learning.
—*KB, REP, LR*

< < < < <
Thinking Maps® is a registered trademark of Thinking Maps, Inc. Information about Thinking Maps® and professional development training may be found at www.think ingmaps.com. We encourage you to visit this website to learn more.
—*KB, REP, LR*

Thinking Maps® provide a common language for teachers to use in culturally diverse classrooms to develop both the critical thinking and language (or "codes of power") needed to strengthen students' ability to construct meaning from text and to communicate their learning. When students use the Thinking Maps® as a language of dynamic and expandable graphics—rather than static graphic organizers—teachers can quickly assess their thinking and identify specific comprehension issues (Hyerle 2004). Figure 16–2 gives an overview of the eight thinking maps.

Thinking Maps® is a language of eight interdependent tools that are internalized by students for their own independent use. While often used together as a language, the following are two discrete examples developed by students. The first helps students situate content area learning in the relevance of their own lives. The second develops language skills by helping students see relationships between words and/or terms.

The Circle Map

One of the maps, the Circle Map, is an extremely powerful prereading tool because it enables teachers to mediate concept development by facilitating students' ability to construct meaning of both concrete and abstract concepts through the students' culture. A simple circle map lets students brainstorm some thoughts about a topic, but situating it within the added "frame" (a square) tells students to put what they know about this topic within their own frame of reference (Hyerle and Yeager 2007). This tool explicitly supports student in surfacing and generating discussion in a holistic way about a full range of different experiences, perceptions, and points of view they have related to a concept being developed.

The Circle Map with a Frame is an essential starting point for generating ideas before introducing a universal concept or unit of study. There's a good reason the Circle Map with a Frame resembles a target: it helps illustrate and maintain what the focus of understanding is (see Figure 16–3).

As shown in this example, students are using a tool to provide examples of the concept from their lives that also supports the development of thinking in context. The Frame then offers students a mental space for showing the influence of background experiences on their thinking. The most provocative question for this discussion is to ask the students why or how the examples in the outside circle relate to or reflect the targeted concept. Students bring their culture (whatever is meaningful and relevant to them) to every learning experience they have. Helping underachieving adolescents analyze the factors that influence their thinking or points of view assists them in unlocking and realizing their smartness . . . again—a smartness lost from a young childhood, when all was possible.

OVERVIEW OF THINKING MAPS BY DAVID HYERLE

Graphic Primitives and Definitions

| primitives | Thinking Maps and the Frame | expanded maps |

The Circle Map is used for seeking context. This tool enables students to generate relevant information about a topic as represented in the center of the circle. This map is often used for brainstorming.

The Bubble Map is designed for the process of describing attributes. This map is used to identify character traits (language arts), cultural traits (social studies), properties (sciences), or attributes (mathematics).

The Double Bubble Map is used for comparing and contrasting two things, such as characters in a story, two historical figures, or two social systems. It is also used for prioritizing which information is most important within a comparison.

The Tree Map enables students to do both inductive and deductive classification. Students learn to create general concepts, (main) ideas, or category headings at the top of the tree, and supporting ideas and specific details in the branches below.

The Brace Map is used for identifying the part-whole, physical relationships of an object. By representing whole-part and part-subpart relationships, this map supports students' spatial reasoning and is for understanding how to determine physical boundaries.

The Flow Map is based on the use of flow charts. It is used by students for showing sequences, order, timelines, cycles, actions, steps and directions. This map also focuses students on seeing the relationships between stages and substages of events.

The Multi-Flow Map is a tool for seeking causes of events and the effects. The map expands when showing historical causes and for predicting future events and outcomes. In its most complex form, it expands to show the interrelationships of feedback effects in a dynamic system.

The Bridge Map provides a visual pathway for creating and interpreting analogies. Beyond the use of this map for solving analogies on standardized tests, this map is used for developing analogical reasoning and metaphorical concepts for deeper content learning.

The Frame

The "metacognitive" frame is not one of the eight Thinking Maps. It may be drawn around any of the maps at any time as a "meta-tool" for identifying and sharing one's frame of reference for the information found within one of the Thinking Maps. These frames include personal histories, culture, belief systems, and influences such as peer groups and the media.

Thinking Maps, Inc. 2007

FIGURE 16–2. *Thinking Maps®: A Language for Learning*

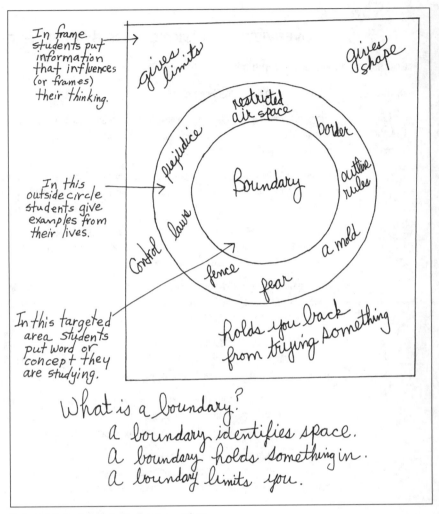

In frame students put information that influences (or frames) their thinking.

gives limits

gives shape

restricted air space

border

prejudice

Boundary

outline rules

In this outside circle students give examples from their lives.

Control laws

a mold

fence

fear

In this targeted area students put word or concept they are studying.

holds you back from trying something

What is a boundary?
A boundary identifies space.
A boundary holds something in.
A boundary limits you.

FIGURE 16–3. *Janelle's Circle Map with Frame*

The Bridge Map

Another very powerful tool within the model is called a Bridge Map. The key to this map is that it guides students as they identify the common factor among the ideas being compared (Hyerle and Yeager 2007). In other words, a Bridge Map actually helps students visualize how analogies work, build their own analogies based on the content they are learning, and use them for driving more meaningful classroom discussions and as linchpins for essay writing. Historically, analogies have been used as teacher-centered devices to guide and leverage students' understanding or as testing instruments on gate keeping exams that we all know so well. Within the Thinking Maps® language, students systematically and creatively learn how to build their own analogies while checking and demonstrating their understanding by writing or reading the analogy as a complete sentence. For example, in Figure 16–4, students in a social studies class discussed the relationship among the following words: *country, planes, acceptance, border, prejudice,* and *restricted air space.* Then they decided that the connection was that one thing was a quality of something else and they created the following analogy: Border is a boundary for a country as prejudice is a boundary for acceptance as restricted air space is a boundary for planes.

As students explore various relationships of language, they build their academic content vocabulary schema as well as improve their abilities to think analogically and metaphorically. Students ready for more challenge can be encouraged to continue finding pairs of words that would fit the pattern. Allowing students to work collaboratively to complete Bridge Maps allows students to hear how others link words or see relationships among the terms. Students literally build a bridge that shows how terms connect as they build a bridge to their own understanding.

Leaving Stereotypes Behind

The needs that adolescents express about turning on their learning are the same needs identified by brain researchers as being crucial to the learning process

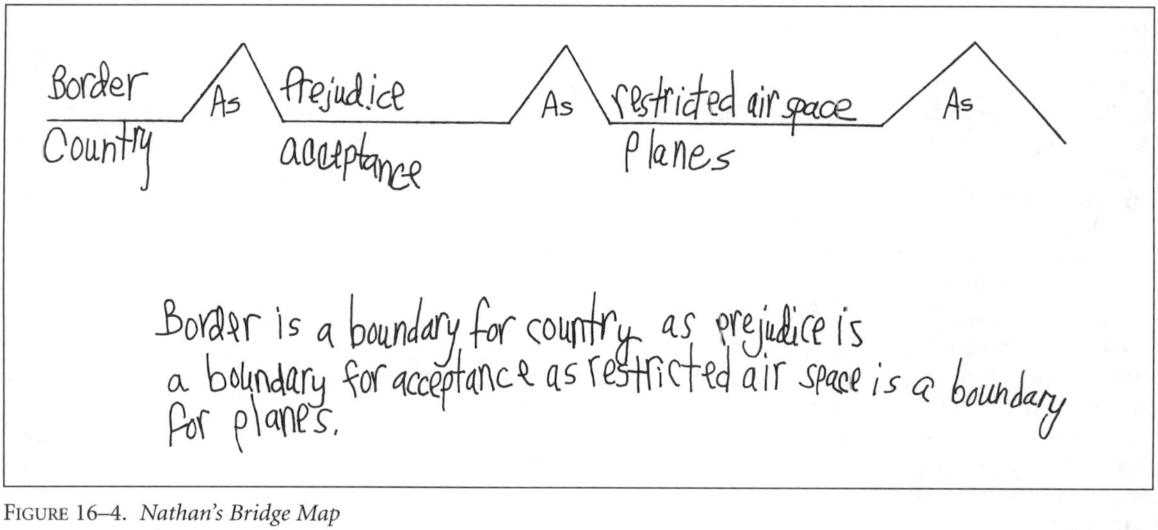

FIGURE 16–4. *Nathan's Bridge Map*

> > > *The belief, determination, and confidence educators bring to the academic experience provide the hope for the students we serve and turn the promise of a generation into the practice of a literate life.*

itself: engagement, relevance, meaningfulness, challenge, and feedback (Jensen 1998). They want us to provide them with

> the invitation and catalysts to explore
> tools to inquire, construct, and communicate meaning and
> venues through which to be heard and appreciated for the knowledge and perspective they bring

What they are asking for (and what we can enable them to do), is to be smart . . . again. We have the ability; now what we need is the will. This means we must be willing to argue against those who believe that some students deserve less because they are less deserving or less able. Without this belief, without a Pedagogy of Confidence, we will continue to lose those seven thousand students each day from our nation's schools. But with it, we will help all students of all colors, of all economic backgrounds, in all locations graduate, prepared for the demands of the world. In *The World Is Flat*, Thomas Freidman (2005) described a world changed to the extent that *all* students needed to be taught the high intellectual skills necessary to compete in a global economy. The intent of this chapter is to suggest some instructional pathways that enable all students to experience the promise of America. The belief, determination, skills, and confidence educators bring to the academic experience provide the hope for the students we serve and turn the promise of a generation into the practice of a literate life.

When you want to know more . . .

Kylene once said that if there were no achievement gap, she wouldn't have felt such compulsion to pull this book together. But there is a gap, and Yvette and Eric have focused intently upon it. Eric has told us before that our beginnings don't necessarily dictate our fate, in his *Voices from the Middle* article "It Begins with Belief: Social Demography Is Not Destiny" (2005), and has worked with several others to edit a collection addressing the same topic, *Teaching All the Children* (Lapp et al. 2004). Yvette has talked about the promise in our underachieving students in "Unlocking the Potential of African American Students: Keys to Reversing Underachievement," from *Theory into Practice* (2005), and "Reversing Underachievement in Urban Students: Pedagogy of Confidence," in *Developing Minds* (2001).

> > > DEVON BRENNER,
        P. DAVID PEARSON, LINDA RIEF

Thinking Through Assessment

FROM THE EDITORS: In the summer of 2006, we—Kylene and Bob—spent time working with teachers who attended the Yale School Development Program Adolescent Literacy Institute. At one point during the week, one teacher left the following note for either or both of us to answer.

> I read one article that says America's students are failing, that more than 60% of secondary students read only at a basic or below basic level; I read another article saying that we can't trust the state assessments or national assessments students take and that our schools (and students) aren't failing. The ACT report [Reading Between the Lines] says schools lack rigor; the SAT report is that scores are on the decline. "Experts" say don't teach to the test and then my principal says if my students don't pass the test, if we don't make AYP, then I'll be fired and/or our school will lose needed funding. One article says assessment is supposed to be authentic and the next says it's supposed to be rigorous but then the school memo says to get kids ready for the state test, which certainly isn't authentic and is only rigorous to those who are behind. You are talking about 21st-century literacy skills, about the literacy in a conceptual age, and about the roles kids will be expected to play in this "flat" world. How does the multiple-choice test that I have designed to measure ability to identify the main idea help prepare a kid for this world you're describing? What is the responsible measure of a student's success and how do I marry that with NCLB, high-stakes tests, a standards-driven curriculum, and demands of the 21st-century workplace?

Deciding where to set a chapter on assessment was far more difficult than we imagined. Why? Assessment guides what we do—so it certainly ought to go first. Assessment makes sense only in the context of what we're teaching—so it certainly ought to fit right in the middle. And assessment is what we pause to do as we reach end points—so it certainly works toward the end of the book. We finally chose the last as our guiding issue, but . . . if the Heinemann folks had let us change our minds just one more time . . .

—KB, REP, LR

We mumbled some answers and then kept the note. This teacher had asked crucial questions that deserved better than our cursory responses. We believe that an issue as complex and critical as assessment deserves thoughtful response. We also know that you teach in a place with its own peculiarities, needs, and restrictions. Those factors help shape what you not only want to do but *can* do or *must* do when it comes to assessment. Therefore, we suggest that providing you with a single answer to questions about assessment is not the best strategy. Instead, we want to provide you with some of the best thinking about this topic from some of the leading minds in adolescent literacy.

Therefore, we turned to Devon Brenner and P. David Pearson. We turned to David and Devon for two specific reasons. First, they had written a wonderful chapter on assessment for Kylene in a book that she and Barbara Samuels coedited, *Into Focus: Understanding and Creating Middle School Readers* (1998). Second, David is now the dean of the College of Education at the University of California, Berkeley, and therefore he is constantly considering what students in that college are learning about assessment. Devon lives on the other side of the country in Mississippi, where she is an associate professor at Mississippi State University. Like David, she too must make sure that her students know a range of assessment strategies. Devon has been working with the Mississippi Department of Education to create a statewide adolescent literacy initiative, so she's been thinking about many facets of assessment. Likewise, David, in his position as dean, is constantly thinking through policy implications of assessment. We like that both are considering assessment from slightly different perspectives. Furthermore, while many of the students from David's program end up teaching in large, urban districts, most of the students in Devon's program teach in rural areas. We liked the geographic contrast David and Devon brought to the conversation as well as the distinct demographics of the schools in which their students will teach.

What follows is the transcript of an online conversation about assessment among Devon, David, and Linda. We hope this conversation jump-starts a similar conversation in your building with your own colleagues.

Initiating the Conversation

Dear David and Devon,

We will begin by offering many thanks to both of you for participating. In preparation for this online conversation, you've already read the letter from the teacher about assessment (email sent to you both on September 6). Her frustration is evident and not unreasonable. We think that much of the teacher's frustration is because of mismatch. There's a mismatch in what teachers know that state assessments should do (measure individual students' growth over time) and what state assessments actually do (measure one group against another from one year to the next). There's a mismatch in what state assessments value (the ability to select the single correct answer) and what twenty-first-century workplace skills demand (the ability to formulate multiple answers to complex problems). There's a mismatch in what policy makers say about assessment ("makes *schools* accountable") and who is punished when scores don't meet a particular point (*students* who are retained or are refused diplomas). And there's a mismatch between what assessment could actually do (celebrate accomplishments) and what high-stakes assessments do (highlight failures).

Assessments ought to help teachers plan instruction for a particular child, but high-stakes tests don't do that. Scores are received near the end or even after the school year is ended, and therefore are of little help to the teacher in shaping the curriculum or instruction for the student. They ought to tell teachers and parents and, yes, even students, something about what students actually know about reading or math or science, but instead they just provide numbers that rarely help parents (and teachers and students) understand what their children actually know. The list of mismatches goes on, but always with the same result: frustration. In the midst of that frustration, the teacher asked it best: *What is the responsible measure of a student's success and how do I marry that with NCLB, high-stakes tests, a standards-driven curriculum, and demands of the 21st-century workplace?*

So what do you say to this teacher?

—Kylene, Bob, and Linda

And the Responses Began

DEVON: What a terrific question. I think that these are the assessment issues we are all grappling with. In Mississippi, our brand-new state frameworks for language arts explicitly address media literacy, technology, inquiry, critical thinking, and so forth. But the new frameworks will be accompanied by a new state test. Because of pressures to return test data quickly, the new test will be all multiple choice—cutting even the few extended-response questions and demanding even more one-right-answer-type questions. So yes, teachers are getting conflicting messages.

While we can lament the fact that standardized tests measure only a narrow slice of literacy and document the ways that the accountability movement seems to seek to actively undermine the very kind of rich teaching Kylene and Bob were advocating in the summer institute and outlined in this book, I wonder if it isn't more helpful to reframe these conflicting messages about assessment as the conflicts that are *always* inherent in assessment. There are multiple reasons to assess:

> so we can communicate with students about their achievements

> so that we can figure out what to teach next, or whether our teaching decisions are working the way we hoped

> so we can communicate with outside audiences—families want to know how their children are doing; administrators want to know if we are fulfilling our role as teacher

> so that we can compare the performance of one group of students with that of another within our school and district and across the state and country

Not all of these purposes and audiences for assessment are particularly helpful for making teaching decisions, but that's not their function. No one way of assessing would ever allow us to accomplish all these different purposes. The assessment that convinces my administrator that I'm meeting all the standards may not convince parents that their students are making progress. The ones that are easy to administer may not provide sufficient information about specific literacy processes. For me, it is helpful to recognize these different purposes and audiences, and to keep them in mind when I am figuring out just what and how to assess. Thinking of assessment in terms of multiple purposes and audiences frees me from putting too much emphasis on one assessment or trying to force daily assessments and project evaluations to do the work of the standardized test.

> > > > >

Devon is making an excellent point as she reminds us that assessment that does not consider the demands of the twenty-first century lead us down wrong paths. Review what Jim Burke has to say about those twenty-first-century demands (Chapter 10).

—*KB, REP, LR*

It also seems to me that the kind of instruction that seems furthest from the test—what your teacher calls literacy for the twenty-first century and a flat world—*does* prepare students for the standardized test. Students who are able to comprehend on the literal, inferential, and critical levels will probably be able to figure out just what the test is asking. Students who read and write copiously and who learn and think about and apply content knowledge, as well as learn a lot of vocabulary, develop strategies for dealing with a variety of texts. Students who are making complex decisions about the content of a Web page or analyzing ads in the media are learning to apply their knowledge and to respond to a variety of questions. I think that these students become prepared for any kind of test.

All this doesn't mean that we don't explicitly study the genre of tests just before the test arises—and there are lots of guides out there for how to prepare for the test. But mostly, we prepare for the test by teaching children complex, thoughtful, multifaceted literacy skills. I've been collaborating with some middle school teachers in my hometown of Starkville, Mississippi, on schoolwide reform. One teacher, Ms. Vanderford, uses problem-based learning (students work in groups to apply a variety of resources to solve real-world problems) and process writing and technology whenever she can. In her district, she's a bit of an anomaly, and she found she was constantly bumping up against policies and tussling with her administrators. Last year, she decided she was tired of being a rebel and that she would closely follow the week-by-week curriculum map that linked the tested part of the old framework—that is, the benchmark—to particular passages in the basal text, activities, and worksheets from the teacher's manual. At the end of a year of doing just what she was told to prepare for the test, her test scores were the worst they've ever been. You can bet your buttons that this year, she's going to be a rebel again!

My colleague, Kay Brocato, has a saying that's become a bit of a mantra for me: the one who is doing is the one who is learning. To me, that's why good teaching actually prepares people for the test. Our students learn a lot when they actually engage in a variety of literacy practices and get lots of feedback about how they're doing.

> < < < < <
> One good place for finding information on helping students prepare for tests is a great book titled *The Literacy Coach's Handbook*, by Walpole and McKenna (2004).
> —*KB, REP, LR*

DAVID: I say *amen* to everything that Devon has said . . . but let me add a little of my own perspective—say it in a different way, if you will. Roger Farr is fond of saying that assessment is useful only when someone or some group has decisions to make or questions to answer. This means that assessment is always a means to an end, never an end unto itself. It's the quality of the decision we make, not the test score, that counts. We have to keep that thought uppermost in our minds in this world of high-stakes assessment because we often treat assessments as if they were ends unto themselves.

Devon is right to put purpose foremost on her assessment agenda. And, of course, audience has to be right up there with purpose; without an audience for the information, there can be no purpose. Instead of using the term *audience*, I like to think of assessment systems as having *clients*, and I would always make students the number one clientele. If our assessments are not helping students answer their basic questions, which I take to be some form

> > > *Assessment is always a means to an end, never an end unto itself. It's the quality of the decision we make, not the test score, that counts.*
>
> —*David Pearson*

of How am I doing? and What do I need to do next? then I think we have failed to serve the major client as educators. But students are not the only clients. So are parents, teachers, administrators, policy makers (school boards and state agencies), and, of course, the general public. And Devon is right to emphasize the fact that each of these clients has very different needs (questions to answer and decisions to make), and thus they each require very different sorts of information. Standardized tests probably do serve the needs of the general public and policy makers when they try to answer the question How are our schools doing? But they don't do a good job of helping teachers track students' progress through a curriculum or even a set of standards. For those purposes and questions, teachers need fine-grained information of the sort that can come only

THE ASSESSMENT NEEDS OF DIFFERENT CLIENTS OF THE ASSESSMENT SYSTEM

Client	Decisions to Be Made / Questions to Be Answered	Assessment Tools
Students	How am I doing? What shall I do next?	Portfolio entries (self-evaluated) and/or feedback from classroom work samples
Teachers	Have the kids met my learning goals? How did my teaching go? How can I help Amy? Should Amy enter X?	Portfolio entries and work samples Curriculum-embedded tests Informal diagnostic tools An array of converging evidence
Parents	How is my child doing? Compared with the average bear?	Portfolios/work samples Norm-referenced tests
Administrators	How effective is our program? How are our teachers doing?	Aggregated data of some sort (portfolios, norm-referenced tests)
Policy makers	How well are schools meeting public expectations?	Trends, over time, on some aggregated data (norm-referenced tests would do just fine)
Taxpayers	How well is our money being spent?	Trends, over time, on some aggregated data (norm-referenced tests would do just fine)

FIGURE 17–1. *Crafting Assessment Table, Developed by P. David Pearson*

from deep analysis of everyday work products. I've tried to capture the notion of a system, with different tools for different folks, in Figure 17–1, reprinted from an earlier piece of mine.

LINDA: I like the distinction amongst clients (what Devon calls audiences) and needs for different kinds of information. As classroom teachers, we are often at odds with all the assessments we are asked to administer because they are, precisely as you say, for different audiences. It is hard for us to remember to keep that in mind, especially when few audiences outside the classroom take the time to look at the evidence that helps guide our instruction and work with students on a day-to-day basis. This evidence is cumbersome and takes time to examine, but good teachers gather it. Good teachers look at the drafts of writing students, how they use comments and suggestions to move from one draft to the next. Good teachers look at the students' responses to reading, to examine how deeply and critically they are entering into a book, or essay, or poem. Good teachers keep anecdotal notes on students and know enough about those kids to suggest ideas for writing and books they might be interested in reading. Good teachers ask open-ended questions that push students to think more deeply about all that their reading brings to mind, about themselves, about the world, and about the intentions of the authors. All of this is assessment on a daily basis. Kids gather this evidence in writing-reading notebooks and portfolios, filled with the drafts and finished pieces of writing, with teacher notes and self-assessments and goal setting. *But*, this is for the student and the teacher, and few other audiences either want to see this or know how to use this information, even when guided through the material. I have sent portfolios and notebooks home along with guided questions for reading and understanding what the parents see. The parents seem grateful yet still don't know quite how to respond to all this information. Administrators don't want to see it. When I've carried portfolios and writing-reading notebooks to sessions with them, they have never once looked at a student's portfolio to see what these students know and are able to do or what I am doing to help them grow as readers and writers.

> < < < < <
>
> For more information on Linda Rief's writing-reading notebooks, take a look at her chapter (13). *And a note from Kylene:* I was lucky enough to visit Linda's classroom in the fall of 2006. While I could have been wowed by a lot, I spent much of my time looking through her students' writing-reading notebooks. I kept thinking to myself, "I want my son to keep one of these!"
>
> —*KB, REP, LR*

That's why we continue to have standardized tests, in order to give the various constituents a number that gives them the information they think they want. The irony is, what do those numbers say, other than, in comparison with other students, your child is wedged in the list of numbers here? The numbers and categories say little that is really a deep understanding of what the child knows and can do, but the audience members believe the number tells them what they want to know.

Somehow we haven't made it clear how and why different assessments are used by a variety of audiences, and why each is sufficient unto itself based on all that audience really wants to know. This is frustrating to teachers,

> > > > *Standardized tests probably do serve the needs of the general public and policy makers when they try to answer the question How are our schools doing? But they don't do a good job of helping teachers track students' progress through a curriculum or even a set of standards. For those purposes and questions, teachers need fine-grained information of the sort that can come only from deep analysis of everyday work products.* —*David Pearson*

though, because few people want the evidence that really shows what kids know. It's complicated and cumbersome and can't be reduced to a number. It is real learning, and it is messy.

The most important thing I want to say, agree with, is that those students who are immersed in reading and writing for real reasons for real audiences, on a daily basis, do fine on any assessment. They are thinkers who can figure out what any audience needs to know and how to convey that information. When assessments that veer from this daily writing are taught as a genre and when we remind students to approach the task as they would any writing or reading task, students still do well. When, on the other hand, teachers and students must spend precious time and energy repeatedly prepping specifically for an assessment, the students are denied opportunities for real problem solving through interaction with texts and tasks in the real world.

I really appreciated hearing the example of Ms. Vanderford. For nearly ten years, I've been working with a district in another state, teaching courses to their teachers for two weeks during the summer and hosting many of them for weeklong observations of writing and reading in my classroom. Despite all they have learned about writing and reading, these teachers have been unable to convince their administrators that they do not have to spend months prepping their kids for the state tests. Three years ago, they asked if I would give my students their state writing test, with no prep. I did. They coded my students' writing so no one would know which pieces came from my classroom. Many more of my students scored in the higher categories and well above their students on this persuasive essay. Ironically, even that did not convince the administrators who mandate test prep.

This even happens in my district. For the first time this year, despite the fact that our students score well above the state and national averages in all categories of state tests, it was suggested we "prepare" the students for the test. I felt guilty. Maybe I should do more than give a forty-five-minute crash course. I downloaded the practice NECAP [New England Common Assessment Program] test from the state department of education's website.

After spending several class periods literally boring the kids to sleep (why would you use a colon, instead of a semicolon; how is your school day compared with that of the Aztecs of 1200 AD; what ingredients are *not* in this recipe; what would you write for just the middle paragraph of this essay) I thought, *I will never do this again*. What I will do is continue to immerse them in writing and reading of all genres, asking them to think deeply and widely about all they do. That's what they had been doing, until I so rudely interrupted them. They were in the middle of investigating health issues, ones they were curious about. They had to present their findings in at least three different formats: PowerPoint, interview, poetry, fictional story, diary, informational pamphlet. Olivia was investigating Alzheimer's disease because her grandfather was diagnosed with it, Jack anorexia because he was worried about a girl on his swim team, and Forrest alcoholism because it is so prevalent in his family and he worries about it. How can I get these kids to care enough about the school day of the Aztecs to show all they are capable of as readers and writers when they can't conjure any passion or interest in that subject?

DAVID: Linda, if I could butt in for just a moment, I'd like to say *amen* and offer a challenge to all of us. I agree with you wholeheartedly that the way to improve scores on standardized tests is to have a first-rate curriculum and set of teaching practices; then we can let the external testing chips fall where they may. But, *and here is the challenge,* as a field, we desperately need to prove precisely your claim. Because until and unless we do, teachers will continue to teach directly to the external, high-stakes tests out there—not just because they are fearful of their own fate (What happens if my class scores are too low?) but also because they won't be 100 percent certain that they are not jeopardizing students' futures, too. (What happens to Tommie or Susie if he or she gets a low score on the high school exit exam?) We need a few schools willing to step up to the plate to do exactly that study—demonstrating that students do just fine on external examinations if they receive thoughtful, individually tailored instruction from highly professional teachers.

> > > *It seems to me that the most useful way to think about assessment to support instruction is by asking, from the outset, two important questions: What is it I want my students to know and be able to do? and What would serve as evidence that students know and can do those things? —Devon Brenner*

LINDA: I think, too, we often associate assessments with an end product, instead of viewing assessment as critical to the decision making right from the beginning of writing or reading. What do I want to write about? Why is one topic or genre more critical than another? Have I said what I need to say in the clearest, most compelling way? What book do I want to read? What can I take from, learn from this reading? As I read, what questions come to mind that need to be answered, more clearly thought out? What is this author saying between the lines? What are other viewpoints? This is where assessment begins, not at the final product.

DEVON: Yesterday, I was invited to Armstrong Middle School Shadow Day. My own son is an eighth grader there, so I shadowed him from band practice to art to English class. Vaughan absolutely hates reading novels but loves reading the conversations in online role-playing games like *Runescape* and *Second Life*. His friend Josh has his own Nintendo web forum with reviews and cheat codes for Nintendo games and the DS Lite. In response to a *use the vocabulary words in a paragraph* prompt, the boys had created a storyboard for a new Xbox game they'd developed; created a jacket and taped it around a box to look like a real game jacket; created a promotional, animated video in QuickTime; and uploaded it to www.youtube.com to show it to the rest of the class. They got all ten points for correctly using the words in context and extra credit for the best project, but the teacher did not have a visible plan for assessing all the other remarkable literacy and inquiry and problem solving the boys had done. I'm thinking of these boys, and their classmates, as I respond to Linda.

Linda, you talk about viewing assessment as critical to planning decisions and instruction right from the beginning, not just as the end product of teaching or learning. I think you are so right. It seems to me that the most useful way to think about assessment to support instruction is by asking, from the outset, two important questions: What is it I want my students to know and be able to do? and What would serve as evidence that students know and can do those things?

I see these two questions rolled into one in the note from Kylene and Bob's teacher that kicked off this conversation, when she asked: "What should be the measure of success?" It seems to me that the measure of success depends on (1) what we want students to learn and (2) the artifacts and activities and observations that might serve as evidence of that learning.

Assessing the traditional, school-based kinds of reading and writing is neither easy nor straightforward. This is partly because standardized tests and even our anthologies and teacher's manuals assess only a fraction of the literacy processes that good teachers care about and partly because literacy processes themselves are complex and intertwined with content knowledge and so on. But there *are* bunches of resources out there for teachers who want to think about assessing literal and inferential comprehension, or ability to form an argument in writing, or revision processes, or vocabulary knowledge. There are rubrics and portfolios and checklists and other tools out there that help us assess many of the literacy practices we care about.

There are fewer resources that have already articulated what to look for and how to find out if students are using the array of literacy practices that are possible when we teach those twenty-first-century literacies. I recently read *Teaching and Learning Multiliteracies: Changing Times, Changing Literacies*, by Anstey and Bull (2006). These authors are from Australia, where they've been teaching these things for a while. This book had great ideas for incorporating multiliteracies in the classroom, but nothing about assessment—*assessment* wasn't even in the index! And I think this is typical of the new-literacies/multi-literacies literature. (I still don't even know what to *call* this kind of teaching!) And yet, if we're going to ask students to engage in inquiry and create websites and use media sources (and if they're already hosting forums and spending hours on Facebook and MySpace), it is imperative that we begin conversations about the literacy practices we hope to see and what those look like.

Individuals and teams of teachers will have to work together (are working together?) to decide—What does comprehension and/or knowledge of narrative structure look like in a video or a rap song about *The Crucible*? What does evaluating sources look like when students create a website about the history of the civil rights movement? What are the criteria for formatting an email to a friend versus an email to a person in Congress? In my own classes, we make movies, and I'm learning to articulate the criteria for demonstrating understanding in a visual form—such as images that go beyond cliché, connections from one part of the movie to the next, and ability to explain (verbally and in writing) the choices of music and color and pictures in the movies. But I've still got a ways to go, a lot to learn about assessing both the new literacy practices afforded by moviemaking and the ways that the movie format allows them to express knowledge of content and writing process and comprehension and vocabulary and such that I've always taught.

LINDA: I worry, Devon, about all the resources for rubrics and checklists that you mentioned. I, too, often see these printed as posters, with kids having little understanding of what these lists mean and how they could use them. Too often teachers use them to assess students with little understanding themselves of how to teach or how to succeed at accomplishing these characteristics or traits. And if they don't know, how can their students figure them out?

DAVID: Posted rubrics can become a fraud, an activity in which we go through the motions of sharing with students the standards for what counts as a quality piece of work without really helping them come to grips with what quality looks like—and, more important, how a quality piece differs from one that falls short. I don't think rubrics have any value unless we involve students in examining what it means for a piece to have a certain feature—say, voice—by involving them in judging when it is present and when it isn't. Otherwise, the standards in rubrics are vague—and cruel—generalities. I have seen some teachers, however, do a good job of deconstructing why some pieces of writing work while others don't. And then, of course, the trick is to get students to shine that light on their own work—recognizing when a piece is working (and when it isn't) and why.

> < < < < <
> You might speculate about what Don Murray would have to say about assessment in the teaching of writing in Chapter 12. Consider in particular the amount of time he would give to writing, revising, re-writing, and then re-writing once again a single piece. We might speculate about what he would have to say about rubrics.
>
> —*KB, REP, LR*

LINDA: I wanted to pick up on Devon's comments about new literacies. In this wave of new literacies, with students knowing and doing more with technologies than most of us as their teachers know and do, maybe we are better off without lists; maybe we should have to develop all the possibilities based on what those kids show us. Wouldn't this be exactly what Don Murray talks about when he says, "We should be seeking diversity, not proficient mediocrity" (personal class notes)? These rubrics almost demand mediocrity. If we already know what we're looking for, and look only for that, we might not see other evidence of learning.

   I am thinking of Devon's son Vaughan and his friend Josh. I am not surprised at what they created. Many of my students will tell me informally that they have written their own games on the computer. John and Nick told me to listen to them on WUNH one night; they would be the disc jockeys for the university radio station. They had to take three courses at the University of New Hampshire and pass FCC regulations before being left in charge of the station and its programming. Two fourteen-year-olds. They had passed. They would be running the station three nights a week. Vaughan and Josh created their own rules and used the list of vocabulary words to create a storyboard. Why do we need a rubric—or visible plan—for assessing that? What if the assessment looked different? Were their classmates engaged by the game? Did the rules make sense? What was to be accomplished in the game? What kind of critical thinking and problem solving did the game require of players? Did the promotional material sell the product in the mind of the consumers? What were the problems they encountered as they created the product and how did they solve them? What do they see as the strengths and weaknesses of what they did (process and product)? What would they do differently next time?

And they did this for themselves and each other. Not the teacher. The very projects, or pieces of writing, that most engage my students are the ones they do for themselves first, not the teacher. Maybe if we admitted to our students that we had some things to learn from them, we would realize they can explain and assess their own learning in ways we haven't begun to think about. What if our assessments included process papers: Tell me how this came to be. What did you do from one draft, one segment to the next? How did you do that? What problems did you encounter? How did you solve them? What did you enjoy most about making or crafting this? What would you do differently next time? Wouldn't that be more valuable information than a number, the ten points for using all vocabulary words in context? (Instead, What decisions did you make about each word as you attempted to use them?)

I think the question we should be asking ourselves now should be not only what do *we* want our students to know and be able to do, but what do *they* need and want to know based on what they already know and are able to do, so that they move forward in their learning.

The artifacts are changing. Standardized tests and handwritten answers to questions are inadequate. Yet simply teaching kids PowerPoint is not enough, either. The content on that PowerPoint or website and whether it's credible, informative, compelling information that moves the viewer to learn and think and feel matter. How the producer of those materials created that product matters also—the process he went through—be it a piece of writing, a video, or a website. How and why does that affect the viewer or listener? Assessment is about the process and the product.

DAVID: I'll go part of the way down that road with you, Linda, but not all the way. I fully agree with what you say about getting the student engaged in the assessment process—that follows from my assertion that the student should be the primary client of the assessment system. But I also agree that others have a stake in evaluating the performance of individuals—the whole process by which society certifies that individuals possess certain types of knowledge, skills, and dispositions is, for example, essential to what we call professional knowledge. So I don't want to back off the idea that when the public interest is

PROCESS PAPER (BACKGROUND HISTORY OF THE WRITING) AND EVALUATION

Name_____ Section _____ Date _____

Title or Topic _____

Tell me everything you can about *how this writing came to be.* You may write on the back of this sheet also.

1. How did you come up with the idea for the piece?

2. What did you do differently (to revise or edit this piece of writing) as you went from each draft to the final draft, and why did you make, or not make changes?

3. What kind of problems did you encounter and how did you solve them?

4. What helped you the most to make the piece as strong as it could be?

5. What do you want me to know about the writing of this that I might not know just from reading it?

6. What parts of this writing are done especially well? (What qualities or characteristics make it an effective piece of writing?)

7. What have you learned to do as a writer from doing this piece?

8. What did you learn/notice/pay attention to with regard to editing comments given to you (or done on your own) about spelling, punctuation, paragraphing, and the construction of sentences in order to write this piece carefully?

Student grades	Teacher grades	Comments
process		
content		
mechanics		

Process Paper by Linda Rief

From *Adolescent Literacy*. Portsmouth, NH: Heinemann. © 1991 by Linda Rief from *Seeking Diversity*. Portsmouth, NH: Heinemann.

at stake, society has the right to impose standards for performance. That said, I think the public interest is best served by open systems of assessment where everyone knows what the rules of the game are. And I also believe that schools have a special obligation to all of us, as learners, to reach the point where we can assess for ourselves, as free agents in this universe, whether the piece we wrote will do the job for the audience we wrote it for or whether the reading I did for a book, a newspaper article, or a menu was good enough for the purpose I had in mind when I read it. And that requires us—absolutely requires us—to let students in on the assessment process.

DEVON: Clearly, good teachers spend a lot of time figuring out what students know and can do. Finding out what students want to know can help us to teach them. And we may not need a plan or rubric from the outset for every project we teach or every unit. Learning in depth about what our students are thinking and doing is idiosyncratic, and moment-to-moment assessing can be powerfully informing. This kind of assessment, with process papers and interviews and portfolios and justifications, can and should inform our teaching. These questions recognize that adolescents do come to our classrooms with amazing literacy practices that often go unrecognized and are undervalued at school—they are able to use rhyme and rhythm and verbal interplay, able to text message faster than lightning (with knowledge of all the symbols and specialized vocabulary of texting), or, like your students and my son, with all kinds of technological literacy skills.

But even though they possess this wide array of literacies, these same adolescents may not be very good text analyzers, critical thinkers, or connection makers. They may be copious writers of emails, but they may not be revisers. They may develop amazing video games and not question how those games position the people who play them or who are portrayed within them. There are literacy practices (or are they ways of thinking?) that seem applicable to all kinds of texts and modes of communication, and I think that it might be useful to hold those literacy practices in our heads (and in our assessment systems) as we ponder that original question, What should be the measure of success?

My co-interviewee here, David, and his colleagues Terry Underwood and Monica Yoo have a chapter (in press) that is based on Luke and Freebody's four resources model of reading (Freebody 1992; Luke and Freebody 1999). Readers, Luke and Freebody explain, take on four intertwining roles, depending on the task at hand and the nature and difficulty of the texts they read:

> code breaker (cracking the code or cipher that maps spellings to sounds and vice versa)

> meaning maker (focusing on the message of the text, including the knowledge required to understand it)

> > > > >
If you're reading this book in order, then what Devon has just said should remind you of comments from Jeffrey Wilhelm and Michael Smith (Chapter 15) as well as Yvette Jackson and Eric Cooper (Chapter 16). If you've not yet read those chapters, a smart thought would be to turn to them next to see how critical student-centered inquiry is to the learning process.
—*KB, REP, LR*

> text user (focusing on the pragmatics of use—what function does a text serve in a social context?)

> text critic (a critical competence that entails unpacking the social, economic, and political *assumptions* behind and *consequences* of using a text) (Underwood, Yoo, and Pearson, in press)

DAVID: Terry, Monica, and I appreciate the plug! Thanks, Devon.

DEVON: To me, it's been very useful to think about these four roles—they're what I've always been working at as a literacy teacher, but I've not articulated them this clearly. I think that for the most part, schools have done a pretty good job creating readers who are code breakers and perhaps meaning makers, but we've been less successful helping students become text users and text critics. And these roles seem particularly crucial as more of us get our knowledge from unregulated sources like Wikipedia and Google. (Just the other day, I was reading about how Google and other search engines have become the arbiters of knowledge and how their logarithms control what we learn and don't learn. They've got so much power in terms of defining the knowledge we have access to. But I'm getting away from the point here.)

> > > *For many of us, it will take remembering that all these technologies are just the tools that deliver the thought and creativity and imagination of a person. The technology is the tool, like a pencil and paper, and we can't give it all the credit. Assessment will always have embedded in it the notion "to sit beside," and that involves a living, breathing person.*
>
> *—Linda Rief*

LINDA: I'm fascinated, Devon, by this notion of four resources and agree with you that schools probably don't do a very good job of teaching kids to be more critical consumers of information, especially on the Internet. There is so much available to them that it is critical that this becomes a priority.

I agree also that there should be a visible assessment that pushes students to analyze, critique, and connect with the literacies of this flat world. For many of us, it will take remembering that all these technologies are just the tools that deliver the thought and creativity and imagination of a person. The technology is the tool, like a pencil and paper, and we can't give it all the credit. Assessment will always have embedded in it the notion "to sit beside," and that involves a living, breathing person. As always, I have more questions than answers. It's the search that keeps me teaching. It's the conversation that keeps me learning.

DEVON: I think this goes back to your question, Linda, about why we need a visible rubric or a system for assessing. I think it is important to think through our assessment systems so that we are assessing (and, in turn, teaching) all of the

**When you want to
know more...**

Assessment is one of our
most difficult issues: some
would say we do too much,
others, not enough, and
almost everyone would like
to do it better. Devon and
David have been dealing with
this for some time, for exam-
ple, in their essay "Authentic
Reading Assessment in the
Middle School," from *Into
Focus: Understanding and
Creating Middle School
Readers* (1998). Devon
talked about the implications
for school reform in "Early
Implementation of School
Reform: How Observation of
Literacy Practices Reveals
the Impact of Accountability
Systems on the Reform
Process," in *Language and
Literacy* (Brenner, Brocato,
and Kurz 2006).

kinds of literacy practices that matter to us. There has to be some interplay between what we learn from and about students as they teach us the new literacies, and our very important role in helping students learn to think, critique, contextualize, and question. So I think we do need a visible plan, or set of plans, to help us assess all the different roles that we want our readers-writers-composers to be able to perform. We need to be able to communicate, to ourselves and to students and to stakeholders, about what counts as evidence of the literacy practices that matter to us. This, for me, is an ongoing task.

LINDA: David, how do we do a better job of accomplishing Devon's goal?

DAVID: It's both the easiest and the hardest job we have as educators. Easy because it's a matter of being clearer, more transparent, more open, more honest, more engaging with students and their parents, letting them in on our little secrets about what we value in student work—whether it is reading, writing, talking, whether we're teaching English, history, science, or math. That, by the way, is the primary motive for rubrics and standards, even with all of their foibles—to be transparent so that no one has an advantage over anyone else by having special access to unwritten rules and standards.

It's hard because it really requires the building of that assessment system. (Remember Figure 17–1 on page 262, where all clients get just the information they need to answer just those questions that matter to them.) And finding just the right piece of information for each and every player in the education game is a very tall order. It will require a lot of trial and error, until we, like Goldilocks, get it just right! But it is worth the effort, and I, like Devon and you, am still learning how to do it.

> > > RICHARD L. ALLINGTON

Effective Teachers, Effective Instruction

ADOLESCENT literacy has recently become a hot topic in both professional and political circles. I am not clear just why this happened at this time, but I think the rising political interest is linked to presumed deficiencies in the literacy abilities of U.S. adolescents as depicted through the results of the National Assessment of Educational Progress (NAEP) and the Program for International Student Assessment (PISA). The typical interpretation of the reading and literacy outcomes from these two assessment schemes seems to be that U.S. adolescents are in big trouble when it comes to reading proficiencies (Schemo 2003). The reasons for this pessimistic interpretation are many.

First, on the NAEP (National Center for Educational Statistics, 2006), neither eighth- nor twelfth-grade reading outcomes have improved since 1971 (though fourth-grade outcomes have shown modest improvements from 1971 to 2002). Second, on the Program for International Assessment—PISA—(NCES 2002), U.S. fifteen-year-olds performed at about the international average, with better performance on narrative text reading than on informational text reading (and average ranking is not the desired status for a world superpower). Third,

In a way, we've been building toward this chapter from the first page. We've placed this topic here for several reasons. First, now with rich ideas and strategies in your mind, it's time to make sure you put them into practice in effective ways. Second, this chapter is an excellent compliment to the chapter on assessment (Chapter 17). Third, it becomes important background knowledge for the following Interlude 5 by Leila Christenbury and the subsequent chapter on literacy coaches by Kathy Egawa (Chapter 19).
—*KB, REP, LR*

> > > > >

We encourage you to spend time looking at the NAEP long-term trends and PISA trends in detail. Go to http://nces.ed.gov/nations reportcard/ for NAEP scores and http://nces.ed.gov /surveys/pisa/ for PISA results.

—KB, REP, LR

both assessments demonstrate huge gaps between the achievement of suburban and urban adolescents, between poor and nonpoor students, and between ethnic majority and minority youth. By huge, I mean that both poor and minority students at twelfth grade read at the same level as eighth-grade nonpoor and nonminority students.

Finally, almost half of the states have now implemented some demonstration of adequate reading ability as a requirement for graduation from high school, and far too many students have been unable to achieve the reading proficiency benchmarks that have been established for a diploma. These new demands have resulted in a recent decrease in high school completion rates (Amrein and Berliner 2003).

Thus, we have seen a proliferation of reports and initiatives focused on enhancing adolescent literacy proficiencies, with most targeting modifications of classroom instruction, particularly instruction in content area classes, so as to better address the reading instructional needs of all adolescents. In general, these reports have emphasized the need for continuing instruction to develop literacy proficiencies, especially the strategies adolescents must acquire to read informational texts of some complexity. Thus, the general goals of most reform initiatives have focused more on the potential changes in the roles of content area teachers, including the warning that literacy development cannot be the sole province of the English department or relegated to remedial reading and special education programs (see Bean and Readence 2002).

There seem to be two broad themes, or foci, within current initiatives addressing adolescent reading. The first is on the development of higher-order literacies (see, for example Langer 2002) in all students. The second is improving the literacy proficiencies of those adolescents who struggle every day with the literacy tasks they confront (see Beers 2002; Tovani 2001). In this chapter, I hope to offer some useful insights for initiatives for either, or both, foci, but because I have studied struggling readers most of my career, the chapter will undoubtedly tend toward a focus on those adolescents who do struggle daily.

> > > *Both assessments [NAEP and PISA] demonstrate huge gaps between the achievement of suburban and urban adolescents, between poor and nonpoor students, and between ethnic majority and minority youth. By huge, I mean that both poor and minority students at twelfth grade read at the same level as eighth-grade nonpoor and nonminority students.*

These insights are derived largely from our work studying effective teachers of literacy in grades 4 through 12 under the auspices of the Center for English Learning and Achievement, one of the federally funded national educational research centers (cela.albany.edu). The insights derive from an oft-neglected aspect of the various initiatives, especially those focused on struggling readers. That neglected aspect is classroom instruction, specifically the nature of the learning environment adolescents encounter all day long (Allington, 2007).

Studies of Exemplary Teachers

The key studies that fostered my insights were the studies known as the "exemplary teacher studies," especially those studies conducted in the upper-elementary, middle school, and high school classrooms. What stood out in these studies was the potential that classroom instruction had for fostering substantial growth in students' literacy proficiencies, especially growth among those who struggled in other classrooms. But the English and language arts teachers we studied seldom produced such growth alone. In many cases, their students also received instructional support from remedial reading or special education teachers every day. It became clear that special intervention programs by themselves are rarely sufficient to meet the needs of the students they serve. In other words, struggling readers needed high-quality instruction all day long, in every class, as well as a well-crafted daily intervention class.

> > > *Struggling readers needed high-quality instruction all day long, in every class, as well as a well-crafted daily intervention class.*

This should not have been so difficult to imagine. Common sense alone would suggest that students would benefit more from five or six hours of daily lessons that addressed their needs than they would from a single period. Still, it was an insight that had largely escaped me to that point in my career, and my discussions with middle and high school teachers over the past ten years suggest that I wasn't alone.

In the remainder of this chapter, then, I attempt to describe what seem to be critical features of the classrooms that worked to develop higher-order literacies and foster substantial growth among the struggling readers. The classrooms we studied were similar in many ways, and that is what I focus on—commonalities. But I must caution readers that these teachers were hardly identical in the manner by which they taught students to read and write. So take from the descriptions what you can, and build a classroom that works better for all *your* students.

A Closer Look

The original planning for the studies of effective literacy teachers was prompted, at least in part, by the "expert" studies reported by Chi, Glaser, and Farr (1988) and the work on expertise and flow by Csikszentmihalyi (1990). Our review of the extant research on effective literacy teachers suggested that (1) there were few studies of any sort focused on literacy learning in upper-elementary, middle school, or high school grades; (2) only a very few studies reported on effective adolescent literacy teachers; and (3) most of these studies had small, local samples and many were surveys or interviews, not observational studies. Thus, we crafted a larger-scale, qualitative, observation and interview study of effective literacy teachers in grades 4 through 12, located in six

< < < < <

If you're not familiar with this concept of flow and want to understand it more fully at this moment, turn to the beginning of Jeff Wilhelm and Michael Smith's chapter (15). If you want to keep reading this chapter and review what they say later, then keep in mind that flow describes the feeling of energized focus when engaged in activity that gives you a high level of enjoyment and fulfillment.

—KB, REP, LR

states (Florida, California, Texas, New York, New Jersey, and New Hampshire) and working typically in urban schools.

We selected teachers for the study based on their excellent reputations. Each of the teachers was observed for at least ten full days. Typically, the minimal observational scheme was five consecutive days in both the fall and spring semesters. We then used a post hoc analysis to provide evidence of substantial effects on student achievement on standardized tests (Allington and Johnston 2002). We also collected evidence of various sorts illustrating student literacy performances (e.g., conversations, compositions, discussions, reading logs, interviews, and so on).

The primary analytic procedure involved independent qualitative analyses, each using contrastive case studies developed from the field notes, interview, and document and records analysis. We created elaborate case studies of the teachers selected to represent the range of geographic sites, school situations, and curriculum plans. The findings have been reported in books and in published professional journal articles (Allington 2002; Allington and Johnston 2002; Allington, Johnston, and Day 2002; Langer 2001); there were other studies reporting other analyses, as well, that extended the case study findings.

> > > > >

We applaud Dick for not backing away from using specific research terms like *contrastive case studies* and *hierarchical linear modeling.* At the same time, we know many of us must think back to stat classes that we've sometimes worked hard to forget to understand those terms. If you need a brief reminder, see the sidebar titled "Research Terms."

—KB, REP, LR

RESEARCH TERMS

Case study is a type of research that is about investigating a single event (or case) in depth and over time (longitudinally). Case study requires a systematic observation and careful data collection and analysis, and results might be reported as either conclusions or as hypotheses that lead to additional research.

Constant comparison method is a type of analysis in which the researcher compares events that were observed with previous events. This constant comparison allows the researcher to code one observable phenomenon and classify it as something and then compare this across other categories. For instance, in research looking at aliterate students, Kylene Beers identified one group of students who said they liked to read but just didn't do it; these students were self-identified as "dormant readers." Kylene then could use that term to look for dormant readers in other situations—home reading and in-school but out-of-classroom reading—to see if that term made sense in other settings. This constant comparison allows the researcher to define the parameters for observed behavior.

Discourse analysis (DA) is a term used to describe the analysis of language—written or spoken. Think of this as the broad term. **Conversational analysis (CA)** is focusing the analysis on interative talk. So, in a classroom, CA focuses on turn taking or patterns of interaction between those doing the talking (so in a classroom setting, between students or between teacher and students, or between teachers, for instance). **Discursive psychology** pushes us to look beyond the face value of words to what people might really mean. So, you look at the banner on the aircraft carrier that says "Mission Accomplished" and ask what (if any) is the hidden political meaning behind that text. You see how certain images are privileged on television concerning the war in Iraq and ask how the images you see clarify (or do not clarify) oppression. In a classroom, you listen to the teacher who says, "Good," to one particular student when an answer is correct but "Excellent" to another for answers that don't appear that much better and ask yourself what's the hidden agenda (known to the teacher or not) behind those responses.

Epistemology is the branch of philosophy that studies knowledge. It focuses on questions such as What is knowledge? and How is knowledge acquired?

Hierarchical linear modeling (HLM) is a type of multilevel analysis that allows the researcher to look at outcomes at different hierarchical levels. This is important because this allows us to see how data look when nested within other things. For instance, in school settings, students don't exist in isolation, but are nested within peer groups, classrooms, grades, schools, districts, and states. HLM lets the researcher analyze the outcome variables at each of those hierarchical levels.

Post hoc analysis is about finding patterns in a sample. After concluding the experiment, it's a way of looking at the data to see what patterns may have emerged that had not been considered before the study began.

Qualitative research is one of the two major research methods; the other is quantitative research. Qualitative research seeks out in-depth understanding of a situation or a behavior. It pushes us to examine the reasons behind behavior. Think of it this way: qualitative research wants to know about the why and how of something while quantitative research is focused on the measurable facts— the what, where, and when. Qualitative analyses are those procedures that allow you to draw conclusions about the why and how of the qualitative research.

In Johnston's (2004) extended analysis of the nature of classroom talk, the analytic frames included discourse analysis, conversational analysis, and discursive psychology. Johnston, Woodside-Jiron, and Day (2001) employed a constant comparative method in their analysis of the impact of teacher epistemologies on student identity and agency as readers. Langer (2002) reported on qualitative cross-site comparisons of effective teachers in more- and less-effective middle and high schools. Applebee, Langer, Nystrand, and Gamoran (2003) used a hierarchical linear modeling technique and found discussion-based classrooms more effective at enhancing reading and writing achievement after controlling for prior achievement and other background variables. In other words, the findings of this project, as one might expect, were broad as well as deep.

Unique Aspects of Effective Teachers' Classrooms and Lessons

Finding that effective literacy teachers were good classroom managers; or that they created a sense of community; or that their students exhibited higher levels of engagement largely confirmed the findings of earlier studies, so we decided to focus on explaining how these teachers accomplished such things. Thus, while our data did, in fact, indicate that effective teachers accomplished all this and more (and we reported such findings), our research methods were an attempt to better understand the strategies by which these teachers achieved these outcomes. This led us to a focus on commonalities, aspects of instruction that we observed over and over again. One commonality was the use of multiple texts.

Multiple Texts

These effective teachers typically created multiple-text and/or multiple-level curriculum plans that offered all students the opportunity to engage in classroom reading, writing, and conversational episodes. There were two huge advantages in using a multitext or multilevel curriculum. First, far more students were routinely engaged in academic work in these classrooms than was the case in more typical classrooms, largely because having a variety of texts available meant that virtually all students could find texts that they were able to read accurately, fluently, and with comprehension. The second advantage was that when students were provided opportunities to select which text(s) they would read for a given topic or unit, their level of engagement in academic work was high and sustained. Giving students such choices is a powerful factor in motivating engagement and fostering achievement, as a meta-analysis reported by Guthrie and Humenick (2004) so powerfully demonstrated. They report very large effects as a result of (1) providing students with a choice of texts to read and (2) offering easy access to interesting texts in classrooms. (Effect sizes on reading achievement were 1.2 and 1.6, respectively.) I would note that we used the term *managed choice* to reflect that, typically, students selected books from an array that the effective teachers had created. In other words, *choice* wasn't free choice—it was choice skillfully managed by the teacher.

> > > *When students were provided opportunities to select which text(s) they would read for a given topic or unit, their level of engagement in academic work was high and sustained.*

SEVEN CHARACTERISTICS OF HIGHLY EFFECTIVE COMPREHENSION TEACHERS

1. Effective teachers take the time to understand their use of strategies while reading.

2. They incorporate comprehension instruction into daily, weekly, and monthly plans and lessons.

3. They ask students to apply strategies in a wide variety of texts (genres, topics, levels).

4. They vary the size of strategy instructional groups: *Large groups* are used to

   > introduce a new strategy, or an old strategy with a new genre

   > do a think-aloud to demonstrate proficient use of a strategy

   Small groups are used to

   > provide more intensive instruction for students who need it

   > introduce more challenging texts to students who have quickly picked up a strategy

   > discuss the books that small groups are reading

   > focus on strategy use

   One-to-one conferences are used to

   > check a student's understanding and application of a strategy

   > provide an intensive strategy lesson for students who need it

   > push a student to use a specific strategy more deeply

5. They gradually transfer responsibility for strategy application to students.

6. They ask students to demonstrate strategy use in a variety of ways (two-column journals, Venn diagrams, charts, skits, sketches, time lines).

7. They understand why they teach strategies and how strategy instruction fits into overall goals for teaching reading and content.

These traits stem from an analysis of exceptionally effective teachers, grades 1 through 12, primarily from urban low-income schools in six states (Keene 2002).

FIGURE 18–1.

It was not the case that every teacher used multiple texts for every lesson or assignment. Use of a single text was regularly observed as well, but in such lessons, these effective teachers provided much scaffolding that allowed struggling readers access to the texts and to the discussions and conversation that followed the reading (Langer 2001).

Strategies for Creating Engagement with Texts

It is not surprising, perhaps, that the effective literacy teachers routinely provided students with useful strategies for engaging the texts. Keene (2002) and Pressley (2006) have reported the same finding. The effective teachers in our study taught students strategies for thinking as well as for doing. For instance, all effective teachers taught students strategies for organizing their thoughts while fewer than one in five of the less effective teachers did so. Because much has been written about the power of useful text strategy instruction in previous texts (Beers 2002; Langer 2002; Tovani 2001; Wilhelm 2002) as well as throughout this volume, I won't dwell on that topic in this chapter. However, I will reiterate what I know has been a critical point throughout this book: comprehension strategy instruction is necessary for developing adolescent readers and writers. Note also, though, that successful strategy lessons require that students use texts that they can read accurately, fluently, and with understanding.

Motivation for Literacy and Learning

We also noted that the students in these classrooms exhibited the sorts of motivational and volitional characteristics typically ascribed to successful readers. That is, effective teachers engaged these students in a substantially greater volume of reading across the school day than has been previously reported as typical. They were likely to be found engaged in sustained reading and writing activity in different subject areas rather than in the short bursts of reading and writing that seem to characterize most upper-elementary, middle school, and high school classrooms. Such engaged reading and writing does require teachers to allocate larger blocks of time for such activity (thirty to forty minutes per fifty-five-minute period). Furthermore, sustaining this sort of engagement requires that students have texts they can read and that they find engaging. The teacher must go beyond the standard single-text curriculum frame that dominates in most schools.

The use of multitext and multilevel curriculum materials typically involved either ignoring the district-supplied curricular texts or using them in some nondominant manner (for example, on Monday and Tuesday only or as one of several reference texts). We found these teachers commonly made interdomain and intertextual connections as they moved beyond the single textbook and taught within the multitext and multilevel framework. They would link aspects of a book stu-

> > > > >
Take a look at Teri Lesesne's chapter (6) for an extensive list of books, Ellin Keene's chapter (4) for a list of books that act as scaffolds to more difficult texts, and Alfred Tatum's interlude (2) for a reminder that if what students are reading isn't meaningful to them, then they will never search hard to find any meaning in it at all.

—KB, REP, LR

dents were reading, say, *The Ransom of Mercy Carter* (Cooney), to social studies content and themes or to science. They asked students to notice those characteristics held in common by fictional characters in the books they were reading and by actual historical figures. The discussions observed in these classrooms created "distributed thinking" (Resnick 1991), thinking as a group phenomenon. The integration of out-of-school knowledge and experience with in-school knowledge and experience helped to foster that intersubjective literacy competence.

Other researchers have documented the importance of distributed cognition—the sharing of the various perspectives of members of the group—and noted that the collaboration of multiple minds through talk creates more complex thought than any of the minds might have produced alone. But fostering distributed cognition requires creating a nonthreatening context in which to advance ideas and a tolerance for opposing ideas. It also requires a shared set of expectations and the intellectual and social ability to engage in such conversation. Helping students develop such proficiencies was part and parcel of the effective literacy lessons.

Literate Conversation

This focus on developing students' competence with literate conversation sets these classrooms apart from less effective literacy teachers (and science and social studies teachers). The less effective teachers often reported that they just didn't have time for such talk. They had material to cover. One secondary school teacher nicely summarized this point of view: "If I allow discussion, there won't be enough time to cover everything. Besides, my students don't know enough to get into discussions" (Langer 2004, 45). But good evidence points to the power of literate conversation—discussion—in fostering both literacy development and the acquisition of content knowledge. Applebee and his colleagues (2003) found discussion-based lessons more effective at enhancing reading and writing achievement after controlling for prior achievement and other background variables. Making high academic demands (e.g., more reading and writing assignments and a greater amount of homework) in the context of discussion-based instruction was more effective at each grade level (7–8 and 10–11) and for students from every achievement group and ethnic group. Despite the demonstrated effectiveness of discussion in the classrooms, however, lower-track classes held discussions less frequently and for shorter duration (an average of 3.7 minutes) than students in high-track classes (14.7 minutes). Even so, in those few lower-track classes where there were more frequent and longer discussions, they resulted in higher achievement. It is difficult to know, however, the full impact that discussion-based lessons might have on lower-achieving student performance since they were less common in those lower-track classrooms.

> < < < < <
> Bob Probst (Chapter 5) takes on the difficult topic of talk in a classroom and Smokey Daniels (Chapter 9) addresses other ways in which teachers might communicate productively with their students. Dick's discussion here about the research of this topic provides a necessary coda to their chapters.
> —*KB, REP, LR*

One way to promote these conversations in lower-track English language arts classrooms might be, for example, simply to focus on the ability to name a favorite author and to discuss the characteristics of this author's books that make them favorites. We see the beginning of real conversation, talk that is something like the discourse of adult readers, when students report ideas such as the following:

> I love Cynthia Rylant because her books are always about families a lot like mine, crazy families.

> Gary Paulsen is my favorite author because he makes you feel like you're in the wilderness, sort of like the olden days.

> I love Paul Langan's books because Bluford High is just like my high school. I mean, he may not write great literature or anything, but his books keep me reading way past when I should be asleep.

Such conversations ask the student to talk like a reader. Is it important that teachers help students acquire this ability, regardless of its impact on achievement test scores? Is helping students to develop the ability to engage in literate conversation, regardless of their level of literacy proficiency, a critical aspect of supporting struggling readers? Is it an essential aspect of effective literacy teaching? I would argue it is. The first step in fostering growth in literacy is to cultivate students who read, write, and respond in a manner approaching their more proficient peers. In other words, the first step in helping a ninth grader who reads at a fifth-grade level to develop as a reader is to foster the sorts of reading behaviors and responses that our best fifth graders exhibit before, during, and after they read.

Perspective Taking/Civil Discourse

These more effective teachers were able to foster the sorts of proficiencies that enable students to engage in civil discourse with others who hold a different perspective. One of these abilities is that of perspective taking, as observed when a student says, "I think I understand what you are saying, LaWanda, but I disagree." Another example: "Ron may be right, but I think we need to remember that the film presented the position of the military forces trying to control the area, and the people who were living there might have felt differently." And another: "The author basically presents just the northerners' point of view in this chapter. I wonder how southerners felt about General Sherman's march across the South?" In each case, the speakers are attempting to consider another perspective, to step outside themselves and imagine how others might respond. That's an important skill for a reader.

It was this regular emphasis on considering multiple perspectives that made the effective literacy teachers' classrooms stand out. This ability to consider one's own stance as one of many—the author's stance, that of another reader, those of various characters in the book—is one of the higher-order literacies that many people consider critical, but one that is still largely absent from many of our school or classroom evaluation schemes.

Success and Identity

What of the ability these teachers demonstrated to create a high level of situational interest—that interest that is temporary and situated in content or

---

SIX FEATURES OF EFFECTIVE HIGH SCHOOL SOCIAL STUDIES CLASSES

Ladwig and King (1992) provide other research support for classrooms that mirror many of the features of the effective literacy teachers we studied. Following is a summary of their findings on the essential characteristics of effective social studies instruction.

1. There is a sustained examination of a few topics rather than superficial coverage of many.

2. The lessons display substantive coherence and continuity. Lessons are designed around systematic inquiry that builds relevant and accurate knowledge and works toward integration of ideas.

3. Students are given an appropriate amount of time to think, that is, to prepare responses to questions. There are periods of silence to reflect, ponder alternatives, and develop more elaborate reasoning.

4. The teacher asks challenging questions and/or structures challenging tasks given the level of preparedness of the students.

5. The teacher is a model of thoughtfulness. Key indicators include showing interest in student ideas and alternative approaches to solving problems, using the think-aloud process to demonstrate how he thinks through a problem, and acknowledging the difficulty of gaining definitive understanding of problematic topics.

6. Students offer explanations and reasons for their conclusions.

FIGURE 18–2.

context instead of personal preference—so that students who had read only under coercion were now eager to open a book? What is the longer-term effect of a decision to work hard to ensure that all students have books they can successfully negotiate all day long across several subject matter areas (Allington 2003)? What is the result when teachers reject the use of a state- or district-provided one-size-fits-all textbook and craft a curricular environment where all students, regardless of their current reading proficiency, can work successfully across the day? With the effective literacy teachers, the observed impact was a classroom where most students were engaged in productive academic work almost all of the time. These students were succeeding, not struggling.

Connections

As these teachers encouraged literate discussion, they also made overt connections between knowledge, skills, and ideas and across lessons, days, units, classes, and grades. Such connections can be built into a curriculum and instructional plan at the school level or by the individual teacher. Almost 90 percent of the effective teachers made three types of connections constantly: within lessons, across lessons, and with both in- and out-of-school applications and activities. None of the less effective teachers made all three types of connections, and the few connections made were most often real-world links to the homes and lives of the students (Langer 2002).

The Intellectual Life of Effective Teachers' Classrooms

If we are interested in a broader view of "intellectual life" (Vygotsky 1978) than is exhibited on standardized achievement tests, then we will also have to consider the use of other tools to better assess a variety of potential outcomes. We need to figure out how to look at students' identities as readers and writers—their sense of agency and efficacy as readers, writers, and learners. High literacy accomplishment also includes, and we will have to assess, literate conversational proficiency; motivational and volitional outcomes; and, perhaps, as Johnston (2004) argues, capacity for civil discourse. All these were part and parcel of the learning in the effective literacy teachers' classrooms (Allington 2002; Allington and Johnston 2002; Johnston, Woodside-Jiron, and Day 2001; Langer 2001, 2002, 2004). Just as the literacy research community has broadened the view from reading to literacies, so, too, must we broaden the schemes we use to evaluate the impact of instruction.

Consider how we might examine the nature of classroom discourse. All teacher talk imputes intentions, positions, and identities as well as communicating curriculum-relevant information. For example, if a discussion group has ceased to function well, has broken down into a sort of mild chaos, consider what the students hear when the teacher says:

> > Get back to work or you'll be headed for after-school detention.
> > You are interfering with the others and making me feel frustrated.
> > This is not like you guys. What's the problem? How can you solve it?

As Johnston (2004) suggests, each of these remarks says something different about student identity and agency. Each has the potential to affect future interactions in this classroom and future learning.

The first suggests a laborer-supervisor relationship, the second a cooperative relationship, and the third a collaborative relationship. These different relationships also indicate different sorts of agency for students (deference to authority, respect for others' rights, collaborative problem solving). In a broader view of literate development, important in a participatory democracy, the ability to function within a collaborative problem-solving culture might be seen as one of the more critical outcomes of school literacy lessons. The effective literacy teachers were observed responding in each of these three ways, but what marked their interactions with students was the greater prevalence of interactions reflecting the cooperative and collaborative relationships. In other words, they fostered students' identities as learners and their sense of agency as participants.

> > > *One accomplishment, then, of the effective literacy teachers we studied was to create student identities as readers, writers, learners; as resource persons for classmates; as engaged learners who can enter and sustain a literate and civil conversation.*

Language is both representational and constitutive. It invites identities, for better or worse. Johnston (2004) notes that teachers might comment on an assignment that was well done by saying:

> > You're so smart.
> > You're so creative.
> > I can see that you've worked hard on this.

Each comment situates students differently as learners. The ways in which teachers talk position both themselves and the students in their classrooms. That positioning can situate a teacher as the giver of information, as in the traditional transmission classroom, or it can position the teacher as a co-collaborator in an inquiry classroom. It can emphasize relatively unchangeable qualities, such as intelligence, or more malleable qualities, such as effort. It can position students as dependent or independent, as classroom resources or as classroom competitors. If we again turn to the Guthrie and Humenick (2004) analysis of characteristics of effective classroom instruction, we find that they identified a focus on both effort and collaborative activities as powerful factors in promoting both classroom engagement with lessons and fostering growth in literacy development.

One accomplishment, then, of the effective literacy teachers we studied was to create student identities as readers, writers, learners; as resource persons for classmates; as engaged learners who can enter and sustain a literate and civil conversation. These are not minor accomplishments, but we have few ways to represent these proficiencies in any current accountability scheme. Perhaps that is one reason accountability issues are better addressed locally than from afar. While I doubt any of the principals in the schools where these teachers worked, or the parents of these teachers' students, could have described these accomplishments of effective literacy teachers, both the principals and the parents knew there was "something special" about these teachers, something beyond high test scores. It was something they just couldn't quite put into words.

But then, the effective literacy teachers, themselves, could not put it into words. Johnston notes:

> I frequently watched teachers accomplish remarkable things with their students and at the end of the day express guilt about their failure to accomplish this or that part of the curriculum. This guilt was, in my view, both unfounded and unproductive. It was due, in part, to the teachers' inability to name all the things they did accomplish. (2004, 2)

> > > > >
Dick does this well—slips in a point that makes you stop and rethink all you do. You might want to mark this paragraph and return to it after reading Randy Bomer's chapter (20).

—KB, REP, LR

Many folks have worried that one effect of the current accountability schemes, given the tight focus on standardized achievement test scores in reading and mathematics, is to narrow the school curriculum to a heavy emphasis on those two curricular areas while neglecting the others (Hillocks 2002; Langer 2002). I'll agree, but would also suggest that largely unnoticed is the potential for narrowing the accountability focus to traditional academic content, thus ignoring many critical literacy and language proficiencies that were part of the Jeffersonian ideal for public education. Consider, for instance, a student's ability to take the perspective of someone of a different social class, age group, religion, or ethnic background. In any diverse society, it would seem that developing this ability is critical.

The effective literacy teacher studies helped me better understand three issues that seem critical in any attempt to enhance adolescent literacy learning (and science, social studies, and math learning, as well).

First, teachers of adolescents should plan for substantial variation in achievement and motivation among their students. Even with the evidence on the effectiveness of early interventions, there is no project or school that has managed to eliminate achievement variation. As Hargis (2006) has noted, fully a quarter of entering high school freshmen read at or below the seventh-grade level and another quarter at or above the twelfth-grade level. Bottom line? Kids differ.

All students, not just the academically talented, need high-quality instruction all day, every school day. Currently our middle and high schools seem to have curriculum plans designed to best serve higher-achieving students. That is, it is those students in the upper quartile of reading achievement who have a locker, or a backpack, full of texts they can read accurately, fluently, and with understanding. They attend classes where the tasks they are asked to undertake can be accomplished with only modest effort on their part. Their teachers are more likely to offer not just texts they can read but opportunities to discuss those texts. In other words, in typical schools and classrooms, the highest-achieving students seem far more likely than the lower-achieving students to participate in lessons that both theory and research suggest will foster literacy achievement.

We can continue to craft curricular plans that will ensure some students will have to struggle. Or we can craft curricular plans that reduce the struggle for almost all students. The effective adolescent literacy teachers chose the latter route, and their classrooms produced not only higher levels of motivation, engagement, and achievement but also lower levels of behavioral and classroom management difficulties.

> > > *I'll argue that such forms of participation foster the development of values, beliefs, practices, and norms that become part of what students are as literate individuals, as literate citizens. These are basic accomplishments that have been too long ignored in the quest for what works in terms of the narrowly focused state assessments. Perhaps the problem is that we have not seriously considered what works for these ends.*

Second, if we continue to define literacy accomplishments as primarily those proficiencies we can sometimes measure (or estimate) from standardized reading achievement tests, we will be selling our students and our nation short. "Failure to recognize important aspects of literate development leaves teachers unaware of the full importance of their work as they apprentice students into a literate democracy" (Allington and Johnston 2002, 203).

Some might argue that many of the accomplishments I have discussed are not really reading, but what is the use of reading without the capacity to engage in literate conversation? Or the ability and inclination to pursue the issue of stance or perspective taking? Others might argue that the real worth of these accomplishments is that they lead to improved test scores, and the research suggests that they probably are correct. But I'll argue that such forms of participation foster the development of values, beliefs, practices, and norms that become part of what students are as literate individuals, as literate citizens. These are basic accomplishments that have been too long ignored in the quest for what works in terms of the narrowly focused state assessments. Perhaps the problem is that we have not seriously considered what works for these ends.

If you want to know more about ...

As this chapter reveals, Dick has been a spokesman for reasonable approaches to assessment and accountability, and sensible teaching of our students. He's written more about it in an *Educational Leadership* article, "You Can't Learn Much from Books You Can't Read" (2002b), and in his book *What Really Matters for Struggling Readers: Designing Research-Based Programs* (2006).

Third, the studies of effective adolescent literacy teachers pointed to a number of characteristics that set these teachers and their classrooms apart from the more typical middle and high school teacher and classroom. Similar characteristics have also been identified by other researchers as critically important if increasing engagement and higher achievement are our goals (Guthrie and Humenick 2004; Keene 2002; Ladwig and King 1992). But in the current political environment of evidence-based education, I continue to be concerned that rich findings such as these will be ignored not only by politicians but also by researchers and practitioners. If so, then America and America's adolescents will be worse for it.

Lessons Learned

>>> LEILA CHRISTENBURY

WHO IS THE GOOD TEACHER?

I learned to be a teacher in the high school classroom, and for me the process was neither an easy nor a graceful one. It was, actually, often terrifying, always humbling. I knew my subject matter, and I was determined to succeed, even excel, as a teacher, but I encountered, day after day, the limits of both my own experience and my own expertise. What made this early struggle bearable was that my students were largely cooperative, even generous with my instructional fumblings, and we began to connect through the reading and the writing. Then there would be in the classroom discovery and surprise, with some laughter thrown in, and after some time, I felt that I could learn this teaching thing. I began to sense that with my students and within the four walls of my classroom, I was, unexpectedly, surprisingly, at home.

I have never taken that feeling of being at home for granted. Becoming a good teacher is a lifetime's work, and it is an ongoing one at that: never finished, never final, never done. New students, new material, and new understandings of oneself and one's content make each teaching event singular and its own particular challenge. Who we are as teachers, who they are as students, what *we* are trying to accomplish in the class, what *they* want to accomplish—

or will allow—in class, and what we have at hand to help are all profound variables with which teachers must work and, if we are conscientious, with which we hope to succeed.

After years in the classroom, I have concluded that there are many ways to be a good teacher, and even now not all of them are ones I have explored or ones I practice. But I do know that watching other teachers, listening to them, being open to them, and thus learning from them is one of the great reciprocities of this profession. Our students teach us a great deal, but I also know that in my life, I have been instructed by a range of teachers with whom I have connected and from whom I have taken wisdom. These are some of the lessons I have learned.

LESSON 1: *Good teachers can be found in many places; look for them and learn from them.*

I have observed much good teaching outside of traditional classroom settings and, in two instances, the teachers were memorable.

Despite numerous lessons and hours on the slopes, I just could not relax enough to ski with rhythm or ease or, more to the point, without risking personal injury and putting myself and anyone skiing near me in mild peril. Discouraged but persistent, I continued to take lessons and finally encountered one teenage instructor who refused to give up. She was aware of the challenge—I even overheard her tell another instructor that I was, hands down, "the tensest skier" she had ever seen. But she kept working with me. One afternoon, she asked me if I ever sang. Yes, actually, I did, and she then told me to try singing as I went downhill. It was an odd request, but I had nothing to lose. Just as she suspected, the extra expense of breath made me calm and gave me something to concentrate on other than my turns and balance. It was a trick, and it was a trick that worked; it changed my entire approach, and I hummed, sang, and skied happily for the next ten years. This teacher did not give up; she individualized her instruction to meet the needs of one extremely disheartened student, and I mastered a skill.

Just this past summer, at dog obedience school with my new six-month-old puppy, I watched the trainer praise even the slightest progress and ignore the evident failure of many in the class to sit, stay, and lie down. Some of the puppies—including mine—were largely out of control, and some could not seem to learn the most basic of commands. But week after week, the trainer found all of the efforts marvelous, all of the puppies fantastic, all of the owners dedicated and conscientious, and the consistent encouragement kept everyone in the class motivated and on task. This teacher was cheerful, upbeat, and kind; she almost willfully ignored mistakes, and her attitude worked. At the end of the class, most of the puppies, including my own bouncy, distracted one, had mastered all of the basic commands, and we left obedience school with a positive attitude and even some manners.

There are good teachers in many unlikely places; look for them, and you will find them. They can teach you about good teaching.

> > > *After years in the classroom, I have concluded that there are many ways to be a good teacher, and even now not all of them are ones I have explored or ones I practice. But I do know that watching other teachers, listening to them, being open to them, and thus learning from them is one of the great reciprocities of this profession.*

LESSON 2: *Good teachers may not look like you or act like you; be open to them.*

Early in my high school teaching years, I had a definite view of what a good teacher should do and even look like. I observed with mild skepticism an older teaching colleague on the precipice of retirement. Dressed in her polyester pants, shapeless tops, and crepe-soled shoes, she was a nice woman, but privately I did not believe she was professional, competent, or effective. Teaching out her last semesters, she decided to move away from the fairly inventive curriculum and new materials common to our English department. What did she have to lose? In the time she had left in the classroom, she resurrected out-of-date and discontinued sets of literature anthologies and the accompanying stacks of her old notes and worksheets. Some of the English teachers knew what she was doing and shook their heads, but no one intervened. As it happened, my daily round of afternoon hall duty took me past Ms. Williams' room on a regular basis, and I saw the results firsthand. In her class were students I knew well—a number had been behavior problems and had also failed my English class. But these students were otherwise unrecognizable. I could see that with the elderly, frumpy Ms. Williams and the old textbooks and conventional assignments, the students were engaged, working from bell to bell, and were content and industrious. Day upon day, as I passed by Ms. Williams' door, I saw no behavior outbursts, no one sleeping or goofing off, but an entire class on task, taking notes, completing work, and cooperating with Ms. Williams and each other in a respectful manner. Students were reading and writing for a full period, something I had not been able to accomplish with many of them.

Ms. Williams did not look or act like the teacher I thought I wanted to be, but she was getting from her students work and commitment. What she did was beyond the copyright date of a textbook and far more important than a repertoire of traditional activities; she clearly knew how to motivate students and how to give them a sense of achievement, and the success she had with her students was a memorable lesson for me.

There are many ways to be a good teacher—another's path may not be your way, but the paths to good instruction are multiple.

Lesson 3: *Good teachers learn and relearn all the time; make this part of your teaching life.*

Don't ever assume that teaching isn't what Lawrence Ferlinghetti called "constantly risking absurdity"—the adventure is never over, and the skill is never finally achieved. Every time I teach, I know there are things I could do differently, more effectively, better. Many of the techniques I use are comfortable to me, but not all of them work with every class and every set of students. What I did continue to do, however, is to make a concerted effort to study my students, study what was and was not going on in the class, and make constant modifications to reach them and to encourage their success.

Just this month, I became worried about the progress of one of my classes. I have taught the topic for years, but it seemed to me that our classroom discussions were too brief, possibly unfocused. While student writing indicated some level of understanding, I fretted about whether or not students were comprehending at the highest levels. Tuesday morning I started class by explicitly outlining what I feared and asked students how they felt. Should we restructure? Were the writing assignments helpful? How were the classroom activities supporting our reading? The students took my concern seriously and offered ideas and encouragement. We promised to revisit the issue during the semester, and I left class feeling not only that we were making progress but that, if necessary, we could make changes as the need arose.

Good teaching must be a moving target. We learn and relearn from our students and our classes.

Lesson 4: *Good teachers have a North Star, and they follow it; find yours and keep your eyes on it.*

One of the consistent concerns of those of us who work in education is the frequent change in emphasis from decade to decade—individualized learning, multiple intelligences, accountability, use of assessment data, use of media, PowerPoint for all lectures, rubrics for all assignments. What good teachers do, however, is hold fast to a central verity, to what they value, to what they believe is the best for their students. These teachers have, despite the pressures, changes, and concerns from the outside, an internal gyroscope that keeps them centered and focused. They have a goal that is central to their instructional life.

For me, it is a vision of a classroom; it is Hemingway's clean, well-lighted space, a classroom where students find a place for reading, for writing, for talking, for thinking out loud. In that classroom, students are taken seriously, and being intellectually curious is the norm. In that classroom, skills are taught—but never to the exclusion of creative activities and spontaneous discussions. Tests are given—but they come directly from what has been taught and what has been learned, and they are used to improve student learning and mastery, never to rank and sort and alienate or humiliate. In that classroom, reading is approached in multiple ways, and literature includes whole texts and classics but also embraces the very contemporary. In this classroom, teachers teach first to students, second for curriculum mastery, and a distant third for test scores. In this classroom, activities are authentic, not school-based busywork. In this classroom, all language has a place, all experience is welcomed. And when students leave this classroom, they want to come back and continue to read and write and make language.

The person who helps create that classroom is the good teacher. Who he or she is varies in age, appearance, and even approach. But the good teacher is absolutely recognizable because the good teacher does what all of us truly wish to do: the good teacher makes a difference.

> > > *The good teacher is absolutely recognizable because the good teacher does what all of us truly wish to do: the good teacher makes a difference.*

When you want to know more...

This book is about the search for our North Star, something to guide us as we work with our students. It's about teaching kids to read, write, speak, think. And it's about the society that we might have if we do our jobs well—and, by implication, about the society we might have if we fail. It's about teaching. That's what Leila writes about so eloquently here as well as in her *Voices from the Middle* article "What Matters About Literacy Now?" (2003) and her book *Making the Journey: Being and Becoming a Teacher of English Language Arts* (2006).

Connecting to my thoughts

Connecting to other texts

On Media Literacy

Golden, John. 2001. *Reading in the Dark: Using Film as a Tool in the English Classroom*. Urbana, IL: National Council of Teachers of English.

Hobbs, Renee. 2007. *Reading the Media: Media Literacy in High School English*. New York and Newark, DE: Teachers College Press; International Reading Association.

Krueger, Ellen, and Mary T. Christel. 2001. *Seeing and Believing: How to Teach Media Literacy in the English Classroom*. Portsmouth, NH: Boynton/Cook.

Ostrow, Jill. 2003. "A Letter to a Niece: Critical Media Literacy, One Child at a Time." *Voices from the Middle* 10, no. 3: 23–27.

> > > KATHRYN EGAWA

Five Things You Need to Know About Literacy Coaching in Middle and High Schools

THIS WAS SUPPOSED to be easy—this teaching of teens. We'd talk about things we felt passionate about. They'd listen passionately. We'd work our hardest to give them our best. They'd work their hardest to give us their best. And at the end of each day, we'd all go home a bit smarter and then return the next morning a bit more eager, ready to teach and learn some more.

Well. One can dream!

And I hope we do dream. I hope we dream constantly of the ways to make education better for the hundreds of thousands of students who drop out of school each year, the several thousand we lose each day. But of course, the dream isn't enough. The dream must turn into actions, or as Kylene, Bob, and Linda have said in the title of this book, the promise must become a practice.

One exciting practice that's helping teaching get, if not easier, then at least better is the addition of literacy coaches to our middle and high school settings.

The preceding two chapters focused on assessment—of students and of ourselves. The same type of assessment occurs across this country daily as teachers, parents, administrators, and policy makers ask, "How are we doing and what can we do better?" One answer, of late, has been to bring someone into the middle and high school setting who has deep knowledge and expertise in the reading process, the literacy coach. It makes sense, then, now that we've done some thinking about assessment, that we turn our attention to this very topic.

—*KB, REP, LR*

Indeed, *literacy coaching* is playing an increasingly prominent role in secondary schools (Sturtevant 2003).

Just what does coaching offer? Coaching expert Cathy Toll proposes that coaching is most productive when it is a "fresh alternative" to what the field of education has traditionally offered. In other words, literacy coaching can involve listening to teachers and partnering with them as they grapple with challenging issues and set goals; such partnerships have been missing in most educational settings, despite the presence of people you might assume would do that kind of work, such as reading teachers, professional developers, and principals (Toll 2007).

When coaching is part of a coordinated and interdisciplinary literacy program, all of these educators can work together to create the real changes needed to support all struggling students. Of course, partnering with teachers is not the only approach to coaching, but, according to Toll, it increases the likelihood of greater teacher thinking and decision making.

But what does a literacy coach actually do? Or, you might wonder, how can a coach help me, a secondary-level biology teacher or a middle school social studies teacher, when the coach is a former elementary school reading teacher? These are important questions that certainly deserve an answer. For this chapter I've taken several of the questions that I'm asked most often about literacy coaching and attempted to provide answers. My hope is that you will, as I have, come to see the value added in having a literacy coach in your school. With the right instructional material and with the right instructional support (from teachers, from administrators, and from this person called a literacy coach), I think our dreams of success for all students will become a reality, and teaching and learning, though never *really* easy, will certainly become better.

> > > > >
Rethink what Dick Allington said about effective teaching and effective literacy programs (Chapter 18) and look again at what Kathy is saying here about the roll of the literacy coach to see how his ideas and her ideas combine.
—*KB, REP, LR*

Starting with a Definition

Our principal recently announced that a literacy coach will be joining our faculty. Just what is a literacy coach and what can I expect?

> > > *But what does a literacy coach actually do? Or, you might wonder, how can a coach help me, a secondary-level biology teacher or a middle school social studies teacher, when the coach is a former elementary school reading teacher?*

Foremost, you can expect the coach to work with teachers in a respectful and collegial way. It is also reasonable to expect that the coach's job responsibilities will be described to your faculty when he is introduced.

You might also find it helpful to think in terms of what a coach will and will not be doing (see Figure 19–1). For instance, there is common agreement that coaches do not supervise or evaluate teachers, although their work may include observing them and conferring with them afterward. Literacy coaches do

GRAPHIC VIEW OF WHAT A LITERACY COACH IS AND IS NOT

This organizer is adapted from the September 2004 issue of the NCTE journal *Voices from the Middle*. It was used to visually represent the various facets of a literacy coaching effort taking place in conjunction with the South Carolina Reading Initiative Middle Grades.*

Literacy Coach:

One who trains intensively by instruction, demonstration, and practice

– dictionary definition of coach

A Literacy Coach is:

- A Learner
- A Facilitator
- A Supporter of Classroom Instruction

Should:

- Demonstrate in Classrooms
- Observe in Classrooms
- Confer with a Teacher

A Literacy Coach is not:

- A Small Group Tutor
- A Writer of Curriculum Maps
- A Substitute Teacher

Should Not:

- Substitute for an Absent Teacher
- Evaluate the Performance of a Teacher
- "Fix" a Teacher

FIGURE 19–1.

* We were pleased that Kathy included this graphic and we encourage you to make a similar is/is not definition for the literacy coaches you want in your building. —KB/REP/LR

support classroom instruction, but not through instructional activities like tutoring small groups of students or by substituting for teachers. They might, however, cover classes so that you can observe each other.

Coaches may lead your building's leadership team and will likely help the faculty review assessment data and set goals to improve student learning. Their work is most successful when it is integrated into the building and district instructional decision-making structures, and just as those differ from place to place, there are many variations on how this work is accomplished. Further, if the role of literacy coach in your district is new, it is common that coaches will be finding their way and shaping some of their work through trial and error.

Boston Public Schools has refined the role of its literacy coaches over an eight-year evolution of the program. Formerly school-based coaches are now district-based and assigned to eight-week coaching cycles based on each school's student population. Interdisciplinary teacher teams of six to eight participants work together with a coach to explore areas of interest, to incorporate new teaching strategies, and to observe each other's teaching. At the heart of the work is data-based cohort selection, teacher identification of the work focus with coaches highlighting district goals, and cohorts often taking up the shared inquiry beyond the eight-week cycle (Kral 2006). The challenge is to maximize the potential that literacy coaches offer and to avoid scheduling their time for administrative or housekeeping tasks.

Next, Understanding How a Coach Helps

What is it that a literacy coach knows that's going to help me? How in the world is she supposed to help in my biology class if she's never taught in my content area?

You're right in thinking that a literacy coach will likely not have the content knowledge to teach in your subject area ("Instructional Coaching Research Conducted by the University of Kansas Center for Research on Learning" 2004). Nonetheless, most coaches familiarize themselves with content and state standards and should be able to talk about learning across many content areas.

One strength that coaches do bring to their role is the ability to recognize successful literacy learning and the knowledge to assess difficulties when learning goes awry. If a number of students aren't making sense of the biology textbook or receive low scores on the state writing test, a literacy coach can help teachers put their heads together to address the issue. Teaching includes thinking about one's practice, and coaches can support that thinking by bringing learning and literacy expertise to enhance your subject matter knowledge. Successful student learning is the ultimate goal you all share.

Leaders in the Reading Apprenticeship network, for instance, begin with helping teachers develop metacognitive conversations about reading. Through participating in experiences like think-alouds that they can take back into their own teaching, teachers from different content areas learn that they read discipline-specific texts very differently. Reading poetry is very different from reading a history or math book. Being more conscious of the strategies they themselves use helps content area teachers teach those strategies more explicitly to students (Greenleaf 2006).

When a content area teacher partners with the literacy coach, there are myriad ways the collaboration can play out. For instance, the two of you may decide to co-teach a lesson, with the coach taking the lead to introduce pre-reading or prewriting strategies. In another class, the coach may closely watch several students who participate halfheartedly during a lesson and strategize about how to get them on board. Again, the context in which you teach and your observations and needs determine how coaches and teachers work together.

Then, Understanding Who Does What

But I'm the English language arts department chair. Shouldn't I be the coach? Or *I'm the media specialist. Is the coach going to replace me?*

In fact, in some instances department chairs do step out of the chair role and serve as coaches. It is likely, however, that the responsibilities of either role preclude the time and maybe the skill to accomplish the other. It is more common that the department chairs and literacy coach will work together on the school leadership team, along with other support staff (ELL teachers, special education teachers, the principal), to bring forth the needs and goals from the different departments to the crafting of a comprehensive school plan.

For Desert Vista High School in Chandler, Arizona, that meant an invitation to the faculty to form a study group with one teacher representative from each content area. Eleven teachers stepped forward to participate in the monthly meetings of what came to be called the Reading Team. After some initial discussion and study, the team planned informational and fun kickoff sessions to invite the faculty on board. The reading team identified a shared focus by surveying and compiling faculty opinions on literacy in their content areas that resulted in areas of concentration for the upcoming two years: incorporating books beyond the textbooks and vocabulary study.

At Desert Vista, the reading teacher, Jean Martorana, stepped into the role of coach for part of her day. The role was a large one to play in addition to her teaching, but it was made easier by the commitment and ownership the faculty assumed. In short order, the plan grew: parents became involved;

< < < < <

We've always thought it interesting that in secondary school (meaning middle and high school), there's been this expectation that the English language arts teachers are the people who will take over the reading instruction for the students in that building. However, as many secondary-certified English language arts teachers have pointed out, they have no more experience in reading instruction than the history or science teacher. The literacy coach comes to the school with that experience, freeing up the English language arts department chair to do exactly what she or he ought to be doing—making sure that the teachers in that department have the support they need to best teach literature and composition. While department chairs should work closely with literacy coaches—after all, department chairs know more about the culture of the school and the skills and talents of individual teachers than coaches who most likely are not members of that school faculty—they should also recognize that having a literacy coach in the building affirms that, like the other content area teachers, their expertise is not expected to be in reading, but in their content area.
—*KB, REP, LR*

the *Research Handbook for Desert Vista High School*, including reading strategies, was revised; and a reading textbook for sophomores was adopted (Martorana 2005).

The lesson here is that no one can accomplish this work alone, and literacy coaches offer a unique role in facilitating the work of other school leaders. There is also a period of uncertainty for most school faculties as the literacy coach begins her work and teachers figure out what is expected from their end. Over time, with a model of coaching that is respectful of teachers and collaboration, each school creates a program that meets its needs and changes the culture of the school. This is how one Boston teacher reflected on the work:

> When I first began [teaching], for years and years and years you never came out of your classroom. You never talked about teaching. You never talked about strategies or lessons or any philosophy you had. . . . We never thought we had the right to say, "I don't really understand. I'm not sure . . ." We always had to pretend for some reason that we knew what we were doing. [Now we ask,] How are we going to teach this? What do we need to do all this? The latest research has truly changed my teaching. (Neufeld and Roper 2003, 41–42)

Then Putting This into Place

How can school leaders create the conditions for adolescent literacy learning described in this book?

This might be the most essential question. Roland Barth (2006) has found that the relationships among the adults in a school have a greater influence on the character and quality of that school and on student accomplishment than anything else. That means how you decide to work together, or not, strongly affects student achievement.

Barth identifies four types of relationships and their effects that occur in schools. The first two—parallel play and adversarial—are negative and counterproductive, yet they occur the most often in schools. The third—congenial relationships—although more positive, does not in itself improve teaching and learning. The fourth—the collegial relationship—is the "gold ticket." It is both the hardest to establish and, Barth contends, the only way to create and enhance a professional learning community.

There is no one way to create a culture of collegiality, but Barth suggests encouraging teachers to engage in two primary activities: sharing their knowledge and observing each other. As you listen to coaching expert Cathy Toll (Toll in press) explain that literacy coaching involves listening to teachers and part-

> > > > >

Developing this culture of collegiality means talking together about many issues. We tried to model what those types of collegial conversations might look like with two chapters in this book: Chapters 8 and 17. In Chapter 8, you see Cindy Aguilar, Danling Fu, and Carol Jago think through issues of English language learners. In Chapter 17, you see Devon Brenner, David Pearson, and Linda Rief discuss—not always agreeing—assessment. In your school, you might begin your own collegial conversations around the same topics, perhaps even discussing the same questions mentioned in those chapters. We've also worked to model another type of collegial conversation by "talking" with you throughout this book via these Editors' Comments. You can do the same thing with online exchanges with colleagues by posting a document (student work? PDF of an article? something you've written?) online and using the "comments" feature under the "insert" tab on your toolbar.
—*KB, REP, LR*

nering with them to help them meet goals and pursue interests, then you begin to see that coaches are an important part of helping to develop that culture of collegiality we want in schools.

Finally, Becoming a Coach

What if I'm interested in being a literacy coach? Where could I find out more information about coaching? What qualifications do I need?

The International Reading Association, in partnership with leaders from the National Council of Teachers of English, the National Science Teachers Association, the National Council of Teachers of Mathematics, and the National Council of the Social Studies, has recently created *Standards for Middle and High School Literacy Coaches* (2005). These outline the kinds of competencies that coaching requires, including skillful collaboration with adults and skillful

COACHING COMPETENCIES			
The Gold Standard	**The Great Choice**	**Good Enough for Now**	**Not Good Enough for Now**
> Masters degree in literacy > Additional credential in coaching > Has had successful teaching experience, especially at the grade level to be coached > Has experience working with teachers > Is an excellent presenter > Has experience modeling lessons > Has experience observing in classrooms	> Masters degree in another area > Has had successful teaching experience, especially at the grade level to be coached > Has experience working with teachers > Is an excellent presenter > Has experience modeling lessons > Has experience observing in classrooms	> Bachelors degree and some graduate level coursework > Has had successful teaching experience > Has had successful collaboration experiences > Is eager > Is hard-working > Is willing to learn	> Placed in the coaching position for reasons other than qualifications to do the job

FIGURE 19–2. *From the "Qualification for Literacy Coaches" by S. Frost and J. Bean (2006).*

> > > *My hope is that you will, as I have, come to see the value added in having a literacy coach in your school. With the right instructional material and with the right instructional support (from teachers, from administrators, and from this person called a literacy coach), I think our dreams of success for all students will become a reality, and teaching and learning, though never really easy, will certainly become better.*

literacy teaching and assessment. You can get a sense of which competencies you have and which need developing by completing the survey of skills needed to be a literacy coach found in Figure 19–2.

Two collections of online resources can also support your exploration of this role. The first is the recently launched Literacy Coaching Clearinghouse, www.literacycoachingonline.org. There you will find a link to the standards mentioned earlier, as well as a white paper on literacy coach qualifications. At http://www.ncte.org/collections/literacycoach you will also find a collection of resources, including an article on strategies to clearly separate coaching from supervision. Both sites offer you the opportunity to participate in discussion forums where you can connect with literacy coaches and others interested in coaching as a fresh alternative for supporting teacher and student learning.

When you want to know more...

As Kathy has suggested, professionals never stop working on their profession, and the profession does what it can to sustain them. Coaching is one of the strategies for helping us continue to grow. For more on this, see the book Kathy and others wrote for the NCTE, *Beyond Reading and Writing: Inquiry, Curriculum, and Multiple Ways of Knowing* (Berghoff et al. 2000). You'll also be interested in *Literacy as Social Practice: Primary Voices K–6* (Vasquez et al. 2004).

>>> RANDY BOMER

The Role of Handover in Teaching for Democratic Participation

WE READ AND WRITE for a wide range of purposes—academic, spiritual, artistic, social, personal. Our literate activity may also serve civic purposes—our participation in a democracy, our actions to make the world better for themselves and others, our testimony to fellow citizens about our own lives and our empathic concerns for the interests of others and of the earth. This latter purpose, civic literacy, is one that is especially suited to schools, because the public school system exists to create publics—to make of every student a citizen.

Reading and writing take on a distinct character according to the purpose of the moment. They draw upon different social and psychological processes when applied to varied intentions and contexts. It is one thing to write in order to reflect on a piece of literature, and it is another to write to protest what is being put into a landfill. The two tasks call upon different skills and knowledge. True, they both involve the alphabet, spelling, and punctuation, but the rhetorics of the situations, the relationships between writer and reader, the actions being performed with literate tools, the processes to be undertaken all vary considerably.

We began this book with Kylene raising concerns about No Child Left Behind legislation that has, in too many places, given a skewed vision of how we should measure success. She concluded her chapter with a vision for what schools must accomplish in this new century, this "flat" world that is filled with new literacy demands. Other authors then presented visions of instruction that address those demands. We've placed Randy's chapter here, as a bookend to Kylene's chapter, as he discusses the critical and ultimate purpose for a literate society showing us our real measure of success.

—KB, REP, LR

Literacy educators—English teachers, reading teachers, writing teachers—especially those in public schools, must be concerned with the development of civic literacy. This agenda is not at odds with the more usual valuing of literary knowing in English language arts. Novels and plays are often concerned with socially significant ideas and issues. But it is not enough to read *The Crucible* (Miller) or *To Kill a Mockingbird* (Harper) or *Cut* (McCormick) and ask students to engage solely as spectators, walled off from the politically boisterous world just outside the school. To read about oppression or racism or self-mutilation and to limit one's response to writing and talking about the book seems oddly truncated—seems, further, to be an education for passivity and docile acceptance of unacceptable conditions. Shouldn't an education for democracy be working to make such apathy unlikely and rare, rather than fostering it?

> > > *It is unlikely that any government, ever, will beg the schools to teach students to struggle for social justice. Teachers are the ones who will advance that idea. Or no one will.*

Students need to learn that writing is an action, that writing—even writing about your life experience—can be an effort to remake the world, through the minds and actions of your readers, more the way you think it should be. Students in literacy classrooms in a democracy need to be learning that through our language, we are creating our shared world. It is true that the bureaucratic priorities of the education system do not position students as competent citizens or teachers as educators for democracy. Then again, the legal system does not always position lawyers as champions of justice; the medical system does not always position physicians as healers. Professions have to assert themselves toward what is right even when pressures try to force their work otherwise. It is unlikely that any government, ever, will beg the schools to teach students to struggle for social justice. Teachers are the ones who will advance that idea. Or no one will.

Teacher-Led Civic Literacy

Many teachers have done important work leading students toward shared projects in civic literacy. Linda Christensen (2000), for instance, invited her students to question and critique the ways varied groups were represented in television and movie cartoons for children. The students detected unjust portrayals of women and unwise messages about violence, as well as conspicuous exclusion of almost all races of people and unthinking reliance on stereotypes. From these inquiries, students developed projects for audiences outside of school that attempted to address the uncritical acceptance of the secret education of children. Similarly, Beverly Busching and Betty Slesinger (1999) initiated an inquiry into social class and poverty through examinations of historical incidents, such as the sinking of the *Titanic*, and literature, like *Mississippi Trial, 1955* (Crowe).

Students' written responses to texts and discussions became points of departure for individually composed letters to politicians as well as business and community leaders about problems the students saw related to their collective studies. Richard Beach and Jamie Myers (2001) tell of a class in Stillwater, Minnesota, that became upset about the destruction of a local neighborhood on the banks of the St. Croix River when the town decided to build a new bridge there. Concerned about the rights of the residents of that neighborhood, students interviewed community members, took photos, and exhibited their work in a local gallery, successfully drawing public attention to the issue. Janet Atkins and Phil Sittnick got their students excited about local environmental issues, Janet in South Carolina and Phil in New Mexico (Atkins 2002). The New Mexico students were concerned about a local uranium mine, a facility involved in the early stages of nuclear fuel production. The South Carolina students investigated a local nuclear weapons plant that was now attempting to clean up trace amounts of radiation at the site. As the two groups of students began communicating via email, they shared aspects of their local investigations, motivating writing in authentic and meaningful ways, and ultimately formed a broader coalition that forced them to look at the larger issue in more systemic ways.

This kind of work brings a class together, creating a shared sense of purpose that enriches all other interactions. It also brings the class as a whole into contact with the community and perhaps other students. It makes each student part of something beyond personal interests, and the class itself becomes an instrument of social action. Students have the opportunity to investigate an issue of real-world importance and to work to affect it, under the mentorship of their teacher. There is nothing more likely to raise the energy of students, even those—perhaps especially those—who do not usually see school as particularly useful or interesting. This study is about real things, about things outside of school; it's about trying to get something done that needs doing.

Handing Over Civic Literacy

In these examples, of course, the students do follow the teacher's lead, and the work's progress depends on the whole class, led by a teacher. Ultimately, however, we can really know what learners are capable of only if they have a chance to take up action without our sponsorship. This class is not always going to be together; it's important that individuals carry away habits that they can use once their teacher is no longer in the room with them. For there to be any hope of transfer of learning to new situations, the important tools, concepts, and habits for thinking have to be handed over to the learner (Wood, Bruner, and Ross 1976). British researchers Edwards and Mercer (1987) found that little handover occurred in the progressive classrooms they observed. They found that students demonstrated "ritual knowledge" about how to perform for the

< < < < <

What Randy is describing here is what all the authors of this book have advocated: significance (Kylene Beers, Chapter 1), relevance (Ellin Keene, Chapter 4), effectiveness (Dick Allington, Chapter 18), inquiry (Jeff Wilhelm and Michael Smith, Chapter 15), passion (Tom Romano, Chapter 11), choice (Teri Lesesne, Chapter 6 and Penny Kittle, Interlude 4), talk (Bob Probst, Chapter 5), engagement (Yvette Jackson and Eric Cooper, Chapter 16),value (Alfred Tatum, Interlude 2), change (Jim Burke, Chapter 10), and . . . well, you see the point. Randy is showing us the promise of what can happen when we give students the tools they need to make things happen.

—KB, REP, LR

teacher's expectations in today's lesson, but they never exhibited "principled knowledge," or an awareness of the fundamental principles that would make a procedure or way of speaking applicable in other settings. This, the researchers argue, was because of the teachers' commitments not to teach through "telling," but to allow understandings to emerge from individual children. Because the students never really understood the principles of what they were doing and why, they never could take it over and do it on their own. The researchers note, "A successful educational process is one which transfers competence to the learner. It is almost as if formal education, for most pupils, is designed to prevent that from happening" (159).

A teacher knows she has achieved handover in civic literacy when a student, without teacher prompting, critiques the racial representations in a book he is reading independently or when, in a notebook entry, a student initiates her own thinking about the ways sports events structure losers as much as they do winners. Handover has happened in social action when a young person notices a problem in the world that needs attention and, without the prompting of authority, by virtue of her own freedom and habits of acting, she tries to do something about it. Handover has been (for the moment) successful when, in a class meeting, students bring each other to consider the justice (or lack thereof) in their treatment of each other. Each student needs the chance, on his own, to exercise new habits of looking at the world more critically, reading with socially significant questions in mind, and self-sponsoring social action.

> > > *Ultimately, however, we can really know what learners are capable of only if they have a chance to take up action without our sponsorship. This class is not always going to be together; it's important that individuals carry away habits that they can use once their teacher is no longer in the room with them.*

I'd like to share a quick summary of a set of procedures that have helped students do exactly what I have described. Readers who want a more elaborated description may want to consult my book with Katherine Bomer called *For a Better World* (2001).

Writing as a Tool for Thinking About the World

Before someone takes action, he must determine what to take action *about*. What in his world is of sufficient importance to warrant the effort? He scans his world and takes note of what attracts his attention as *something someone ought to work on*. In order to help develop the habit of mind that regards the world as containing issues calling for action, it is helpful for students to use writing as a device for noticing and reflecting on what is happening around them. In writer's notebooks, for example, which are similar to journals, students write about what is going on around them—in school, in the news, at home, on the street—with an eye toward fairness or justice. They interpret everyday events, looking for ideas to which the public—people in the community—should pay more attention.

There are two important purposes for this writing. One is that the topics for social action projects will come from these notebooks, so they are just a first step in a process that will lead to more extensive writing. Second, and just as important, doing this writing is as close as we can possibly come to teaching kids how to think critically about their world, to look at it with enough love to believe it might be better. The teaching, then, is partly about the writing process and partly about how to think. When Lee notices a mother being perhaps overly stern with her child in a store and writes about it that night, she is thinking about whether the idea of fairness applies to this situation and wondering if this might become the basis for her social action project. She is taking a step toward choosing a topic, but she is also applying a social or political lens to everyday events in her world, which is an intrinsically important habit of mind.

> > > *Handover has happened in social action when a young person notices a problem in the world that needs attention and, without the prompting of authority, by virtue of her own freedom and habits of acting, she tries to do something about it.*

When students have kept journals or writer's notebooks before beginning this particular unit of study (see Bomer 1995), they look back through their previous entries in order to evaluate whether some contain the traces of social issues. Jerold rereads the entries about his constant bickering with his little sister, and in the margins of his notebook, he wonders whether the troubles stem from the different ways boys and girls are treated in his family. Shareesa reads an entry she wrote after watching a movie about war, mostly an emotional reaction. Writing a new entry, she takes up the topic of war as an issue that is hard for entire nations to agree about. What was a personal response becomes a careful consideration of a critically important concept.

Once students have applied a social lens to their previous writing and to their world, they can reread their notebooks in order to see *what they have been thinking most or best about.* They examine their own thinking to see what topics pull at them to continue working in a more sustained manner, what ideas warrant their action toward other people in their world. They decide, out of all the things they've written about, what they would like to take on as their own issue for social action.

< < < < <
Look back to the handwritten journal entry Tom Romano shares with readers (Figure 11–1 in Chapter 11) or to Don Murray's comments about his own writing habits (Chapter 12) to see how they, as Randy is suggesting here, use writing as a way of thinking, a way of knowing. Then, turn to Linda Rief's chapter (13) to see how she guides students through creating their writer's notebooks.

—KB, REP, LR

Getting Ready for Action

Choosing a topic on their own, however, is not necessarily where social action begins. Social action is least effective when it is boxed into solitary individual efforts. To learn to take action in a democracy, citizens must learn to enlist others into caring about their issue and negotiate people's diverse agendas in order to involve more people in their projects. Having determined topics that are important to them, students then find—or create—common ground with some of their peers, building coalitions to work together on an issue. The fact that they have chosen a topic and may even have convinced some classmates of the importance of the topic does not mean that anyone in the group necessarily knows much about it. They probably do not know many facts about the issue at all. They almost surely do not know the decision makers and holders of purse strings to whom they must appeal. Even if there are groups who have been working on this topic for fifty years, chances are the kids won't know about that, either. Therefore, deciding exactly what to research helps to narrow their topic and their potential message. The research itself serves as a basis for framing arguments and developing action plans.

It is not necessary that they know everything in the world about the topic prior to planning and executing some action. Beginning the action, even with imperfect knowledge, will reveal many things they need to find out with further research—the kinds of questions that would not have occurred to them before they began working to persuade an audience. But a week or two of research, even as they begin making plans for their activity, will equip them with evidence, develop their perspectives on that evidence, suggest possible allies, identify significant audiences for their writing, and help to focus their purposes and goals for their writing.

Taking Action Through Language

Because almost all students are neophytes at writing for social action, groups benefit from composing action plans—written descriptions of what they plan to do and how their activities all fit together. Within these plans, varied genres of writing are necessary. A few that are more common are posters, pamphlets, flyers, websites, letters to the editors of newspapers or periodicals, letters to congressional members, query letters and letters of support to organizations working on similar issues, requests for information from government officials, editorials, opinion papers, press releases, surveys, and petitions. Because there are so many forms of writing possible in the name of social action, there are hundreds of possible topics for minilessons during the writing workshop.

These varied genres also go out to varied audiences. Sometimes, a student's audience is her peers in the school building—people she is trying to make equally passionate about her issue. Other times, she is writing to the mayor. It quickly becomes clear that different tones of voice—or registers of writing—are important for different readers. A kid's first impulse might be to address the chief of police with considerably less courtesy than he would use with his own friends. Of course, such a rhetorical strategy is doomed to failure. The teacher and other group members, then, are essential in helping students imagine the perspectives of the people they are addressing in their varied texts. There is, perhaps, no place in a writing curriculum where the essential and complex rhetorical issues of audience and register can be as explicitly taught.

"Illegal Amigos"

As an example, let's visit Deb Kelt's students in Austin, Texas. Late in the spring of 2006, Deb led her students through a unit of study on learning and writing for social action, following something like the basic procedure I have just outlined. During that same season, a national debate was heating up about immigration (Aizenman 2006), specifically undocumented workers from Mexico in the United States—so-called illegal immigrants. Most of the students in Deb's class were Mexican American, and some of them were passionately interested in the way this story was playing out in the media and in public dialogue. One group in particular believed that much of the discourse contained veiled racism, a view shared by many commentators, including some Latino/a community leaders (Navarrette 2005). The literacy project they undertook to affect people's attitudes and the nature of the public dialogue was a blog (teenraza.blogspot.com), which they started easily on the www.blogger.com website. They titled their blog Illegal Amigos, a reference to a controversy the previous fall wherein John Roberts, then nominee for chief justice of the U.S. Supreme Court, was revealed to have used the phrase in papers he composed when working in the Reagan administration. Needless to say, he offended many Latinos.

Their first blog post began with an image of the flag of the United Farm Workers Union and this text:

> How many of you are interested in immigration issues, but just don't know what to do, or how to get involved? Well we're teens just like you trying to get a message out to each and every one of you. We're trying to change the world for the better, not only for immigrants but for Americans as well. We know what you're thinking. Why in the world care for something that has nothing to do with us? Well that's where you're wrong.

Mindful of the ethos or relationship they are constructing with their audience, the writers carefully position themselves as particular kinds of people speaking to other specific kinds of people. It's hard to imagine them doing that so carefully if they were not writing for a real audience about something that matters so much in their lives. They almost immediately begin anticipating objections, specifically apathy in this case, and they are prepared to explain why this issue should matter to their readers. These are important rhetorical strategies that school literacy rarely demands of students. The bloggers go on to discuss the immigration reform bill then before the House of Representatives, arguing that immigrants do jobs that others do not want to do and that getting tomatoes picked without the use of undocumented workers would raise the cost of tomatoes. They end this first post with this:

When you want to know more...

Randy shows us vividly how important literacy is for a democracy. If we can't read, write, and think, our whole society is on shaky ground. He's developed that idea further in other writings, among them *For a Better World: Reading and Writing for Social Action* (2001), which he coauthored with Katherine Bomer, and an article in *Research in the Teaching of English*, "You Are Here: The Moment in Literacy Education" (2006).

We should stop treating them like scum we scraped off our shoes and start treating them like the glue that holds this nation together. I end this by saying that immigrants are human beings. "We're not animals. . . . We're people who have rights just like anyone else." This blog is not just a school assignment, it's a way to express our feelings and our actions towards trying to change what we don't think is right. *But we can't do it ourselves, we need all the help we can get!!!!!* We need ideas, so if you have any ideas please let us know.

In this one post, they move from ethos through logos to pathos—from presenting themselves as particular kinds of people to a presentation of a rational cost analysis for the loss of immigrant workers to pure feeling. They take up, here for the first time, the actual voice of those for whom they are advocating, placing it in quotation marks, though they will drop that distancing in the next post. And they end by once again addressing readers directly.

Deb, their teacher, was concerned that they needed a real audience to address and worried that no one would read their blog. Through me, she got in touch with a teacher from New York who was also having her students experiment with blogs, and students from Queens began reading and commenting on the Illegal Amigos blog. That first post received eighteen comments, more than most bloggers ever get, and over the next couple of weeks, their blog saw a total of seventy-nine comments, both affirming and challenging. This was a real rhetorical situation with an audience of real citizens who needed help to understand this issue. The project provided a rich environment for teaching a variety of issues in language, audience, purpose, and rhetorical strategy.

It turns out that democracy is a pretty good medium for teaching writing, and language a pretty good medium for learning democratic participation. As literacy educators, our choices about what kinds of literacy we emphasize are especially significant, because those choices create the meaning of reading and writing in the lives of students. Too often, students have experienced reading and writing as demonstrations of compliance with authoritarian norms, rather than as ways of acting in the world, tools for doing something real. Could it be that when they are uninterested in literate activity, it's because of what they think literate activity is *for*? What if they thought that literacy were a tool for improving the world they share, a means of making a better future? Our world needs to hear them, needs them to speak, to tell what their lives are like, to participate in democracy, to transform the culture into a more promising environment for human growth. What if we can convince them that the world is listening—and enable them to speak?

> > > > >
Randy's chapter has to remind us of Louise Rosenblatt and her unwavering commitment to democracy and to the vital importance of a literate, thinking public if we are to have any hope of preserving our freedoms. On her death, at the age of one hundred, her son Jonathan told us that the best tribute his mom could receive would be the continued efforts of teachers who respect the power of literacy to develop that power in their students. We applaud our readers for being teachers who work daily to do just that.
—KB, REP, LR

Afterword

I BEGAN TEACHING English to ado-
lescents in 1973. Along the way, I have witnessed big changes in how students
write and read in American secondary schools. Janet Emig (1971), Donald
Graves (1975), and Donald Murray (1968) sparked a revolution that introduced
writing process to middle and high schools; at the same time, the theories of
Alan Purves (1972), Louise Rosenblatt (1978), and Frank Smith (1971) about literature, literary response, and reading brought young adult tradebooks into our
classrooms, along with opportunities for students to read independently and talk
about their reactions. I can't imagine a better time to have been a secondary
English teacher, as so many of us shelved the *Warriner's* handbooks and textbook
anthologies and invited students to think and act as writers and readers.

I also experienced, albeit at a bit of a distance, the revolution in classroom
technology. Although I still compose by hand, and I can't remember how to
turn on the computers that line the walls of my classroom, my kids know everything that matters, and one writer can troubleshoot for another when the technology goes haywire. My seventh- and eighth-graders word process at least
second drafts of all their work, and email has made publication a given—press
"Send" and off goes a CD review to Amazon.com, a memoir to Grandma in

We asked Nancie Atwell to
close this book for us, though
the reality for many readers of
this book is that she helped
open your thoughts to a new
way of teaching. Her work,
grounded in the realities of the
day-to-day teaching of middle
schoolers, reminds each of us
of the critical role of the
teacher as we work to turn
each student's promise into a
reality.

—*KB, REP, LR*

California, a letter to the editor of the local paper. For instance, when I recently came across a call for student poetry for a contest with a postmark deadline on the following day, it took interested writers about ten minutes to bring up their folders, select poems, reformat them according to contest guidelines, print them, and stuff the submissions in a mailer. Without technology—both computers and Internet connections—it would have eaten up days of class time to try to get student voices raised beyond the walls of our rural schoolhouse.

And as recently as five years ago, I was still including within the pages of my books for teachers lists of recommended titles for middle-level classroom libraries. These were out of date before the ink dried, as new books and authors emerged and student tastes changed. Now, each June I ask every reader to write in response to this question: *What ten to twelve books do you love so much you think they might convince a girl or boy who's a lot like you—except that she or he doesn't read much—that books are great?* Nominated titles appear on the school website—www.c-t-l.org—on a "Kids Recommend" page that's culled and updated every summer and available to our students and their parents, as well as other middle school teachers across the United States.

A final insight about technology: My students did check out ebooks, but they aren't buying. As one eighth grader put it, they missed "the geography of reading"—of skimming effortlessly back and forward again across pages and chapters, of dog-earing pages to keep their places, and, most significantly, of measuring with their eyes and between their hands how much of a book's territory they had covered and how near an author was to the end of his or her story.

What hasn't changed since 1973 are adolescents themselves. They still crave meaning; they still respond voraciously when significance is a regular part of the classroom diet. They want their writing and reading to matter to them and to matter now, not in some nebulous someday. They seek personal sense and satisfaction, and the secondary English teacher's job is to invite our students to understand, appreciate, and participate in one of the best things about being an adult: all the ways that literate grown-ups can experience other lives and compose our own.

Weaving through *Adolescent Literacy: Turning Promise into Practice*, I found all manner of pedagogic threads that secondary students might follow to meaningful ends. These are methods that ask and allow teens to read a lot and feel pleasure, to write a lot and feel satisfied, and to talk a lot and feel significant. Their English teachers want to matter, too—to be remembered by kids not for their assignments, personalities, ties, or earring collections, but for who the students became, how they thought about themselves and the world beyond school, and what they accomplished as writers and readers during their time in the classroom.

This means that personal preference—choices of books to read and topics to write about—looms huge in the secondary English curricula described in this volume. It also means that the teacher response that fuels the best writing

> > > > >
This notion of change has been addressed throughout the book. Review what Teri Lesesne (Chapter 6) says about adolescents and change. It's possible, we think, that you will find truth in what both authors offer: adolescents (and adolescence) have both changed and remained the same. That contradiction helps create the tension you might feel as you step into the classroom.
—*KB, REP, LR*

and reading comes during acts of writing and reading, in those moments when a student—experimenting, struggling, soaring, or stuck—could use the eye and ear of a knowledgeable grown-up. And it means that in order to become the kind of knowledgeable grown-ups to whom students will wish to apprentice themselves, teachers of adolescents must read, must write, and must teach from our literate experiences and literary passions.

Donald Murray's chapter in this book, one of his final gifts to teachers, reminds us again to find our writing voices—our *differences*—in order to attend and teach to the differences among our student writers. His powerful influence is explicit throughout *Adolescent Literacy* as other famously effective writing teachers echo Murray's call for English teachers to write because our effectiveness in the classroom begins in the insights we glean from our own literacy. No one is asking teachers to produce the next great American novel. But when confronted with a student who scrawls a dismal first draft and calls it finished, teachers who write can *teach from our writing*.

On overhead transparencies and in PowerPoint presentations, teachers who write show kids who don't know how—or why—to revise their drafts what writing-as-process looks like. We walk kids through examples of the messes that grown-up writers make when we think on paper—as we doodle plans, generate options, choose some, and reject others. And we answer for our students the single most important question about writing: why would anyone want to do it?

Students in my writing workshops have never been enlightened or convinced by the books I've published. Their eyes and minds were opened by the drafts of a poem I wrote as a present for my daughter's birthday, the drafts of a memoir about my obsession with candy, the drafts of a letter to their parents in which I tried to untangle the minutiae of an overnight field trip. Nothing helps blocked student writers become unblocked like showing them examples of my plans—the sheets of paper on which I play around with ideas and language before I begin any draft, or that I turn to when a draft has bogged down, so I can solve as many of my writing problems as possible off the page. And nothing prepared me for the response when one day, as I composed in front of the class on an overhead transparency, someone asked, "How come you keep going back and reading over what you've written so far?" What? They didn't do this when they wrote? Many said no, and this began to explain the lack of coherence in some of the drafts we were conferring about. A poster showing the steps of the writing process, which I'd hung on the wall of my classroom, didn't feature continuous rereading and recasting. My demonstration shed light on a hidden but essential behavior in the repertoire of someone who's trying to write well.

Even as a technophobe, I understand that the technology of literacy will continue to improve as savvy writers and teachers figure out new ways for it to meet their needs: before he died in late 2006 at age eighty-two, Don Murray was on the verge of launching his own website. But a critical need of our teenaged students

> < < < < <
> We're glad to see Nancie connect rereading to the writing process. Kylene Beers has been a strong advocate of rereading as a comprehension process and encourages teachers to help students see rereading as a part of the reading process and to go as far as to borrow words from the writing process with phrases like "your first read is your first draft of understanding" and "as you reread this section, revise your understanding." Here, Nancie reminds us that rereading is also an integral part of composing.
>
> —*KB, REP, LR*

will remain constant—the desire to apprentice themselves to their teachers as writers and readers. Effective teaching of English at the secondary level, whatever the methodology, is grounded in what a teacher knows and loves of writing, literature, and adolescents. I think three kinds of teacher knowledge—compellingly illustrated by the individual chapters of this book—provide a foundation for developing practices that have promise.

> > > *The goal of this superb volume is never a standardized curriculum or a teacher-proof methodology. Rather, it speaks to the human, heartening premise that it's teacher knowledge . . . that will help adolescent students reach their promise as writers and readers.*

First, there's the teacher's own work and play as a reader and writer: our plans, drafts, revisions, and editions; our encounters with other writers' novels, essays, memoirs, and poems; and our reading about the discoveries of other teachers and researchers about literature, reading, writing process, and teaching practice.

Then there's the teacher's firsthand observations of the needs, tastes, challenges, and obsessions of the population of writers and readers whom we teach. Who are our students? What books and poems will resonate for them? Who are the writers they love? The characters? What themes will they respond to? Which genres might meet their needs or represent their next, best challenge? What lessons, examples, and language will help reveal essential concepts of craft and usage that these students can grasp and put to work to strengthen their writing?

Finally, teachers need to figure out how to structure our teaching so that it's possible to know, and reach, individual kids. What does he care about? What does she understand? Not get yet? Need help with right now? What does this student do—and not do—as a writer, reader, and critic?

The contributors to *Adolescent Literacy: Turning Promise into Practice* speak directly to teachers about diverse populations of middle and high school students and about the myriad ways we might rethink our roles, accumulate a wealth of these three essential kinds of knowledge, and put it to work in our classrooms. The goal of this superb volume is never a standardized curriculum or a teacher-proof methodology. Rather, it speaks to the human, heartening premise that it's teacher knowledge—not intuition, adoption, technology, ritual, or tradition—that will help adolescent students reach their promise as writers and readers.

When you want to know more . . .

Nancie's work with middle school students has led to several very important books for teachers of writing and reading at all levels. *In the Middle: New Understandings About Writing, Reading, and Learning* (1998) is the one you know best. You also might want to look at her more recent book, *Naming the World: A Year of Poems and Lessons (6–9),* published by *first*hand, Heinemann.

References

ACT. 2006. *Reading Between the Lines: What the ACT Reveals About College Readiness in Reading.* Iowa City, IA: ACT.

AGUILAR, C., C. MOROCCO, C. PARKER, and N. ZIGMOND. 2006. "Middletown High School: Equal Opportunity for Academic Achievement." *Learning Disabilities Research & Practice* 21 (3): 159–71.

AIZENMAN, N. C. 2006. "Immigration Debate Wakes a 'Sleeping Latino Giant.'" *Washington Post*, April 6, A-1.

ALLEN, J. 1999. *Words, Words, Words: Teaching Vocabulary in Grades 4–12.* York, ME: Stenhouse.

———. 2004. *Tools for Teaching Content Literacy.* Portland, ME: Stenhouse.

ALLINGTON, R. L. 2002a. "What I've Learned About Effective Reading Instruction from a Decade of Studying Effective Literacy Elementary Classroom Teachers." *Phi Delta Kappan* 83 (June 10): 740–47.

———. 2002b. "You Can't Learn Much from Books You Can't Read." *Educational Leadership* 60 (3): 16–19.

———. 2006. *What Really Matters for Struggling Readers: Designing Research-Based Programs.* 2d ed. Boston: Pearson/Allyn and Bacon.

———. 2007. "Intervention All Day Long: New Hope for Struggling Readers." *Voices from the Middle* 14 (4): 7–14.

ALLINGTON, R. L., and P. H. JOHNSTON, eds. 2002. *Reading to Learn: Lessons from Exemplary 4th Grade Classrooms.* New York: Guilford.

ALLINGTON, R. L., P. H. JOHNSTON, and J. P. DAY. 2002. "Exemplary Fourth-Grade Teachers." *Language Arts* 79: 462–66.

ALVERMANN, D. E. 2005. "Literacy on the Edge: How Close Are We to Closing the Literacy Achievement Gap?" *Voices from the Middle* 13 (1): 8–14.

————. 2006. "Technology Use and Needed Research in Youth Literacies." In *Handbook of Literacy and Technology*, 2d ed., ed. M. McKenna, L. Labbo, R. Kieffer, and D. Reinking, 327–333. Mahwah, NJ: Lawrence Erlbaum.

ALVERMANN, D. E., and A. J. EAKLE. 2006. "Dissolving Learning Boundaries: The Doing, Re-doing, and Undoing of School." In *International Handbook of Student Experience in Elementary and Secondary School*, ed. D. Thiessen and A. Cook-Sather, 143–66. New York: Springer.

ALVERMANN, D. E., K. A. HINCHMAN, D. W. MOORE, S. F. PHELPS, and D. R. WAFF, eds. 2006. *Reconceptualizing the Literacies in Adolescents' Lives*. 2d ed. Mahwah, NJ: Lawrence Erlbaum.

AMERICAN DIPLOMA PROJECT. 2004. *Ready or Not: Creating a High School Diploma That Counts*. Washington, DC: Achieve.

AMIT-TALAI, V., and H. WULFF, eds. 1995. *Youth Cultures: A Cross-Cultural Perspective*. New York: Routledge.

AMREIN, A. L., and D. C. BERLINER. 2003. "The Effects of High-Stakes Testing on Student Motivation and Achievement." *Educational Leadership* 60 (5): 32–38.

ANDERSON, R. C., and P. FREEBODY. 1981. "Vocabulary Knowledge." In *Comprehension and Teaching: Research Reviews*, ed. J. Guthrie, 77–117. Newark, DE: International Reading Association.

ANDERSON, R. C., and W. E. NAGY. 1992. "The Vocabulary Conundrum." *American Educator* (Winter): 14–18, 44–47.

ANSTEY, M., and G. BULL. 2006. *Teaching and Learning Multiliteracies: Changing Times, Changing Literacies*. Newark, DE: International Reading Association.

APPLEBEE, A. N., J. A. LANGER, M. NYSTRAND, and A. GAMORAN. 2003. "Discussion-Based Approaches to Developing Understanding: Classroom Instruction and Student Performance in Middle and High School English." *American Educational Research Journal* 40: 685–730.

APPLEMAN, D. 2000. *Critical Encounters in High School English: Teaching Literary Theory to Adolescents*. New York: Teachers College Press.

————. 2001. "Unintended Betrayal: Dilemmas of Representation and Power in Research with Youth." Paper presented at the meeting of the American Educational Research Association, Seattle, WA, April.

————. 2006. *Reading for Themselves: How to Transform Adolescents into Lifelong Readers Through Out-of-Class Book Clubs*. Portsmouth, NH: Heinemann.

ARMAS, G. C. 2005. "'Go to Your Room!' Sends Many Kids to Multimedia Hub." *The Seattle Times*, March 10. Retrieved March 20, 2005, from archives.seattletimes.nwsource.com/cgi-bin/texis.cgi/web/vortex/display?slug=mediakids10&date=20050310&query=Armas.

ARTESEROS, S., ed. 1992. *American Voice: Best Short Fiction by Contemporary Authors.* New York: Hyperion.

ATKINS, J. 2002. "Asking the Hard Questions: Writing About Environmental Risks for Rural Communities." In *Writing to Make a Difference,* ed. C. Benson and S. Christian, 141–56. New York: Teachers College Press.

ATKINSON, C. 2005. *Beyond Bullet Points: Using Microsoft PowerPoint to Create Presentations That Inform, Motivate, and Inspire.* Redmond, WA: Microsoft.

ATWELL, N. 1987. *In the Middle: Writing, Reading, and Learning with Adolescents.* Portsmouth, NH: Boynton/Cook.

———. 1998. *In the Middle: New Understandings About Writing, Reading, and Learning.* 2d ed. Portsmouth, NH: Boynton/Cook.

AUGUST, D., and T. SHANAHAN, eds. 2006. *Developing Literacy in Second-Language Learners: Report of the National Literacy Panel on Language-Minority Children and Youth.* Mahwah, NJ: Lawrence Erlbaum.

BARRETT, M. T., and M. F. GRAVES. 1981. "A Vocabulary Program for Junior High School Remedial Readers." *Journal of Reading* 25 (November): 146–50.

BARTH, R. 2006. "Improving Relationships Within the Schoolhouse." *Educational Leadership* 63 (6): 9–13.

BAUMANN, J. F., and E. J. KAME'ENUI. 1991. "Research on Vocabulary Instruction: Ode to Voltaire." In *Handbook of Research on Teaching the English Language Arts,* ed. J. Flood, J. M. Jensen, D. Lapp, and J. R. Squire, 604–32. New York: Macmillan.

———. 2004. *Vocabulary Instruction: Research to Practice.* New York: Guilford.

BAUMANN, J. F., E. J. KAME'ENUI, and G. E. ASH. 2003. "Research on Vocabulary Instruction: Voltaire Redux." In *Handbook of Research on Teaching the English Language Arts,* ed. J. Flood, J. Jensen, D. Lapp, and J. R. Squire, 752–85. New York: Macmillan.

BEACH, R., and J. MYERS. 2001. *Inquiry-Based English Instruction: Engaging Students in Life and Literature.* New York: Teachers College Press.

BEAN, T. W., and J. E. READENCE. 2002. "Adolescent Literacy: Charting a Course for Successful Futures as Lifelong Learners." *Reading Research and Instruction* 41 (3): 203–10.

BECK, I. L., and M. G. MCKEOWN. 1983. "Learning Words Well: A Program to Enhance Vocabulary and Comprehension." *The Reading Teacher* 36 (March): 622–25.

———. 1985. "Teaching Vocabulary: Making the Instruction Fit the Goal." *Educational Perspectives* 23 (1): 11–15.

———. 1991. "Conditions of Vocabulary Acquisition." In *Handbook of Reading Research,* vol. 2, ed. R. Barr, M. Kamill, P. Mosenthal, and P. D. Pearson, 789–814. New York: Longman.

BECK, I. L., M. G. MCKEOWN, and L. KUCAN. 2002. *Bringing Words to Life: Robust Vocabulary Instruction.* New York: Guilford.

BECK, I. L., M. G. McKEOWN, and E. McCASLIN. 1983. "All Contexts Are Not Created Equal." *Elementary School Journal* 83: 177–81.

BECK, I. L., C. A. PERFETTI, and M. G. McKEOWN. 1982. "Effects of Long-Term Vocabulary Instruction on Lexical Access and Reading Comprehension." *Journal of Educational Psychology* 74: 506–21.

BECKER, W. C. 1977. "Teaching Reading and Language to the Disadvantaged: What We Have Learned from Field Research." *Harvard Educational Review* 47: 518–43.

BEERS, K. 1998. "Listen While You Read: Struggling Readers and Audiobooks." *School Library Journal* 44 (4): 30–35.

———. 2002. *When Kids Can't Read: What Teachers Can Do: A Guide for Teachers 6–12*. Portsmouth, NH: Heinemann.

———. 2004. "Hearing Zach: Matching Reluctant and Struggling Readers with Books." *English Journal* 93 (5): 119–23.

———. 2005. "With Equality for All." *Voices from the Middle* 13 (1): 4–5, 82.

BERGHOFF, B., K. A. EGAWA, J. C. HARSTE, and B. T. HOONAN. 2000. *Beyond Reading and Writing: Inquiry, Curriculum, and Multiple Ways of Knowing*. Urbana, IL: National Council of Teachers of English.

BEREITER, C. 2004. "Reflections on Depth." In *Teaching for Deep Understanding: What Every Educator Should Know*, ed. K. Leithwood, P. McAdie, N. Bascia, and A. Rodrigue, 8–12. Toronto: OISE/UT and EFTO.

BIANCAROSA, G., and C. E. SNOW. 2004. *Reading Next—A Vision for Action and Research in Middle and High School Literacy: A Report from Carnegie Corporation of New York*. Washington, DC: Alliance for Excellent Education.

BLACHOWICZ, C. L. Z., and P. FISHER. 2000. "Teaching Vocabulary." In *Handbook of Reading Research*, vol. 3, ed. M. Kamil, P. Mosenthal, P. D. Pearson, and R. Barr, 502–23. Mahwah, NJ: Lawrence Erlbaum.

———. 2004. "Keep the 'Fun' in Fundamental: Encouraging Word Awareness and Incidental Word Learning in the Classroom Through Word Play." In *Vocabulary Instruction: Research to Practice*, ed. J. F. Baumann and E. J. Kame'enui, 218–37. New York: Guilford.

BOMER, R. 1995. *Time for Meaning: Crafting Literate Lives in Middle and High School*. Portsmouth, NH: Heinemann.

———. 2006. "You Are Here: The Moment in Literacy Education." *Research in the Teaching of English* 40 (3): 355–72.

BOMER, R., and K. BOMER. 2001. *For a Better World: Reading and Writing for Social Action*. Portsmouth, NH: Heinemann.

BOOTH, W. 1988. *The Company We Keep: An Ethics of Reading*. Berkeley: University of California Press.

BRANSFORD, J. D., A. L. BROWN, and R. R. COCKING, eds. 1999. *How People Learn: Brain, Mind, Experience and School*. Washington, DC: National Academy Press.

BRENNER, D., D. K. BROCATO, and T. B. KURZ. 2006. "Early Implementation of School Reform: How Observation of Literacy Practices Reveals the Impact of Accountability Systems on the Reform Process." *Language and Literacy* 8 (2). Retrieved October 27, 2006 from http://www.langandlit .ualberta.ca/archivesDate.html.

BRENNER, D., and P. D. PEARSON. 1998. "Authentic Reading Assessment in the Middle School." In *Into Focus: Understanding and Creating Middle School Readers*, ed. K. Beers and B. Samuels, 281–312. Norwood, MA: Christopher-Gordon.

BRISK, M. E., and M. M. HARRINGTON. 2000. *Literacy and Bilingualism: A Handbook for All Teachers*. Mahwah, NJ: Lawrence Erlbaum.

BRUNER, J. S. 1960. *The Process of Education*. Cambridge, MA: Harvard University Press.

BURKE, J. 2001. *Illuminating Texts: How to Teach Students to Read the World*. Portsmouth, NH: Heinemann.

———. 2006. *50 Essential Lessons: Tools and Techniques for Teaching English Language Arts*. Portsmouth, NH: Heinemann, Firsthand.

BUSCHING, B., and B. SLESINGER. 1999. "Third Class Is More Than a Cruise-Ship Ticket." In *Making Justice Our Project: Teachers Working Toward Critical Whole Language Practice*, ed. C. Edelsky, 191–208. Urbana, IL: National Council of Teachers of English.

BUSTLE, L. S. 2004. "The Role of Visual Representation in the Assessment of Learning [Media Literacy Department]." *Journal of Adolescent & Adult Literacy* 47 (5). Retrieved Nov. 7, 2005, from www.readingonline.org /newliteracies/lit_index.asp?HREF=/newliteracies/jaal/2-04_column /index.html.

CAINE, R. N., and G. CAINE. 1994. *Making Connections: Teaching and the Human Brain*. Menlo Park, CA: Addison-Wesley.

CAZDEN, C. B. 2006. "The Value of Principled Eclecticism in Education Reform: 1965–2005." *Pedagogies: An International Journal* 1: 93–104.

CHI, M. T. H., R. GLASER, and M. J. FARR. 1988. *The Nature of Expertise*. Hillsdale, NJ: Lawrence Erlbaum.

CHRISTENBURY, L. 2000. *Making the Journey: Being and Becoming a Teacher of English Language Arts*. 2d ed. Portsmouth, NH: Boynton/Cook Publishers.

———. 2003. "What Matters About Literacy Now?" *Voices from the Middle* 10 (3): 46–47.

———. 2006. *Making the Journey: Being and Becoming a Teacher of English Language Arts*. 3d ed. Portsmouth, NH: Heinemann.

CHRISTENSEN, L. 2000. *Reading, Writing, and Rising Up*. Milwaukee: Rethinking Schools.

COOPER, E. J. 2005. "It Begins with Belief: Social Demography Is Not Destiny." *Voices from the Middle* 13 (1): 25–33.

COOPER, J. D. 2006. *Literacy: Helping Children Construct Meaning.* 6th ed. Boston: Houghton Mifflin.

COPE, B., and M. KALANTZIS. 2000. Introduction. *Multiliteracies: Literacy Learning and the Design of Social Futures.* New York: Routledge.

COPELAND, M. 2005. *Socratic Circles: Fostering Critical and Creative Thinking in Middle and High School.* Portland, ME: Stenhouse.

CRAWFORD, P. 2004. "A Novel Approach: Using Graphic Novels to Attract Reluctant Readers." *Library Media Collection* (February): 26–28.

CSIKSZENTMIHALYI, M. 1990. *Flow: The Psychology of Optimal Experience.* New York: Harper and Row.

CUNNINGHAM, A. E., and K. E. STANOVICH. 1991. "Tracking the Unique Effects of Print Exposure in Children: Associations with Vocabulary, General Knowledge, and Spelling." *Journal of Educational Psychology* 83: 264–74.

DALE, E., and J. O'ROURKE. 1986. *Vocabulary Building: A Process Approach.* Columbus, OH: Zaner-Bloser.

DANIELS, H. 2001. *Literature Circles: Voice and Choice in Book Clubs & Reading Groups.* Portland, ME: Stenhouse.

DANIELS, H., and N. STEINEKE. 2004. *Mini-Lessons for Literature Circles.* Portsmouth, NH: Heinemann.

DANIELS, H., and S. ZEMELMAN. 2004. *Subjects Matter: Every Teacher's Guide to Content-Area Reading.* Portsmouth, NH: Heinemann.

DANIELS, H., S. ZEMELMAN, and N. STEINEKE. 2007. *Content Area Writing: Every Teacher's Guide.* Portsmouth, NH: Heinemann.

DAVIS, F. B. 1972. "Psychometric Research on Comprehension in Reading." *Reading Research Quarterly* 7 (4): 628–78.

DELPIT, L. 1995. *Other People's Children: Cultural Conflict in the Classroom.* New York: New Press.

DEWEY, J. 1933. *How We Think.* New York: D. C. Heath.

"Diplomas Count: An Essential Guide to Graduation Policy and Rates." 2006. *Education Week* 25 (41S).

DRUCKER, P. 1999. *Management Challenges for the 21st Century.* New York: HarperCollins.

DYSON, A. H. 1983. "The Role of Oral Language in Early Writing." *Research in the Teaching of English* 17 (1): 1–30.

EDWARDS, D., and N. MERCER. 1987. *Common Knowledge: The Development of Understanding in the Classroom.* London: Methuen.

EISNER, E. 1994. *Cognition and Curriculum Reconsidered.* New York: Teachers College Press.

ELBOW, P. 1998. *Writing Without Teachers.* New York: Oxford University Press.

ELLER, R. G., C. C. PAPPAS, and E. BROWN. 1988. "The Lexical Development of Kindergarteners: Learning from Written Context." *Journal of Reading Behavior* 20 (1): 5–24.

EMIG, J. 1971. *The Composing Processes of Twelfth Graders.* Urbana, IL: National Council of Teachers of English.

FIELDING, L. G., P. T. WILSON, and R. C. ANDERSON. 1986. "A New Focus on Free Reading: The Role of Tradebooks in Reading Instruction." In *Contexts of School-Based Literacy*, ed. T. E. Raphael, 149–60. New York: Random House.

FOUCAULT, M. 1984. "Nietzsche, Genealogy, History." In *The Foucault Reader*, ed. P. Rabinow, 76–100. New York: Pantheon.

FREEBODY, P. 1992. "A Socio-cultural Approach: Resourcing Four Roles as a Literacy Learner." In *Prevention of Reading Failure*, ed. A. Watson and A. Badenhop, 48–60. Sydney: Ashton-Scholastic.

FREEMAN, Y. S. and D. E. FREEMAN. 2002. *Closing the Achievement Gap: How to Reach Limited-Formal-Schooling and Long-Term English Language Learners.* Portsmouth, NH: Heinemann.

FRIEDMAN, T. L. 2005. *The World Is Flat: A Brief History of the Twenty-first Century.* New York: Farrar, Straus and Giroux.

FRONING, M. F. 2006. "Recruiting, Preparing, and Retaining Urban Teachers: One Person's View from Many Angles." In *Recruiting, Preparing, and Retaining Teachers for Urban Schools*, ed. K. R. Howey, M. L. Post, and N. L. Zimpher, 67–82. New York: AACTE.

FROST, S., and R. BEAN. 2006. "Qualifications for Literacy Coaches: Achieving the Gold Standard." Sept. 27. Denver, CO: Literacy Coaching Clearinghouse. Retrieved January 26, 2007 from www.literacycoaching online.org/briefs/LiteracyCoaching.pdf.

FRY, E. B., D. L. FOUNTOUKIDIS, and J. K. POLK. 1985. *The New Reading Teacher's Book of Lists.* Englewood Cliffs, NJ: Prentice-Hall.

FU, D. 2003. *An Island of English: Teaching ESL in Chinatown.* Portsmouth, NH: Heinemann.

———. In press. "Teaching Writing to English Language Learners at the Secondary Level." In *The 21st Century's Writing: New Directions for Secondary Classrooms*, T. Newkirk and R. Kent, eds. Portsmouth, NH: Heinemann.

FUEYO, J. A. 1991. "Language Arts Classrooms: Spaces Where Anything Can Happen." *Writing Teacher* (Sept.).

FURTH, H. G. 1981. *Piaget and Knowledge.* Chicago: University of Chicago Press.

GARDNER, H. 1999. *Reframing Intelligence: Multiple Intelligences for the 21st Century.* New York: Basic.

GEE, J. P. 1990. *Social Linguistics and Literacies: Ideology in Discourse.* London: Falmer.

———. 2003. *What Video Games Have to Teach Us About Learning and Literacy.* New York: Palgrave/Macmillan.

GORMAN, M., and J. SMITH. 2003. *Getting Graphic: Using Graphic Novels to Promote Literacy with Preteens and Teens.* Worthington, OH: Linworth.

GOULDEN, R., P. NATION, and J. READ. 1990. "How Large Can a Receptive Vocabulary Be?" *Applied Linguistics* 11: 341–63.

GRAVES, D. H. 1975. "The Child, the Writing Process, and the Role of the Professional." In *The Writing Processes of Students,* ed. W. Petty. Buffalo: State University of New York.

GRAVES, M. F. 1986. "Vocabulary Learning and Instruction." In *Review of Research in Education,* vol. 13, ed. E. Z. Rothkopf and L. C. Ehri, 49–89. Washington, DC: American Educational Research Association.

———. 2000. "A Vocabulary Program to Complement and Bolster a Middle-Grade Comprehension Program." In *Reading for Meaning: Fostering Comprehension in the Middle Grades,* ed. B. M. Taylor, M. F. Graves, and P. van den Broek, 116–35. New York: Teachers College Press.

GRAVES, M., and B. GRAVES. 1994. *Scaffolding Reading Experiences: Designs for Student Success.* Norwood, MA: Christopher-Gordon.

GREENLEAF, C. 2006. "Fostering Metacognitive Conversation in Professional Learning Communities and in Subject-Area Classrooms." *The Exchange* 18 (3): 4–7.

GRISHAM, D. L., and T. D. WOLSEY. 2006. "Recentering the Middle School Classroom as a Vibrant Learning Community: Students, Literacy, and Technology Intersect." *Journal of Adolescent and Adult Literacy* 49 (8): 648–60.

GROSS, F., and C. M. AGUILAR. 1999. "Affinity Groups: A Different Kind of Co-Curricular Activity." *Schools in the Middle,* 9 (2): 23–26.

GUTHRIE, J. T., and N. M. HUMENICK. 2004. "Motivating Students to Read: Evidence for Classroom Practices That Increase Motivation and Achievement." In *The Voice of Evidence in Reading Research,* ed. P. McCardle and V. Chhabra, 329–54. Baltimore: Paul Brookes.

HAGOOD, M. C. 2003. "New Media and Online Literacies: No Age Left Behind." *Reading Research Quarterly* 38: 387–91.

HARGIS, C. 2006. "Setting Standards: An Exercise in Futility?" *Phi Delta Kappan* 87 (5): 393–95.

HERRNSTEIN, R. J., and C. MURRAY. 1994. *The Bell Curve: Intelligence and Class Structure in American Life.* New York: Free.

HIDI, S., and J. M. HARACKIEWICZ. 2000. "Motivating the Academically Unmotivated: A Critical Issue for the 21st Century." *Review of Educational Research* 70: 151–80.

HILLOCKS, G. 2002. *The Testing Trap: How State Writing Assessments Control Learning.* New York: Teachers College Press.

HOLDEN, J., and J. S. SCHMIDT, eds. 2002. *Inquiry and the Literary Text: Constructing Discussions in the English Classroom.* Urbana, IL: National Council of Teachers of English.

HUBBARD, R. S., and V. SHOREY. 2003. "Worlds Beneath the Words: Writing Workshop with Second Language Learners." *Language Arts* 81 (1): 52–61.

HUNT, C. L. JR. 1957. "Can We Measure Specific Factors Associated with Reading Comprehension?" *Journal of Educational Research* 51: 161–71.

HYDE, A., S. ZEMELMAN, and H. DANIELS. 2005. *Best Practice: Today's Standards for Teaching and Learning in America's Schools*, 3d ed. Portsmouth, NH: Heinemann.

HYERLE, D., ed. 2004. *Student Successes with Thinking Maps.* Thousand Oaks, CA: Corwin.

"Instructional Coaching Research Conducted by the University of Kansas Center for Research on Learning." 2004. Lawrence, KS: KU-CRL. Retrieved January 30, 2007 from www.instructionalcoach.org/research.html.

International Reading Association in collaboration with the National Council of Teachers of English, the National Council of Teachers of Mathematics, the National Science Teachers Association, and the National Council for the Social Studies. 2005. *Standards for Middle and High School Literacy Coaches.* Newark, DE: International Reading Association.

JACKSON, Y. 2001. "Reversing Underachievement in Urban Students: Pedagogy of Confidence." In *Developing Minds*, vol. III, ed. A. Costa, 222–28. Alexandria, VA: Association for Supervision and Curriculum Development.

———. 2004. "Closing the Gap by Connecting Culture, Language, and Cognition." In *Student Successes with Thinking Maps*, ed. D. Hyerle. Thousand Oaks, CA: Corwin.

———. 2005. "Unlocking the Potential of African American Students: Keys to Reversing Underachievement." *Theory into Practice* 44 (3): 203–10.

JACKSON, Y., J. LEWIS, R. FEUERSTEIN, and R. SAMUDA. 1998. "Linking Assessment to Intervention with Instrumental Enrichment." In *Advances in Cross-Cultural Assessment*, ed. R. Samuda, 162–96. Thousand Oaks, CA: Sage.

JAGO, C. 2002. *Cohesive Writing: Why Concept Is Not Enough.* Portsmouth, NH: Heinemann.

———. 2004. "Stop Pretending and Think About Plot." *Voices from the Middle* 11 (4): 50–51.

JENSEN, E. 1998. *Teaching with the Brain in Mind.* Alexandria, VA: Association for Supervision and Curriculum Development.

JOHNSON, D. D., and P. D. PEARSON. 1984. *Teaching Reading Vocabulary.* 2d ed. New York: Holt, Rinehart and Winston.

JOHNSON, D. D., S. TOMS-BRONOWSKI, and S. D. PITTELMAN. 1982. *An Investigation of the Effectiveness of Semantic Mapping and Semantic Feature Analysis with Intermediate Grade Children.* Program Report 8303. Madison: Wisconsin Center for Educational Research, University of Wisconsin.

———. 1983. "Fundamental Factors in Reading Comprehension Revisited." In *Reading Research Revisited*, ed. L. Gentile and M. Kamil. Columbus, OH: Charles Merrill.

JOHNSON, S. 2005. *Everything Bad Is Good for You.* New York: Riverhead.

JOHNSTON, P. H. 2004. *Choice Words: Talk in Literacy Learning Communities.* York, ME: Stenhouse.

JOHNSTON, P. H., H. WOODSIDE-JIRON, and J. DAY. 2001. "Teaching and Learning Literate Epistemologies." *Journal of Educational Psychology* 93 (1): 223–33.

KAGEYAMA, Y. 2005. "Literature on the Move." *The Post and Courier*, March 19, B9.

KAJDER, S. B. 2006a. *Bringing the Outside In: Visual Ways to Engage Reluctant Readers.* Portland, ME: Stenhouse.

———. 2006b. "Meeting Readers: Using Visual Literacy Narratives in the Classroom." *Voices from the Middle* 14 (1): 13–19.

KAMIL, M. 2003. *Adolescents and Literacy: Reading for the 21st Century.* Washington, DC: Alliance for Excellent Education.

KAUFMAN, D. 2000. *Conferences and Conversations.* Portsmouth, NH: Heinemann.

KEENE, E. O. 2002. "From Good to Memorable: Characteristics of Highly Effective Comprehension Teaching." In *Improving Comprehension Instruction: Rethinking Research, Theory, and Classroom Practice*, ed. C. C. Block, L. Gambrell, and M. Pressley, 80–105. San Francisco: Jossey-Bass.

———. 2006. *Assessing Comprehension Thinking Strategies.* Huntington Beach, CA: Shell Educational.

KEENE, E. O., and S. ZIMMERMANN. 1997. *Mosaic of Thought: Teaching Comprehension in a Reader's Workshop.* Portsmouth, NH: Heinemann.

KITTLE, P. 2005. *The Greatest Catch: A Life in Teaching.* Portsmouth, NH: Heinemann.

———. 2006. "Stories Along the Way: Postcards from My Classroom." *Voices from the Middle* 14 (2): 54–55.

KRAL, C. 2006. "Keys for Successful Literacy Coaching at the Secondary Level." A panel presentation at the annual meeting of the International Reading Association, Chicago, May 2.

KUTZ, E., and H. ROSKELLY. 1991. *An Unquiet Pedagogy: Transforming Practice in the English Classroom.* Portsmouth, NH: Heinemann.

LABOV, W. 1973. "The Boundaries of Words and Their Meanings." In *New Ways of Analyzing Variation in English*, ed. C. Bailey and R. Shuy. Washington, DC: Georgetown University Press.

LADSON-BILLINGS, G. 2001. *The Dreamkeepers: Successful Teachers of African-American Children*. San Francisco: Jossey-Bass.

LADWIG, J. G., and M. B. KING. 1992. "Restructuring Secondary Social Studies: The Association of Organizational Features and Classroom Thoughtfulness." *American Educational Research Journal* 29: 695–714.

LANGER, J. A. 2000. *Beating the Odds: Teaching Middle and High School Students to Read and Write Well*. CELA Research Report Number 12014. 2d ed. Albany: National Research Center on English Learning and Achievement.

———. 2001. "Beating the Odds: Teaching Middle and High School Students to Read and Write Well." *American Educational Research Journal* 38: 837–80.

———. 2002. *Effective Literacy Instruction: Building Successful Reading and Writing Programs*. Urbana, IL: National Council of Teachers of English.

———. 2004. *Getting to Excellent: How to Create Better Schools*. New York: Teachers College Press.

LANKSHEAR, C., and M. KNOBEL. 2003. *New Literacies: Changing Knowledge and Classroom Learning*. Buckingham, UK: Open University Press.

LAPP, D., ET AL., eds. 2004. *Teaching All the Children: Strategies for Developing Literacy in an Urban Setting*. New York: Guilford.

LEGUIN, U. K. 1985. "She Unnames Them." *The New Yorker*, Jan. 21, 27.

LESESNE, T. S. 2003. *Making the Match: The Right Book for the Right Reader at the Right Time, Grades 4–12*. Portland, ME: Stenhouse.

———. 2006. *Naked Reading: Uncovering What Tweens Need to Become Lifelong Readers*. York, ME: Stenhouse.

LESKO, N. 2001. *Act Your Age! A Cultural Construction of Adolescence*. New York: Routledge Falmer.

LUKE, A., and P. FREEBODY. 1999. "Further Notes on the Four Resources Model." *Reading On-Line*. Retrieved Aug. 12, 2006, from www.reading online.org/research/lukefreebody.html.

MAKLER, A., and R. S. HUBBARD. 2000. *Teaching for Justice in the Social Studies Classroom: Millions of Intricate Moves*. Portsmouth, NH: Heinemann.

MARSHALL, J. D., P. SMAGORINSKY, and M. W. SMITH. 1995. *The Language of Interpretation: Patterns of Discourse in Discussions of Literature*. Urbana, IL: National Council of Teachers of English.

MARTORANA, J. 2005. Personal communication with Katherine Egawa. May.

MARZANO, R. 2004. *Building Background Knowledge for Academic Achievement: Research on What Works in Schools*. Alexandria, VA: Association for Supervision and Curriculum Development.

MARZANO, R., D. J. PICKERING, and J. E. POLLOCK. 2001. *Classroom Instruction That Works: Research-Based Strategies for Increasing Student Achievement.* Alexandria, VA: Association for Supervision and Curriculum Development.

MATA-AGUILAR, C. and F. GROSS. 1999. "Affinity Groups: A Different Kind of Co-Curricular Activity." *Schools in the Middle,* October: 23–26.

MCCANN, T. M., L. R. JOHANNESSEN, E. KAHN, and J. M. FLANAGAN. 2006. *Talking in Class: Using Discussion to Enhance Teaching and Learning.* Urbana, IL: National Council of Teachers of English.

MCINTOSH, P. 1990. "White Privilege: Unpacking the Invisible Knapsack." *Independent School* (Winter). Retrieved Oct. 23, 2006, from www.case.edu/president/aaction/DailyEffectsOfBeingWhite.pdf.

MCKEOWN, M. G., and I. L. BECK. 2004. "Direct and Rich Vocabulary Instruction." In *Vocabulary Instruction: Research to Practice,* ed. J. F. Baumann and E. J. Kame'enui, 13–27. New York: Guilford.

MCKEOWN, M. G., I. L. BECK, R. C. OMANSON, and M. T. POPLE. 1985. "Some Effects of the Nature and Frequency of Vocabulary Instruction on the Knowledge and Use of Words." *Reading Research Quarterly* 20: 522–35.

MEZYNSKI, K. 1983. "Issues Concerning the Acquisition of Knowledge: Effects of Vocabulary Training on Reading Comprehension." *Review of Educational Research* 53: 253–79.

MOJE, E. B. 2000. "'To Be Part of the Story': The Literacy Practices of Gangsta Adolescents." *Teachers College Record* 102: 651–90.

MOORE, D., T. BEAN, D. BIRDYSHAW, and J. RYCKIK. 1999. "Adolescent Literacy: A Position Statement for the Commission on Adolescent Literacy of the International Reading Association." Newark, DE: International Reading Association.

MOORE, D. W., and S. A. MOORE. 1986. "Possible Sentences." In *Reading in the Content Areas,* 2d ed., ed. E. K. Dishner, T. W. Bean, J. E. Readence, and D. W. Moore, 174–79. Dubuque, IA: Kendall/Hunt.

MORGAN, W. 1997. *Critical Literacy in the Classroom.* London: Routledge.

MOROCCO, C. C., N. BRIGHAM, and C. M. AGUILAR. 2006. *Visionary Middle Schools: Signature Practices and the Power of Local Invention.* New York: Teachers College Press.

MURRAY, D. M. 1968. *A Writer Teaches Writing: A Practical Method of Teaching Composition.* Boston: Houghton Mifflin.

———. 1982. *Learning by Teaching: Selected Articles on Writing and Teaching.* Portsmouth, NH: Boynton/Cook.

———. 1990. *Shoptalk: Learning to Write with Writers.* Portsmouth, NH: Heinemann.

———. 1996. *Crafting a Life in Essay, Story, Poem.* Portsmouth, NH: Boynton/Cook.

―――. 2004. *A Writer Teaches Writing.* Rev. ed. Boston: Thomas/Heinle.

MYERS, M. 1996. *Changing Our Minds: Negotiating English and Literacy.* Urbana, IL: National Council of Teachers of English.

NAGY, W. 1988. *Teaching Vocabulary to Improve Reading Comprehension.* Newark, DE: International Reading Association.

NAGY, W. E., and P. A. HERMAN. 1987. "Breadth and Depth of Vocabulary Knowledge: Implications for Acquisition and Instruction." In *The Nature of Vocabulary Acquisition,* ed. M. G. McKeown and M. E. Curtis, 19–35. Hillsdale, NJ: Lawrence Erlbaum.

NATIONAL CENTER FOR EDUCATIONAL STATISTICS (NCES). 2002. *Highlights from the 2000 Program for International Student Assessment.* Retrieved Feb. 18, 2002, from nces.ed.gov/surveys/pisa.

―――. 2006. *National Assessment of Educational Progress, Selected Years, 1971–2004 Long-Term Trend Reading Assessments.* Retrieved July 16, 2006, from nces.ed.gov/nationsreportcard/ltt/results2004/nat-reading-scale-score.asp.

NATIONAL COMMISSION ON WRITING IN AMERICA'S SCHOOLS AND COLLEGES. 2003. *The Neglected R: The Need for a Writing Revolution.* Washington, DC: College Entrance Examination Board.

NATIONAL ENDOWMENT FOR THE ARTS. 2004. *Reading at Risk: A Survey of Literary Reading in America.* Research Division 46. Washington, DC: National Endowment for the Arts.

NATIONAL GOVERNORS ASSOCIATION CENTER FOR BEST PRACTICES. 2005. *Reading to Achieve: A Governor's Guide to Adolescent Literacy.* Washington, DC: National Governors Association.

―――. 2006. *Results That Matter: 21st Century Skills and High School Reform.* Washington, DC: Partnership for 21st Century Skills.

NATIONAL WRITING PROJECT (NWP) and C. NAGIN. 2003. *Because Writing Matters.* San Francisco: Jossey-Bass.

NAVARRETTE, R. 2005. "Roberts Is No Friend of Latinos." *San Francisco Chronicle,* Sept. 22, B-9.

NEUFELD, B., and D. ROPER. 2003. *Year II of Collaborative Coaching and Learning in the Effective Practice Schools: Expanding the Work.* Cambridge, MA: Education Matters.

NEW LONDON GROUP. 2000. "A Pedagogy of Multiliteracies." In *Multiliteracies: Literacy Learning and the Design of Social Futures,* ed. B. C. M. Kalantzis, 9–37. London: Routledge.

NICKERSON, R. S. 1985. "Understanding Understanding." *American Journal of Education* 93: 201–39.

NIETO, S. 1996. *Affirming Diversity: The Sociopolitical Context of Multicultural Education.* White Plains, NY: Longman.

NO CHILD LEFT BEHIND ACT OF 2001. PL 107-110, 115 Stat.1425, 20 U.S.C. 6301 *et seq.*

NORWOOD, J., Chair of the Study Group. 2006. *Reading at Risk: The State Response to the Crisis in Adolescent Literacy, the Report of the NASBE Study Group on Middle and High School Literacy.* Rev. ed. Alexandria, VA: National Association of State Boards of Education.

NYSTRAND, M. 1997. *Opening Dialogue: Understanding the Dynamics of Language and Learning in the English Classroom.* New York: Teachers College Press.

———. 2006. "Research on the Role of Classroom Discourse as It Affects Reading Comprehension." *Research in the Teaching of English* 40 (4): 392–412.

O'BRIEN, D. 2003. "Juxtaposing Traditional and Intermedial Literacies to Redefine the Competence of Struggling Adolescents." *Reading Online* 6 (7). Retrieved Jan. 20, 2004, from www.readingonline.org/newliteracies/lit_index.asp?HREF=obrien2.

O'BRIEN, D. G., and E. B. BAUER. 2005. "New Literacies and the Institution of Old Learning." *Reading Research Quarterly* 40: 120–31.

OHIO DEPARTMENT OF EDUCATION. 2001. *Academic Content Standards K–12 English Language Arts.* Columbus, OH: Ohio Department of Education

PARTNERSHIP FOR 21ST CENTURY SKILLS. 2003. *Learning for the 21st Century: A Report and MILE Guide for 21st Century Skills.* Washington, DC: Partnership for 21st Century Skills.

PEARSON, P. D. 1998. "Standards and Assessment: Tools for Crafting Effective Instruction?" In *Literacy for All: Issues in Teaching and Learning,* ed. F. Lehr and J. Osborn, 264–88. New York: Guilford.

PINK, D. 2005. *A Whole New Mind: Moving from the Information Age to the Conceptual Age.* New York: Riverhead/Penguin.

———. 2006. *A Whole New Mind: Why Right-Brainers Will Rule the Future.* New York: Riverhead.

PITTELMAN, S. D., K. M. LEVIN, and D. D. JOHNSON. 1985. *An Investigation of Two Instructional Settings in the Use of Semantic Mapping with Poor Readers.* Program Report Number 85-4. Madison: Wisconsin Center for Educational Research, University of Wisconsin.

PRENSKY, M. 2001. "Digital Natives, Digital Immigrants." *On the Horizon* 9 (5). Retrieved Nov. 1, 2005, from www.marcprensky.com/writing/default.asp.

PRESSLEY, M. 2006. *Reading Instruction That Works: The Case for Balanced Teaching.* 3d ed. New York: Guilford.

PROBST, R. E. 2000. "Literature as Invitation." *Voices from the Middle* 8 (2): 8–15.

———. 2004. *Response and Analysis: Teaching Literature in Secondary School* Second Edition. Portsmouth, NH: Heinemann.

PURVES, A. 1972. *Literature and the Reader: Research in Response to Literature, Reading, Interests, and the Teaching of Literature.* Urbana, IL: National Council of Teachers of English.

RAY, K. W. 1999. *Wondrous Words: Writers and Writing in the Elementary Classroom.* Urbana, IL: National Council of Teachers of English.

RESNICK, L. 1991. "Shared Cognition: Thinking as Social Practice." In *Perspectives on Socially Shared Cognition,* ed. L. B. Resnick, J. Levine, and S. Teasley, 1–20. Washington, DC: American Psychological Association.

———. 2000. "Literacy in School and Out." In *What Counts as Literacy: Challenging the School Standard,* ed. M. A. Gallego and S. Hollingsworth, 27–41. New York: Teachers College Press.

RICHARDSON, W. 2006. *Blogs, Wikis, Podcasts and Other Powerful Web Tools for Classrooms.* Thousand Oaks, CA: Corwin/Sage.

RIEF, L. 1992. *Seeking Diversity: Language Arts with Adolescents.* Portsmouth, NH: Heinemann.

———. 2003. *100 Quickwrites: Fast and Effective Freewriting Exercises That Build Students' Confidence, Develop Their Fluency, and Bring Out the Writer in Every Student.* New York: Scholastic Teaching Resources.

———. 2006. "What's Right with Writing." *Voices from the Middle* 13 (4): 32–39.

ROMANO, T. 2000. *Blending Genre, Altering Style: Writing Multigenre Papers.* Portsmouth, NH: Boynton/Cook.

———. 2004. *Crafting Authentic Voice.* Portsmouth, NH: Heinemann.

———. 2005. "The Power of Voice." *Educational Leadership/The Best of EL.* Alexandria, VA: Association for Supervision and Curriculum Development.

ROSENBLATT, L. 1978. *The Reader, the Text, the Poem: The Transactional Theory of the Literary Work.* Carbondale, IL: Southern Illinois University Press.

SCHEMO, D. J. 2003. "4th-Grade Readers Improve, but 12th-Grade Scores Decline." *New York Times,* June 23: 16.

SCHWARZ, G. E. 2002. "Graphic Novels for Multiple Literacies." *Journal of Adolescent & Adult Literacy* 46 (3). Retrieved January 30, 2007 from www.readingonline.org/newliteracies/lit_index.asp?HREF=/new literacies/jaal/11-02_column/index.html.

SCOTT, J. A., and W. NAGY. 1997. "Understanding the Definitions of Unfamiliar Verbs." *Reading Research Quarterly* 32 (2): 184–200.

SELIGMAN, D. 2005. "Gapology 101." *Forbes* (Dec. 12). Retrieved January 30, 2007 from www.forbes.com/free_forbes/2005/1212/120.html.

SHORT, K., and G. KAUFFMAN. 2000. "Exploring Sign Systems Within an Inquiry System." In *What Counts as Literacy: Challenging the School Standard,* ed. M. A. Gallego and S. Hollingsworth, 42–61. New York: Teachers College Press.

SMITH, F. 1971. *Understanding Reading.* New York: Holt, Rinehart & Winston.

SMITH, M. W., and J. WILHELM. 2002. *"Reading Don't Fix No Chevys": Literacy in the Lives of Young Men*. Portsmouth, NH: Heinemann.

———. 2006. *Going with the Flow: How to Engage Boys (and Girls) in Their Literacy Learning*. Portsmouth, NH: Heinemann.

SPRING, J. 2006. "Pedagogies of Globalization." *Pedagogies: An International Journal* 1 (2): 105–22.

STAFFORD, K. 2003. *The Muses Among Us: Eloquent Listening and Other Pleasures of the Writer's Craft*. Athens: University of Georgia Press.

STAFFORD, W. 1978. *Writing the Australian Crawl*. Ann Arbor: University of Michigan Press.

STAHL, S. A. 1987. "Three Principles of Effective Vocabulary Instruction." *Journal of Reading* 29: 662–68.

———. 1999. *Vocabulary Development: From Reading Research to Practice*. Newton Upper Falls, MA: Brookline.

STAHL, S. A., and M. M. FAIRBANKS. 1986. "The Effects of Vocabulary Instruction: A Model-Based Meta-Analysis." *Review of Educational Research* 56 (1): 72–110.

STAHL, S. A., and K. A. D. STAHL. 2004. "Word Wizards All! Teaching Word Meanings in Preschool and Primary Education." In *Vocabulary Instruction: Research to Practice*, ed. J. F. Baumann and E. J. Kame'enui, 59–78. New York: Guilford.

STAHL, S. A., and S. J. VANCIL. 1986. "Discussion Is What Makes Semantic Maps Work." *The Reading Teacher* 40: 62–67.

STANOVICH, K. E. 1986. "Matthew Effects in Reading: Some Consequences of Individual Differences in the Acquisition of Literacy." *Reading Research Quarterly* 21: 360–407.

STREET, B. V. 1995. *Social Literacies: Critical Approaches to Literacy in Development, Ethnography and Education*. London: Longman.

STURTEVANT, E. 2003. *The Literacy Coach: A Key to Improving Teaching and Learning in Secondary Schools*. Washington, DC: Alliance for Excellent Education.

TATUM, A. W. 2005. *Teaching Reading to Black Adolescent Males: Closing the Achievement Gap*. Portland, ME: Stenhouse.

———. 2006. "Engaging African American Males in Reading." *Educational Leadership* 63 (5): 44–49.

TATUM, B. 1997. *"Why Are All the Black Kids Sitting Together in the Cafeteria?": And Other Conversations About Race*. New York: HarperCollins.

TOLL, C. 2007. *Lenses on Literacy Coaching: Conceptualization, Functions and Outcomes*. Norwood, MA: Christopher-Gordon.

TOVANI, C. 2001. *I Read It, But I Don't Get It: Comprehension Strategies for Adolescent Readers*. Portland, ME: Stenhouse.

TROTTER, A. 2006. "Minorities Still Face Digital Divide." *Education Week* 26 (3): 14.

U.S. DEPARTMENT OF EDUCATION. 2006. "Striving Readers." Retrieved Oct. 21, 2006, from www.ed.gov/programs/strivingreaders/index.html.

UNDERWOOD, T., M. YOO, and P. D. PEARSON. In press. "Understanding Reading Comprehension in Secondary Schools Through the Lens of the Four Resources Model." In *Secondary School Reading and Writing: What Research Reveals for Classroom Practices*, ed. L. S. Rush, A. J. Eakle, and A. Berger. Urbana, IL: National Council of Teachers of English.

VACCA, J. L., R. L. VACCA, and M. K. GOVE. 1987. *Reading and Learning to Read.* Boston: Little, Brown.

VACCA, R. T., and J. L. VACCA. 1996. *Content Area Reading* 5d. New York: HarperCollins.

VADEBONCOEUR, J. A., and L. P. STEVENS, eds. 2005. *Re/constructing "the Adolescent": Sign, Symbol, and Body.* New York: Peter Lang.

VASQUEZ, V., K. A. EGAWA, J. C. HARSTE, and R. D. THOMPSON, eds. 2004. *Literacy as Social Practice: Primary Voices K–6.* Urbana, IL: National Council of Teachers of English.

VYGOTSKY, L. 1978. *Mind in Society: The Development of Higher Psychological Processes.* Cambridge, MA: Harvard University Press.

WALPOLE, S., and M. C. MCKENNA. 2004. *The Literacy Coach's Handbook: A Guide to Research Based Practice.* New York: Guilford.

WEINSTEIN, S. 2002. "The Writing on the Wall: Attending to Self-Motivated Student Literacies." *English Education* (Oct. 2002): 21–45.

WHITE, T. G., J. SOWELL, and A. YANAGIHARA. 1989. "Teaching Elementary Students to Use Word-Part Clues." *The Reading Teacher* 42: 302–8.

WILHELM, J. 2002. *Action Strategies for Deepening Comprehension: Role Plays, Text Structure Tableaux, Talking Statues, and Other Enrichment Techniques That Engage Students with Text.* New York: Scholastic.

———. 2007. *Engaging Readers and Writers with Inquiry.* New York: Scholastic.

WILHELM, J., and B. EDMISTON. 1998. *Imagining to Learn.* Portsmouth, NH: Heinemann.

WILHELM, J., and M. W. SMITH. 2006. "What Teachers Need to Know About Motivation." *Voices from the Middle* 13 (4): 29–31.

WOOD, D., J. S. BRUNER, and G. ROSS. 1976. "The Role of Tutoring in Problem Solving." *Journal of Child Psychology and Child Psychiatry* 17: 89–100.

ZEMELMAN, S., H. DANIELS, and A. HYDE. 2005. *Best Practice: Today's Standards for Teaching and Learning in America's Schools.* 3d ed. Portsmouth, NH: Heinemann.

Trade Resources

What follows is a list of the trade books that were mentioned throughout this book. The point of this list is to give you a way to look at-a-glance at all the books that the authors of this text mentioned or discussed in some way, but not necessarily endorsed. Remember, sometimes books were mentioned for what they didn't offer readers. Consequently, we don't encourage a blanket copying and distributing the list to would-be readers. Instead, peruse the list, check-off the ones you've read, and note what needs to be added to your summer reading list. If you want to remind yourself what the author said about a particular book or author, you'll find the chapter number at the end of each title.

We didn't include full bibliographic information because that information changes as books move from hardback to paperback or from one printing to the next. However, with your favorite search engine, we're convinced that with title and author you can find the books easily.

Abbott, Tony. *Firegirl*. (6)
Anderson, Laurie Halse. *Fever, 1793*. (15)
Anderson, Laurie Halse. *Prom*. (6)
Anderson, Laurie Halse. *Speak*. (6)
Anderson, M. T. *The Astonishing Life of Octavian Nothing*. (6)
Anonymous. *Go Ask Alice*. (6)
Armstrong, Alan. *Whittington*. (6)
Arnold, Nick. *Disgusting Digestion*. (7)
Arteseros, Sally, ed. *American Voice: Best Short Fiction by Contemporary Authors*. (12)

Astor, Gerald. *The Greatest War.* (13)

Avi. *Nothing But the Truth.* (6)

Bauer, Joan. *Hope Was Here.* (6)

Bauer, Joan. *Stand Tall.* (6)

Blackwood, Gary. *Second Sight.* (6)

Blackwood, Gary. *Year of the Hangman.* (6)

Block, Francesca Lia. *Weetzie Bat.*(6)

Bloor, Edward. *London Calling.* (6)

Bloor, Edward. *Tangerine.* (6)

Blume, Judy. *Are You There, God? It's Me, Margaret.* (6)

Blume, Judy. *Forever.* (6)

Brashares, Ann. Sisterhood of the Traveling Pants (series). (6)

Burgess, Melvin. *Doing It.* (6)

Camus, Albert. *The Plague.* (14)

Camus, Albert. *The Stranger.* (15)

Canales, Viola. *The Tequila Worm.* (6)

Chambers, Aidan. *Postcards from No Man's Land.* (6)

Cisneros, Sandra. *The House on Mango Street.* (Interlude 3)

Cole, Babette. *Hair in Funny Places.* (6)

Cooney, Caroline. *The Ransom of Mercy Carter.* (18)

Cormier, Robert. *The Chocolate War.* (6)

Crowe, Chris. *Mississippi Trial, 1955.* (15, 19)

Crutcher, Chris. *Stotan!* (6)

Curtis, Christopher Paul. *Mr. Chickee's Funny Money.* (6)

Cushman, Karen. *Catherine Called Birdy.* (6)

Cushman, Karen. *The Midwife's Apprentice.* (6)

Davis, Anthony, and Jeffrey Jackson. *"Yo, Little Brother . . .": Basic Rules of Survival for Young African American Males.* (Interlude 2)

Davis, Sampson, George Jenkins, and Rameck Hunt. *The Pact: Three Young Men Make a Promise and Fulfill a Dream.* (Interlude 2)

de la Pena, Matt. *Ball Don't Lie.* (6)

Defoe, Daniel. *Journal of a Plague Year.* (15)

Deuker, Carl. *On the Devil's Court.* (6)

Ellis, Deborah. *Parvana's Journey.* (6)

Farmer, Nancy. *The House of The Scorpion.* (6)

Fitzgerald, F. Scott. *The Great Gatsby.* (Interlude 3)

Flinn, Alex. *Breathing Underwater.* (6)

Flinn, Alex. *Diva.* (6)

Gallo, Donald R. *On the Fringe.* (6)

Gantos, Jack. *The Love Curse of the Rumbaughs.* (6)

Garden, Nancy. *Annie on My Mind.* (6)

Garden, Nancy. *Endgame.* (6)

Giles, Gail. *Shattering Glass.* (6)

Going, K. L. *Fat Kid Rules the World.* (6)

Golding, W. *Lord of the Flies.* (Interlude 4)

Gratz, Alan. *Samurai Shortstop.* (6)

Gray, Farrah. *Reallionaire: Nine Steps to Becoming Rich from the Inside Out.*
    (Interlude 2)

Green, John. *Looking for Alaska.* (6)

Haduch, Bill. *Food Rules.* (7)

Hajime, Ueda. Q-KO-CHAN. (6)

Halls, Kelly, Rick Spears, and Roxyanne Young. *Tales of the Cryptids:*
    Mysterious Creatures That May or May Not Exist. (7)

Harris, Robie. *It's Perfectly Normal.* (6)

Harris, Robie. *It's So Amazing.* (6)

Hartinger, Brent. *The Geography Club.* (6)

Hautman, Peter. *Godless.* (6, 14)

Hawthorne, Nathanial. *The Scarlet Letter.* (Interlude 3)

Head, Ann. *Mr. and Mrs. Bo Jo Jones.* (6)

Hemingway, Ernest. *The Old Man and the Sea.* (Interlude 3)

Hinton, S. E. *The Outsiders.* (6)

Hoffman, Alice. *Green Angel.* (6)

Holt, Kimberly Willis. *When Zachary Beaver Came to Town.* (6)

Horowitz, Anthony. *Evil Star.* (6)

Hurston, Zora Neal. *Their Eyes Were Watching God.* (Interlude 3)

Janeczko, Paul. *Top Secret: A Handbook of Codes, Ciphers, and Secret Writing.* (7)

Jenkins, A. M. *Damage.* (6)

Jian, Ji-li. *The Red Scarf Girl.* (6)

Jones, Patrick. *Nailed.* (6)

Kadhota, Cynthia. *Kira Kira.* (6)

Keizer, Garret. *God of Beer.* (6)

Knowles, John. *A Separate Peace.* (Interlude 3)

Konigsburg, E. L. *A View from Saturday.* (6)

Koss, Amy Goldman. *Poison Ivy.* (6)

Lee, Harper. *To Kill a Mockingbird.* (Interlude 3)

Levine, Gail Carson. *Cinderellis and the Glass Hill.* (6)

Levine, Gail Carson. *Ella Enchanted.* (6)

Levine, Gail Carson. *Fairest.* (6)

Levine, Gail Carson. *Fairy Dust and the Quest for the Egg.* (6)

Levithan, David. *Boy Meets Boy.* (6)

Levithan, David. *The Realm of Possibility.* (6)

Littman, Sarah. *Confessions of a Closet Catholic.* (6)

Lord, Cynthia. *Rules.* (6)

Lowry, Lois. *The Giver.* (6)

Lubar, David. *Punished.* (6)

Lupica, Mike. *Travel Team.* (6)

Lynn, Tracy. *Rx.* (6)

Martel, Yann. *The Life of Pi.* (Interlude 3)

Martin, Ann M. The Baby-Sitters Club (series). (6)

Martin, Ann. M. Baby-Sitters Little Sister (series). (6)

Masoff, Joy. *Oh, Yuck! The Encyclopedia of Everything Nasty.* (7)

McCormick, Patricia. *Cut.* (6)

McCormick, Patricia. *Sold.* (6)

Meyer, Stephenie. *New Moon.* (6)

Meyer, Stephenie. *Twilight.* (6)

Miller, Arthur. *The Crucible.* (20)

Moody, Anne. *Coming of Age in Mississippi.* (15)

Morrison, Toni. *Remember: The Journey to School Integration.* (4)

Moseley, Walter. *47.* (6)

Murphy, James. *An American Plague: The True and Terrifying Story of the Yellow Fever Epidemic of 1793.* (15)

Myers, Walter Dean. *Fallen Angels.* (6)

Myers, Walter Dean. *Handbook for Boys: A Novel.* (Interlude 2)

Myers, Walter Dean. *Shooter.* (6)

Myers, Walter Dean. *Street Love.* (6)

Myracle, Lauren. *ttyl (Talk to You Later).* (6)

Na, An. *A Step from Heaven.* (6)

Napoli, Donna Jo. *Crazy Jack.* (6)

Napoli, Donna Jo. *Spinners.* (6)

Napoli, Donna Jo. *The Beast.* (6)

Nelson Bibles, Inc. *Revolve: The Complete New Testament.* (6)

Nolan, Han. *A Summer of Kings.* (6)

O'Brien, Tim. *The Things They Carried: A Work of Fiction.* (Interlude 3)

Orwell, George. *Animal Farm.* (Interlude 3, 6)

Park, Linda Sue. *A Single Shard.* (6)

Paterson, Katherine. *Bridge to Terabithia.* (6)

Paulsen, Gary. *The Amazing Life of Birds.* (6)

Perkins, Lynne Rae. *Criss Cross.* (6)

Peters, Julie Anne. *Luna: A Novel.* (6)

Philbrick, Rodman. *Freak the Mighty.* (6)

Pilkey, Dav. Captain Underpants (series) (15)

Portman, Frank. *King Dork.* (6)

Randle, Kristen. *Slumming.* (6)

Reinhardt, Dana. *A Brief Chapter in My Impossible Life.* (6)

Rice, Ann. *The Vampire Lestat* (Vampire Chronicles series). (6)

Ripley Inc. *Ripley's Believe It or Not* (published yearly). (7)

Rowling, J. K. Harry Potter (series). (6)

Roy, Arundhati. *The God of Small Things.* (Interlude 3)

Salinger, J. D. *The Catcher in the Rye.* (Interlude 3)

Shakespeare, William. *Romeo and Juliet.* (Interlude 4)

Shepard, Jim. *Project X.* (6)

Shusterman, Neal. *Dread Locks.* (6)

Shusterman, Neal. *Duckling Ugly.* (6)

Shusterman, Neal. *Red Rider's Hood.* (6)

Smith, Jeff. Bone (series). (6)

Spiegelman, Art. *Maus: A Survivor's Tale.* (6)

Steinbeck, John. *Of Mice and Men.* (Interlude 3)

Stine, Catherine. *Refugees.* (6)

Stone, Tanya Lee. *A Bad Boy Can Be Good for a Girl.* (6)

Strasser, Todd. *Give a Boy a Gun.* (6)

Taylor, Mildred. *Roll of Thunder, Hear My Cry.* (15)

Trueman, Terry. *Cruise Control.* (6)

Trueman, Terry. *Inside Out.* (6)

Trueman, Terry. *Stuck in Neutral.* (6)

Voigt, Cynthia. *Izzy Willy-Nilly.* (6)

Volponi, Paul. *Black & White.* (6)

Vrettos, Adrienne. *Skin.* (6)

Whelan, Gloria. *Homeless Bird.* (6)

Yolen, Jane. *The Devil's Arithmetic.* (6)

Zindel, Paul. *The Pigman.* (6)

Zusak, Markus. *The Book Thief.* (6)

Appendix A: **Templates**

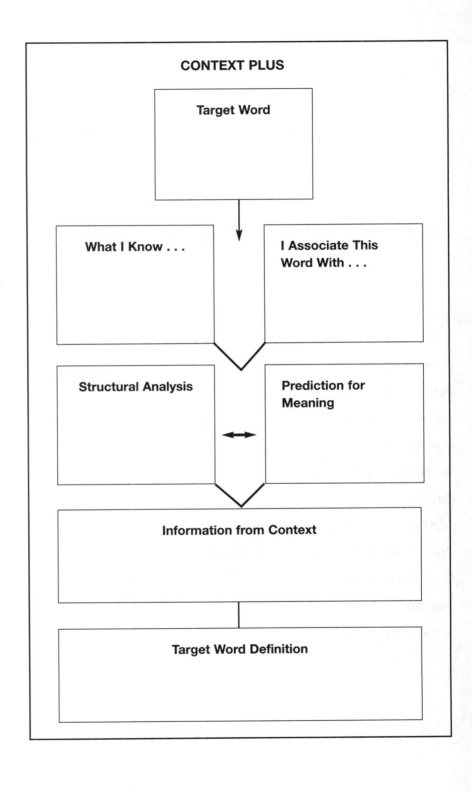

PORTABLE WORD WALL FOR _____

A-B	C-D	E-F	G-H
I-J	K-L	M-N	O-P
Q-R	S-T	U-V	WXYZ

Word Notes:

POSSIBLE SENTENCES: _____
Topic

The following words appear in our chapter on _____. Work with a partner to write sentences that you think we could possibly find when we read this chapter. Use only two or three words in each of your possible sentences.

_____ _____   _____   _____

_____ _____   _____   _____

_____ _____   _____   _____

_____ _____   _____   _____

Possible Sentences
1.
2.
3.
4.
5.
6.
7.
8.
9.
10.

Using Sentences as a Guide/Modifying Predictions
Each day when you're finished reading, mark each of the possible sentences with true, false, or unknown. When you've finished reading, return to your sentences and see how you could modify them so that they are accurate in terms of the content of the passage you have read. In other words, rearrange the words in the sentences so they are true in the context of our reading.
1.
2.
3.
4.
5.
6.
7.
8.
9.
10.

CONCEPT CIRCLES: _____

Describe the meaning and relationships between and among the words in the sections of the concept circles.

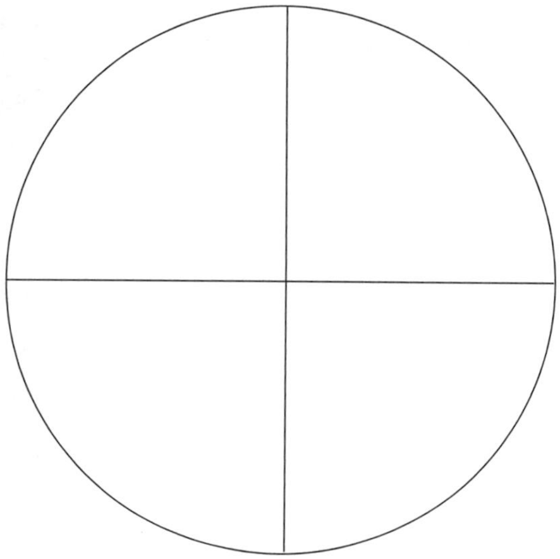

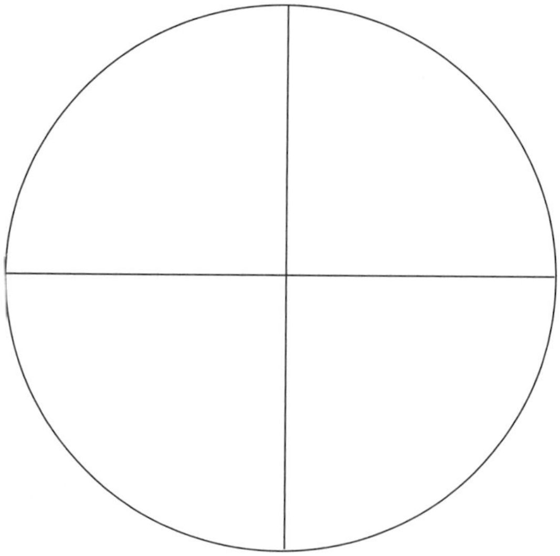

_____

_____

_____

_____

_____

_____

_____

_____

_____

_____

_____

_____

_____

_____

_____

_____

_____

_____

_____

_____

CIRCLE MAP WITH FRAME

Describe the meaning and relationships between and among the words in the sections of the concept circles.

In frame put information that influences your thinking.

In the outer circle, give examples from your life.

In the center circle, put the word or concept you're studying.

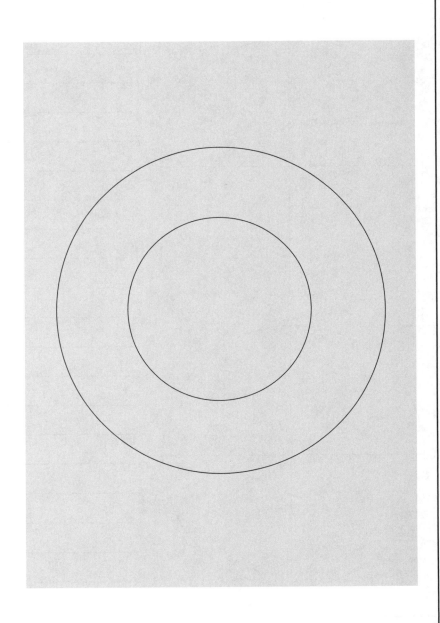

PROCESS PAPER (BACKGROUND HISTORY OF THE WRITING) AND EVALUATION

Name_____ Section _____ Date _____

Title or Topic _____

Tell me everything you can about *how this writing came to be.* You may write on the back of this sheet also.

1. How did you come up with the idea for the piece?

2. What did you do differently (to revise or edit this piece of writing) as you went from each draft to the final draft, and why did you make, or not make, changes?

3. What kind of problems did you encounter and how did you solve them?

4. What helped you the most to make the piece as strong as it could be?

5. What do you want me to know about the writing of this that I might not know just from reading it?

6. What parts of this writing are done especially well? (What qualities or characteristics make it an effective piece of writing?)

7. What have you learned to do as a writer from doing this piece?

8. What did you learn/notice/pay attention to with regard to editing comments given to you (or done on your own) about spelling, punctuation, paragraphing, and the construction of sentences in order to write this piece carefully?

Student grades	Teacher grades	Comments
process		
content		
mechanics		

From *Adolescent Literacy.* Portsmouth, NH: Heinemann. © 1991 by Linda Rief from *Seeking Diversity.* Portsmouth, NH: Heinemann.

THE ASSESSMENT NEEDS OF DIFFERENT CLIENTS OF THE ASSESSMENT SYSTEM

Client	Decisions to Be Made Questions to Be Answered	Assessment Tools
Students	How am I doing? What shall I do next?	Portfolio entries (self-evaluated) and/or feedback from class room work samples
Teachers	Have the kids met my learning goals?	Portfolio entries and work samples
	How did my teaching go?	Curriculum-embedded tests
	How can I help Amy?	Informal diagnostic tools
	Should Amy enter X?	An array of converging evidence
Parents	How is my child doing?	Portfolios/work samples
	Compared with the average bear?	Norm-referenced tests
Administrators	How effective is our program? How are our teachers doing?	Aggregated data of some sort (portfolios, norm-referenced tests)
Policy makers	How well are schools meeting public expectations?	Trends, over time, on some aggregated data (norm-referenced tests would do just fine)
Taxpayers	How well is our money being spent?	Trends, over time, on some aggregated data (norm-referenced tests would do just fine)

CRITERIA FOR THE EVALUATION OF DISCUSSION

The student/class . . .	Notes:
1. comes prepared to engage in the work of the classroom by having read, written in the journal, conducted interviews, and sought out relevant information or experience.	
2. supports the ongoing discourse of the classroom by contributing to the talk, listening attentively to the offerings of others, and helping, when necessary, to draw others into the discussion.	
3. accepts responsibility for the success of the talk by refraining from sarcasm or insult that silences others and by tolerating digressions from his/its immediate concerns.	
4. is willing to probe and question, to speculate, to take risks.	
5. tolerates the missteps, meanderings, and recursiveness typical of discussion, and explores the possibilities in ideas offered.	
6. attempts to build upon and extend the thoughts of others.	

CRITERIA FOR THE EVALUATION OF DISCUSSION *(continued)*

7. questions others, exploring the potential of their contributions, and offers clarification and elaboration upon her/its own ideas when necessary.	
8. assumes some of the work necessary to maintain discussion and push it along—i.e., helps by summarizing issues, raising questions, extracting significant points, making connections, setting agenda.	
9. assumes the responsibility for independent and individual summary and closure.	
10. looks for connections—between texts, the ideas offered by other students, and experiences outside the classroom.	
11. acknowledges the structure of the discussion and abides by the patterns implicit in it (brainstorming, storytelling, responding, and problem solving all imply different sorts of talk).	

CONFERENCE SHEET

Conference Sheet Name _____ Section _____

Date	How can I help you? Articulated by writer	Like/Hear/Stays with me Written by listener	Questions? Written by listener	What if you . . . ? Written by listener	What will you do next? Articulated by writer

Dialogue with
a Poem

Dialogue with
a Poem

Dialogue with
a Poem

Dialogue with
a Poem

Please read the poem, and take a moment or two to reflect on it. Then turn to the next page and begin. Take a few minutes—as much as you need or want—with each question. Please reflect on each question for a moment or two, perhaps jotting down brief notes, before discussing it. Some may be more productive than others for you, and you may wish to give those more time. There is no rush, no need to finish them all. Please don't glance ahead in the booklet.

Please read the poem, and take a moment or two to reflect on it. Then turn to the next page and begin. Take a few minutes—as much as you need or want—with each question. Please reflect on each question for a moment or two, perhaps jotting down brief notes, before discussing it. Some may be more productive than others for you, and you may wish to give those more time. There is no rush, no need to finish them all. Please don't glance ahead in the booklet.

Please read the poem, and take a moment or two to reflect on it. Then turn to the next page and begin. Take a few minutes—as much as you need or want—with each question. Please reflect on each question for a moment or two, perhaps jotting down brief notes, before discussing it. Some may be more productive than others for you, and you may wish to give those more time. There is no rush, no need to finish them all. Please don't glance ahead in the booklet.

Please read the poem, and take a moment or two to reflect on it. Then turn to the next page and begin. Take a few minutes—as much as you need or want—with each question. Please reflect on each question for a moment or two, perhaps jotting down brief notes, before discussing it. Some may be more productive than others for you, and you may wish to give those more time. There is no rush, no need to finish them all. Please don't glance ahead in the booklet.

Introduce yourself to your partners—where are you from, where do you teach, what are your interests, and so on. Ask any questions you wish.

Introduce yourself to your partners—where are you from, where do you teach, what are your interests, and so on. Ask any questions you wish.

Introduce yourself to your partners—where are you from, where do you teach, what are your interests, and so on. Ask any questions you wish.

Introduce yourself to your partners—where are you from, where do you teach, what are your interests, and so on. Ask any questions you wish.

What is your first reaction or response to the poem? What feelings or emotions did you have as you read the poem? Describe or explain briefly.

What is your first reaction or response to the poem? What feelings or emotions did you have as you read the poem? Describe or explain briefly.

What is your first reaction or response to the poem? What feelings or emotions did you have as you read the poem? Describe or explain briefly.

What is your first reaction or response to the poem? What feelings or emotions did you have as you read the poem? Describe or explain briefly.

What did you see happening in the poem? Paraphrase it—retell the event briefly. When you discuss, see if there are differences in the paraphrasing.

What did you see happening in the poem? Paraphrase it—retell the event briefly. When you discuss, see if there are differences in the paraphrasing.

What did you see happening in the poem? Paraphrase it—retell the event briefly. When you discuss, see if there are differences in the paraphrasing.

What did you see happening in the poem? Paraphrase it—retell the event briefly. When you discuss, see if there are differences in the paraphrasing.

What memory does the poem call to mind—of people, places, events, sights, smells, or even of something more ambiguous, perhaps feelings or attitudes?

What memory does the poem call to mind—of people, places, events, sights, smells, or even of something more ambiguous, perhaps feelings or attitudes?

What memory does the poem call to mind—of people, places, events, sights, smells, or even of something more ambiguous, perhaps feelings or attitudes?

What memory does the poem call to mind—of people, places, events, sights, smells, or even of something more ambiguous, perhaps feelings or attitudes?

What idea or thought was suggested by the poem? Explain it briefly.

What idea or thought was suggested by the poem? Explain it briefly.

What idea or thought was suggested by the poem? Explain it briefly.

What idea or thought was suggested by the poem? Explain it briefly.

What is the most important word in the poem?

What is the most important word in the poem?

What is the most important word in the poem?

What is the most important word in the poem?

What sort of person do you imagine the author of this poem to be?

What sort of person do you imagine the author of this poem to be?

What sort of person do you imagine the author of this poem to be?

What sort of person do you imagine the author of this poem to be?

Did you feel involved with the poem, or distant from it?

Did you feel involved with the poem, or distant from it?

Did you feel involved with the poem, or distant from it?

Did you feel involved with the poem, or distant from it?

How did your reading of the text differ from that of your discussion partners? In what ways was it similar?

How did your reading of the text differ from that of your discussion partners? In what ways was it similar?

How did your reading of the text differ from that of your discussion partners? In what ways was it similar?

How did your reading of the text differ from that of your discussion partners? In what ways was it similar?

How did your understanding of the text or your feelings about it change as you talked?

How did your understanding of the text or your feelings about it change as you talked?

How did your understanding of the text or your feelings about it change as you talked?

How did your understanding of the text or your feelings about it change as you talked?

Does this poem call to mind any other literary work (poem, play, film, story—any genre)? If it does, what is the connection you see between the two?

Does this poem call to mind any other literary work (poem, play, film, story—any genre)? If it does, what is the connection you see between the two?

Does this poem call to mind any other literary work (poem, play, film, story—any genre)? If it does, what is the connection you see between the two?

Does this poem call to mind any other literary work (poem, play, film, story—any genre)? If it does, what is the connection you see between the two?

What did you observe or learn about your discussion partners as the talk has progressed?

What did you observe or learn about your discussion partners as the talk has progressed?

What did you observe or learn about your discussion partners as the talk has progressed?

What did you observe or learn about your discussion partners as the talk has progressed?

If you were asked to write about your reading of this text, on what would you focus? Would you write about some association or memory, some aspect of the text itself, about the author, or about some other matter?

If you were asked to write about your reading of this text, on what would you focus? Would you write about some association or memory, some aspect of the text itself, about the author, or about some other matter?

If you were asked to write about your reading of this text, on what would you focus? Would you write about some association or memory, some aspect of the text itself, about the author, or about some other matter?

If you were asked to write about your reading of this text, on what would you focus? Would you write about some association or memory, some aspect of the text itself, about the author, or about some other matter?

Dialogue with a Text

Dialogue with a Text

Dialogue with a Text

Dialogue with a Text

Please read the text, and take a moment or two to reflect on it. Then turn to the next page and begin. Take a few minutes—as much as you need or want—with each question. Please reflect on each question for a moment or two, perhaps jotting down brief notes, before discussing it. Some may be more interesting than others for you, and you may wish to give those more time. There is no rush, no need to finish them all. Please don't glance ahead in the booklet.

Please read the text, and take a moment or two to reflect on it. Then turn to the next page and begin. Take a few minutes—as much as you need or want—with each question. Please reflect on each question for a moment or two, perhaps jotting down brief notes, before discussing it. Some may be more interesting than others for you, and you may wish to give those more time. There is no rush, no need to finish them all. Please don't glance ahead in the booklet.

Please read the text, and take a moment or two to reflect on it. Then turn to the next page and begin. Take a few minutes—as much as you need or want—with each question. Please reflect on each question for a moment or two, perhaps jotting down brief notes, before discussing it. Some may be more interesting than others for you, and you may wish to give those more time. There is no rush, no need to finish them all. Please don't glance ahead in the booklet.

Please read the text, and take a moment or two to reflect on it. Then turn to the next page and begin. Take a few minutes—as much as you need or want—with each question. Please reflect on each question for a moment or two, perhaps jotting down brief notes, before discussing it. Some may be more interesting than others for you, and you may wish to give those more time. There is no rush, no need to finish them all. Please don't glance ahead in the booklet.

What is your first reaction or response to the text? What thoughts did you have as you read? Describe or explain briefly.

What is your first reaction or response to the text? What thoughts did you have as you read? Describe or explain briefly.

What is your first reaction or response to the text? What thoughts did you have as you read? Describe or explain briefly.

What is your first reaction or response to the text? What thoughts did you have as you read? Describe or explain briefly.

What did you see happening in the text? Paraphrase it and retell the event briefly. When you discuss, see if there are differences in the paraphrasing.

What did you see happening in the text? Paraphrase it and retell the event briefly. When you discuss, see if there are differences in the paraphrasing.

What did you see happening in the text? Paraphrase it and retell the event briefly. When you discuss, see if there are differences in the paraphrasing.

What did you see happening in the text? Paraphrase it and retell the event briefly. When you discuss, see if there are differences in the paraphrasing.

Does the text call to mind anything else you have read about or learned on this topic or related issues?

Does the text call to mind anything else you have read about or learned on this topic or related issues?

Does the text call to mind anything else you have read about or learned on this topic or related issues?

Does the text call to mind anything else you have read about or learned on this topic or related issues?

What is the most important word or phrase in the text?	What is the most important word or phrase in the text?
What is the most important word or phrase in the text?	What is the most important word or phrase in the text?

What sort of person do you imagine the author of this text to be? What do you think the author wanted you to learn in this selection? Is the author trying to persuade you to do something after reading this?

What sort of person do you imagine the author of this text to be? What do you think the author wanted you to learn in this selection? Is the author trying to persuade you to do something after reading this?

What sort of person do you imagine the author of this text to be? What do you think the author wanted you to learn in this selection? Is the author trying to persuade you to do something after reading this?

What sort of person do you imagine the author of this text to be? What do you think the author wanted you to learn in this selection? Is the author trying to persuade you to do something after reading this?

Was the text interesting? Why or why not? (Think, too, about the graphics, charts, vocabulary, topic, and page layout as you answer this question.)

Was the text interesting? Why or why not? (Think, too, about the graphics, charts, vocabulary, topic, and page layout as you answer this question.)

Was the text interesting? Why or why not? (Think, too, about the graphics, charts, vocabulary, topic, and page layout as you answer this question.)

Was the text interesting? Why or why not? (Think, too, about the graphics, charts, vocabulary, topic, and page layout as you answer this question.)

How did your understanding of the text differ from that of your discussion partners? In what ways was it similar?

How did your understanding of the text differ from that of your discussion partners? In what ways was it similar?

How did your understanding of the text differ from that of your discussion partners? In what ways was it similar?

How did your understanding of the text differ from that of your discussion partners? In what ways was it similar?

How did your understanding of the text or your feelings about it change as you talked?

How did your understanding of the text or your feelings about it change as you talked?

How did your understanding of the text or your feelings about it change as you talked?

How did your understanding of the text or your feelings about it change as you talked?

Does this text remind you of anything else you have read, seen, or heard? Think of newspaper articles, television, movies, books, and music. If it does, what is the connection you see between the two?

Does this text remind you of anything else you have read, seen, or heard? Think of newspaper articles, television, movies, books, and music. If it does, what is the connection you see between the two?

Does this text remind you of anything else you have read, seen, or heard? Think of newspaper articles, television, movies, books, and music. If it does, what is the connection you see between the two?

Does this text remind you of anything else you have read, seen, or heard? Think of newspaper articles, television, movies, books, and music. If it does, what is the connection you see between the two?

If you were to be asked to write about this text, on what would you focus? Would you write about some association or memory, some aspect of the text itself, about the author, or about some other matter?

If you were to be asked to write about this text, on what would you focus? Would you write about some association or memory, some aspect of the text itself, about the author, or about some other matter?

If you were to be asked to write about this text, on what would you focus? Would you write about some association or memory, some aspect of the text itself, about the author, or about some other matter?

If you were to be asked to write about this text, on what would you focus? Would you write about some association or memory, some aspect of the text itself, about the author, or about some other matter?

Appendix B:
Surveys

In this section you'll find five surveys. The first four are for teachers to help them assess their educational beliefs and practices. The final one is for principals or supervisors to use as a tool to evaluate teacher and administrator/supervisor practices.

WHAT YOU DO COUNTS: A SURVEY OF YOUR PRACTICES

Please respond to each statement below by placing a check in the appropriate box. *Strongly Agree* indicates that you do something on a very regular (every week), consistent (all year) basis with a high degree of expertise. *Agree* indicates that you do this often and have some level of expertise. *Disagree* indicates that you rarely do something and have only basic knowledge about the topic. *Strongly Disagree* indicates that you never do something and lack knowledge of this topic. If you answer *Neutral*, please briefly explain in the box why you chose that answer.

Statement	Strongly Agree	Agree	Neutral	Disagree	Strongly Disagree
Comprehension					
I spend instructional time helping students develop their own list of fix-up strategies.					
I spend instructional time helping students identify their reading miscues so they can learn how to self-correct.					
I require that my students read a range of self-selected material throughout the school year.					
I directly teach comprehension processes (predicting, visualizing, questioning the text, clarifying, summarizing, inferring, summarizing), showing students how to apply these processes to any text.					
I provide time for daily sustained silent reading with texts at students' independent reading level.					
Assessment					
I know how to determine a student's instructional reading level and use that information to help match students to texts.					
I use miscue analysis to help assess a student's strengths and weaknesses as a reader.					
I use assessment data to put selected students into flexible instructional groups.					
I use assessment data to help me decide which professional development opportunities I need.					
Writing					
I complete all writing assignments I give to my students.					
I share my own frustrations with writing with my students and we work through solutions together.					
I model my revision process for my students.					
I share my own writing with my students.					
I give students an opportunity to share their writing with other students.					
I return student writing in a very timely manner with more than a letter or numerical grade and comments that highlight powerful writing.					
I have students write each week.					

SURVEY *(continued)*

Statement	Strongly Agree	Agree	Neutral	Disagree	Strongly Disagree
Professional Development					
I meet on a regular and consistent basis with teachers in my building to discuss reading, writing, and technology strategies.					
I read at least three professional books a year.					
I read at least one professional journal on a regular basis. (If strongly agree or agree, list journal[s]).					
My principal supports building-level professional development by bringing in speakers or providing regular time for departmental meetings.					
I pay my own way to professional development conferences/institutes when my school will not.					
Classroom Practices					
My instruction is guided primarily by student needs.					
My instruction is guided by building-level decisions about what I should teach.					
My instruction is guided by district- or state-level standards.					
I have a range of texts to use with struggling readers.					
Students work in small- and large-group settings on a regular basis.					
I use mini-lessons to share information the whole group needs and then work primarily with individuals or small groups.					
Twenty-first-Century Learning Skills					
I understand what this term implies.					
I use a range of technology to support my teaching and student learning.					
I have access to a computer, an LCD projector, a printer, and the Internet in my classroom.					

Next Steps

1. Where do you see the most need for growth?

2. What's your plan for improving in those areas?

3. Discuss your survey results with other colleagues. Are there patterns of response in your school that suggest areas of growth for the entire faculty?

SURVEY OF PROFESSIONAL BELIEFS AND PRACTICES

Directions: Rate the importance of each statement twice. For the first rating, *circle* the number that represents what you believe. For the second rating, *underline* what you actually do.

1. How important do you believe each of the following is? Circle the number. ◯ 2. How often do you do each? Underline __	Scale of Importance				
	Not at all	Not very	No opinion	Somewhat	Extremely important
Read professional journals on a regular basis.	1	2	3	4	5
Read professional books on a regular basis.	1	2	3	4	5
Meet with other members of your department on a regular basis to *discuss professional matters.*	1	2	3	4	5
Meet with other content area teachers on a regular basis.	1	2	3	4	5
Participate in ongoing professional development regarding reading instruction.	1	2	3	4	5
Participate in ongoing professional development regarding writing instruction.	1	2	3	4	5
Keep up with research concerning adolescent literacy.	1	2	3	4	5
Work collaboratively with others to develop a schoolwide plan for improving adolescent literacy.	1	2	3	4	5
Develop an interactive website for students to use to help them with the subject you teach (not just a place where you post assignments and required materials).	1	2	3	4	5
Participate with your professional organization (e.g, National Council of Teachers of Mathematics, National Council for the Social Studies, National Council of Teachers of English, National Science Teachers Association, National Council for Geographic Education) by reading the organization's journals, attending state and local affiliate meetings, attending national conventions, or checking the website to see what information is offered there.	1	2	3	4	5
Meet individually with students several times a year to discuss progress and set goals.	1	2	3	4	5
Contact parents on a regular basis through email, online newsletters, links to website, phone calls, or letters home.	1	2	3	4	5

Next Steps

Identify those areas in which your beliefs do not match your practices. Consider what it means for them to be out of alignment. If there are multiple areas where beliefs and practices do not match, decide which area needs your immediate attention. Next, think through what you need to do to better align your beliefs and practices.

WHAT COUNTS IN TEACHING ENGLISH WITH TECHNOLOGY?

Directions: Read each statement twice. First, *circle* the number that represents what you believe. For the second rating, *underline* what you actually do.

1. How important do you believe the following is? Circle the number. ◯ 2. How often do you do each? Underline __	Scale of Importance				
	Not at all	Not very	No opinion	Somewhat	Extremely important
Integrate technologies other than a word processor (e.g., MS Word) or a multi-media presentation tool (MS PowerPoint) into your teaching.	1	2	3	4	5
Provide students with an opportunity to use technologies as readers and writers during class time.	1	2	3	4	5
Critically evaluate the technologies that you are required to use in your teaching—or that are provided in your lab, media center, classroom, and so on.	1	2	3	4	5
Keep up with the technologies your students are using outside of the classroom.	1	2	3	4	5
Evaluate and articulate what literacy means within your teaching, the tasks you ask students to complete, your classroom culture and environment, and the models that you provide.	1	2	3	4	5
Work alongside students to evaluate how emerging technologies work as reading and writing tools.	1	2	3	4	5
Read blogs.	1	2	3	4	5
Post comments on others' blogs.	1	2	3	4	5
Maintain (regularly) your own blog.	1	2	3	4	5
Provide students with opportunities to create multimodal texts (e.g., digital story, digital video, digital book trailer) in response to what they read or in response to a prompt.	1	2	3	4	5
Require students to use and cite online sources when researching a topic.	1	2	3	4	5
Discuss searching strategies with students prior to integrating online sources into a research project.	1	2	3	4	5
Listen to podcasts.	1	2	3	4	5
Provide students with opportunities to write, record, and upload their own online content (e.g., book reviews, podcasts, wiki postings, weblog posts, digital stories).	1	2	3	4	5
Provide students with opportunities to interact with authentic audiences.	1	2	3	4	5
Use technologies (e.g., epals, podcasts, e-mentoring, fanfiction writing) to connect students with authentic audiences for their work.	1	2	3	4	5
Collaborate with other teachers (or students) to design technology-infused curricula or assignments.	1	2	3	4	5
Learn a new strategy, tool, or structure for integrating technology transparently and effectively into your teaching to do something you could not previously do.	1	2	3	4	5

Adapted from Kylene Beers' What Matters to You? *survey.*

LANGUAGE SURVEY

Name: _____

Phone: _____

Email: _____

Dear Student,

I would like you to complete the survey below so that I can be a better teacher to you. Forgive me if I seem to be prying, but the more I know about you, the better I will be able to teach you. Please feel free to skip any question you don't feel comfortable answering.

Sincerely,

Language Survey

What languages do you speak? _____

_____

_____

What languages can you write and read? _____

_____

_____

What language do you speak at home? To parents? Grandparents? Brothers or sisters? _____

_____

_____

What language are you most comfortable in? Explain. _____

_____

_____

_____

LANGUAGE SURVEY *(continued)*

Have you gone to school in another country? Where? Through what grade? _____

_____

_____

_____

If your first language wasn't English, how did you learn English? _____

_____

_____

_____

Do you ever watch TV or listen to the radio in another language? Explain. _____

_____

_____

_____

When you have children, what language do you plan to speak to them? What language(s) do you want them to be able to speak? Explain. _____

_____

_____

_____

Comments about your experience being bilingual and/or biliterate? _____

_____

_____

_____

_____

What else do I need to know about you to be an effective teacher to you? _____

_____

_____

_____

_____

QUICK ASSESSMENT FOR PRINCIPALS

Teacher Name:

Class:

Observation Dates:

Supporting a Range of Learners

☐ Teacher uses a diversity of texts (meaning type and difficulty) for instruction.

☐ Teacher uses a variety of instructional formats, including small-group work, on a regular basis.

☐ Teacher uses formative and summative assessments to guide instruction.

Comprehension Strategies

☐ Teacher exhibits ability to determine instructional, independent, and frustrational reading levels for students.

☐ Teacher uses a range of prereading strategies that determine prior knowledge and actively front-load meaning needed for text comprehension.

☐ Teacher consistently models a range of during-reading comprehension strategies that students can use to clarify confusions (fix-up strategies).

☐ Teacher uses a range of after-reading strategies that help students comprehend a range of texts.

Writing

☐ Teacher writes with students, modeling his or her own writing process, throughout the school year.

☐ Teacher has students write several times a week on a variety of topics and for a variety of purposes, although not all pieces of writing will move to completion.

☐ Teacher has students keep a writing portfolio in which students not only keep drafts and completed, edited pieces of writing but also keep their reflections on writing.

Technology

☐ Teacher has basic technology—computer, Internet, printer, LCD projector—available for use in his or her classroom.

☐ Teacher uses technology to support learning in various ways: conducting research, creating multimodal texts, using class blogs to promote discussion.

☐ Teacher uses technology regularly to support teaching in various ways.

Leadership

☐ I consistently model for this teacher research-based best practices that help in the teaching of comprehension and writing and the use of technology in classrooms.

☐ I meet regularly and consistently with this teacher to discuss specific strategies to improve reading, writing, and technology skills of adolescents.

☐ I regularly read journal articles and/or professional texts on adolescent literacy and share findings with this teacher.

Notes:

Contributors

CYNTHIA MATA AGUILAR is a Managing Project Director for Education Development Center, Inc. (EDC) in Newton, Massachusetts, and is the Adolescent Literacy Specialist for the New York and New England Comprehensive Centers. Her expertise includes adolescent literacy, diversity and antiracism training, and middle and high school reform. She has many publications, including *Visionary Middle Schools: Signature Practices and the Power of Local Invention*. She can be reached at caguilar@edc.org.

JANET ALLEN is a teacher, writer, researcher, and literacy consultant. She is the author of *Recorded Books' Plugged-in to Reading: Audio-Support Literacy Workshop*. Her professional books include *It's Never Too Late; Yellow Brick Roads; Tools for Teaching Content Literacy;* and *Words, Words, Words*. She can be contacted at www.janetallen.org or jallen3219@aol.com.

RICHARD L. ALLINGTON is Professor of Education in the Literacy Studies Program at the University of Tennessee. He is author of a number of books, including *What Really Matters for Struggling Readers*. He can be reached at rallingt@utk.edu.

DONNA E. ALVERMANN, formerly a classroom teacher, is an appointed Distinguished Research Professor of Language and Literacy Education at the University of Georgia, where she teaches courses on young people's multimodal literacies. Her research focuses on the role of media and popular culture in adolescents' learning. She can be reached at dalverma@uga.edu.

DEBORAH APPLEMAN is Professor of Education Studies at Carleton College. A high school teacher for nine years, she works weekly in high schools. She is the author of *Critical Encounters in High School English* and *Reading for Themselves* and coauthor of *Teaching Literature to Adolescents*. She can be reached at dapplema@carleton.edu.

NANCIE ATWELL teaches seventh- and eighth-grade writing, reading, and history at the Center for Teaching and Learning in Edgecomb, Maine. Her book *In the Middle* won the NCTE David H. Russell Award and the MLA Mina Shaughnessy Prize for distinguished research in the teaching of English. She is also the author of *Lessons That Change Writers*, *Naming the World: A Year of Poems and Lessons*, and *The Reading Zone: How to Help Kids Become Skilled, Passionate, Habitual, Critical Readers*.

KYLENE BEERS is the Senior Reading Advisor to Secondary Schools with the Reading and Writing Project, Teachers College, Columbia University. Currently serving as vice president of the National Council of Teachers of English, she is a former editor of the NCTE journal *Voices from the Middle*. Recipient of the NCTE Richard Halle award for outstanding contributions to middle-level education, Kylene can be reached at kbeers@prodigy.net.

RANDY BOMER is Associate Professor at the University of Texas at Austin. He is a past president of the National Council of Teachers of English, and he is the author of *Time for Meaning* and *For a Better World*. He can be reached at rbomer@mail.utexas.edu.

DEVON BRENNER is Associate Professor of Reading and Language Arts at Mississippi State University. She is researching the role of opportunity to read in literacy achievement and teacher education policy making. She lives in Starkville, Mississippi, with her son, Vaughan, and daughter, Ruby, where she can be reached at devon@ra.msstate.edu.

JIM BURKE teaches English at Burlingame High School. He is the author of numerous books, including *The English Teacher's Companion* and *ACCESSing School*. Recipient of the NCTE Intellectual Freedom Award and Conference on English Leadership Award, he has served on the National Board for Professional Teaching Standards Committee on Adolescence and Young Adulthood English Language Arts Standards. He can be reached at www.englishcompanion.com.

LEILA CHRISTENBURY is Professor of English Education at Virginia Commonwealth University, Richmond. A past president of the National Council of Teachers of English and former editor of *English Journal,* she is the author of *Making the Journey,* now in its third edition. She can be reached at lchriste@vcu.edu.

ERIC J. COOPER is President of the National Urban Alliance. He received his doctorate from Columbia University. He has received a MacArthur Foundation Award, a Community Advocacy Award from Connecticut Voices for Children, and an ABCD Community Service Award from Connecticut. Eric is also a producer of documentaries for PBS. He can be reached at NUA4556@aol.com.

CHRIS CRUTCHER is a writer and family therapist best known for his books for young adults. Among his works are the novels *Stotan!, Staying Fat for Sarah Byrnes,* and *Chinese Handcuffs* and his recently published autobiography, *King of the Mild Frontier.* He has supported teachers of the English language arts for years, both through the books he has offered them and through his frequent visits to schools and conferences. His work has won many awards, including the American Language Association's Margaret A. Edwards Lifetime Achievement Award and NCTE's National Intellectual Freedom Award. He can be reached at Stotan717@aol.com.

HARVEY DANIELS is Professor of Reading, Language, Secondary Education and Interdisciplinary Studies at National-Louis University in Chicago. Much of his time now is spent with the Center for City Schools, where he works with a network of fifteen elementary schools in Chicago. He is the author of *Literature Circles: Voice and Choice in Book Clubs and Reading Groups* (2002).

KATHRYN EGAWA lives in the Pacific Northwest and works as a literacy consultant with literacy coaches and teachers throughout the country. She is a founding member of the Literacy Coaching Clearinghouse National Advisory Board and is an advocate of listening carefully to the interests and concerns of teachers. A former columnist for the NCTE journal *Voices from the Middle,* Kathy can be reached at kegawa@gmail.com.

DANLING FU is a Professor of Literacy and Language at the University of Florida, Gainesville. Since 1990, she has been working and researching in schools and communities in New Hampshire, San Francisco, and New York City, where there are large populations of new immigrant students. She can be reached at danlingfu@coe.ufl.edu.

YVETTE JACKSON is the CEO of the National Urban Alliance. Yvette is passionate about changing misperceptions about underachieving students of color. Her research in literacy, gifted education, and the cognitive mediation theory of Dr. Reuven Feuerstein is the basis for her Pedagogy of Confidence. She can be reached at DRJNUA@aol.com.

CAROL JAGO has taught for thirty-two years in the Santa Monica Unified School District and directs the California Reading and Literature Project at University of California, Los Angeles. She is author of *Papers, Papers, Papers* and *Sandra Cisneros in the Classroom* and received a 2006 NCTE Classroom Excellence Award. She can be reached at jago@gseis.ucla.edu.

SARA B. KAJDER is Assistant Professor of English Education at Virginia Tech. A former middle and high school English teacher, she received the first National Technology Leadership Fellowship in English/Language Arts. She is the author of *The Tech Savvy English Classroom* and *Bringing the Outside In*. She can be reached at sara.kajder@louisville.edu.

ELLIN OLIVER KEENE consults with schools and districts throughout the country and abroad on issues related to literacy teaching and learning and leadership. She is a coauthor of *Mosaic of Thought: Teaching Reading Comprehension in a Reader's Workshop* and the author of the forthcoming *To Understand*. She can be reached at ellinkeene@earthlink.net.

PENNY KITTLE teaches writing at Kennett High School in Conway, New Hampshire, directs the mentor teacher program, and is a literacy coach in local elementary schools. Penny is the author of *The Greatest Catch* and *Public Teaching* and coauthor with Donald Graves of *Inside Writing*. She can be reached at pennykittle@adelphia.net.

TERI S. LESESNE is a Professor in the Department of Library Science at Sam Houston State University in Texas, where she teaches classes in literature for children and young adults. Teri is the book review column editor for *Voices from the Middle* and writes an author interview column for *Teacher Librarian*. She is the author of *Making the Match: The Right Book for the Right Reader at the Right Time* and *Naked Reading: Uncovering What Tweens Need to Become Lifelong Readers*. She can be reached at lis_tsl@shsu.edu.

DONALD M. MURRAY was a Pulitzer Prize–winning journalist, a columnist for *The Boston Globe*, and Professor Emeritus of English at the University of New Hampshire. Teachers will know him through his books on writing and its teaching—among them *Learning by Teaching* and *Expecting the*

Unexpected—but he has also served as an adviser to several national news-papers. Don was also a poet, and has published in such prestigious journals as *Poetry*.

P. DAVID PEARSON is Dean of the Graduate School of Education at the University of California, Berkeley, and faculty member in the Language, Literacy, and Culture Program. His research focuses on reading instruction and reading assessment policies and practices. He has served as editor of *Reading Research Quarterly* and the *National Reading Conference Yearbook*, as president of the National Research Council, a member of the International Reading Association's board of directors, and the founding editor of the *Handbook of Reading Research*. Those contributions have earned him several awards, among them the IRA's William S. Gray Citation of Merit (1990) and NCTE's Alan Purves Award (2003). He can be reached at ppearson@berkeley.edu.

ROBERT E. PROBST is Research Fellow at Florida International University, College of Education, Center for Urban Education and Innovation, after serving many years at Georgia State University. He is the author of *Response and Analysis: Teaching Literature in Secondary School*. He can be reached at probstre@gsu.edu.

LINDA RIEF, eighth-grade teacher at Oyster River Middle School in Durham, NH, and instructor in the University of New Hampshire's Summer Literacy Institute, is still *seeking diversity* with her adolescent writers and readers. She is an author, a former NCTE editor, and a national and international presen-ter on adolescent literacy issues. Linda can be reached at editlin@comcast.net.

TOM ROMANO teaches at Miami University in Oxford, Ohio, and each summer at the Literacy Institute at the University of New Hampshire. He got the writing bug in seventh grade and the teaching bug at twenty-one. He has never recovered from either. He can be reached at romanots@muohio.edu.

RUTH SHAGOURY has taught children from preschool through high school. She is the Mary Stuart Rogers Professor of Education at Lewis & Clark College, where she coordinates the Language and Literacy Program. She is a coauthor of *The Art of Classroom Inquiry*. She can be reached at shagoury@lclark.edu.

MICHAEL W. SMITH is a Professor in the Department of Curriculum, Instruction, and Technology in Education at Temple University. Together with Jeffrey Wilhelm, he received the 2003 David H. Russell Award for Distinguished Research in the Teaching of English. He can be reached at mwsmith@temple.edu.

ALFRED W. TATUM is Assistant Professor in the Department of Literacy Education at Northern Illinois University. His book *Teaching Reading to Black Adolescent Males: Closing the Achievement Gap* and received the James Britton Award given by NCTE. He provides professional development to schools across the nation. He can be reached at atatum@niu.edu.

JEFFREY D. WILHELM is a Professor of English Education at Boise State University. His book *You Gotta BE the Book* won the NCTE Promising Researcher Award, and *"Reading Don't Fix No Chevys"* (coauthored with Michael Smith) won the David Russell Award for Distinguished Research. He is the author of fifteen books on teaching reading, writing, and literacy. He can be reached at jwilhelm@boisestate.edu.

Acknowledgments

A mind stretched by a new idea can never go back to its original dimensions.

—Oliver Wendell Holmes

WHILE IT IS THE collective voice that gives us community, it is the individual voice that gives us strength. This book offers readers both—community and strength—only because many individuals committed themselves to this project. The thank-you list is long and begins with sincere gratitude to each contributing author.

Contributing authors had a difficult task. Each had to write a chapter or an essay on lessons learned that would stand alone and yet fit alongside other chapters. We asked authors to consider their own body of work and then to contextualize that work alongside the demands of the twenty-first century. We asked some to work over the summer, some to work over holidays, some to work while traveling, some to work while completing other writing projects and their own teaching assignments. We pushed each to revise, reconsider, re-vision, and rethink. We needed authors to make chapters shorter or make them longer or make them more about this point or that one. And with each request, authors said *yes*. They said yes not only because they believed in this project but because they understand that the promise of each student is tied to the practices of each teacher. Furthermore, they each believed in the importance and power of a highly qualified teacher long before a legislative mandate decided this was critical. We applaud the entire body of work these authors bring to the educational community and thank each for the contribution he or she has made through this book.

Heinemann staff supported this book from our first conversations. Lisa Luedeke, our editor for this project, began nodding her head yes when we first approached her with this idea. Lisa helped with any task, from finding email addresses, to serving as a critical reader, to pushing our thinking about the organization of the book. We became better editors as we watched her work, and we appreciate her willingness to share her expertise with us. Lynne Costa, the production editor, had the challenging task of keeping the three of us moving together, at the same pace, at the same time, about the same topic. She managed this task with skill, with grace, and with charm, and we know this book made deadlines because of her commitment to the project.

The cover of this book is the result of the brilliant talent of Lisa Fowler. "Give us something with energy," one of us said; "Highlight each contributing author," another said. "Make it different from all the other covers" was the final request. With those comments that perhaps offered vision but certainly little direction, she set to work. In short order, she returned a cover that captured all that we wanted. Though we have all been told not to judge a book by its cover, we know readers do. Our thanks to Lisa for giving us a cover that beckons readers to the pages within.

Others at Heinemann also played a critical role: Olivia Reed worked through some difficult permission issues; Eric Chalek created the promotional copy; Leigh Peake kept us thinking about the audience for the book; and Lesa Scott, president of Heinemann, supported the project with smart questions and smarter comments from the beginning. We thank each of them.

Carol Schanche, a production editor for several of the journals of the National Council of Teachers of English, has long been a first reader for everything Kylene writes. She served in that critical role again as she read chapters, asked questions, made suggestions, and helped us think through issues. Her comments and suggestions most certainly made this a better book.

We each thank our families, who not only gave us the space and time to begin and work through a project of this magnitude but also gave us the needed encouragement to finish. Spouses—Brad Beers, Wendy Probst, and George Rief—patiently listened to each of us talk about this project. They offered suggestions, delivered coffee, and nodded with understanding when family time was set aside or cut short so we could work on this book. A particular thanks to

Baker Beers, who was a high school freshman when the book began and a sophomore when it was published. He understood that when a chapter arrived or when Bob or Linda called his home, it was likely that Mom would forget that dinner was cooking. More important, he served as the first teen we'd turn to with many of our questions: How many teens do you know who have a blog? What's happening in your school that really makes you think? What worries you most about tomorrow? What do you wish teachers understood better? We most certainly asked other teens these same questions, but Baker was a captive audience, and he answered us not only with wit but with wisdom.

Finally, we thank *you*, the readers of this book. You are the ones who, in spite of all the difficulties and challenges teachers now face—from overcrowded curriculum to underfunded mandates—walk into classrooms each day with the conviction to teach not to the test but to each student. You offer, for so many students, the promise of a better tomorrow through the practices you show them today. We are proud to call you colleagues.

Kylene, Bob, and Linda

Index